Eighty Knots to MACH 2

Forty-five Years in the Cockpit

Richard Linnekin

Eighty Knots to *MACH 2*

Forty-five Years in the Cockpit

Naval Institute Press
Annapolis, Maryland

Library of Congress Cataloging-in-Publication Data

Eighty knots to mach 2 : forty-five years in the cockpit / Richard
Linnekin.
    p.   cm.
Includes index.
ISBN 1-55750-500-4

1. Linnekin, Richard. 2. United States. Navy—Aviation—
Biography. 3. United States. Navy—Aviation—History. I. Title.
II. Title: 80 knots to mach 2.
VG93.L55   1991
359.9′4′092—dc20
[B]   90-28950

REMEMBERED

LIEUTENANT ROBERT THAYER RICH, USN

COMMANDER JAMES M. HEFFERNAN, USN

CAPTAIN JAMES HERVEY MILLS, JR., USN

Contents

Preface

WHAT FOLLOWS IS A RECOLLECTION, a kind of diary. The writer has lived through and so far survived a unique era in the quest for flight. Neither past nor future generations of pilots can expect to experience the spectrum of flying machines that was around from the late 1930s to the present. From stick-and-wire fabric-covered biplanes to Apollo and the space shuttle is quite a transition!

Admittedly, I started at the tail end of the fabric-covered biplane era. My World War II trainer was an N2S, a "Yellow Peril" that was closer to the Sopwith Camel and Fokker D-VII of World War I than to the all-metal Wildcats that fought early in the large war. And I stopped in the Mach 2.3 Phantom II, reaching seventy-seven thousand feet in a ballistic zoom climb but well short of extra-atmospheric exploration, which is what space flight is all about. Nevertheless, some seventy airplanes and forty-five years later, I recall an interesting gaggle of airplanes.

There is no pretension here of either truly unique personal flight experience or anything approaching what the trailbreakers did in the same time frame. It gets back to the motivation of the diary writer: The flying was fun. There was excitement, purpose, and fulfillment combined in a way infrequently experienced in this world. It would be a shame to lose the memory because of a failure to record.

History records the significant. The less significant gets shorter shrift. If there are any fellow short-shrifters out there who would like to share one man's impression of some interesting airplanes, stick around. The writer has a minor distinction in having acquired less flight time in more different airplanes than most folks.

A few remarks about organization. For the most part each chapter is dedicated to a single airplane. The exceptions are evident from the chapter titles. There is no essential dependent continuity; one can look at these airplanes in any order. In each case, one may expect the following:

—A general description of the airplane, including its historical significance, if any.

—How it flew. This includes the sort of stuff each machine was expected to do in its operational environment.

—Professional anecdotes aimed at the characteristics of the airplanes and their pilots while flying them.

—Occasional personal anecdotes about the folks who flew the airplanes: straight arrows, wild hairs, or whatever in between they may have been while they were *not* flying airplanes.

Anecdotes are inescapable in an aviator's life; references to individuals are unavoidable. The stories that follow are intended to be positive. Some of the more colorful, cranky airplanes required colorful, cranky masters—pilots who survived their airplanes' crankiness and did good things.

Acknowledgments

*F*IRST, Captain Rosario "Zip" Rausa, USN, naval aviator, editor, and author, for his editorial suggestions and other good advice—not least of which was sharing his knowledge of the intricacies of the publishing business with a neophyte.

Mary Beth Straight of the U.S. Naval Institute Photo Library; and H. J. "Shoney" Schonenberg and his colleagues, Lois Lovisolo and Peter Kirkup, of the Grumman History Center. The old fighter pilot knows where all the old photographs and line drawings are buried, as well as the bodies.

Two of the new breed, for reading and commenting on certain chapters and sections: F/A-18 pilot Lieutenant Stephen N. Frick, USN; and A-4M and AV-8B pilot Captain Richard B. Linnekin, Jr., USMC.

The unofficial Macintosh computer guru at Westinghouse, John De Frank, whose assistance in formatting, reformatting, and reproducing the manuscript went right past *invaluable* on the way to *essential.*

Finally, my best friend, who survived being, in turn, daughter, wife, widow, wife again, and mother to four different naval aviators and still found a path to establish herself as a professional teacher and recognized fine artist.

Eighty Knots to MACH 2

Forty-five Years in the Cockpit

Prologue

*I*T WAS THE TYPICAL WARM-FRONT WEATHER you can expect in the early fall in Virginia Beach. It moves in with low stratus, fog, and drizzle. After about a week, you are convinced that it will move out, that the oncoming cold front will produce clearing skies. Then the low-pressure cell stalls offshore. For a few more days there is an effort by the elements to produce something like sunshine. During the day the weather tries to clear, but by late afternoon the easterly wind brings a fresh batch of moisture over the land. The stratus and drizzle move back in. The cycle continues.

In 1964, the bad weather wasn't entirely disqualifying, depending on what kind of flying you wanted to do. But for the VC (*C* for composite) squadron, it was enough to cancel some missions. The squadron had a mixed bag of airplanes to fulfill its mission of providing target and other services to the fleet squadrons: F-8 Crusaders to be the basis for a backup fighter mission, and S2Fs to perform a variety of other services. With this kind of visibility, there was certainly going to be no banner towing today for either air-to-air or surface-to-air gunnery. The S-2s, with their high-visibility paint jobs, and the dull gray F-8 Crusaders sat on the ramp. Still, the weather wasn't truly rotten; a couple of the F-8s—high-flight-time, many-times-reworked F8U-1s, now called F-8As—might get to do something.

There was a mile and a half to two miles' visibility. The ragged lower level of clouds was about a thousand feet. The next layer appeared to be about four thousand. There were light spots, suggesting several other layers. If the tops weren't too high, it might be possible to provide fighter and bogey targets for the radar intercept trainees at Dam Neck.

The visiting captain sat in the nearly empty ready room, listening intently to the Operations Officer of the squadron brief him and his flight leader, Lieutenant (jg) Lee Prost. The captain, a former F-8 skip-

1

per, was exercising a privilege that is probably no longer viable in the 1990s: he was delaying becoming permanently deskbound after leaving his last squadron. The commander of the VC squadron, a friend dating from Test Pilot School at Patuxent, was conspicuously low key. He was also very much present.

"How's it going?" he asked. (Translation: "You sure you want this flight?")

The captain smiled, interrupting the note taking. "Great. This a good operation you've got here." (Translation: "I can handle it. Piece of cake.")

"It's all skill and leadership," the skipper said. "These guys were garbage before I showed up."

Lee Prost's relaxed attention to his own knee pad suggested that he understood the exchange. Visiting firemen occasionally showed up to fly. So far the skipper hadn't picked any duds, but you never knew about these gray-headed old men.

The briefing completed, the captain and Prost manned their airplanes. They went through the complicated starting procedure, which involved at least two separate pieces of yellow ground equipment. No standalone airplanes these; they required support! The pretaxi procedure was even more complicated. The F-8 represented the height of system sophistication for its time, with dual-redundant everything plus emergency backup. It had hydraulically powered controls with a decidedly finicky electrical trim system. The most bizarre feature was a variable-incidence wing—actually a two-position wing. The idea was to provide the angle of attack needed for landing and takeoff without rotating the fuselage through a large angle. Another advantage was that it permitted reasonably short landing gear.

When he was ready to taxi, the captain held his right thumb up for Prost to see, confirming his readiness over the squadron's tactical UHF radio channel. Prost tapped his hard hat over his ear and held up two fingers. That meant "Shift to Ground Control frequency," the second of a series of radio channels they would use on this flight. Prost would do all the communications for the flight to the outside world. As long as they operated in a two-plane section, all between-airplane communications would depend on hand signals or simple nods.

Ground Control directed them to the duty runway. Having already filed for a standard instrument departure and climb-out, they switched to the control tower for takeoff clearance. When cleared, they moved into the takeoff position in two-plane formation. They went through final preflight checks, mostly checking engine rpm, pressure ratios, and temperatures to ensure that adequate thrust was available. Prost looked over at the captain and held up his right thumb: I'm ready, are you? The captain held up his left thumb, the one Prost could see: Ready.

Porst leaned his head against the headrest. He advanced the throttle, then held up his other hand where it could seen, whirling two fingers in an arc. His hand disappeared from view. He nodded forward as he released the brakes. The two aircraft moved forward as one. Prost nodded to the right: Burner. He moved his head to the left: Now! With that coordinating motion both pilots hit afterburner. There was a barely discernible explosive sound in the cockpit, a loud bang outside. The impact of acceleration drove each pilot back into his seat, even those old F-8As really moved out in a burner takeoff. Prost eased his throttle back to the fully modulated position to give the captain the maneuvering power to fly formation. They broke ground, landing gear moving up almost immediately. Prost's head went back to the headrest. As he moved his head forward, he actuated the wing-down handle. Without that coordinating signal his wingman might have found it impossible to transition and still stay in formation. Another head signal took them out of burner and into a basic engine climb.

They quickly passed through the thousand-foot scattered cloud layer. Approaching the four-thousand-foot layer, now broken, the captain moved closer. They were in the clouds. He moved closer yet, confirming the angular and distance relationships he identified as a good wing position. Prost was getting hard to see. The captain moved closer yet into a real air show parade formation. If he lost sight of Prost, he was going to have to break away, forcing Departure Control to control two flights to "on-top" instead of one—embarrassing at best.

He must concentrate exclusively on Prost. He must ignore his own instruments, never take his eyes off the other airplane. Maintain the formation longitudinal and lateral position with throttle and rudder. Duplicate the lead aircraft's wing position (bank angle) at all times. Follow the rules, and the leader could take you through anything, from a simple instrument climb like this one to the most extreme coordinated aerobatics. Ignore the rules, and one possibility was metal-to-metal contact that no one would enjoy.

The captain felt an acceleration that told him Prost was starting a turn to the right. He knew they were cleared for an arcing departure to put them on the designated radial for the long climb to "on-top," which was reported to be an altitude in excess of thirty thousand feet. He felt the acceleration that he himself created by banking his airplane to match the other. Experience told him that from now on he could not trust any messages from his own body, his own inner ear, his own sensations. He was operating in a kind of aviator's never-never land, flying both formation and instruments—formation, in the sense that he maintained the angular and distance relationship to the lead airplane visually; instruments, in the sense that the other airplane was his gyro horizon. That "horizon" was literally relative. If the lead airplane chose to turn, climb, descend, even fly through a three-dimensional maneuver like a loop, a good wingman would duplicate the entire maneuver with no awareness of what was going on with respect to the natural "earth" horizon.

The captain knew that. Not then flying every day and having been leader more often than wingman, perhaps he could be excused for listening, even peripherally, to his inner ear. "What the hell is this kid doing?" he thought. "I feel like I've been in a 45-degree bank for half an hour!" As demanding of concentration as the close formation was, he stole a quick glance at his own instruments, then back to the leader. The stolen look told him that he was in a smooth coordinated climb, wings level, nose up, just as he was supposed to be; no bank at all; no g's on the airplane. With a feeling of guilty chagrin, he slid into an even tighter wing position.

At least his formation instincts were OK. Nothing had changed during the seconds the furtive cockpit peek had taken. He wasn't on the verge of either running into his leader or losing him in the stratus. Now he could enjoy it. The flight leader knew what he was doing. The exercise was demanding, but it posed neither a threat to life nor, the fighter pilot's dread, the prospect of looking bad while surviving.

They popped into the clear. A crystal-clear blue expanse of sky was above them. The many-times overhauled F-8s with their dull gray civil servant–applied paint jobs glistened brilliantly in the sunshine. Thirty thousand feet of dank warm-front moisture had given them the momentary allure of a twelve-coat custom car lacquer job. The clean, functional sleekness of the F-8's supersonic profile stood out against the solid white cloud deck below and the vibrant blue sky above.

The formation climb through thousands of feet of dense stratus had had the cleansing effect of dissolving layers of accumulated deskbound-pilot rust. The captain had been comfortable in the steady-state portion of the long climb, skills and reactions reasserting themselves. He felt like a pilot again, maybe even like a fighter pilot. Then this reward: the tingling excitement and overpowering beauty of the sky providing a limitless arena for two airplanes and two pilots. For the next hour the arena was their playground. As far as they could see the only inhabitants of the universe, they were allowed, even required, to cavort about the sky in supersonic airplanes. They weren't even obliged to feel guilty; they were providing essential services for earthbound colleagues who even then peered at the greenish glow of radar scopes in the smoke-filled gloom of a training CIC (combat information center), far below.

Oh, I have slipped the surly bonds of earth
And danced the skies on laughter-silvered wings;
Sunward I've climbed and joined the tumbling mirth
Of sun-split clouds and done a hundred things
You have not dreamed of, wheeled and soared and swung.

"High Flight," John Magee

Is it any wonder man flies?

Chapter 1
N2S Stearman

I **REMEMBER MY EARLY ROMANTIC NOTIONS** about flying as well as my early experiences, those first airplane rides. In the early 1930s, when I was eleven and twelve, my father periodically undertook, with me in tow, the trek on the Long Island Railroad from Manhattan to Roosevelt Field in Mineola, Long Island. Roosevelt Field was one of the departure points for a number of the early transatlantic attempts, both before and after Lindbergh's flight. There was a small museum featuring a well-preserved S.E.5 and a Fokker D-VII. Occasionally there would be an air show, a special event indeed. There was never an entrance fee, unless one insisted on sitting in the temporary bleachers. For the depression it was good, cheap entertainment—not much burden for an indulgent father, except time. As best I can tell, today Roosevelt Field lies underneath a shopping mall.

One Sunday afternoon I explored the hangars and even crawled into the cabin of an unlocked staggerwing Beechcraft. The seats of that fascinating machine were leather of a thickness and luxuriousness not to be duplicated today—physically duplicated, perhaps, but not to match the memory of an eleven-year-old's forbidden trespass into the gloom of an unguarded hangar. The aura of comfortable, adventurous magnificence was overpowering. It smelled seductive and romantic.

The instrument panel and exotic-looking handles and levers conjured up something like what today's youngsters must feel when looking at a simulation of a shuttle cockpit. But today's youngsters have had preparation; they have already seen *Star Trek*. I was gloriously unprepared. My visual preconceptions were all from imagination, inspired by lurid descriptions in pulp magazines and an occasional fuzzy reproduction in *Model Airplane News*.

I don't know how many instruments there were. Having since seen the panel of a restored staggerwing Beech, I could now be deceived into remembering that there were ten or twelve. But that would not be an honest recollection. In honest recollection there were a large number of round instruments, one or two of them bigger than the rest. At least one appeared to be the size of a softball.

Along with the luxury and opulence of this functional machine was its incredible sleekness. There was one feature—practical then and now—that conveyed an automatic, emotional impression of high performance: retractable landing gear. Once machines began to go really fast, retractable gear became a necessity. At some point the advantages are minimal; the weight and complexity penalty for 5 to 10 knots of airspeed leads to a trade-off decision. Piper and Cessna, among others, have made money selling retractable-gear versions of 180- to 200-horsepower general aviation airplanes whose performance barely equals that of their fixed-gear cousins. For the staggerwing, however, that feature alone gave it instant recognition as a "hot" airplane.

Back out in the sunshine, I found a surprise in store. The around-the-pea-patch two- to five-minute airplane ride had been pioneered by the post–World War I barnstormers for about a dollar the trip. It was still going on in the early 1930s, but the price had risen to five dollars. On this day there was a single-engine Fairchild that held four or five passengers in-line in an enclosed cabin. For the sum of ten dollars the pilot would take a full load of passengers for a tour of lower Manhattan and back to Roosevelt Field. The flight took almost half an hour. The pilot had about four hundred hours of flight time, as my father ascertained before committing his only son to this venture. Moreover, ten dollars was a lot of money, two or three years into the depression. I little understood that at the time, but that first time off the ground in an airplane I understood, and appreciated, plenty else! I sat in the forward passenger seat and thus was able to look out the windows with a minimum of obstruction. Equally exciting, I could see part of the instrument panel. The only instrument I could see clearly and interpret was the airspeed indicator. It went up to about 170 mph, but even then I thought that 140 mph might be more attainable. In flight the needle never got close to either number. Everything else, though, was better than I had imagined. Flying was fun, even for a passenger.

I had two other hook-setting experiences in the late spring of 1934. The DC-2 was then new on the scene and would eliminate its competition within a year or so. The competition was a late, reasonably clean-looking, version of the Curtiss Condor biplane, a smallish Boeing 247 monoplane, and the Ford trimotor. I rode in two of those three.

First, I rode in a Condor from Newark (New Jersey) Airport—then among the busiest in the world—to Buffalo, New York. It may be difficult to perceive any biplane as "clean," but if biplanes represent most of the flying machines you have ever seen, the differences within the breed are significant. What to look for is the number and design of various protuberances. Smooth is better than rough. Enclosed is better than hanging out in the breeze. The earlier version of the Condor had four liquid-cooled engines. The one I rode in ("rode in," not "flew"—the difference is important) had two efficiently cowled Pratt & Whitney radial engines. For those who know the lovely low-drag profiles of the in-line, liquid-cooled, Merlin-engined Spitfires and Mustangs of World War II, it may be hard to think of any radial engine as low-drag compared with a liquid-cooled engine, but some were—at least in comparison with the blunt, flat-nosed descendants of things like the Liberty engine of World War I. Another thing that helps in a biplane is to cut down on the number and variety of the struts and wires that hold the whole thing together. Smoothly fairing the struts you can't eliminate helps, too; that was one of the secrets of the staggerwing Beech. The Condor was wonderfully roomy, too—eighteen seats, compared with about twelve for the trimotor and only fourteen for the DC-2.

The Curtiss Condor flew me to Buffalo with a passenger stop at Elmira. The operator was American Airways. The AA logo on the blue side of the fuselage was essentially the same as the familiar American Airlines insignia. The seats were roomy and, of course, leather. The uniformed stewardess was a registered nurse, as almost all flight attendants were in those days. She paid special attention to the boy traveling alone. From somewhere she produced the equivalent of a Sectional Chart and tried to show me how to orient myself. I couldn't take my eyes off her. The minute she was gone I was lost, both emotionally and geographically, madly in love and completely disoriented ("disoriented" is what we pilots call it when we are lost). I couldn't read the chart at all, or at least I couldn't correlate what I saw on the ground with what I saw on the chart. That trip cost my father twenty-one dollars.

I made the trip back in a Ford trimotor. It was nonstop—we skipped Elmira—and American Airways again, because that was the only airline serving both Buffalo and Newark. Having been introduced to the sophisticated modernity of the most advanced and luxurious of the biplanes, I was not enthusiastic about this retrograde step to the trimotor, all-metal monoplane design notwithstanding. Not that I objected, but I already liked that other airplane. How soon one becomes opinionated where airplanes are involved!

The trimotor had two rows of seats on either side of a reasonably sized aisle. The seats were not leather but wicker, that funny cane stuff they used to make lawn and patio furniture before cheap aluminum became available, before plastic was invented. Altogether it was a much more primitive environment than the fabric-covered Condor biplane. It was also noisier; it shook and vibrated like hell. Perhaps some of my recollection is conditioned by later experience. Then, the trimator compared unfavorably only with the most recent example in my newly acquired airborne impressions. Years later I speculated on the difficulty of keeping two, let alone three, engines synchronized so as not to shake out your wisdom teeth before constant-speed propellers.

I was not off the ground in an airplane again until 1943, when I was first allowed to touch the controls of a Curtiss SOC floatplane. I didn't do it in earnest until my introduction to the N2S Stearman in 1944.

General Description

The Boeing-Wichita plant produced over ten thousand primary trainers for the Army and the Navy during the war years. A close cousin, the N3N, was turned out by the Naval Aircraft Factory in significant numbers, but by 1943 essentially all the Navy's primary trainers were Boeing-produced N2S Stearmans. They were powered by either Continental R-670s or Lycoming R-680s. In either case the R designates a reciprocating engine, with displacement given in cubic inches. Hence, the R-670 was a reciprocating engine with a displacement of 670 cubic inches.

The airplanes were fabric covered, a good grade of canvas over a rigid framework. Spars, the main structural members of the wings, were

N2S-3 Boeing Stearman, appropriately parked on the grass. Official nickname Kaydet, never heard out loud. Yellow Peril sometimes. Usually just Stearman. (USNI Photo Library)

spruce. There was wood at the wing tips too. The fuselage structure, simple but efficient trusses, was metal. In other words, they were very different structurally from the last generation of World War I airplanes. The engines, however, were literally an order of magnitude better. They were smaller cousins of the big radials that powered most of the good American airplanes throughout World War II. Aerodynamically better also, the Stearmans were pulley and cable controlled. The upper wing was attached by struts and wires. The lower wing was securely butted to the fuselage, but its relation to the upper wing was in turn controlled by a complex network of struts and wires. Physical twist could be controlled by adjusting tension on the wires, which in turn controlled the loading on the struts. Arcane expressions like *wash-in* and *wash-out* described how one rigged a biplane. (If that seems bizarre, think of the Wright brothers. Their famous Flyer had no ailerons. Lateral control was maintained by actually twisting or "warping" the wings in flight.) The objective of rigging was to make the airplane as close to a hands-off machine for the pilot as possible. What was accomplished was to vary the lift along the wingspan so as to compensate for engine torque and also to prevent the wing from stalling all at once. The same effects are achieved today, as in the more enlightened monoplanes of World War II, by varying the aerodynamic sections—that is, the rib profiles—as a function of wingspan location.

The Stearmans were, in the modern expression, tail draggers—"modern" because from the time that wheels replaced skids for the support of an airplane on the ground, there was a third thing, usually in back. It was a long time before that thing graduated from skid to wheel and even longer before it moved to the front of the airplane. The Stearmans were open-cockpit machines, two-seaters. They were balanced so that the pilot rode in the second seat solo. In that respect they were closer to the post–World War I mail, cargo, and (occasionally) people carriers than to the two-seat combat machines of that war. The Bristol Fighter and the notorious de Havilland D.H.4—the "Flying Coffin" of between-the-wars pulp fiction—were representative of the front-seat pilot, rear-seat gunner/observer configuration that extended through a good number of the dive-bomber/attack airplanes of World War II.

The N2S coexisted with some relatively sophisticated machines. None of the major powers fought World War II with biplanes, although most of the major combatants had them engaged somewhere. The Stearman was an admirable trainer, eminently suited to its job of training pilots throughout World War II. Its use as a simple trainer was consistent with the notion that pilots should learn the fundamentals from the beginning; besides, it was cheap. Only at the end of the war was the N2S

Stearman retired as a Primary trainer in the Navy in favor of the SNJ, a retractable-landing-gear metal monoplane.

How It Flew

There was a between-the-wars training film produced by the Navy that showed a 1920s ground instructor addressing a class of Pre-Primary flight students. Among his words of wisdom were, "It is not deemed feasible to install brakes on airplanes." The statement provides no grounds for optimism about the ground-handling characteristics of airplanes before tricycle landing gear became common. In the classic tail dragger the pilot sits well aft, with a relatively large engine in front of him. The fuel is in the center section of the wing, close to the airplane's center of gravity. On the ground the pilot cannot see directly forward. The contraption sits tail-low, of course, and the tail wheel, if present instead of a skid, is no bigger than necessary to keep the fuselage from bumping along the ground while taxiing. Without brakes and, classically, with a tail skid, no wheel at all, the machine could be a monster on the ground; that is why you see all those wing walkers and grabbers in old photographs. If you wanted to turn the airplane on the ground, the thing to do was to kick the hell out of the rudder at the same time that you gave a burst of power.

That old-time instructor was wrong. Airplanes *do* have brakes. By the time of the N2S, tail skids had given way to tail wheels. However, the center of gravity was still behind the main wheels. This means that there was an inherent tendency for the airplane in motion to swap ends. The resulting maneuver is called a ground loop—exciting, unpredictable, and no fun at all. A tail skid offers some resistance to sideways sliding, partial help in avoiding a ground loop. A fixed, noncastered tail wheel provides similar resistance but is even harder to maneuver than a skid. There are two alternatives: first, a tail wheel that can be selectively locked or unlocked on command, unlocked for taxi and other ground maneuvers and locked for takeoff and landing; second, a tail wheel that is somehow steerable. There are advantages and disadvantages for each.

Efficient ground maneuvering of airplanes awaited the installation of effective differential brakes. Airplane brakes are activated by the rudder pedals. The pedals are conveniently hinged at the bottom and connected to hydraulic cylinders. When the pilot depresses the top portion of a rudder pedal with his toe, the motion activates the brake on that wheel. At the same time he can apply rudder pressure to the pedal with the heel of the same foot. The arrangement makes it possible to apply brake and/or rudder to each wheel separately and selectively with only two feet. Brakes introduce a new problem. The center of gravity is still behind the main landing gear, and what works in the horizontal plane also works in the vertical plane: there is the same tendency to swap ends. If, while in significant forward motion, one applies both brakes at the same time, the result may be a tail dragger standing on its nose or, worse yet, on its back. Think of those pictures of vintage airplanes in various states of disrepair, on their noses or on their backs! That embarrassment can be avoided by never applying the brakes simultaneously unless you are completely or almost completely stopped.

Since you can't see directly in front of the airplane, you must make your taxi path a constant series of S-turns, alternately uncovering the right and left views ahead by swinging the nose back and forth out of the way. The combination of wheel brakes and movable tail wheels made that possible, if not easy. Although ground handling is not what airplanes are about, maneuvering on the ground is necessary to get oneself into the air. Most airplanes make such lousy automobiles that a budding aviator can be too intimidated and humiliated by his pre-takeoff performance to learn much on his first flight.

I was to appreciate that in the fall of 1944 at Naval Air Station Ottumwa, Iowa. This was a Primary Training base crowded with yellow Stearmans. There were two runways adjacent to a large macadam mat and two separate wings of Stearmans parked in neat rows on the tarmac.

Flight line of N2S-3s, NAS Jacksonville, Florida. (USNI Photo Library)

The students operated out of a large ready room with an adjacent parachute-issuing room; you drew a parachute for each flight and carried it out to the flight line. There were a couple of big blackboards on the flight line where student, aircraft, and instructor assignments were recorded in chalk, with plenty of erasers for the constant changes.

We wore flight suits, gloves, goggles, and cloth helmets with Gosports plugged into the earpieces. The Gosport was a one-way communications system. The theory was that a student didn't have anything constructive to say, and that anything he said would only disrupt the business at hand. The Gosport resembled a stethoscope. It was a Y-shaped rubber hose with two branches leading to earpieces built into the student's helmet. The trunk part of the hose either plugged into a metal tube in the rear cockpit or was long enough to lead into the front cockpit; in either case the instructor could plug into it. The instructor's portion ended in what resembled a small oxygen mask held in place by an elastic headband. He talked, and the student listened. All other communication depended on hand signals or an occasional shout into the slipstream. The system led to misunderstandings; one critical misunderstanding could lead to a screwed-up flight. The Gosport was not popular with students.

There were no radios in these airplanes. All takeoff, landing, and traffic pattern signals were given by light from the tower, when such signals were deemed necessary. For the most part we operated much like an uncontrolled but closely monitored airfield. Considering the large number of airplanes flying, it worked well.

Once a student with all that gear was at his airplane, he would put on his parachute and await the instructor. If this was not a first flight, he might get into the airplane and strap himself in to save time. There would be little preflight briefing. The preflight of the airplane was minimal compared with what the modern general aviation pilot must do. The ground crew had already done most of the preflighting, and the aircrew's inspection merely confirmed what the sailors had already performed.

The cockpit of the N2S was simple, even Spartan. There were a stick, rudder pedals, a throttle—where it belonged, on the left—and a small lever, the elevator trim tab control. The cockpit didn't have a complete floor, just metal channels for your heels to slide along. If you happened to drop a glove, it landed in the bilge, gone for the flight—not serious in mid-October, but in December enough to cancel a flight for fear of frostbite. The seat had a considerable height adjustment. There was a little glass or Plexiglas windscreen—just like in the movies—for each cockpit. Suitably strapped in, the student could see the back of the instructor's head and, in a mirror mounted on the bottom of the upper wing, the instructor's eyes staring at him. The Gosport mask covered most of the instructor's face. For the moment the instructor's goggles might be pushed up on his head; once in the air the student wouldn't even have the eyes to read, only that voice through the Gosport tubes.

The instrument panel was spare, matching the rest of the cockpit. There was a magneto switch that did not have or provide for a key. There were a tachometer, oil pressure and temperature gauges, altimeter, airspeed indicator, and magnetic ("wet") compass, but no gyro instruments and no needle-ball (turn and bank indicator).[1] One was supposed to learn coordinated flight literally by the seat of one's pants; a needle-ball was perceived to be an unnecessary crutch that might actually inhibit a student's efforts to develop a properly sensitive behind. By the time I was flying solo it was already cold in Iowa. We put on more and more clothes, and the more the layers, the more sensitive the butt had to be. I was pleased to discover that if I raised the seat to the maximum height, I could see the instrument panel of the empty front cockpit, where there was a turn and bank indicator. Now I could calibrate my behind so that I might recognize coordinated flight when I saw it. I didn't think of the obvious question: If the dumb student in the back seat didn't need that instrument, why did the smart instructor in the front seat have one?

The fuel gauge was a float in a sight gauge below the center section of the upper wing, where the fuel tank was. The starter was an inertial device that had to be hand cranked before being engaged by the pilot in the cockpit. It could be cranked by one person on the ground, outside the airplane, but it was better to have help. The enlisted ground crew did a lot of cranking, but so did the students, especially in the winter months. Woe to the student in the cockpit who fouled up the starting procedure so that it had to be repeated! When it got really cold, the starter couldn't do the job, and we resorted to a daisy chain of people on a long rope attached by a bungee cord to a leather sleeve that fit over a propeller blade. With this thing you might start an otherwise recalcitrant engine, but not often and hardly ever on the first try. The icy tarmac provided its own element of danger: it is not healthy to slip and fall in the vicinity of whirling propellers.

With the airplane finally started and running, the enlisted plane captain would give hand signals to taxi the airplane out of the chocks. The student pilot would taxi straight ahead, eyes glued to the plane captain. The instructor, who had better forward vision than the student, would surreptitiously ride the brakes, knowing better than to trust the student completely. Clear of the chocks, the airplane would taxi between rows of airplanes to the main taxiway. The student would find the airplane a handful, not even realizing that he was getting help. By the time he reached the taxiway where the last taxi director waved him on his way, there would be two other trainers behind him. The student would turn the airplane and follow a line of N2Ss winding their serpentine way to the takeoff mat.

Enough power was used to move the airplanes ahead at a speed approximating a brisk walk, just as the instruction books say to this day. The student pilot would taxi slower because of the proximity of other aircraft, particularly the ones ahead. He had a blind spot dead ahead of 60 to 80 degrees—that is, 30 to 40 degrees either side of the centerline—because of the engine, nose, forward fuselage, and, of course, the head and shoulders of the instructor. To compensate the pilot would negotiate a series of controlled S-turns by the use of power, rudder, and brakes. Each time he swung the nose through his intended direction of travel, he would crane his neck to see what lay in front; he wanted to make sure that his propeller was not about to chew up the tail of the next airplane ahead.

Not many of us felt comfortable or in control that first time out. Compared with modern general aviation trainers, the Stearman is a big airplane. It has a relatively long fuselage, which constitutes a sizable lever arm, and the linkage from the rudder pedals to our "steerable" tail wheel felt sloppy. It was a constant case of undercontrol followed by overcontrol. Too much overcontrol would break the tail wheel loose into full swivel. When that happened, getting back into steerable mode required engine power plus brute force applied judiciously to brake and rudder; often, the instructor had to get things squared away. Then when the student *wanted* to get into full swivel, the machine became part mule. First tentatively, then with increasing use of full rudder, full brake deflection, and increasing power, the student would try to swing the tail around. When the tail wheel finally broke loose, the machine would be hell-bent on turning all the way around before it could be stopped. The N2S was not a confidence builder on the ground. It was designed to fly, not to be a three-wheel taxicab.

Eventually we arrived at a paved mat for takeoff. A "mat" was a roughly circular, rectangular, trapezoidal, or blob-shaped area where a gaggle of airplanes could land and take off virtually simultaneously. The Navy has historical film clips, occasionally seen spliced into training films ending with the Blue Angels, of mass takeoffs from places like North Island in San Diego. Four, six, or more airplanes taking off abreast from a mat was feasible and not uncommon at the larger airfields. As long as everyone recognized the wind direction and accurately aimed into that wind while taking off and landing, a paved mat could accommodate a lot of airplanes.[2]

On a first takeoff the instructor assumed responsibility for wind direction and airplane alignment. He was more concerned about a ground collision than the student was, who already had as much to think about as he could handle. The takeoff roll was unremarkable, except for the problem of going straight. The student pilot had peripheral vision of the only pavement visible, that part ahead of the lower wing on either side of the fuselage. Once he added full power, rudder control was almost immediately available. Counteracting the torque of the radial engine at full power required appreciable right rudder. Takeoff entailed permitting the stick to assume a roughly neutral position—trim was supposed to take care of that initially. This was in marked contrast to taxi, for which, except in the case of a strong wind from astern, the stick had to be all the way back. The idea was to avoid the ultimate ignominy: the airplane standing on its nose or, worse yet, upside down. We took off from a three-point attitude. The airplane accelerated quickly and flew off in a surprisingly short distance.

For most of us this was the first time in actual control of an aircraft. *Control* may be used loosely here; I had once held the yoke of a PBY in my hands, and the previous spring I had spent perhaps fifteen minutes at the stick in the back seat of an SOC floatplane, part of the aviation detachment of the cruiser USS *Louisville*, in the lagoon of Majuro atoll in the Marshall Islands—not exactly meaningful prior experience. This first takeoff and first flight were all new.

The first specific piece of flight instruction I received was the same as I had received from my shipmate in the SOC: nose position—that is, pitch—controls airspeed; throttle controls altitude or rate of descent. This controversial old chestnut[3] was an item of faith for carrier aviators in the days of high-drag airplanes that did almost everything at the same airspeed; *high-drag* especially means the biplanes. My instructor specified a climb speed and "talked" to me until I found a pitch attitude that more or less bracketed that speed. The next order of business was rudder. In that fixed-pitch-propeller machine with no rudder trim, there was never enough right rudder in a full-power climb. It was especially challenging for a novice to find just the right amount of rudder without the benefit of a turn and bank indicator. I was supposed to know by feel: "You're flying in a skid! Can't you *feel* that?"

Eventually we leveled off at the designated altitude. Except for predictable "hunting" in altitude and heading, I approximated straight and level flight to the instructor's satisfaction.

Motion pictures of the time portrayed the first flight of a military aviator as a collection of highly visible, erratic gyrations representing incipient loss of all control. Reality was different; most of us did reasonably well, fairly soon. We were introduced to stalls, spins, and simulated emergencies from the beginning. "A" Stage consisted of eight flights of about one and a half hours' duration. At the end of that time, with about twelve hours' total flight time, we were expected to be ready for solo. Therefore, the instructors tried to introduce us to all the hazards we might be subject to when flying by ourselves and to show us how to recover from the consequences of our own misdeeds.

We did many stalls and spins in "A" Stage. The stall characteristics of the Stearman were straightforward, predictable, and repeatable,[4] though they might be startling to the modern Cessna or Piper pilot. The Stearman's stall really broke, with or without a wing drop. A manageable left wing drop was common. There was no need for argument or discussion as to when or if stall had occurred. (The closest general aviation equivalent I can think of is a Mooney 201.) The stall was easily recovered from, however. Brisk, forward motion of the stick, rudders neutral, add power. Do not attempt to level the wings with aileron; it won't work and may throw you into a spin. At slow speed or when actually stalled, rudder is much more effective for roll as well as yaw control. That phenomenon is the basis for the falling leaf maneuver. The falling leaf is performed with full back stick, power at idle, and alternate applications of full left and full right rudder, causing the nose to yaw spasmodically from one side to the other with an abrupt accompanying wing drop. It is a semiviolent back-and-forth maneuver that actually resembles the motion of a falling leaf.

Spins were performed as a precision maneuver. They were entered the same way as power-off stalls. Just before the stall, kick full rudder in the desired direction of the spin. Hold full aft stick and full rudder until you want to recover. The approved technique was to initiate the spin over a road or a recognizable section line. (This was Iowa; the whole state is divided by section lines.) About a quarter turn of spin goes by before you know what is going on; that gives you time to pick up the road or section line over the nose at the half-turn mark. One-half, one, one and a half, two, two and a half turns—recover! Should you want to recover precisely at two and a half turns, lead the recovery by about a quarter turn. To recover, apply forward stick, full rudder, against the spin. Hold these control positions until the rotation stops, then neutralize the controls. When the airplane is flying—above stall speed, that is—bring the nose up to the horizon, wings level. Do this gradually so as not to get into another spin, but not too gradually, because you do not want to exceed the maximum allowable speed of the airplane. As the nose comes through the horizon, add full power and climb back up to maneuvering altitude for another go. The airplane spins fine in either direction. The left spin is a little more active; even at idle, that not insignificant engine and the consequent rigging details make it easier to turn, and to spin, to the left. (This left-spin tendency gets more pronounced with the large reciprocators; the Corsair and Hellcat are notable examples. The spin recovery technique I have described is generally valid for every Navy airplane I can think of, with only minor variations up to—but definitely not including—the Vought F8U Crusader.)

Another major survival tool was the simulated emergency, usually a "cut gun" administered by the instructor when he thought you were least prepared to deal with it—commonly on takeoff or out in the practice area. The point of the quotation marks is to emphasize that the engine was never really shut down, and this for all sorts of reasons, including that the instructor and his butt were also riding in the airplane. The simulated engine failure was simply a "throttle to idle" by the instructor. The way it usually worked was that the throttle under your left hand assumed a life of its own and abruptly went to idle. This was followed by the instructor's voice over the Gosport: "This is an emergency!"

The rules of safety/survival don't change; the correct actions in 1944, or 1924, were the same as they are today. First, keep the airplane flying, then find a place to put it. If you have time—but *only* if you have time— try to restart. In most of our drills that last was not a viable option, for the low altitudes did not allow time for restart. We did not lack potential landing sites, however; Iowa farmland provided plenty of fields. An emergency on takeoff, then and now, means keep the airplane flying, land essentially straight ahead, and try not to hit anything hard.

There were no simulated emergencies in the traffic pattern, and for good reasons. The first is that in "A" Stage all landings were made at idle power from five hundred feet. We chopped throttle at that altitude when we were abeam the point of intended landing, slowed the airplane to an indicated 65 knots, and made a graceful 180-degree turn to a full-stall, three-point landing on what would have been the numbers, if there were numbers. That was the idea. While we were doing this, a bunch of other guys were in the pattern trying to do the same thing. There was little airspace available for innovative variations on a standard approach. The other reason for there being no simulated emergencies in the landing pattern was that there was a special exercise called "small field procedure." That consisted of flying a specified pattern altitude— eight hundred to a thousand feet—around a rectangular grass field. We flew an oblate pattern such that when the instructor pulled the throttle to idle anywhere in the pattern, there was a feasible approach path to a normal landing. But that exercise came in a later stage. In "A" Stage the theory was that it would be nice to get into the field of choice, but the important thing was simply to get the airplane down safely somewhere.

Landings are what "A" Stage is all about. The Navy's approach to flight training was heavily conditioned by the characteristics of the biplanes with which naval aviation started and by the specialized requirements of getting airplanes on and off aircraft carriers. Since the laws of aerodynamics are more or less immutable, they don't change with scale effect or even with materials. How one adapts to scale effect, materials, speed, and aerodynamic configuration of a specific vehicle is a different matter. The way we were taught to fly in the Stearmans was expected to be applicable to anything we were to see in the fleet. That was largely true up through the straight-wing jets and the straight-deck carriers.

The traditional premise of carrier landing was that you flew the whole landing approach at an airspeed slightly above stall speed, ideally between power-on and power-off stall. When right before the numbers (the round-down of the aft end of a carrier deck) you took a "cut" (chopped the throttle to idle) and let the airplane fall out of the sky as gracefully as you could manage. This got you down as precisely as possible, as slow as possible, in an airplane that was absolutely, positively not flying anymore. If you did it right, you would get that lovely deceleration signifying that you had caught a wire. That was the end game that dominated Navy flight training from the very first flight. With changes, it still does today.

The emphasis in Primary Training was controlled, slow-speed, low-altitude approaches to precision touchdowns. Every landing was full-stall, three-point, stick all the way back in your lap, and you better land within a hundred feet of your selected aim point. Some lack of precision on touchdown was permitted in "A" Stage, but the landings were judged critically. They didn't have to be judged by the instructor; the airplane itself communicated error to a less-than-skillful student more quickly and dramatically than even the most articulate instructor. That did not, however, inhibit instructors from expressing their impressions of student performance. It made for noisy cockpits and sometimes ingenious contributions to a more picturesque speech.

I was a relatively slow learner when it came to landing an airplane. Somewhere along the line you have to get it, like the proverbial light coming on in a dark room. It may not work that way for everyone, but it did for me. You have to understand what is required and relate your reactions in a systematic way to making it happen. When the object of the exercise is to land a noisy, smallish but still-roaring monster of a tail-dragging biplane on a specific, restricted piece of real estate, you must first learn to get close to doing it right. When you finally see it you say to yourself something like, "So that's what he meant. I can do that!" The *it* that you finally see is a recognition of when to establish a "flare," that is, stop the rate of descent and establish the pitch attitude from which you would like the airplane to land. The standard tail-wheel airplane goal is a three-point touchdown when the airplane makes the decision that it is time to land. From that point on you try to get in as many landings as you can, perfecting your technique until some check pilot will let you proceed to the next stage.

Making it to solo in less than twelve hours was not easy. Shortly before I reported to flight training in 1944, the attrition rate was in excess of 90 percent. Most of the student pilots were bagged (washed out of the program, no physical harm) before their first solo. (Demand had a lot to do with it. The Navy didn't lose as many pilots after the Battle of Midway as had been anticipated. They didn't slow down the program input until they started producing more pilots than they could absorb.) With all respect to modern general aviation pilots—an impressive community and a national resource abominably unrecognized—learning to fly in a Cessna 150/152 or Piper Warrior just ain't the same thing.

Initial aptitude was a real driver in wartime military flight training; the system was geared to the fast learner. Sometimes special motivation hurt rather than helped. If you are super-motivated, you tend to try too hard. It is a little like golf or learning to catch a ball: the harder you try, mentally directing each muscle to achieve some complicated coordinated end, the less success you seem to have. Ultimately you have to relax. Let your mind observe and simply watch your instincts at work, making only modest corrections when required. The instructor can scream, "Hold it off! Hold it off! Don't let it land! There, you got it. For God's sake keep it straight. Stick back! Stick back!" (that last comment was frequently punctuated by a sharp rap of the stick against the seat pan; if you were sufficiently prudent, or lucky, no part of your person extended forward of the seat pan). You can hear it a hundred times, but it doesn't mean anything until perception finally, magically occurs. Until you finally see when to break the glide, pull the nose up to a proper landing attitude, and know enough to hold that attitude—knowing all the while that you are finally doing it right—and persist until the bird finally sighs itself onto the ground with or without a bounce, until you manage that for the first time, you are not really flying. From then on it is all refining technique and going on to new adventures.

If you managed to get through the presolo check ride with your

instructor and the subsequent first solo unscathed—with not even
minor damage to yourself or the airplane—you entered "B" Stage. The
new maneuvers here included wingovers, S-turns to circles, and turns
around pylons. There was constant review of what had already been
learned. The small field procedure described earlier was in "B" Stage.
"B" Stage included many of the current Federal Aviation Administration
Commercial Pilot requirements. Among other things, the maneuvers
were preparation for the acrobatics of the next stage.

The Navy wingover was essentially an exaggerated or extended lazy
eight, a climbing turn followed by a diving turn during which a 180-
degree change of direction is achieved. If you let your imagination run
free enough, it can be visualized as a leaning or inclined eight. The
biggest difference between the Navy and FAA versions is the steepness
of the dives and climbs and the maximum angle of bank that is reached.
A reasonable maximum bank angle for the civilian maneuver is 45 degrees, but 30 degrees is recommended. In the Navy—and, I presume,
the Army/Air Force version at the same time—the maximum bank was
90 degrees, which occurred at the 90-degree turn point with the nose
passing through the horizon.

The easiest way to visualize the wingover is to consider a series of
coordinated climbing and descending turns starting from straight-and-
level flight. Like virtually all flying maneuvers that flow smoothly as a
coordinated continuum, the wingover is awkward to describe as a series
of attached "step-functions." As a training and learning experience, the
maneuver is best performed in a series as the pilot gets the feel of it.
The wingover is one of the best of all coordination maneuvers. Everything is changing all the time. Constant rudder adjustments are required
for variations in airspeed and aerodynamic loads to maintain truly "coordinated" flight. The Stearman presented no special problems in the
maneuver, except for relatively heavy control forces.

The chandelle was not significantly different from the modern Commercial Pilot rating maneuver. Essentially a climbing turn resulting in
a 180-degree change of direction, it was one of the first tactical maneuvers to evolve in aerial combat during World War I. Pylon turns were
unremarkable as well, except that the rules affecting both entry and
maneuver performance were considered extremely important. But some
of the maneuvers peculiar to the Navy of the day had elements of in-
trinsic interest or could be bizarre in both interpretation and consequence. Among these were the two precision landing maneuvers, S-turns
to circles and slips to circles.

These two maneuvers had the same basic objective: to land in the
middle of a one-hundred-foot circle from a cut-gun (idle throttle) approach from the 180-degree (beam) position. The circles were marked

with something like whitewash in the middle of outlying grass practice fields. Instead of the standard Navy semicircular approach path, as viewed from above, the path over the ground resembled an S with one lobe bigger than the other. The S-turn approach involved crossing the wind line on final at an acute angle, deliberately high. The plan was to overshoot and come back, playing your radius of turn and bank angle such that the airplane arrived over the circle almost fully stalled and therefore ready to land. The slip approach started the same way. The wind line on final was again intercepted deliberately high, but instead of overshooting the pilot entered a forward slip to dissipate altitude. He recovered from the slip at an appropriate low altitude in a semi-stalled attitude, ready to land the airplane in the middle of the circle. In each case the approach is designed to prevent an undershoot by deliberately coming in high. The excess altitude is then dissipated by the prescribed technique so as to accomplish a precision landing. Thus, one more accommodation to the demanding task at the end of the line: landing on an aircraft carrier.

S-turns to circles were a part of "B" Stage. They didn't trust us to do slips to landings until "C" Stage, with good reason. While S-turns involved coordinated flight all the way, the transition from a slip to a full-stall landing in slips to circles was more demanding. We practiced both for hours, but only after some instructor decided that we could practice them by ourselves without undue hazard to life, limb, and machinery. I don't think any of us was especially concerned about risk. We knew that unfortunate things happened in aviation, but we worried more about not getting through the program.

That meant avoiding a "down," or unsatisfactory check ride. There is no such thing as a good down. The least it meant was more attention than any of us wanted. If you got a down, you had to fly two consecutive up-checks with new instructors covering the same material. The instructor who gave you the first recheck already knew that you had been given a down by one of his colleagues. If you were brilliant on that second check flight, you qualified for the third, deciding attempt. In practice instructors tended to corroborate each other's view of an errant pilot. After you collected a second down, if you were lucky the student review board looked at the record and decided that you deserved another chance. This meant two refresher dual flights given by someone other than your regular instructor and two solo flights, followed by two more check flights, also given by two people with whom you had not previously flown. A chancy business. We all were afraid of that first down.

There were two parts to the problem—not just in precision landings to circles, but in the whole syllabus. The first was actually learning to fly, acquiring the necessary skills. The other part was to guarantee performance on demand good enough to pass flight checks. Even the best of us had his awkward moments in the course of a flight check. An axiom of flight training at all levels says that there is no such thing as a perfect flight check: any check pilot can give any flight student a down on any given flight. Except in the rarest of instances this applies to every flight student, however good. There are occasions when a check pilot would have to be totally unreasonable to issue a down, but he might find a way.

There are countless stories of the hard-nosed instructor who is shown the error of his ways. A typical tale involving the local "Downcheck Charlie" goes like this: Charlie's buddies get a new, particularly talented instructor pilot whom Charlie doesn't know. They dress him up in the uniform of a cadet and send him out to the flight line for a check with Charlie. Cadet Doe has his helmet and goggles on, and he keeps his face averted to avoid casual recognition. They fly. Cadet Doe flies, with absolute perfection, the best performance his hours of flight time and years of experience can muster. Charlie gives him a down anyway. At this point Charlie is confronted with incontrovertible evidence of his unfair, if not unreasonable, standards. His supposedly unsatisfactory "student" flew at least as well as he and met or exceeded all reasonable flight performance standards. Thereafter, so the legend goes, Charlie rejoins the human race to the delight of his students and the satisfaction of his fellow instructors.

In the training environment most of us were sure that we could, and probably would, give any check pilot grounds for a down check in the course of a one-and-a-half-hour "examination" flight. We hoped that our overall ability was such that the check pilot would overlook the overlookable, meaning no major transgressions, certainly none affecting "safety of flight." "Unsafe" allowed no defense; "a little rough on the controls," on the other hand, might be acceptable. What this meant was that just landing in the middle of that damn circle could be more important than how you got there—provided you didn't scare the hell out of the instructor while you were doing it.

Surviving "B" Stage was a prerequisite for the most enjoyable phase of Primary flight training: "C" Stage and acrobatics. "C" Stage was fun, and the best part was acrobatics. The Stearman was capable of all accepted acrobatic (or "aerobatic") maneuvers. In addition to spins, wingovers, and chandelles, "C" Stage included the snap roll, split-S, barrel roll, falling leaf, slow roll, and Immelmann maneuvers. For maximum utilization of time we combined maneuvers into variations like the basic squirrel cage: split-S to loop to Immelmann or Cuban eight.

(The latter is really a separate maneuver combining elements of loops and aileron rolls.)

In retrospect, the maneuvers came fairly easily to me, with two significant exceptions: the slow roll and the snap roll. They were difficult for very different reasons. The slow roll may have been the hardest for most of us to master. In theory the slow roll is a precise rotation about the longitudinal axis of the airplane, with that longitudinal axis pointed at a selected point in space. Since the sky is not loaded with finite aim points, that usually meant finding a piece of cloud to point at. Since we are dealing with a high-drag, relatively low-powered airplane with manual, cable-operated controls, we were faced with, among other things, an energy problem.

The airplane is not going to roll quickly; it is probably going to require full control deflections at least part of the time. Therefore, we better start with enough speed to sustain the maneuver. Eighty-five knots was the magic number for entry into a slow roll. You dropped the nose below the horizon to accelerate to entry speed, then brought the nose above the horizon toward an imaginary aim point, adding full throttle in the process. Next, apply full aileron in the direction of roll. As you start to roll, apply increasing opposite rudder until the 90-degree roll position, while applying increasing forward stick so as keep the nose on the point. From that position to 180 degrees (upside down), you decrease rudder application so as, in the first part of that 90-degree segment, to keep the nose up to the point in pitch and, in the second part, to keep the nose from drifting off the point in yaw. At the same time, you coordinate stick motion so that by the time you are on your back the stick is well forward, to keep the nose above the horizon and on the point.

The second part of the roll, from upside down (the 180-degree position) to right side up, is a mirror-image replication of what you did to get upside down in the first place. On the way you pass through the 270-degree position, where your wings are vertical. You are holding essentially full top (left) rudder and whatever elevator it takes to keep the nose on the point. As the roll continues, you decrease rudder and apply increasing back stick.

I am trying to describe a smooth, coordinated exercise—or perhaps a coordinated exercise in contra-coordination, with all that cross-controlling—one step at a time, when in fact several things were going on at the same time. A lot of muscle was required, as well as precise coordination, to do such maneuvers. We had to visualize what was supposed to happen before actually performing the feat in the air. As is evident from the description, it is easier to see and interpret than to delineate with words.

My Primary flight instructor was Lieutenant (jg) Whitney. He was quiet-mannered, a nice guy, a good instructor, and relatively unflappable. (For me, that was good. I don't do well with screamers, as if anyone does, and flying was so important to me that I tended to work too hard at it.) Whitney was a former aviation cadet, an AVN in Navy terminology, *A* standing for aviation, *V* for heavier-than-air craft,[5] and *N* for training. AVNs had been through the entire Navy training program and were fully qualified naval aviators.

However, many instructors, all of whom wore the standard Navy pilot wings, were AVTs. That is the same kind of nomenclature, except that the *T* also stood for training. These men instructed only in Primary. There was a considerable spectrum of experience and background among these instructors. Some were relative old-timers, crop dusters and the like, who had spent their lives in and around the tenuous business that was pre–World War II aviation. They brought time-tested skills to the Navy, and after some indoctrination they started training Navy flight students. Another group of AVTs were young guys, about the same age as the commissioned officer students. Before being commissioned they had accumulated flight experience varying from a few hundred to several hundred hours, and Commercial Pilot licenses. When the instructor shortage was at its height, the Navy induced them to serve as instructors for some period of time before proceeding with the full Navy syllabus. As it turned out, many of them left Primary Training at about the same time I did and were friends and colleagues throughout the rest of the program. Typically, they were excellent pilots.

Both groups of AVTs, products of the unstructured world now called general aviation, were shy on the niceties of teaching theory. There was a lot of empirical Old Aviators' Wisdom, especially among the middle-aged fliers. The AVNs—the regular-program naval aviator types—seemed better at communicating with neophytes. Whitney, who was an AVN, solved my initial difficulties with the slow roll because he was able to track through the peculiar thought and reaction process that produced my mistakes. But some of my friends had problems with their ex–crop duster AVT instructors. On the entry to the split-S, for instance, Lieutenant Crop Duster, USNR, might advise, "You just flip it over on its back. Let the nose fall through. You know, like the back half of a loop." Flip it over on its back? How do you do that? That advice might be helpful to a "natural pilot," whoever he might be. But me? I was glad I had Whitney instead of one of those other guys. (It reminds me of a cartoon that was circulating in the Training Command at the time. Two instructors are talking in the foreground. In the background, three Marines in full combat gear are prodding with their bayonets an obviously reluctant student toward an early F4U Corsair, unofficially nicknamed the Ensign Eliminator. *First instructor:* "It's a new approach. Start them in fighters and eliminate all but the natural aviators.") There was nothing fundamentally wrong with Lieutenant Crop Duster's instruction on the split-S maneuver, but his tendency was to tell the student *what* to do rather than *how* to do it. Some of the old-timers had figured these things out for themselves; most of us needed more specific information on the incremental elements that made up the maneuvers.

The split-S is a combination of the first half of a snap roll followed by the second half of a loop. It may be easier to visualize if we look at those two maneuvers first. Let's start with the second part of the maneuver, the loop. The loop is essentially a vertical circle, or as close to a vertical circle as you can make it; in practice it tends to be oblate, sort of egg-shaped. It is best to select a straight-line ground reference, like a road, railroad track, or section line.[6] You enter with a moderate dive angle over and parallel to the reference, initially with cruise power. Accelerate to 25 percent greater than cruise speed, retarding throttle so as not to over-rev the engine. In a Stearman, that puts you at about 120 knots. Ease the stick back smoothly. We had no g-meters, but 3 to 3½ g's is about right. As the nose comes up through the horizon, add full throttle. This is the last good reference for a while, so check your heading and wing position carefully. You should still be right over your reference line. Keep the wings level coming through the horizon and you won't lose heading. Keep the power and g-forces constant up through the vertical. As you pass the vertical, tilt your head back as far as you can. Start looking for the horizon coming up the other side. You can start easing the back pressure on the stick. As you get upside down, the weight of the airplane is helping the vertical turn; it wants to point toward the ground. That literally adds an extra g, so you don't need to apply as much back stick pressure. Besides, the airplane has been slowing down ever since you came up through the horizon; the airspeed is decreasing toward stall speed. As you pass through the completely inverted position, let the nose fall through rather than pulling through. Start easing off power so as not to overspeed the engine. You should have regained the horizon and your ground reference by now. Check alignment and wings-level; if you keep wings level throughout the maneuver, alignment will take care of itself. Passing back through the vertical, you should have reacquired most of the original g-loading. Correct power is whatever it takes to keep rpm within permissible limits, probably close to idle. As you bring the nose back toward the horizon, add power back toward cruise setting. If you want to regain altitude for another try, add full power and establish a climb; you gave up some altitude on the entry.

The loop is easier to do than to describe, and it's fun (but don't mess with this stuff on your own without a qualified acrobatic instructor and a certified acrobatic airplane, both of which may be hard to find). When it's done right, you experience a perceptible *thunk* as you hit your own slipstream near the bottom of the loop. (This occurs whether or not the wind is blowing, by the way. You are flying in a moving air mass.)

The other half of the split-S, the entry, is a partial snap roll. (The split-S can also be entered with a half slow roll or a half aileron roll, but the snap roll entry is preferable because it provides the slowest top-of-the-loop entry speed.) A snap roll is a one-turn spin in a horizontal plane. Like all acrobatic maneuvers, the snap roll is begun at an altitude that allows plenty of room for recovery. A proper clearing turn is mandatory before starting. Establish a slow-cruise airspeed, 80 knots in the Stearman. Ease the nose slightly above the horizon. Start the stick moving aft smoothly. Then snap it back the rest of the way to the seat pan as vigorously as you can while applying full, abrupt rudder in the intended direction of roll. As the stick approaches the seat pan, vigorously apply full aileron in the direction of roll. Hold these controls! The airplane will start a modest pitch up and will then snap into a roll. This is different from a slow roll, in which the longitudinal axis of the airplane points to an imaginary point in space throughout the maneuver. The airplane will rotate about an axis, but the nose will never be aligned with that axis. That is, while you are rolling the nose will be pointing at some angle away from the actual axis of rotation. This is basically what happens in a normal, upright vertical spin. You describe a helical path about the actual motion vector of the airplane.

Having initiated the maneuver, you are now rolling. What are you going to do about it? You need to recover from this horizontal spin. Apply forward stick first, followed by full rudder against the roll; this will unstall the wings and stop the rotation. Neutralize the controls, and you are ready to try again. Deciding when to initiate the recovery is the hard part. This varies with the airplane, the pilot, and the speed of rotation. It takes a little experimentation, but you initiate the recovery so that it will be complete at precisely the time the airplane approaches wings-level, upright. It isn't very difficult. After a few tries, you can be good at it. If it were that hard, how could all those World War II pilots make it through flight training? The key to the exercise is the application of the controls. It is more than brisk; it is more like Bang! Bang! Bang! or One! Two! Three! This is true for recovery as well as for initiation.

For one reason or another very few modern airplanes either can, or are certified to, perform snap rolls. This applies to modern fighter aircraft as well as general aviation airplanes. (The last military airplane

I flew for which the snap roll was authorized was the SNJ in the Army, the T-6; in the RAF and Fleet Air Arm, the North American Texan). The maneuver was not authorized for the Hellcat, the Bearcat, or, especially, the Corsair.[7] In the straight-wing jets, the combination of lower structural limits, the essential violence of the maneuver under higher speed (higher "q" or dynamic pressure) conditions, the almost spooky aura of the unknown in the early jet years, and published limitations kept most of us from experimenting. But from the end of World War I until World War II, virtually all single-engine airplanes, unless specially designed for some load-carrying job—and not many were—had the inherent strength and maneuverability to perform what the between-the-wars military regarded as the basic maneuvers. Some of them, the chandelle and the Immelmann in particular, evolved as tactical, one-on-one dogfight maneuvers. Others, such as the loop and split-S, were already known but were adapted for combat. I refer here to "military acrobatics." The categorization is useful to distinguish these maneuvers from the exotic stuff the acrobatic competition folks do and what modern military flight demonstration teams do. These maneuvers were considered part of the skills and techniques that any competent pilot was supposed to have. Hence, they were taught in Primary flight training to all military pilots regardless of what dedicated tactical flying they were to do later on. Even the bomber pilots!

There were other maneuvers. Some, though not required by the syllabus, were the favorites of individual instructors. These included gems like Cuban and Chinese eights and the Whifferdill, the Whifferdill being any weird maneuver that someone invented or stumbled onto. In an otherwise routine dual-acrobatic flight, "This one isn't required, but see if you can do it!" might suddenly come over the Gosport. Among the required maneuvers, on the other hand, was the Immelmann. Essentially a half roll on top of a loop, it was invented by Max Immelmann, one of the German fighter aces of World War I. As a tactical maneuver, it had the then-spectacular advantage of producing a 180-degree change in direction with an increase in altitude. That is, of course, still a very good thing to be able to make happen in one-on-one aerial combat. The problem is that everyone knows how to do it. Also, it is easy to follow; if you start out on the tail of someone making an Immelmann, you can very easily stay on his tail throughout the maneuver. But when Max dreamed up the maneuver, nobody even knew it was possible, let alone what it was. He got rid of a few threatening folks that way, winding up in a position to slide down onto their tails, and that's what helped him become an ace.

The Immelmann, or Immelmann turn, begins with a shallow dive similar to that for the loop. (In a modern high-performance airplane it would be entered from level flight. Early airplanes didn't have sufficient thrust or power.) Gain more airspeed than for the loop, enough that at the top of this "loop" you can use full aileron deflection without danger of stalling. Why not a half snap? Remember the object of the maneuver. You want to have enough speed when it is all over to do something else, like maneuver to a position of tactical advantage against the opponent you just escaped; that usually means on his tail. At best, a snap roll on top would leave you very slow, perhaps too slow to maneuver effectively. You might even stall out and lose the altitude you just worked so hard to attain.

If you think of the characteristics of the three vertical-plane maneuvers, something may occur to you: they can be converted into a series. Start with the split-S. When the nose comes up to the horizon on recovery, don't stop! Keep going and complete a loop. At the bottom of the loop, keep the pressure on and the speed up so that you can continue up and over on your back again. Roll out, and you have performed a form of the squirrel cage: split-S to loop to Immelmann. This is a fun and efficient way to practice all three maneuvers. It is also a common practice tail-chase series in fighter squadrons in modern aircraft. We used to do it in Hellcats with up to eight airplanes in trail (without the forbidden snap entry to the split-S, of course).

The student pilot was exposed to all of these maneuvers in Primary flight training. The final items were cross-country and formation flying. The requirements of the latter dictated that we finally get into the front seat, which is where the pilot sat in all tactical military two-seaters. This was part of "D" Stage. The transition to the front seat was trivial in terms of difficulty. The view, not to mention overall visibility, was much better when in front. It was also nice to have a couple of extra instruments. One necessary but unremarkable condition for solo flight was to carry a sandbag strapped into the rear seat to keep the N2S's center of gravity within limits. We didn't know what the consequences of forgetting the sandbag were, but I don't recall anyone ever forgetting his.

The cross-country syllabus was short and featured only one solo cross-country flight. It did, however, present challenges. Once more I refer to Iowa geography. Here we were, each alone in an airplane without communication radios, let alone radio navigation aids. We navigated by dead reckoning and some ancestor of the modern Sectional Chart. *Sectional* is an apt word. Don't forget the ubiquitous section lines that were the ultimate boundaries of all those farms. Iowa looked as if it had been laid out by a heavenly Rand McNally who, having laid out the grid system, got lazy and decided not to put in any physical recognition features such as mountains, rivers, forests, lakes, or peninsulas. The celestial cartographer did, however, sprinkle in some variations of color that created a great patchwork quilt in earth tones.

It was easy to get lost. The good news was that those farm spreads made good landing fields in extremis, as when running out of gas. In the fall and winter—before the snow fell!—the fields were at their accommodating best as landing fields. Even last season's cornstalks were gone. There were no recent furrows, and the ground was hard. Getting lost was more a psychological hazard than a reality. We learned every idiosyncrasy of the terrain on the routes to the few known training destinations. Landing at a strange field on a macadam strip instead of the familiar NAS Ottumwa mat proved enlightening. How was that cross-wind landing technique supposed to go?

The introduction to formation flying in the Stearman signaled the end of Primary. When I tried to fly in formation in the N2S, I had no standard of comparison. It was difficult to learn, but not disqualifyingly difficult. Nobody I knew ever washed out in formation phase; formation flying just wasn't easy to perform gracefully. The object is to maintain a constant bearing and distance from the lead airplane. This is accomplished by utilizing a combination of visual references, control applications, and power. The visual references consist of aligning some part of your airplane with a part of the "lead" so as to maintain a predetermined angular bearing, like 45 degrees aft of a side-by-side or beam position. In general, longitudinal—that is, fore and aft—distance is maintained by applications of power. Side-to-side or lateral distance is maintained with rudder, skidding or slipping while maintaining wings exactly parallel to the leader's. This means cross-controlling with rudder and aileron. Up and down is controlled with stick back or forward, as required. Obviously, all of these control applications are interdependent; application of one control always affects the others. Once more, the endeavor is a controlled continuum. The closer to the ideal position, the smaller the necessary control corrections and the easier it becomes. For instance, if you are close to where you should be, a little back stick to raise your altitude a foot or so will cause a minimum increase in drag. The further off position you are, and the greater the required corrective stick displacement, the more you must immediately follow with a power application to keep from drifting behind—that is, losing ground in the longitudinal or fore and aft direction.

We always flew in three-plane sections. Initially there was an instructor in each airplane. Students were in the front seats, which was mildly unnerving to the instructors. The three-plane arrangement was common until famed Navy fighter pilot John S. "Jimmy" Thach and others demonstrated the advantages of the two-plane section for fighters. Still, the three-plane section remained the basic element for the V-of-V's formations that were most prevalent for large numbers of bomber aircraft, regardless of service or nationality, throughout most of the war. That was the setup for all those B-17 and B-29 formations seen on the *Late Show*. It was also the basic formation element used by the Japanese Navy carrier striking force at Pearl Harbor and by the Imperial Japanese Army Air Force in virtually simultaneous strikes against the Philippines.

Since we were flying biplanes, we flew step-up rather than step-down. This means that the wingmen were slightly higher than the leader. The upper wing of a biplane, or a high-wing monoplane, is usually forward of the cockpit. Thus, the pilot's view up and forward is restricted. The lower wing is staggered behind the upper wing so that the pilot's view down and forward is relatively unobstructed. There are maneuverability and tactical penalties associated with this arrangement. It is just as well that the low-wing monoplane took over before we were seriously involved in aerial combat.

In any formation flight it is important that the lead airplane fly smoothly and predictably. It is always difficult for a wingman when the leader turns into him. For the wingman turned away from there is the potential embarrassment of being left behind. For the one turned into there can be the real problem of getting the hell out of the way before unplanned metal-to-metal contact. The latter problem is more easily dealt with when you are step-down in a low-wing monoplane than when you are step-up in a biplane. From the step-up position, if you really have to work at getting out of the way, you have a long way to go down. The biplane is a slow reactor. If you elect to go up, you must bank away from an initially high position, thereby risking losing sight of the airplane you are trying to avoid, in an airplane that doesn't climb very well under the best of circumstances.

With all of that going—or not going—for us, those Stearman formation flights were designed to be gentle and nonthreatening. Nonthreatening they were; gentle they were not. Think of working an old-fashioned lever-operated water pump: that is a fair representation of throttle activity on the first couple of flights. The good guys were moving the throttle as if they were pumping water, or trying to, with an unprimed pump. The less talented were turning it into a two-position throttle— on or off—and this at a very high cyclic rate! The wingmen's airplanes appeared to be bouncing up and down like little string-operated toys in the hands of erratic children. There was a common inclination to overcontrol power in the early phase of formation flying, but we became relatively proficient in a remarkably short time. It wasn't long before we were making three-plane-formation takeoffs and landings.

The Primary Training syllabus ended with formation and cross-country work. Successful survivors could say goodbye to the N2S and move on to the all-metal, low-wing, retractable-gear, constant-speed-propeller SNJ, what the general aviation community refers to today as a "complex airplane." At this point we had 100 to 125 hours of total flying time. We left for Pensacola or Corpus Christi with scarcely a nostalgic glance at the Yellow Perils we left behind. Now, a couple of generations of pilots later, I guarantee that there are few if any of us who would not like to get back into one of those airplanes.

It was a cold fall and winter in Iowa. I got my cheeks frostbitten in the back seat of a Stearman and my ears frostbitten one Saturday morning outside a hangar, waiting for Captain's Inspection. I was still nursing my cheeks at Christmas. A few weeks later I finished Primary flight training. It was time for a change of scenery and a new airplane.

Chapter 2
SNJ Texan

General Description

THE NAVY PROCURED ABOUT FIVE THOUSAND SNJs from 1939 through 1945. They were built by North American Aviation, now Rockwell International, the successor to the Berliner Joyce company. Berliner Joyce, originally in Baltimore, Maryland, had built tactical and trainer aircraft in the 1920s and 1930s—up to 1934. The SNJ metal, low-wing, retractable-landing-gear airplanes were "hot" aircraft for trainers. Most were powered by Pratt & Whitney R-1340 "Wasp" engines rated at 550 hp. Most Navy SNJs were procured under U.S. Army contract as "AT-6s" (for example, the Army AT-6C was the Navy SNJ-4).

The SNJ series was a follow-on to the prototype NJ-1, a fixed-gear, fabric-covered airplane that looked very similar. The SNJ was a tandem-cockpit two-seat aircraft with stick and rudder controls. The pilot normally sat in the front seat, the instructor in the back seat. This was a significant difference to us Stearman-trained pilots. Solo flights were always conducted from the front seat in the SNJ. This arrangement was consistent with the normal tactical arrangement of fleet airplanes, with the pilot in front and the crewman, whatever his function, in back.

The cockpits were covered by a long greenhouse canopy, each cockpit with its own sliding section for access or ventilation. There was much open-canopy flying in World War II–era airplanes, especially in the Pacific. Aircraft controls were essentially the same in both SNJ cockpits. Each had a complete instrument panel as well as communication and navigation radios. The latter were necessary for one of the missions of the airplane: Instrument Training. For Instrument Training—the first phase of SNJ training—the instructor pilot sat in front, from where he could monitor what was going on in the outside world, while the student suffered under the "bag" in the rear seat. The bag was a canvas cover on a metal frame that was normally stowed out of

SNJ-5, shinier than most Navy trainers. (USNI Photo Library)

the way, accordion-like, behind the rear cockpit; it was not unlike a small convertible top for an automobile. The student could pull it over his head by the upper frame and latch it to the top of his instrument panel, creating a canvas canopy within and below the airplane Plexiglas canopy. The student was then in his own little tent where he could see and have access to all controls and instruments but not the outside world. Only the student could rig the bag, but the instructor had a quick release with which he could pop it open.

One of the exciting things about the SNJ was its appearance: it looked like a hot airplane. By U.S. standards it was small for a radial-engined airplane, compact, sleek. Its low, tapered wings ended in squared-off tips. The overall appearance, especially the relationship of the forward cockpit to the engine cowling and the shape of the vertical tail, gave it a superficial resemblance to the Japanese Mitsubishi Zero fighter. That resemblance has been taken advantage of in a dozen or so motion pictures about World War II. The most recent may be *Final Countdown*, currently on videotape and cable. Recognition features? The big giveaway for the phony Zero of movies is the square wing tips. Also, the SNJ canopy is a little too long. One film went to the trouble of dummying up some "real" Zeros. *Tora! Tora! Tora!* used airplanes that were good replicas, at least cosmetically; the producers started with SNJs and used plastic and epoxy in the transformation. In the early days of the Blue Angels, when they flew Hellcats and Bearcats, the demonstration included a simulated attack on a "Zero," née SNJ. The climax was a smoke-generator "fire" in the critically damaged "Zero" followed by a parachuting "enemy pilot," in reality a dummy with a barometrically or lanyard-opened parachute thrown out of the airplane on cue.

In common with most other airplanes of the era, these were tail-wheel airplanes. Some of them had fully swiveling, lockable tail wheels; others had the "steerable" variety I complained about in the Stearmans. They had rudder as well as pitch trim tabs. This was an innovation that had real merit for fledglings dealing with the relatively high engine torque produced by the SNJ power plant.

The prototype NJ-1 was advertised to have a top speed of 176 mph (about 152 knots) with a radius of 810 statute miles.[1] The SNJ was advertised to have a top speed of 210 mph (183 knots), a cruise speed of 196 mph (170 knots), and a range of 900 statute miles.[2] (Those numbers come from wartime sources. Note that *radius* was used to describe the NJ-1, *range* to describe the SNJ. *Range* is the correct term.) The principal difference between the two airplanes was retractable gear and metal skin (SNJ) versus fixed gear and mostly fabric skin (NJ-1). It is reasonable to expect perhaps a 10 percent difference in range and 10 to 15 knots' difference in speed attributable to retractable landing gear. The difference in drag between retractable versus fixed gear, then as now, is partially offset by increased weight. The SNJ was about 800 pounds heavier.

Neither airplane in service flew close to those published numbers, at least not to the cruise values. We normally flew the SNJ at about the same speeds as the SBD, around 128–32 knots indicated airspeed. Top speed was a lot better, close to the advertised. Entry speeds for some acrobatic maneuvers approached 170 knots.

The "J" was a fine airplane and an excellent trainer. Indeed, it performed better than many "service type" or fleet airplanes in use at the beginning of the war. The all-metal, retractable-landing-gear airplane was just coming into its own when World War II started. The Japanese and Germans flew fixed-gear dive-bombers throughout the war. It was not, then, de rigueur to insert a fledgling pilot into a hot, modern, metal monoplane—with retractable landing gear, yet!—until late in his training. Thus, we all started out in Stearmans. The next step for most wartime trainees had been the SNV Vultee Valiant, more commonly called the Vultee Vibrator. The SNV was used for Basic flight training and instruments. The SNJ was reserved for Advanced Training, which was really tactical and combat training. Operational Training, in which pilots were introduced to their fleet aircraft, came after that. Of these, only Operational Training was invented during the war; before that, fleet pilots learned to fly their service airplanes on reporting aboard their first squadron.

My group was among the first to transition directly from the Stearman to the sophisticated SNJ with its fighterlike performance. We were excited and apprehensive but ready for the challenge. A classmate, George C. Watkins,[3] on first viewing the flight line at Naval Auxiliary Air Station Cabaniss Field, Texas, was heard to say, "Retractable gear. I bet you can really fly low in those things!"

How It Flew

On arrival at Cabaniss Field—or Cuddihy, or Waldron—we did not promptly leap into the blue in these interesting new airplanes. Ground school occupied half our time, and a good chunk of that came before we even got near an airplane. These airfields were part of a supporting complex that extended outward from "Mainside," which was Naval Air Station Corpus Christi; the satellites were Naval Auxiliary Air Stations. There were so many students and so many flights ongoing that there was a lot of waiting before getting started in the flying syllabus.

We were fed large doses of navigation, instruments, aircraft systems, and Morse code—radio and blinker. Pilots were not expected to read radio code except in extremis. However, some theorized that we should be able to read and transmit blinker, so we carried signal mirrors and flashlights as standard survival equipment to send flashing-light code. There was also radio range theory and tortuous hours in the venerable Link Trainer.

Before elaborate cockpit simulators were invented, the indoctrination one received before climbing into an airplane consisted primarily of a cockpit checkout. This was routinely conducted by a flight instructor who would rather have been doing something else. The cockpit checkout typically included a dozen students. Instead of each of us in turn sitting in the airplane and getting familiar with the controls—followed by a "blindfold" cockpit checkout where we identified all the major controls with our eyes covered—only a couple of us actually got to sit in the airplane; the rest crowded around trying to see. The instructor droned away. The guys in the back didn't have the foggiest idea what was going on. Most of us went back on our own later and spent time in the cockpits, to satisfy ourselves that we knew where the important items were and how to reach them.

We did ultimately fly, though, and not only in the back seat under a hood where we were mesmerized by dials and gauges. Eventually we moved into the front seat of the airplane. One day, by ones and twos, we shambled out to the flight line, carrying our parachutes by the straps over our shoulders: "By the leg straps, Mister, not the risers. You might have to use that thing!" Between the parachutes and our clothing, it was hard not to shamble. We wore the ubiquitous, baggy cotton khaki-colored flight suits. They had more zippers and pockets in unlikely places than the law should allow. (Except for new materials and better zippers, today's flight suits are similar. They are better tailored now, and Velcro fasteners have replaced the buttons.) We wore cloth helmets with real radio earphones—no more Gosports! The earpieces were set in flapped pockets in the helmet. The interconnecting wires teed into a longer wire ending in a phone plug that mated with a still longer wire in the airplane.

And we wore goggles, usually pushed up on our foreheads. They were loosely attached to the helmet by a loop around the elastic. The goggles themselves had smallish metal frames, hinged in the middle, surrounding real glass that was supposedly shatter resistant. Foam rubber pads around the eyepieces made them endurable, if not comfortable. With each pair of goggles we received replacement lenses for different applications: clear, tinted, and amber. Changing lenses was so difficult that we seldom attempted it; we stuck with what we had if at all possible (except for night flying, when you needed clear lenses), or we simply left the goggles perched on top of the head. The lenses were roughly oval, confirming a line from one of comedian Sid Caesar's routines: "The Americans wore round goggles. The Germans wore square goggles." According to Hollywood, Caesar was right. The rectangular look in goggles was the air-warfare equivalent of the black hat. This was the real World War II–look for aviators, right out of *Baa, Baa Black Sheep*, Marine Corps ace Pappy Boyington style.

Overwhelming confidence was not a common commodity for most of us before the first SNJ flight. With the assistance of a plane captain, the student put his parachute in the front cockpit. My experience was typical. I normally did that chore myself, followed by a walk-around preflight inspection—admittedly cursory, because the line crew had looked the airplane over carefully before I even showed up. Once in the cockpit I got squared away. The plane captain made sure that I was properly strapped in and that my headphones were plugged in; the mike was hand-held, its normal home a receptacle with a retaining clip on the side of the cockpit. Then there was nothing to do but look around and wait for the instructor.

Like most trainers the SNJ was yellow, although some had aluminum-colored fuselages and tail sections; the high-gloss, natural-metal look was almost exclusively Army Air Corps. The inside of the airplane was predominantly green—not a nice healthy nature green, but a sickly zinc-chromate green. Zinc chromate was to naval aviation what red lead paint was to the surface Navy, the universal coating for everything that didn't move.

This cockpit was far different from that of the N2S Stearman. It was as sophisticated and complicated as any World War II–era single-engine airplane. The instrument panel was black, contrasting with the overall green interior. The gauges and dials were large. By daylight all the numbers and needles were white against a black background. The significant exception was the gyro horizon, now usually called the attitude gyro. The lower half represented the earth and was black; the upper half represented the sky and was white. Those white needles and lettering were like luminous-dial wristwatches. They glowed in the dark or low ambient light levels. They really came to life when lit by ultraviolet light. The SNJ featured a detachable swivel light that illuminated the panel with ultraviolet light.

The stick and rudder controls were conventional, not significantly different from the Stearman's except that the black-ended stick was more businesslike, incorporating both a trigger for the single 30-caliber machine gun firing through the propeller and a small button, or "pickle," for releasing bombs or other wing-mounted stores. In Basic and Instrument Training we had no need for either. At the pilot's left, conveniently positioned for the left hand, was the throttle quadrant on which was mounted the throttle and the propeller pitch and mixture controls. This was the standard arrangement for virtually all single-engine, single-cockpit or tandem-seat airplanes. It is the same today for fighter and light attack airplanes, although the propeller and mixture controls have disappeared with the advent of jet engines.

For the budding SNJ pilot the most important controls on the right side were the trim controls. The Stearman had only a pitch trim control. It helped relieve the work load by eliminating excessive pitch control forces, but most of us didn't use it as often as we should. By modern Cessna and Piper standards the Stearman control forces were heavy. In the Stearmans we were constantly changing both flight path and airspeed, so we could do without the nicety of being properly trimmed. Steady-state flight was rare. The SNJ was going to be different, but not about changing flight path and airspeed. "Straight and level" was a theoretical concept, not something to be experienced often in the Training Command. The big difference was that the torque and aerodynamic forces in the SNJ were great enough that it was important to approach hands-off trim at the outset.

The takeoff setting was particularly important in the SNJ. The trim controls were two round, rotatable metal disks, coaxially mounted side by side on the right side of the cockpit. The disks were oriented fore and aft, located so as to be easily reached by the pilot's right hand.

Each had a notch in the periphery that served as a point of reference; it amounted to a zero setting when the notch was exactly centered on top of the disk. For takeoff we rolled the outer control forward (right rudder) until the notch was about 45 degrees forward of center. Similarly, we rolled the inboard control aft (nose-up trim) until the notch was about 45 degrees aft of the center position. The rudder trim ensured that the torque that accompanied full power for takeoff didn't instigate a turn to the left that might be followed by a wild ride off the runway. In the same way, the pitch trim ensured a comfortable three-point take-off attitude. This was accepted technique for single-engine tail draggers in the Navy.

The Navy emphasized proper and frequent use of trim tabs. Trim minimizes the varying control forces the pilot must contend with in flight. Trimming out as much control force or pressure as possible is desirable. (Some people prefer a small continuous pull force, others a push force while flying.) It is not necessarily true that a lazy pilot is a good pilot, but it makes sense not to load oneself unnecessarily, if for no other reason than to reduce fatigue. Then there is the importance of retaining as much control effectiveness or authority as the airplane is capable of providing. In many modern airplanes, particularly those with flying tails where the entire horizontal stabilizer moves, available control travel, as well as control effectiveness, is enhanced or inhibited by trim position. A pilot can get into mischief by running out of available control travel or discovering that he is simply not strong enough to move the controls where he needs to.

There were other new features in the SNJ cockpit such as a control for adjusting flaps for landing and takeoff. The most significant of the innovations was retractable landing gear. The gear went up and down by actuation of a simple lever. The motivating power was provided by a hydraulic system. The SNJ had a lazy hydraulic system. In its normally quiescent state it just sat there, taking a nap from which it could be awakened only by actuation of the power-push, a different lever. One push would activate the system. It stayed on line long enough to operate both gear and flaps for a landing approach. However, if we took too long to move the gear-actuating handle or if a broken habit pattern caused us to recycle something, the system would drop off after its programmed time interval, and that interval was short. You can imagine the booby-trap aspects of such a lash-up, an embarrassment waiting to pounce on an unsuspecting student. He moves the landing gear or flap handle, certain that he has activated the hydraulic system, and nothing happens. But he is under stress, otherwise the time interval wouldn't have elapsed in the first place. He doesn't notice that nothing has occurred, even though all retractable-landing-gear airplanes have a warning system—audible, visual, or both. An unintentional wheels-up landing was not an unusual result. Later, the student would try to explain: "Well, yes, Commander, I think I did just barely hear something about 'landing gear' on the radio. But there was a loud noise in the airplane, like a horn. It made so much noise I couldn't really make out what the tower was saying. . . ."

The SNJ starting mechanism is unique in my experience. It was a sophisticated variant of the inertial starter in the Stearman. Instead of the manpower, a euphemism for sailor or flight-student power, that was required to crank the traditional inertial starter—getting the flywheel up to speed—the SNJ had a two-position foot-operated device. It looked like something off a shoeshine stand but was corrugated so that the pilot's foot wouldn't slip. When it was pressed down a clutch would engage. The flywheel wound up, audibly. After an estimated time interval, or when it sounded right, the pilot rocked his foot forward and pressed with his toe the forward part of the pedal. The starter engaged, the propeller turned, and, other prestart procedures having been taken care of, the engine began to run.

I didn't go through the first starting procedure by myself. The instructor helped as I dutifully read off each item on the checkoff list. From the instructor's viewpoint there was something special about the SNJ: he couldn't see very well from the back seat, especially when on the ground. The visibility out of the rear cockpit was acceptable in the air when performing normal and sometimes not-so-normal flight maneuvers, but operations on the ground or when approaching the ground required courageous patience on his part. It was for many instructors an unnerving experience. Old rule: what is unnerving for the instructor will prove to be unnerving for the student. My instructor was a good pilot and a nice guy, maybe even charming, but in the back end of that bird he was nervous, and a shouter. I never did well with shouters.

Getting the SNJ out of the chocks, onto the taxi strip, and eventually to the takeoff spot was not difficult. It was easier than the first time in the Stearman. The airplane had the dreaded steerable tail wheel, and I was apprehensive about the power and control response. Through this part of the evolution the instructor was relatively calm, although I noted his high-pitched voice; it would get higher. The airplane was quite easy to taxi. The visibility from the front seat was excellent. There was no upper wing or struts to get in the way. The front cockpit was far forward and comfortably high. Even for a comparative shorty like me, the seat would adjust high enough to put my head at canopy level or higher. My companion was not so fortunate. As I S-turned my way to the runway, I could see him vigorously craning his neck and head as the nose swung back and forth, trying to determine what we had almost hit that time. Being able to see him in *my* rearview mirror on the upper part of the windshield bow was a refreshing change!

In simple airplanes the power instrument is the tachometer, the rpm indicator. (Most of us flying airplanes today for which we pay the costs are flying "simple" airplanes.[4] Constant-speed props cost money.) The higher the rpm, the more power being delivered. As long as an engine has excess power available, the pilot has control over the power delivered to the propeller. Under varying loads with a fixed-pitch propeller the rpm varies, even at a constant power setting (throttle position). Because of that physical fact, formation flying in the N2S was a study in speed instability. The whole notion of the variable-pitch, or constant-speed, propeller is that it enables the pilot effectively to select the proper "gearing" for what he is trying to do. A controllable-pitch propeller for an airplane accomplishes much the same thing that selectable gears do for an automobile. There are times when one wants high torque to get a machine from a standing start to some desired cruise condition, which may include a desired altitude as well as a desired cruise speed. Good acceleration performance is required, for which it may be acceptable to endure the high revs, engine wear, and fuel consumption that go with all that turning and burning. After all, this a transient condition.

Once you get to cruise configuration, however, you want sustaining performance with relatively low rpm. For takeoff and climb you want the engine turning like hell with the propeller set to take a lot of small bites of air very quickly; at cruise you want the propeller to take very large bites of air at the slowest turning rate you can manage. It really is a lot like a stick-shift automobile. Envision what happens if you get it wrong. Can you imagine trying to get a high-performance car away from a stoplight in an overdrive fifth gear? Same thing as trying to take off or climb in an airplane in high pitch (low rpm). How about trying to cruise at highway speeds in first gear? Same thing as trying to cruise at altitude in low pitch (high rpm). Neither works very well, and both are not at all kind to the power plant's mechanical condition.

A reason for devoting attention to this feature of a whole class of airplanes is that the SNJ had a special distinction. It was a very noisy airplane—although I didn't notice the noise in the cockpit, probably because I was too busy and apprehensive. Besides, I was wearing one of those old-fashioned helmets with the insulated earpieces. It was when one was outside the airplane, watching from the ground, that the full effect was apparent. On takeoff, with full power, full low pitch, the airplane was loud. It was an attention getter with few peers. If a hapless solo student got airborne and climbed much above a thousand or fifteen hundred feet without adjusting propeller pitch, he would not be able to hide it; when he got on the ground, he would find out that the whole world knew.

Every pilot of that era learned early on the sound effect of the SNJ's prop pitch control when shifted back and forth from high to low pitch at low altitude. Even more civilized airplanes went through a distinctive, easily recognizable frequency and amplitude change. During the war it was a matter of pride to be able to identify individual models of airplanes by the noise they made. (Frederic Wakeman uses this as a conversation device with a couple of his principal characters in *Shore Leave*, perhaps the raunchiest tale of World War II naval aviation.) But identifying an SNJ was no challenge; the most distinctive sounding of all, it could be identified by everybody.

Meanwhile, there I was, about to fly one of these birds for the first time. I taxied onto the runway and lined up with the centerline. I rolled forward a couple of feet to center the tail wheel and came to a complete stop. With my feet firmly on the brakes, stick back in my lap, I added full power. I released the brakes, allowed the stick to move forward to a neutral position, and was off and rolling. I was conscious of the need for right rudder as I started to roll, but since I had adjusted the rudder trim, the pressure required was not excessive. Acceleration was not exactly neck snapping, but I knew I had a different beast on my hands. While I adjusted to a variety of new sensations, the plane got airborne as if anxious to get into its own element.

Then the instructor began instructing: "Get the gear up. Make your clearing turn. Pull the manifold pressure back to 30 inches. Prop pitch! Prop pitch! Climb setting! Watch your airspeed. That's not what you were told to climb at." I had myself a talker. We made it to two thousand feet and leveled off. I tried to remember the various control settings as I had been briefed, but it didn't matter, because they were being repeated to me in exhaustive detail. After leveling off I had to retard the throttle to designated cruise manifold pressure, then retard the propeller pitch to cruise rpm. Do this in inverse order, and excessive manifold pressure might result; "overboosting" was the dreaded result. Thankfully, it was difficult to abuse an SNJ engine either accidentally or on purpose. We were being trained to establish good, safe habits, not just for this airplanes but also for the more powerful, less forgiving ones we would fly later on.

However much I deplored his style, my instructor was following a time-honored method: teach procedures, procedures, procedures; skill would come in due course. With carefully conditioned, ingrained procedures, we would learn instinctively to do the right thing, the safe thing, in all kinds of conditions. My group was fortunate that the survival pressure had considerably abated compared with what it had been even six months before. Program survival, that is. Physical survival was not in question, unless it was possible to be shouted to death by the guy in the back seat.

After some time devoted to straight and level flight, turns, climbs, and descents—the four basic airplane evolutions—we slowed the SNJ down and performed stalls. (At that stage we did not spin the airplane; spins were reserved for Advanced Training.)

We proceeded to one of the outlying practice fields for what our British cousins refer to as "circuits and bumps." The airplane was immediately easy to fly. The control forces were heavier than I was used to, but the bird felt so stable and smooth that I was barely conscious of having to pull or push harder. There was an unmistakable feeling of higher performance in this airplane.

The practice fields were grass, quite similar to those in Iowa except that the Texas ones were naturally bigger. Again, we were always part of a crowd when we used one. The traffic pattern was full and called for discipline while we attempted to master a whole set of new procedures in a new airplane. There were many more levers, handles, and knobs to worry about. Another significant difference was the number of imaginary points around the pattern, from the moment of adding power for takeoff to touching down for landing. At each point we were supposed to take a particular action or achieve a designated flight condition.

The pattern required a slight jog to the right immediately after takeoff, followed by landing gear retraction. That little turn was important. In naval aviation, all procedures are geared to aircraft carrier operations. This was a clearing turn. It is designed to point the wake of a departing aircraft somewhere other than in the face of the next airplane to take off. That little turn, followed almost immediately by its counterturn in the opposite direction, effectively sidestepped each departing aircraft from directly in front of the ship. While operating aircraft from an aircraft carrier, it is desirable to have the relative wind a few degrees off the port bow so that the turbulent wake of departing aircraft—taking off at intervals of only seconds—is quickly blown clear of the deck. Having the wind off either bow would accomplish that. However, if aircraft are landing simultaneously, it is necessary also to avoid fouling the landing area with other turbulence—such as from the wind shadow of the island structure. Wind with a component from the port side averted the problem, since American aircraft carriers always have the islands on the starboard side.

Hours of practice in the landing pattern made the clearing turn virtually automatic. After gear retraction on takeoff the throttle was retarded to reduce manifold pressure to climb power. Reduction in propeller rpm was next. The pilot tried to control airspeed and monitor altitude while he was doing this. After passing through three hundred feet or so, he began a climbing turn to the left to intercept the downwind leg. (There is no crosswind leg in the Navy.) The climb continued to pattern altitude, where the pilot made another transition, to slow cruise configuration. That involved changes in manifold pressure, rpm, airspeed, altitude control, and trim, always trim. By then it was time to start the prelanding checklist.

Somehow I got through the pattern on my first landing approach, unhappy both with my performance and with the vocal response from my instructor in the back seat. I found myself on final approach, checklist complete, on airspeed and glide slope. I looked at the field coming up at me. Aware of helpful advice from the rear, which I largely ignored, I landed. Not bad! This really isn't that difficult, I thought. Then the shouting from the back seat went up again on the roll-out. That is the way it went throughout the touch-and-go landings.

I returned from that first flight with mixed emotions. I knew I could fly the airplane. I was sure I could land it consistently. I knew I could master the procedures, but could I master them fast enough for my impatient instructor? The question loomed large, so large that I began to believe that I knew the answer, and I didn't like it. Events proved me wrong, but until almost the instant he finally gave me the "up," clearing me for solo in the SNJ, I remained convinced that he wouldn't pass me. That was the last time I felt serious concern about washing out of the training program (which is not to say that I never again carried the baggage of apprehension).

A major part of the Basic syllabus was an introduction to formation flying in a low-wing monoplane. We could fly step-down now, just like the big guys. The constant-speed propeller eliminated most of the speed instability that had plagued us in the Stearmans. We still flew in three-plane sections. We revisited the section evolutions and maneuvers, including cross-unders, echelons, and formation landings and takeoffs. New to us were break-ups and join-ups, which are essential to maneuvering large numbers of aircraft effectively.

Break-ups are the easier of the two evolutions. The lead airplane of a three-plane section signals the others into echelon, either right or left; right echelons were predominant. The lead pilot raises his right arm in a fist, making sure that his left wingman can see him. When he receives an acknowledgment, he waggles his wings. The left wingman drops down by retarding throttle and adding a little forward stick. He keeps his wings level, using rudder to slide underneath the lead airplane and the other wingman. When he reaches the proper lateral position, he stops the slide with rudder, adds throttle, and, with a little back stick, pops up gently into echelon. This is the basic cross-under. Now both wingmen are stacked, stepped down on the leader's right. To break, the leader holds up two fingers and makes a circular whirling motion; this signifies that the break-up is pending. He taps his head and points to the wingman, the next closest airplane in the echelon. At that point the wingman becomes the new leader. The former leader banks sharply away from the formation. The new leader passes the signal and repeats the maneuver after a brief interval, usually a few seconds. Thus it goes down the line until all aircraft have broken.

Break-ups may be followed by individual airplanes entering a landing traffic pattern about a field or carrier. To keep aircraft from stretching out over the horizon, it is customary to stack major elements vertically: divisions, flights, or squadrons, with individual divisions dropping down into the break-up altitude pattern as it empties below them. For drill in training, we simply stretched our three-plane divisions/sections in trail until the signal was given for join-up.

The join-up signal was a short series of small zoom/dive oscillations by the lead, created by a slight fore and aft motion of the stick, followed by an approximately 30-degree banked turn. This turn will continue through 180 degrees, one complete course reversal; by the end of that turn, all hands are supposed to be on board—joined up! The trick for the "joiners" is to delay starting the join-up turn until the lead is 30 to 40 degrees off the nose of their airplanes. Then, start a turn, adjusting bank angle and throttle so as to close on the leader on a constant bearing line, 45 to 60 degrees behind his wingtip. The join-up must be timed just right so that you approach the final position v-e-r-y s-l-o-w-l-y on a heading approximating that of the lead aircraft. It is also considerate to stop your relative motion at least one plane width away from your intended final position; that way the leader is comfortably aware that you are not going to try to fly through him (it has happened). From that position you can perform a cross-under to a position on the leader's other side or simply fly into position on the same side. A common priority is for early joiners to take the outside positions to make things easier for the late joiners. That priority also makes it easier for the lead to keep track of who has and who hasn't joined yet.

There is plenty of room for error in join-ups. If you, the joiner, come in at an angle too far forward on the lead airplane, it is almost certain that your heading will not be the same as the lead's. This can result in a high rate of closure that cannot be easily stopped. One way to salvage the maneuver is to throw up a wing and enter a steep bank away from the leader. What makes this technique fraught with trauma for all hands is that (1) the joiner can no longer see the leader (the leader is supposed to keep doing what he is doing; the joiner is supposed to make it all come out right); and (2) the joiner probably can't kill the rate of closure right away with that convulsive, last-ditch bank maneuver. So there you are, closing on some guy you can no longer see. And there he is, semi-immobilized, perhaps, because of people already flying close formation on him, watching the belly of this projectile—that's you, the joiner—coming right at him. How does he get out of the way? And if he gets out of the way, how does he know that you won't hit somebody else?

Obviously, that is not an acceptable technique. What is merely troublesome with, say, three airplanes can be severely embarrassing at a squadron or air group level. If you have misjudged badly, there is no graceful solution. Whack off power. Level your wings. Go well under everybody else, well to the outside. Then come back as best you can. You are almost guaranteed to be Tail-end Charlie for a while, as well as being late joining up. You might even hear some constructive suggestions when you get back on the ground.

Join-up errors in the other direction may have the same result, but without scaring the hell out of everybody in the process. Suppose, for instance, that you start your turn late: the turn is too shallow, or you are not carrying enough power. The bearing line on which you are trying to close the leader is now too far aft. You wanted to be somewhat behind his wing tip but have wound up closer to being on his tail, essentially behind him. (Old nautical expression: "A stern chase is a long chase.") Instead of being inside the leader in a turn, which would have let you fly an arc with a shorter radius than the leader's, you now are forced to catch him with extra speed.

Nothing good is going to come of this. If you are the last pilot to join the formation, the leader can either set out on his intended course to wherever he wanted to take the flight in the first place, or he can continue the join-up turn past 180 degrees to help you. If he chooses the former, you burn a lot of extra fuel, as well as time, trying to catch up to everybody. Roaring up from behind, you get to look at a lot of tails. That is all you can see, and it is the worst view you can have of an airplane for determining relative position by either depth perception or perspective. Naturally, you are impatient to get out of this position of embarrassment, so you are going like the devil when you finally approach the other airplanes. The probable consequence is that you will overshoot. Now you slide to the outside of the formation, frantically trying to kill off excess speed so that you don't go past the whole outfit. You look off to the left to see the skipper's eyes boring holes into you: "You were supposed to be on the other side of me a long time ago," those eyes are saying. You can't blame him. If he had chosen the other alternative, continuing the turn for your convenience, the other airplanes would be burning both fuel and time waiting for you, and that's poor airmanship.

If you were not the last wingman to join, there are other possibilities. At some point in the evolution, the people behind you who are doing it right can't see you in your "sucked"[5] position. Having concluded from your performance that you are unpredictable, they are going to be reluctant to take their eyes off you. This occurs at a time when they should be concentrating on the leader, not worrying about you. You have become very noticeable at a time when it is better not to be noticed.

The final flight in the Basic formation syllabus was the check ride. The instructor/check pilot was a Marine I had flown with before. He rode in my airplane. Instead of rotating the formation lead among the three of us, he let me keep it the whole time. Not only did I not screw up, I made an absolutely grease-on landing at the end of the flight. You are not supposed to be able to do that out of a full-stall or approach-to-stall landing. It reminded me of the apocryphal quotation of the old-time airline pilot who probably got his experience in the stiff-legged DC-2, a notoriously difficult airplane to land well: "One grease-on landing in a row is an accident. Two grease-on landings in a row is a miracle. Three grease-on landings in a row, somebody's lying!"

The completion of Basic and Instrument Training meant farewell to Cabaniss Field, although I was to revisit the place. The next stop was NAAS Kingsville and Advanced Training. Until now the emphasis had been individual skills and individual performance. For the rest of the program, including Operational Training in fleet-type airplanes, the emphasis shifted to group endeavors, section and division exercises in which we learned to fly tactically. There were new individual skills to be acquired and graded, of course. The object was to learn to use the airplanes as weapons, with minimum risk to ourselves and to our instructors.

Kingsville, Texas, is about forty miles south of Corpus Christi. In the late spring of 1945 the sign at the "city" limit indicated a population of about seventy-eight hundred. It was somewhat larger in the fall of 1985 when I revisited, but not much. Kingsville is also about eighty miles north of Brownsville and its companion community across the border, Matamoros, Mexico. These facts were not immediately known to me on reporting aboard Kingsville, but they became of more than passing interest later.

Aside from being out in the boonies even by Texas standards, Kingsville was a good, well-equipped base with excellent runways. But in those days before air conditioning, late spring and summer in southeast

Texas were hotter than bloody hell. We lived in temporary wooden buildings, four or six to a room. During the working week, we flew, went to ground school, and played a lot of handball on the outdoor courts. We went occasionally to a base movie, rarely to the Officers' Club, almost never into town. Part of the problem was the "working week," which varied as a function of student load and weather delays. For much of the time we worked seven or eight days on and two days off. Our "weekends" were on a sliding scale that only periodically coincided with actual Saturdays and Sundays. Transportation was a problem. Gas rationing was very much in effect, and only a few of us had cars, barely enough to get us all back and forth to the flight line without being totally dependent on the ubiquitous "cattle car" station buses.

It was a relatively Spartan existence; it was, after all, wartime, although there was no longer any doubt of the outcome. But we were in the United States, and, perhaps most important, we were actually getting paid to fly airplanes. We sustained morale in different ways. Wooden .50-caliber ammunition boxes with their metal liners and screw-on wooden lids made excellent beer coolers; they were positioned throughout our less-than-palatial quarters and rarely were allowed to go empty.

Despite the emphasis on tactics and formation flying, there were a couple of hurdles to negotiate before we could get on with real tactics. First was aerobatics in the SNJ, and the first step to that was inverted spins. The "J" was close to an unrestricted airplane for maneuvers. The flip side is that there was virtually no such thing as an "unusual attitude." Anything a pilot could do with it was permissible, if not strictly usual. That includes the consequences, such as an inadvertent inverted spin. What is the big deal about an inverted spin? A couple of things. The first is that control responses, both intentional and unintentional, are different when you are upside down. When you are on your back, you pull back—not forward—on the stick to make the nose go down; if you try a coordinated turn upside down, you must actually cross-control stick and rudder. The second problem is recognition. In order to recover from a spin, you must know what kind of spin you are in, for the recovery techniques required vary.

We weren't supposed to perform the insidious inverted spin on purpose, and no self-respecting, life-respecting instructor wanted to demonstrate one in an SNJ. An acceptable alternative was an inverted spin demonstration in an N2S. There was a suspiciously small number of instructors who seemed to be available for that particular syllabus hop, even though every student had to have the demonstration flight before starting the acrobatic syllabus in the SNJ. There was a fair amount of apprehension on the part of both student and instructor on approaching the inverted spin hop. Our peers had prepared us for the experience with exaggeration, witchcraft, and just plain B.S. The actual flight lacked trauma, in part because the instructor let the spin develop just far enough for proper identification and recovery.

The other diversion from the real object of Advanced Training was Instruments. The Advanced phase of Instrument Training was more oriented toward overall ability to fly instruments than the more specific training we had undergone at Cabaniss. For that or some other reason the Instrument Training in Advanced was subject to certain procedural abuses. The biggest was that we hardly ever actually flew instruments. We did a lot of you-do-one-I'll-do-one dual acrobatics and more than a little flat-hatting and cow chasing over the King Ranch. There may even have been a little sitting in the shade under the wing of an SNJ at an outlying field discussing instruments instead of flying them.

I was scheduled for an instrument flight one day. The instructor was a guy who had been two years ahead of me in Lincoln High School in Jersey City, New Jersey. This lieutenant (junior grade) remembered me and saw no reason to make things difficult. On the contrary, he had decided that this was to be your basic goof-off flight—after he determined that I was not actually dangerous on instruments, that is.

We were flying a brand-new SNJ-6, the first time I'd ever been in a new airplane. Aside from its incredible newness, this airplane had a major visual difference from the SNJ-3s and -4s we were used to: the finish on the fuselage was that lovely shiny aluminum that we Navy types associated with the Army Air Corps, leading me to believe that we must have got in on the tail end of an Army contract. (I didn't know that virtually all Navy SNJs were procured under Army contracts.) I got under the bag as the instructor taxied onto the runway for takeoff. Following instructions, I set my directional gyro to zero, zero, zero, as to have a good directional reference for the anticipated instrument takeoff (using the actual runway heading would work, but minor deviations of heading would be harder to detect). I carefully adjusted the little airplane symbol on the artificial horizon (attitude gyro).

Artificial horizons were basically similar in appearance to those common in general aviation airplanes today; all in all, not too different even from those in many of the more sophisticated of today's airplanes.[6] This round instrument represents the outside world. There is a white horizon line across the middle to denote the difference between up and down. There is a little airplane symbol that represents your aircraft. If it is parallel with the horizon line, your wings are level. If not, you are in a bank and consequently turning. The upper part of the round indicator, above the horizon, is white; the bottom is black. Before gyro horizons were invented, pilots had to deduce their airplane's attitude,

Formation flight of SNJ-6s out of NAS Pensacola in 1951, no longer shiny under new paint. Note the clear plastic bubble at the end of the canopy, compared with the SNJ-5 birdcage. (USNI Photo Library)

up or down, turning or not turning, by scanning and interpreting other instruments.

World War II–era gyro horizons were gimbal limited. In other words, they would physically tumble in their mounts if you exceeded about 110 degrees of bank or 80 degrees of climb or dive. They could, however, be locked or "caged." The caging function had a dual purpose: you could cage before an acrobatic maneuver to protect the relatively delicate instrument from damage; and you could cage and uncage to reset if an obvious error developed (all gyros precess with time, and these things needed periodic resetting).

I performed the instrument takeoff as directed, one of my better efforts. My instructor took control of the airplane. I don't recall if he told me to cage my gyros or not, but the next thing I knew we went into three unannounced snap rolls with me still under the bag. While I was adjusting to the trauma, he turned the aircraft over to me to fly on instruments out to the practice area. But surprise! On the first roll the brand-new gyro in this brand-new airplane had self-destructed. It slammed over to one side and lay there like a gut-shot duck, purely dead. The upshot was that I flew the airplane "partial panel" (no gyros, that is), without informing my instructor. Fortunately, this turned into a sea-stories-under-the-wing-in-the-shade flight as soon as we reached the first outlying field.

The SNJ was such an honest airplane that there was little in the Advanced syllabus that was unique to that airplane; it was mostly a revisit to what we had seen before, with the new stuff fed to us in digestible chunks. This is true of all teaching/learning processes, although in naval aviation the chunks are not always so easily digestible. Acrobatics were much easier in the SNJ than in the N2S. The benefits of higher thrust, engine torque, and relatively low drag were apparent in the SNJ. The airplane was forgiving, although not completely docile; it was, after all, a tail-wheel airplane. It was easily recoverable from the consequences of the mistakes that most pilots made. (I don't know that anyone had occasion to rely on the special inverted spin training. At least I never heard anyone *admit* having got into an inverted spin.)

The continuing formation work was supplemented by an introduction to bombing and air-to-air gunnery. The latter consisted of runs on towed banners without ammunition. The principal benefit of the gunnery flights was to teach us the necessary time-space-logistic evolutions to get three to six airplanes rendezvoused with a towplane and its escort in an area where gunnery runs were permissible; we didn't learn much about actual gunnery. We were exposed to at least two of the basic canned runs: high sides and low sides. Since we didn't even carry gun cameras, we didn't know if we ever hit the sleeve or not. The runs were judged on form and spacing. We learned to run a flowing, daisy chain pattern without endangering ourselves or the towplane, in itself a considerable achievement. We did actually operate the single .30-caliber machine gun, firing through the propeller arc,[7] on the last gunnery flight. About half the guns didn't fire, and they hadn't bothered to give us color-coded ammunition. But accuracy was not the object of the exercise. We would work on that when we got into Corsairs and Hellcats.

Gaining confidence that we would actually become naval aviators, we just wanted to get our wings and get out of there. But the weather did not cooperate. Clear airspace was needed for the formation and tactical work, but for days at a time the sky was often 40 percent or more saturated with swelling cumulus clouds. We played a lot of handball in those days and wore a path to Brownsville and Matamoros. That was when I first heard of the "Bermuda High" as the principal villain for any adverse weather effects in the American South and Southwest. (The Bermuda High, as in high-pressure area, is not to be confused with the so-called Bermuda Triangle.)

Unless the swelling cumulus developed into thunderstorms, the sky generally cleared up at night, so at least we could get in the night flights. Unfortunately, there were only a few of those, and they came late in the syllabus. They were run more like survival drills or cross-country flights than anything operationally useful. They kept us apart—no formation flying at night; that would come with Operational Training in fleet airplanes. We spent most of each night period flying a racetrack pattern at a designated altitude, ensuring that we neither overran or were overrun by our shipmates.

Our only references were the lights of the other aircraft. These flights were conducted over a sparsely populated part of Texas, where under the best of circumstances there were not many lighted landmarks, perhaps an occasional burn-off at an oil rig or the lights of the air station in the distance. All that Instrument Training began to make sense. With essentially no visible horizon and a minimum of outside references, we relied on the gauges to stay properly oriented, not to mention right side up. Nor did we have anything that qualified as dependable communication: primitive medium-frequency radios, with broad-band "coffee-grinder" receivers and a couple of preselected transmit channels. Once in a while we actually heard something, but only rarely could we communicate. So we stayed in our racetracks by the clock. If we were in the higher racetrack pattern, we carefully watched the lights of the other aircraft, those below and those at the same altitude. At the appropriate time, generally a third of the way through the flight, each of us gingerly let down. We established ourselves at the new altitude and again tried to establish an interval on the pilot ahead, occasionally S-turning to see how close the airplane behind was. If we were in the lower racetrack, we broke away and headed, single file, toward the bounce (touch-and-go landing) pattern.

Night touch-and-go landings in the Stearmans had been a chancy exercise at best. They were not confidence building. In common with most aircraft at the time, the Stearman had no landing lights. No big deal, except that we didn't land on a proper—that is to say, lighted—runway. In the middle of the macadam mat that was our usual landing area they simply laid out a landing strip marked by kerosene flare pots. Back in the dark ages similar pots had marked road construction areas, a task for which they were better suited. Establishing an intended glide slope when using flare pots for reference was difficult; determining one's precise altitude so as to initiate a flare to a full-stall landing was a true challenge. Visualize a runway lighted by birthday cake candles: it was like landing in a black hole.

In Advanced Training, the airplane and the environment were better. The airplanes had landing lights, one in the leading edge of each wing, separately selectable. And the runways were generally lighted by permanently installed electric lights. What a difference! Runway lighting is not judged by the same standards as, say, the lighting of an athletic field for a game involving a ball. Runway lighting is intended merely to outline the area of arrival. Flare pots accomplished that, but just barely; electric lighting, however inefficient, provided the extra illumination that made all the difference.

Flying SNJ airplanes out of Kingsville, we discovered that we could see runway texture in the pools of illumination around the lights just before touchdown, even without landing lights. It may not sound like much, but that single visual reference was a great confidence builder. We at least knew where we were for certain while there was still time to make corrections. It made a big difference to me. After that I was never again apprehensive about night landings on a field. After a number of years of flying tactical aircraft, I even regard landing lights as unnecessary—as long as the runway lighting meets certain minimum standards. That was all well and good for initial takeoffs and final landings at NAAS Kingsville. Unfortunately, our night bounce periods took place at outlying fields, where it was back to flare pots. Here, the SNJ's landing lights proved invaluable.

Professional Recollections

It is a tribute to the basic honesty and stability of the airplane that I am at a loss to recall any horror stories, entertaining or otherwise, involving the SNJ. There were, of course, the occasional wheels-up landings one might expect with a retractable-gear airplane, but I managed to avoid that embarrassment, as did my friends.

However interminable the process seemed, eventually we completed the Advanced Training syllabus. Leaving Kingsville was by no means a farewell to the J-Bird; the airplane was around for many more years in the Training Command and as a proficiency and instrument trainer in the fleet. For us, it was on to newer and greater things. The attrition in Advanced Training was minimal. Almost all of us survived to confront the last remaining obstacle between us and those wings of gold: Pre-Operational Training in the SBD Dauntless dive-bomber. Pre-

SBD-5 Douglas Dauntless. This late version was the transition airplane in Pre-Operational Training. Technologically no advance over the SNJ, it was bigger and more powerful. This version carries a new radar in a pod under the right wing. (USNI Photo Library)

Operational consisted of nearly thirty hours, mostly formation tactics and navigation. All but the anxious pessimists among us decided that we were home free; I stubbornly refused to join the optimists.

Virtually coincident with our completing Advanced Training, the Pacific War ended.

Chapter 3
F6F Hellcat

O N 14 NOVEMBER 1945, after a short interlude flying SBD Dauntless dive-bombers at Beeville, Texas, I finally received the coveted wings of gold. I wore one set of wings on my Aviation Winter Working Green Uniform jacket. I wore another set on my shirt so that when I took the jacket off the world could still see that I was a naval aviator. If it hadn't been so scratchy, I probably would have worn a third set on my T-shirt. If I could have found a removable, painless way to tattoo pilot wings on my chest, I might have gone that route too. Along with the wings I received orders to Sanford, Florida, for Operational Training in Grumman Hellcats.

I didn't believe it was real until I checked into my new duty station and saw a flight line of the stubby beasts that had done so much to win the Pacific War. I did not say "little" stubby beasts; for World War II fighters these were large airplanes. That flight line was in Opa Locka, north of Miami. Naval Air Station Sanford, which had been a Wildcat and a Hellcat base, was among the early casualties of demobilization. I actually had to travel to Sanford to discover an empty flight line and a skeleton staff on the field to make that discovery. In the ways of bureaucracy the Sanford trip by train and bus was probably unavoidable. I did have orders to Sanford. I couldn't travel, instead, to Opa Locka. Who in Miami would endorse my orders as having actually arrived at Sanford or, perhaps harder, modify my orders to the Miami area? They couldn't give me a change of orders unless I had checked in. I couldn't check in unless I had orders. I presume that is clear.

The aspiring Hellcat pilots shared the field with a Corsair training squadron. The Corsair squadron had come from Lee Field south of Jacksonville. Florida had so many training fields during and right after the war that it is a wonder it didn't sink beneath the waves of the Gulf and the Atlantic Ocean. Considering the mean elevation of Florida, maybe it was trying to.

General Description

Grumman—then the Grumman Aircraft Engineering Corporation (GAEC)—produced about twelve thousand F6F-3 and -5 Hellcats from 1942 to 1945. The Hellcat was designed to be superior to or at least competitive with the Mitsubishi A6M Zero fighter. Among the attributes needed for the airplane were more speed, greater rate of climb, greater range, and, if possible, better turning capability than its predecessor. The Wildcat, especially the earlier models, was markedly inferior to the Zero. The success of some of our Wildcat pilots against the Zero was remarkable but far from common. The Marines, led by Major Joe Foss with twenty-six kills in the Wildcat, did well enough to have several pilots with double-digit scores. These victories were not all against Zeros, but many were.

In discussing the capabilities of any aircraft, particularly fighter aircraft, the definitive question is, Compared with what? In the Pacific War, "what" was always the Zero. This remarkable airplane first saw combat in China in the summer of 1940. The facts surrounding the airplane are impressive enough without the associated mythology. Pilots who were nationals of virtually all of the Allied and most of the Axis countries involved in World War II had seen the Zero in combat over China months before Pearl Harbor. The fact that information concerning the airplane failed to penetrate the intelligence circles of any of these nations provides telling support for all the bad jokes about "military intelligence."[1]

For the United States, the existence and performance of the Zero constituted an unpleasant surprise—a surprise that had to be dealt with effectively and quickly. Grumman responded. In June of 1942 Grumman test pilot Bob Hall first flew the prototype XF6F-1.[2] In September of 1943 I rode the USS *Louisville* (CA-28) into Pearl Harbor under a virtual umbrella of various carrier aircraft. This was when the "fast carriers" still operated out of Pearl. The most numerous airplane was one I had never seen before.

The new airplane was peculiarly American. The norm for World War II fighters was smallish, short-range machines like the British Hurricane and Spitfire. (The Zero fit the mold for size.) That meant a wingspan of about 35 feet, perhaps 6,000 pounds gross weight, loaded, or a little more. The Hellcat had a wingspan of over 42 feet, grossed over 12,000 pounds in combat configuration, and was powered by a big radial engine, a Pratt & Whitney R-2800, with eighteen cylinders in two banks of nine. In its various versions that engine powered all the Hellcats, the Corsairs, the Republic P-47 Thunderbolts (also a large fighter), later the Grumman AF series of antisubmarine airplanes, the Bearcats, and many other airplanes. The *R* stands for radial, with the number signifying displacement in cubic inches.

Not a small engine, the R-2800 presented a formidable frontal area, which meant a lot of drag. The airplane was significantly different from the European design approach, which sought to achieve high performance with minimum power and size, emphasizing low drag, particularly low frontal area or form drag. Airplanes like the Spitfire, Hurricane, Me-109, and our own P-40s, Mustangs, and Airacobras come to mind. The Spitfires were lineal descendants of the Supermarine seaplane Schneider Cup racers of the mid- and late 1930s, the fastest of which were capable of 400 mph when most of the world's fighters could barely achieve 200 mph. These airplanes had large in-line liquid-cooled engines characterized by low frontal area, ideal for skinny, pointy-nose low-drag profiles.

There was good reason for the Hellcat approach. Displacement is the most straightforward way to increased power. (Old race car adage: "There is no substitute for cubic inches.") The penalties resulting from engine size and drag are largely manifested in airframe size. In the Pacific, where long range and endurance and load-carrying capability were important, airframe size brought some good things to the party. The Hellcat, with 250 gallons of internal fuel divided among three tanks, had inherently good range and endurance characteristics, even with a fuel consumption at fast cruise of about 60 gallons per hour. The commonest combat configuration included a well-streamlined 150-gallon external belly tank, for a total of 400 gallons. This turned out to be an ideal load. It provided not only excellent range performance for long-range escort of strike groups but also a solid four hours of "loiter" speed on a combat air patrol (CAP) station, leaving more than sufficient combat reserve if it had to fight at precisely the time when it would normally recover.

The idea was that the belly tank would be used first and then could be jettisoned for combat. Most of the time pilots retained the tanks even when empty. Fighter combat was not and is not usually fought at maximum speed where drag is critical. If you have access to the Navy's film *The Fighting Lady*, or the exciting aerial combat footage from the old television series *Victory at Sea*, you will notice that most of the Hellcats are wearing their belly tanks.

It is noteworthy that the Hellcat achieved its objective of besting the Mitsubishi A6M Type Zero (Japanese designation; the Allies called it Zeke for identification and reporting). However, it didn't beat its designated opponent by a lot. And it was a much larger airplane. There are no combat rewards for fighting out of your weight class, but the Zero

F6F-3 Hellcat with early–World War II national insignia. The prewar red disk inside the star has been eliminated to avoid confusion with the Japanese Rising Sun "meatball"; rectangular "ears" have not yet been added to the star. This aircraft has drag-reducing fairings around the .50-caliber gun muzzles, not to my knowledge seen in service aircraft. (Grumman History Center)

was a remarkable machine. Barrett Tillman presents an interesting comparative table.[3]

The Hellcat was 15 to 55 statute miles per hour faster than the Zero, depending on altitude. (Consider a reasonable combat envelope to extend from sea level to about twenty thousand feet. With its three-stage supercharger, the Hellcat improved up to twenty thousand to twenty-five thousand feet.) The Zero had a marginally higher service ceiling—over thirty-eight thousand, compared with about thirty-six thousand feet. Time to climb to twenty thousand feet was roughly the same for the F6F-3, the F6F-5, and the A6M5. The slightly heavier F6F-5 may have taken marginally longer to get there. The initial rate of climb of the Zero (at sea level) was better. The small, lightweight A6M had phenomenal range for its class and its time, something over a thousand statute miles. The -3 Hellcat excelled here, but only marginally. The -5 reportedly had at least two hundred miles more range, but I am not sure that the comparison is valid—the 150-gallon external tank may have got into the equation.

It was an unpleasant surprise to the Chinese and their mercenary AVG (American Volunteer Group) air force when Japanese bombers were accompanied by Zeros over their targets. American Navy and Marine pilots had difficulty understanding how fighters from near Rabaul could penetrate almost as far south and east as Guadalcanal. The Zero was more maneuverable than the Hellcat within its operating envelope, but the stronger, heavier Hellcat was better in a sustained dive and had more structural strength. The appellation Grumman Iron Works started with the Hellcat's structural ruggedness and persists to this day among pilots of Grumman products.[4] (At least the fighters. Lest this sound like a Grumman commercial, the Hellcat was by no means the perfect fighter plane. However, it appeared on the scene at an opportune time with the right attributes to make it effective.)

Some of the later Japanese fighters narrowed the gap, but the Hellcat maintained its qualitative superiority until the end of the war. There were other characteristics too that ultimately made it "no contest" for the Japanese. Besides the factors of increasing American numerical superiority, armor plate, self-sealing fuel tanks, and greater margin of structural strength, the increasing skill and experience level of our pilots made a significant difference. The Japanese never recovered from the loss of skill and experience that they suffered at the Battle of Midway. Good as the Japanese Army pilots were, the cream of Japanese tactical aviation went down with the Japanese aircraft carriers sunk off Midway. Superior American numbers and tactics essentially neutralized any maneuvering and speed advantage of the newer Japanese airplanes as the war wound down.

The F6F-5 earned its right to be called a "400-mph airplane," at least at one altitude. It also had a combat, water-injection mode that gave it five minutes' worth of augmented combat performance, not a trivial advantage in a fight. For those of us who never fought the airplane, the -5 had another seductive advantage: an honest-to-God continuous crank starter! No more accursed shotgun shells. I went through training in the -3s, which did have shotgun starters.

There were about ten thousand late-model Zeros (A6M5) manufactured, compared with over twelve thousand F6F-3s and -5s. There is another number worthy of note: in March of 1945 Grumman delivered to the Navy more than six hundred Hellcats, almost twenty a day for a thirty-one-day month.

How It Flew

In June of 1944 I was standing gunnery watches aboard the USS *Louisville* (CA-28) shooting at the still-disputed island of Saipan at the time that certain exciting events were taking place several hundred miles to the west. If they hadn't taken place, the older fire support cruisers and battlewagons, including the *Louisville*, and the amphibious ships of the landing force off Saipan would shortly have been in serious jeopardy. These events included the spectacular night recovery of Task Force 58 "fast carrier"[5] airplanes after a maximum-range strike against what remained of the Japanese Carrier Strike Force. Also included was the "Marianas Turkey Shoot," in which Dave McCampbell, flying a Hellcat, shot down nine Japanese airplanes in one flight. Commander McCampbell was CAG (Commander, Air Group) 15 at the time. He became the Navy's leading ace with thirty-four kills, all in Hellcats.

In 1944 when a "fast carrier" strike did not conflict with a landing operation, the *Louisville* often got to travel with the first team. As a "treaty cruiser" (Washington Naval Arms Treaty),[6] the 8-inch-gunned *Louisville*'s protective armor was essentially nonexistent, but she was fast and had good range. We were with Task Force 58 on the second Truk strike, the first Palau strike, and the covering operation for the landings at Hollandia, New Guinea. How did we escape a fire support mission at Hollandia? Possibly because a lot of Army and the Seventh Fleet were involved. (The 5 in 58 stands for Fifth Fleet.)

In those operations we observed the strike aircraft and their escorts going and coming. I saw returning Hellcats maintaining position in formation with large holes in various vital parts, occasionally with a critically important part, like a horizontal tail surface, mostly blown away. The Hellcat made a favorable impression on me. (At the same time the Vought Corsair, because of various unsolved carrier suitability problems, was mostly land based.)[7]

My favorable impression of the Hellcat continued. In October of 1944, by which time I was in Primary flight training at Ottumwa, Iowa, Commander Dave McCampbell came through on what could be termed a "morale tour." To a packed audience in the station auditorium he gave an appropriately low-key speech about his recent Pacific experiences. He also brought a color print of *The Fighting Lady*.

"The Fighting Lady" herself was the second carrier named the *Yorktown* (CV-10). The film was a full-color documentary covering the year just past when the Navy's combat forces had moved from Pearl Harbor to the Western Pacific. If not actually "based," our carriers staged through places like Ulithi and Eniwetok. The motion picture was a full-blown Hollywood-type production, narrated by Robert Taylor, in Navy uniform for the duration. As an actor he wasn't in a class with Robert Redford or Paul Newman, but at the time he had equivalent name recognition. The film took the viewer from the *Yorktown*'s commissioning, with later-Admiral "Jocko" Clark as the first skipper, through the "fast carrier" raids—some of which I had experienced from the safety of a task group formation hundreds of miles away from the action—to the

Marianas Turkey Shoot. The movie was put together in about the time it took me to get back to the States and flight training! What made the film different and exciting was its extensive use of combat gun camera film in good color. For those who remember the twenty-episode television series *Victory at Sea*, a prisoner of black and white because of its time, much of the good carrier aviation footage was borrowed from *The Fighting Lady*. The aerial combat footage is remarkable, and all the U.S. fighters in the film are Hellcats.

In that crowded auditorium at NAS Ottumwa in the fall of 1944, with an audience already enthusiastic about carrier flying, the response to the film was Super Bowl style, especially since it was preceded by a short talk from the Navy's leading ace. At the conclusion of the movie, Commander McCampbell answered a few questions. There were many flight students present, with aviation cadets substantially outnumbering officer students. There were station personnel, officer and enlisted, and members of the training squadrons. The latter included enlisted and commissioned ground instructors, many of whom were nonaviators, as well as instructor pilots. A commissioned officer arose with this question: "What are the chances of an instructor getting out into the carrier fleet?"

I don't know if the good commander was engaging in a putdown or missed the point. The house lights were up by then, but the questioner was pretty far back. Maybe McCampbell really couldn't see that he was wearing wings. There was no doubt in my mind that the question was the appeal of a frustrated-fighter-pilot flight instructor who wanted to get out of the Training Command and into action. After a moment of thoughtful reflection, "Well, Lieutenant"—apparently he could see the rank insignia—"I'm afraid the answer is, we can't all be pilots."

It brought the house down.

It was over fourteen months later when I saw my first flight line of Hellcats. The initial view of a new base with different airplanes carries a mystique. The less experienced the observer, the stronger the impression. The airplane is a mystery, a challenge. With exposure to many different kinds of airplanes that feeling may change, but it is always there at some level. When you have been inside the cockpits of only three different kinds of machines as I had, the impression is strong.

This day in early January of 1946, I watched a flight of F6Fs taxi into the chocks and shut down. The airplanes seemed huge, and noisy. I watched the pilot of the second airplane in line. He secured his engine. When the prop stopped turning, his head bobbed down. Inside the cockpit he moved various levers and switches that were part of the postflight procedure. With professional casualness and economy of motion, he unsnapped his seat belt, threw back the shoulder straps, and, with a touch of weariness, climbed out of the cockpit, carefully balancing the awkward parachute that threatened to hang up on the cockpit sill. He found the steps in the side of the fuselage with his toes, as if he knew where they were, and dismounted from the airplane. I recognized the pilot, a classmate from the Naval Academy: Earl "Buddy" Yates.[8] I had been behind Buddy throughout the whole program. This time there was no envy. I was *here*. I was going to fly this thing too!

That did not happen immediately. There was a considerable "pool" of pilots when I got to Opa Locka in December of 1945. A few weeks later, which included a welcome Christmas leave, I was assigned to a flight and got into the active program. When I did, I found myself all strapped in, bent over in the cockpit like some kind of symmetrical Quasimodo. (The problem was a parachute with short risers, further shortened by a four-inch life raft under the seat pad.) Fortunately, the Hellcat seat has a lot of up and down travel so that even foreshortened I could raise it until my head was virtually against the Plexiglas canopy. That had the advantage of enabling me to see partially over the nose of the airplane, thus allowing a limited ability to taxi straight ahead or at least to minimize the eternal sine-wave taxi path endemic to tail-wheel airplanes. There is enough rudder pedal adjustment in the airplane that virtually anyone who meets the minimum height require-ments—it used to be about five feet five inches—can reach the rudder pedals and also get full rudder throw with full brake deflection.

The cockpit was roomy and not intimidating for the novice. I man-aged to get started and out of the chocks with no memorable difficulty. All that ground school and a couple of accumulated hours in the cockpit beforehand didn't hurt. I even negotiated the dreaded shotgun starter. The problem with that device was that the engine had to be put in a state of optimal readiness for starting—somewhat reminiscent of the old hand-propping days, when just one swing of the propeller through a quarter of a turn was enough to get an engine going. Not often on the first try!

The advantage of the alternative, continuous cranking, is that the cylinders, revolution by revolution, purge themselves of any combina-tion of fuel and air the pilot may have thrown into them by mismanaging the induction system to begin with. After such purging, the engine may very well start if the mixture setting and throttle opening are where they should be.

My apprehension about actually getting the engine to fire and keep firing stemmed from the very first Hellcat I saw close up. It was at Cabaniss Field when I was just starting Basic Training in the SNJ. A fleet or ferry pilot had brought in a brand-new F6F-3. The airplane was

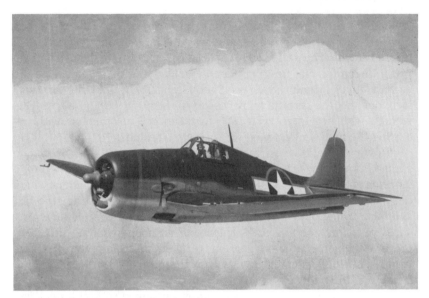

F6F-3 Hellcat. (Grumman History Center)

wearing the usual "sea-blue gloss" paint. (The color was closer to "navy" than "sea" blue. Grumman's paint jobs were neither the best nor the most durable in the aviation world, but when new they looked good.) I was appropriately dazzled by the airplane and hung around the flight line as the pilot prepared for departure. Preparations included starting the engine. It did not go well. I watched expectantly as a single puff of smoke signified the firing of the starter. The three-bladed propeller moved through the better part of a turn. Nothing. There was some scurrying about as the pilot instructed the ground crew where to get another shell. Presumably they knew how to install it from the previous try. The shells, perhaps five or six, were kept in pockets of a heavy web canvas holder on the inside of the starter access door. The pilot used all of them. At one point there was an answering puff or two from the engine, but no start. In retrospect, he must have been a ferry pilot who was unfamiliar with the R-2800 engine, or at least with that particular installation. When last seen, the pilot was sitting dejectedly in the cockpit while someone went looking for a new supply of starter cartridges. They were not readily available on an SNJ base.

One of the secrets, besides proper priming and initial throttle setting, had to do with the mixture control. The starting position was out of the idle cutoff position. If the engine was known to be either "cold" or "hot" there were thumb rules for the amount of prime. It was not recognizing—or, perhaps more serious, actually causing—a "rich" or flooded condition that caused most problems. Without continuous cranking there was no convenient way of purging the cylinders of a flooded engine. The preferred, or at least a generally effective, technique was to listen for that first or second cylinder to fire, then advance the mixture control rapidly, even precipitously, all the way to the "full rich" stop, opening the throttle as necessary to keep the engine going. This worked with nearly every R-2800 installation I am familiar with, including the more enlightened direct crank varieties.

However tentative on that first starting attempt, I got the engine started. I know I was tentative taxiing. I sat behind, nearly on top of, a monster of an engine capable of 2,000 hp. A major hazard, about which there were repeated warnings, was the consequence of taxiing too fast and then trying to stop abruptly. Applying both brakes simultaneously could result in standing the airplane on its nose, resulting in a bent propeller and engine "sudden stoppage." I taxied the airplane at a slow crawl, allowing too much interval on the airplane ahead of me and frustrating the pilots in the airplanes behind me.

In the run-up area, there was room for people to taxi around me to the runway. There was no significant procedural difference in the pretakeoff checklist compared with other airplanes, particularly my last prior experience, the SBD. The Dauntless was, after all, a "service" airplane too. In the Hellcat there was a three-position supercharger to cycle through. That was the biggest new item. (I chickened out there: it is easy to get bollixed up with "stages" versus "speeds" where superchargers are concerned. There is also the difference between turbo and direct drive.) The Hellcat's supercharger had "neutral," "low," and "high" positions. It was not turbine driven. (There was an experimental Hellcat version with a turbocharger late in the war, but it never saw production.) It was easy even for a fighter pilot to realize that "neutral" blower was there all of the time, like it or not. The other positions were to be selected when reaching appropriately high altitudes. (Without the blower the airplane would have been "normally aspirated" and therefore capable of pulling no more than about 30 inches of manifold pressure, or whatever ambient pressure happened to be. At sea level the R-2800 in the F6F was good for something on the order of 55 to 60 inches. By contrast, some of the bigger in-line engines, like the Rolls-Royce Merlin in the Spitfires and Mustangs, were reputedly capable of 80 or 90 inches of manifold pressure.)

The biggest difference in the run-up was a kind of scale effect. It is one thing to sit in a Cessna 152 at full power and cycle through the relatively few items there are to cycle—or a Piper Arrow with its different level of sophistication. It is quite another to sit with the stick in your lap—it better be in your lap, touching the seat pan if you can get it there—with 2,800 cubic inches of roaring, vibrating radial engine seemingly trying to self-destruct. This goes on while you systematically fiddle with things like magneto switches, propeller pitch control, and supercharger select. It was possible to check mags at a substantial throttle opening without the airplane either sliding forward against the locked brakes or trying to nose up, but you better hold those brakes and keep the stick all the way back!

An important thing to worry about when going from one airplane to another in those days was takeoff trim setting. The Hellcat was relatively forgiving in that a significantly incorrect trim setting could be overcome by the pilot on takeoff roll—unlike such machines as the Mustang, Corsair, and Skyraider. Nonetheless, the pilot didn't really know this on the first ride; "know" is not the same as "being told." The settings called for a little back (nose up) trim, substantial right rudder, and right aileron. There were numbered tick marks on all three trim control knobs. We used precise, recommended values.

Finally came the moment of truth. There I was on the runway, all by myself in the airplane. I was ready for the very first time to fly this 400-mph fighter that had defeated the mighty Zero and led the way to winning the Pacific War. With only one seat in the airplane, I had to be alone. Later it became the practice for an instructor to "chase" each first-time student in another airplane. In January of 1946—and for some time thereafter, even with Bearcats—it was different; you flew your first flight essentially unsupervised. The drill was to go out to some designated practice area, familiarize yourself with the airplane, and then come back to shoot landings.

Standing on the brakes in takeoff position, I added full power. When the engine came up to speed, I checked the gauges and released the brakes, anticipating the need for right rudder for directional control. I was tense. I braced my head against the headrest to minimize the shock of the inevitable neck-slapping acceleration.

Slowly, à la SBD, the airplane moved forward and began to pick up speed. I wasn't going as fast as I expected. This was years before Danny Kaye made *The Secret Life of Walter Mitty*. Nonetheless, rolling down the runway, "ta-pocketa-pocketa-pocketa" came to mind, perhaps because I had read the James Thurber story. Moving out of this initially lumbering start, the machine accelerated in reasonably good shape. I was not expecting it to become airborne when it did, but this was hardly the exhilarating experience I was prepared for. A thought came: "This is the airplane that won the Pacific War?"

More or less automatically, I cleaned up to climb configuration and headed out to the practice area. There wasn't that much to clean up: pull the gear up as you break ground (flaps weren't used for takeoff);

pull the manifold pressure back to climb power, reduce rpm, and adjust cowl flaps and the oil cooler door. I began to enjoy the airplane.

The idea of the familiarization flight was to explore the handling characteristics at speeds from normal cruise down to slow flight. This entailed speed changes, altitude changes, turns at various bank angles, turns to heading, and, in general, evolutions designed to enable the pilot to get comfortable with the overall feel of the aircraft. So-called slow flight was important because this was a carrier airplane. Navy pilots are supposed to land slow—but not too slow. That means that stalls and approach-to-stall maneuvers are very important. In the real world, once you got out by yourself in a new airplane, a common custom was to go through all that thoroughly—and as fast as possible. The rest of the time you spent finding out what the machine could really do.

It would not be appropriate to read too much into my reaction to that first takeoff. Obviously, I had been oversold on some aspects of Hellcat performance. It was an impressive airplane that I came to like almost immediately. Its performance was far superior to anything I had been in before. The forgiving nature of the machine has been praised by virtually everyone who has flown one. (Barrett Tillman describes a fifty-year-old Leroy Grumman flying a Hellcat in 1944, after having not flown anything for several years. Fifty-year-olds just didn't fly fighters in those days!)[9]

However, for all its amazing combat record—a 19-to-1 overall kill ratio is impressive for any airplane in any theater—the Hellcat was somehow never one of the glamour machines. It was better than most of its opponents, archetypically the Zero, but not spectacularly better. Perhaps some Hellcat proponents were excessive in their zeal to get the F6F a little respect. In view of performance figures now available,[10] that the Hellcat needed defending at all is a tribute to the quality of reporting in general and aviation reporting in particular. Among the myths prevalent during and immediately after World War II—some of them extant to this day—are the following:

1. Carrier-based airplanes, by definition, are inferior to their land-based counterparts.
2. The European air war was essentially fought by the first team of all participating nations. What went on in the Pacific was important, but the air war and its airplanes were second rate (except for those airplanes that also fought over Europe).
3. The Battle of Britain was won by a combination of skill and determination of the British fighter pilots, made possible by the qualitative superiority of their airplanes.
4. A corollary to number one: Some of the most effective aircraft

in the Pacific theater would not only have been ineffective over Europe, they would have been barely survivable.

It may be conceded that raw performance numbers do not reliably explain aircraft effectiveness (as weapons); the comparative success of some airplanes in some theaters and the relative ineffectiveness of the same airplanes in other theaters attest to that. However, if weapon effectiveness were the sole criterion, the historical esteem of the Hellcat as an airplane would never be in question.

If there is any question concerning my simple assertion as to number one, "T'aint so!" I respectfully suggest that the reader look elsewhere for verification; I submit that the empirical evidence is overwhelming. I further submit that numbers two, three, and four are also incorrect. Number three is especially sticky because it has become an article of almost religious faith in the British Isles. The fact is that the Hawker Hurricane, which was the principal British fighter in the Battle of Britain—the numerically inferior Spitfire was not really the determining factor—performs about like the lowly Wildcat. Even the "Spit" was, in speed, marginally inferior to the later Me-109s, though somewhat superior to the most numerous 109s in the Battle of Britain. Both British airplanes were extremely agile and maneuverable, however. The German fighters in that battle were characteristically at the limit of their range and endurance at the time of engagement. Qualitatively, it was close to a wash, except that the Hurricane apparently performed better than was reasonable to expect. This suggests that the "qualitative superiority" that was involved had a lot more to do with the human beings in the cockpits and on the ground than with the airborne machinery. All of this should be quite enough for British pride. The real object of the exercise in the Battle of Britain was to get rid of the bombers and V-1 missiles; the German fighters were just something that had to be disposed of to accomplish the mission. The Royal Air Force pilots did both in near-miraculous fashion.

It may be appropriate to examine the F6F's performance in the context of other contemporary aircraft. The Hellcat's performance numbers are as good as or better than every European theater airplane mentioned in the preceding paragraphs. The -5 was a legitimate 400-mph airplane at altitude. The F6F also had, characteristically, twice the range of the European theater airplanes. The most numerous Spitfire in the Battle of Britain was the Mk V, about 375 mph. The Mk XVI was a 400-mph airplane. The Mk XIV, a later airplane, was reportedly capable of 450 mph. There weren't really that many 400-mph-plus airplanes around, and it is questionable whether top speed, as such, ever got utilized in a fight. Certainly the ability to accelerate, as opposed to simply go fast, either to catch somebody or to escape, is valuable. Some other 400-mph-plus airplanes were the Mustang, the late Fw-190s, the P-38 Lightning, the P-47 Thunderbolt, and the F4U Corsair.

The Corsair, at most "useful" altitudes, was as fast as any and had substantial range and substantial load-carrying capability. If you could figure out some measurement scale that people would agree to, you could find support for the idea that the Corsair may have been the best/ most effective fighter in all of World War II—until you factored in how many Corsairs were wrecked operationally by their own pilots. Oh well, nobody's perfect!

That "useful" altitude reference is in honor of the P-47, which is difficult to categorize. The N version is credited with something on the order of 469 mph, but at thirty-two thousand feet. What reciprocating-engine airplanes actually fought at thirty-two thousand feet? It may be useful to fly that high, but at what cost? The P-47 was a very good airplane with a fine combat record. It was not, however, lauded as a sterling performer. I contrast that high-altitude performance with con-temporary reports that some versions of the P-47 were dogs below ten thousand feet. On the other hand, the people who fought in the airplane swear by it. I have a neighbor who was a twenty-one-year-old ace flying Thunderbolts. It's possible that the P-47 is the Air Force version of the Hellcat in the don't-get-no-respect department. Its nickname was, after all, "The Jug." The airplane had a huge turbo supercharger that, by a combination of drag and mechanical power bleed-off, must have caused a substantial performance degradation at other than optimum altitudes. I know a couple of people in a Bearcat squadron who had an inadvertent encounter with four late-model P-47s one day in 1947. (Inadvertent, hell. The Bearcats jumped them. What did you expect? The P-47s were there.) It was no contest—partly because the Bearcat, below ten thousand feet, could do absolutely everything better than anything else with a propeller and at low altitudes could out-accelerate most contemporary jets. None-theless, our guys said that AD Skyraiders and even SB2C Helldivers flown aggressively had at other times given them as much trouble as the P-47s.

The true test of an airplane is how it measures up to the mission it is required to perform. How pilots feel about the airplane is also a valid measure. Does the pilot feel comfortable, secure, in control? Does he have to work like hell to fly it? Does the machine frighten him? Does it inspire him? If the answer to the last is a resounding yes, you may have a great airplane. Raw performance numbers and reputations es-tablished through the press can be irrelevant.

Judged by those criteria, the Hellcat may qualify for greatness by virtue of having precisely the right attributes for what it was asked to do, where it was asked to do it. Its limited combat record in Europe suggests that it would have done very well in that theater too. Moreover, the domestic European theater airplanes[11]—even the hot rods that achieved their 400-mph performance late in the war, having evolved from earlier versions—didn't have the range to get into many of the Hellcat's most critical fights. Really? Really: Me-109—410 miles; Hawker Hurricane—460 miles; Spitfire Mk VC—470 miles; Fw-190-D9 (420-mph version—520 miles;[12] F6F-5 Hellcat—1,300 miles; A6M5 Zero—1,090 miles.[13] To compete you first have to be there!

Back at NAS Opa Locka, I went through the familiarization stuff just the way I was supposed to. The airplane flew fine, but there were some differences from other airplanes I had known. Control forces were definitely heavier, particularly in roll. Grumman expended considerable effort throughout the intense production period to do something about aileron response and control forces. There were minor changes to the ailerons, much tweaking and fiddling. The final attempt involved spring tabs. The idea of spring tabs—one on each aileron—is that initial stick deflection in roll actuates only the tabs. When you run out of that initial, incremental travel such that you then start moving the ailerons themselves, the tabs are supposedly already moving, actually "flying" the control surfaces in the direction you want. I must have flown spring tab -5s somewhere along the line, since VBF-3 (Bombing, Fighting Squadron Three) was flying Hellcats, late Hellcats, when I joined them in the summer of 1946. The tabs must not have made a lot of difference, because I retain an impression of heavy control forces in roll. Pitch control forces were heavy also, but you expect that with higher speed. That is why there is elevator trim.

An extensive combat comparison of the Hellcat and Zeke (our old friend, A6M Zero) was made in 1944 at what is now the Naval Air Test Center, Patuxent River, Maryland—the Navy's test activity having moved from NAS Anacostia near Washington. The results are documented in a Royal Navy tactical note dated December of 1944.[14] It contains the familiar affirmations of the Zero's agility and maneuverability along with a prohibition against attempting to dogfight with— that is, try to out-turn—Zeke. That turning advantage disappeared with higher speed. Above 200 knots, the Hellcat was superior because of the Zero's "high control forces" above 175 knots.

The Hellcat's control forces were heavy compared with slower airplanes, but by no means disqualifyingly so. With mechanical control systems, that is predictable and unavoidable. The Hellcat's handling characteristics throughout the authorized flight regime were straightforward, almost docile. Stall characteristics were downright benign. The airplane did not want to stall. Recovery was easier and quicker than in the SNJ. There was no overt tendency to spin. Recovery from a left spin, even from multiple turns, was as close to instantaneous as the most nervous pilot might desire. Right-hand spins were something else again. The Hellcat simply wouldn't spin to the right. You could get as slow as possible without actually stalling, then aggravate matters by pointing the nose up in the air, hold the stick all the way back in your lap, then kick the right rudder as far as it would go and hold it there; even throw in full right aileron. The airplane would slop around to the right in an unenthusiastic spin. Relax any pro-spin control deflection (which is what I have just described about all three axes)—especially rudder—and the spin would degenerate into a kind of half-assed spiral.

As far as it goes, that is a neat collection of qualities. A pilot is extremely unlikely to spin-in in the groove in a Hellcat, especially to the right. There is, however, no free lunch in aviation; there is always a price. In the slow-flight condition the Navy demands for carrier approaches, the Hellcat has atrocious right rudder forces and not nearly enough right rudder trim to compensate. While Grumman devoted all that effort trying to correct aileron forces, I wonder why the company didn't try to solve the rudder problem as well. These forces were not trivial! Imagine a short pilot, with right leg almost fully extended, trying to hold a precise rudder deflection as fatigue sets in—all in the course of one carrier approach. Ultimately, the leg begins to tremble and vibrate in tune with the airplane.

It was easier to start the pass in a skid, head hanging out the side of the airplane, railroad engineer style, until the Landing Signal Officer picked you up with the paddles. Then before he started kicking his foot at you—the LSO signal for an unwanted slip or skid—add right rudder to the most comfortable position you could maintain. (I exaggerate; it wasn't that bad.) The classic carrier approach is a somewhat oblate semicircle with essentially no straight final. You level your wings and land. Because you were turning, you saw the LSO by looking out the side of the airplane. You didn't really need to hang your head out; with the open canopy the breeze just made it feel that way. With the advent of the mirror landing system and jet airplanes, the approach was substantially modified. Since then, there has been a discernibly straight final leg of the approach. In learning to fly the Hellcat, I found insufficient available right rudder trim to be the most objectionable characteristic of the airplane.

One might expect, along with that right rudder deficiency, a hellacious tendency to torque roll to the left, especially with the sudden application of go-around or wave-off power. Not so, perhaps because of the very lack of acceleration I noticed on my first takeoff. The Hellcat wanted neither to flip you over on your back nor to drop you into the spud locker. ("Spud locker"? A euphemism for the back end of an aircraft carrier, well below flight deck level, an area traditionally populated by potato-peeling, mess-cooking sailors—not designed for landing airplanes.)

Fast cruise was achieved with a power setting of 30 inches of manifold pressure and 2,000 rpm. That "30-and-20" combination was common to many R-2800 engine installations. The significance was that 30 inches was the maximum allowable manifold pressure without increasing rpm above 2,000. Revolutions determine fuel consumption. Further increase of manifold pressure would overboost the engine beyond its design and service limitations. More economical power settings were available at lower rpm settings, but the Hellcat had a to-avoid lower rpm vibration range that limited the effectiveness of decreased rpm as a fuel-saving technique. The alternative was to reduce power and consequently speed. At the 30 and 2,000 power setting, depending on altitude and configuration, the Hellcat would indicate from 165 to 175 knots. For comparison, the F4U Corsair at a similar power setting cruised at 180 to 190 knots. At low altitude the F8F Bearcat, with a later version of the same engine, indicated 230 to 260 knots at 32 inches and 2,200 rpm. The F8F-1 was somewhat faster than the F8F-1B and F8F-2. (A real danger in the fighter business is to "improve" performance out of later versions! Most changes to airplanes result in increases in weight or airplane surface area, both of which lower performance.)

There are some not so subtle qualifiers in that last paragraph, words like *indicated airspeed, knots*, (versus *statute miles per hour*), *depending on configuration*, and *at low altitude*. Primarily I use *knots* in this text for a couple of reasons. First, I am more familiar with the term *knots*, and second, virtually all modern airplanes have airspeed indicators calibrated in knots. Note that a nautical mile is precisely equal to one minute of latitude (or one minute of longitude at the equator). Since a knot equals one nautical mile per hour—knots per hour, which you occasionally see in the print media, is not a speed at all but an acceleration, a very slow acceleration!—knots and nautical miles are very handy units for long-range navigation, particularly over water. Miles per hour, on the other hand, are fun when you are trying to make an airplane sound fast but a pain in the tail when converting the unit to something more useful.

"Indicated airspeed" is what the airspeed indicator says. At sea level it is equal to "true airspeed," except for instrument and position errors. The relationship between "true" and "indicated" airspeed varies as a function of altitude, specifically as a function of the square root of the outside air density as you ascend. This sounds complicated. An example: At forty thousand feet true airspeed is approximately twice the indicated airspeed at that altitude. (The relationship is accurate for "calibrated" airspeed, a close relative of "indicated" airspeed.) Most of us get to that altitude only on commercial airliners, but it emphasizes the numerical trend. The principle operates the same way at the lower altitudes with which most of us are familiar.

The differences between "cruise" speed and "maximum" speed, between "miles per hour" and "knots," and between "true" and "indicated" airspeeds are significant. The result is that discussions of airplane performance tend to be imprecise. The saying "The first liar doesn't have a chance" may be appropriate.

The cruise speed that my 30-and-20 Hellcat power setting gave me on the way to the practice area that day in 1946 was less than dazzling but certainly greater than the 120 to 135 knots I was used to. The overall sense of the power and size of the F6F was impressive. I was reluctant to add power, especially enough manifold pressure to force me out of the 2,000-rpm range. This was no problem as long as I was performing required maneuvers: stalls, slow flight, even spins and steep turns. I was reluctant to use full throttle in any power plant. This was born of Training Command conditioning, which I may have taken more seriously than some of my peers.[15] The general prudential rule was "Take care of your engine and it will take care of you." The SNJs at Cabaniss and Kingsville had been either tired or brand-new, not much in between. In either case, pilots were encouraged to treat them gently. The SBDs at Beeville were very tired, both airframes and engines. The Wright R-1820 engine in the SBD was basically reliable but unforgiving of mismanagement. The dire consequences of abusing one's engine had been described ad nauseam in graphic, occasionally grisly terms. With that background I tended to be gentle with throttle and propeller pitch. The Hellcat performed impressively without using full power.

A good first acrobatic maneuver is a loop. The loop is straightforward. There is no requirement for difficult coordination or cross-controlling. Point the airplane's nose down and gain speed until you are satisfied that you won't run out of airspeed before you can get the airplane pointed back down again. It works as easily in the F6F as in the Stearman, except that you make a bigger circle. Depending on altitude and entry speed, you may have to decrease power on the way down to avoid overspeed (airplane, not engine). Unlike the fixed-pitch-propeller machines, this power plant will maintain its power setting.

It was difficult to perform a really good 360-degree slow roll in the F6F. The Hellcat's aileron effectiveness was acceptable but control forces were substantial, as has been noted. The trick was to aim the nose above the horizon, preferably at a recognizable reference like a distant cloud, apply full aileron, and hold it there. Roll the airplane with

F6F-5s with 150-gallon belly tanks. The national insignia on the fuselage has evolved into a borderless design. Open-canopy flying was common in the Pacific at low altitudes and slow speeds. (Grumman History Center)

full lateral stick deflection, left or right, followed by appropriate rudder and stick control inputs, that is, right and left rudder and fore and aft stick, as required to keep the nose on the selected point until you are right side up again. When it is done correctly, the only constant is the full aileron deflection until the maneuver is completed. Rudder and fore and aft stick vary continually. Smooth cross-control coordination is required. Many of us learned to fake the slow roll by entering at a higher-than-normal entry airspeed and using just enough stick and rudder to accomplish an aileron roll, which was a kind of modified, tighter barrel roll.

There is no fooling a knowledgeable observer. I remember bumming a ride in a photo Hellcat (F6F-5P, an air group airplane temporarily based ashore during an in-port period) out of Wheelus Air Force Base, near Tripoli. Naturally, I did a slow roll on takeoff. Why not? It was an Air Force field. The takeoff direction was toward the Mediterranean, where my squadron skipper, Duke Windsor, and Operations Officer, Bob Hoppe, were enjoying the beach. They didn't object to the roll on takeoff; it was the execution they gave me hell about. According to them, I scooped out of the bottom of the roll so badly that the locals ran up warnings for high winds and surf. Porpoises in the area were traumatized. The Hellcat was not the easiest airplane in which to do classic slow rolls, but I disclaim responsibility for any trauma-induced genetic defects in marine mammals, in the Mediterranean Sea or anywhere else.

The tactics phase of Operational Training in Hellcats presented no surprises. There was much formation flying, including variations on the theme of two-plane sections, which, joined together in the usual pairs, constituted four-plane divisions. It was all related to tactics conceived and developed by people like John S. "Jimmy" Thach and James Flatley. The tactics worked; the tactics our fighter pilots fly today are derived from them.[16] Even the most rudimentary form of discipline in an aerial free-for-all can produce positive results. That is a stuffy way of saying that if, for instance, you can turn a four-against-four engagement into four two-against-one engagements, you have a good chance of bringing home more of your folks than the other guy. An appropriate amount of such discipline might even win the day against superior airplanes. That may explain the successes of machines like the Wildcat and Dauntless against the Zero.

We flew a lot of formation and exercised many variations on the Thach weave in single-plane and two-plane section evolutions. In this sense, the notion of formation doesn't relate to the parade stuff of ground troops, or to the parade routines of modern drill teams, or to the formal infantry battle lines that were blown into history by the massed cannons of World War I. Formation represents the difference between every-man-for-himself aerial chaos and an organized effort by a number of airplanes to accomplish a specific task. Each section should behave as a unit, maneuvering to support whichever section has the lead. Within the section, the leader has primary responsibility for doing what the section is assigned to do. The wingman has the responsibility for making it possible for the leader to do that. In graphic terms, the wingman was supposed to keep some outsider from shooting his leader's ass out of the sky. The other side of that coin is that the leader got the first shot at anything that got in the way of accomplishing the mission—or anything that got in the way, period! With no disrespect to the likes of Dave McCampbell, that is a partial explanation of why a CAG, like Commander McCampbell, had the opportunity to get thirty-four kills while his relative by marriage, Wayne Morris, frequently a wingman, got eight kills. (They both had to be good, opportunistic shooters!)

I marvel at the Eighth Air Force heavy bombardment airplanes that operated out of Britain, particularly before D-Day. The notion of hundreds of B-17s taking off from dozens of primitive airfields and then going through an arduous, time-consuming rendezvous process before even starting toward Europe and their assigned targets is almost beyond the ken of this former tactical pilot. The before and after part of those missions must have been longer than some of the airplanes I flew could stay in the air. Newspapers and newsreels of the day referred to thousand-plane raids as if they were commonplace.

The essential problem was the same: get the birds off, collected, and on their way as quickly as possible. The next thing you know you are going to have to recover them back aboard the ship; those you can't recover in time will wind up in the water. Unlike the British Isles, the middle of an ocean has no spare airfields. With that premise, everything else tactical was eventually subordinated to good formation flying. The only thing that had higher priority was preparation for carrier landings. I don't imply that anything was neglected—only that specific weapons training was always associated with formation flying. Section and division tactics got more emphasis than one-on-one individual combat tactics. That last is a euphemism for dogfight training, of which we got very little.

We did a modicum of bombing training, strictly Mark 1, Mod 1 eyeball fixed-sight stuff using miniature bomblets with shotgun shell marking charges. The difference between fighter squadrons and fighter-bomber squadrons as the war wound down became blurred to invisibility; everybody learned how to bomb.

The most exciting part of fighter Operational Training was gunnery. For the first and only time in the whole training cycle, we were exposed to a complete spectrum of gunnery approaches to a real target. We fired live ammunition against towed nylon sleeves. Gunnery provides the best fun a fighter pilot can experience in a training environment. It has a little bit of everything. The flying itself crosses well over any defined boundary for "acrobatic" flight. It is a great test of skill and coordination, flying an airplane at high speed through a complex pattern while maintaining precise control of speed and position with respect to another moving object. Then there is the competition. Flying the pattern in full, if not exactly continuous, view of your peers leaves you equally exposed to praise and ridicule. The payoff in personal satisfaction can be that you are doing the whole thing for score. That is not the object of the exercise, of course; you are supposed to be up there acquiring a demanding professional skill that has military utility. They do, however, keep score. Everybody is firing color-coded ammunition, an esoteric way of saying that the nose of each round of ammunition—each bullet—has been dipped in paint. The paint is not completely dry.[17] Each pilot is shooting a different color. When a round goes through the nylon sleeve, it leaves a ring or mark of paint. Count the different-colored holes at the end of the flight, and you have a winner! Not to mention a loser or, more correctly, several who did not score as well as the winner.

The drill was for a colleague to drag a nylon sleeve attached to one F6F Hellcat off a runway. That colleague, duly escorted by another colleague in a similar airplane, was supposed to arrive in a piece of airspace reserved for gunnery at about the same time as the rest of the flight. The flight included an instructor, who was obliged to keep track of what up to eight still-learning aviators were going to do in the next thirty minutes or so. All of these folks are flying high-performance, combat-proven fighter airplanes. The tow pilot—understandably concerned lest one of his fellows fail to remember that the towplane is pulling, not pushing, the target—is a special case. He alone does not have a minimum of one hundred rounds of ammunition for each of two (out of a possible six) .50-caliber machine guns. He alone does not shoot. His job is to fly straight and level while his buddies shoot at that white sleeve he is pulling through the sky. For the most part, those guns could—and did—shoot real bullets with impressive reliability. This gaggle of airplanes, led by the towplane's tour up and down a designated path, is going to make firing runs on the sleeve until the time is up or until everyone has exhausted his ammunition. Then the towplane is going to drop the sleeve over an airfield, probably not the one from which everybody took off; it will be an "outlying field."

It takes experience in a lot of outlying fields before one feels the necessity for quotation marks! The irony will become evident in a moment. A typical outlying field in wartime and postwar southern Florida was a kind of hexagonal wagon wheel. The six spokes were three runways, each about two thousand feet long, crossing in the middle in what can be thought of as a hub. The rim of the wheel was six straight segments that served as an uninterrupted taxiway around the perimeter. With the Navy emphasis on short field landings and takeoffs, it is normally no big deal to land and stop an airplane in two thousand feet. But a typical gunnery flight might take only about forty-five minutes, not enough time to make a serious dent in the 250 gallons of fuel you started out with; that fuel weighs about six pounds per gallon. Suppose you didn't quite get rid of all that ammunition either. And suppose it is a hot day when the wind is calm. Or suppose, for whatever reason, everybody is landing downwind when you get there. Suppose you are still a novice in the airplane. It just might be a real challenge to get down and stopped before either running out of pavement or standing the bird on its nose.

Forget the supposing; that was me after my first gunnery flight, although I managed not to do either of those bad things. I couldn't wait to get on the ground to count holes in the sleeve, if there were any, reload, and try it again. That, of course, is why we used the "outlying" fields. They were close to the range. All that was needed were facilities for reloading and refueling—and, of course, the capability of recovering and launching target sleeves.

"Launching target sleeves" fails to communicate what was involved. One didn't "launch" the sleeve, like an inanimate object, to proceed on its own to some location where it would behave in a prescribed manner while young men attempted to puncture it with rounds of .50-caliber ammunition. Someone had to drag that sleeve. The draggers were us. Each of us in turn had to fly the towplane.

The first problem was to get the sleeve off the ground. It really was a kind of sleeve, much like a long wind sock. It was intended to stream symmetrically behind the towplane and present the same aspect in plan, side, or overhead view to an attacking airplane. I remember the first time I observed the operation—impartially, because I was well away from the action. One couldn't just make a normal takeoff with the sleeve and all that line dragging behind, willy-nilly, until everything finally got airborne. The line was carefully flaked out—laid out in elongated strips folded back alongside each other, on or next to the runway, so as to avoid fouling. The idea was to get as much of the line into the air as possible before any real tension was applied. That way the sleeve would be smartly yanked into the air rather than dragged along the grass or pavement. Otherwise the sleeve would be demolished or torn off before it left the ground, or the line/cable would part.

What I saw that first time was a Hellcat going like hell on the ground, well past normal takeoff speed, and then depart the runway with the nose pointed dramatically skyward. The angle of climb would have been unremarkable for a modern afterburning jet fighter, capable of virtually vertical climb, complete with continuous aileron rolls, until it disappears from sight. But jet fighters in significant numbers were still years into the future. For a roaring, barrel-shaped, piston-powered World War II–era fighter to emulate even the front part of such a maneuver was startling. My first reaction was, "God, what a performer!" Immediately followed by, "He can't do that. He's going to bust his ass!" Just when it seemed inevitable that the airplane would stall and make an even more spectacular descent, the pilot pushed the nose over sharply. The sleeve left the ground. Then it was back to "ta-pocketa-pocketa" as the pilot reverted to a laborious, slow climb to altitude and proceeded toward the range. What I had observed was a special case of a high-performance takeoff, a gross extenuation of the "short field takeoff" technique that every pilot learns today in pursuit of the FAA Private Pilot certificate.

The towplane was escorted by a wingman who flew abeam or a

little behind the sleeve. His function was to alert other airplanes to the danger of a small, hard-to-see piece of nylon at the end of a long piece of line and cable. A collision with that cable would not be good for the collider. High-speed collisions with any part of a towline have been known to cause airplane losses and bodily injury.

The towplane has by now reached a position on the gunnery range that is confirmed clear. Unambiguous confirmation is mandatory before entering the firing range, let alone before starting to shoot. The tow escort has now joined the flight. Seven Hellcats, led by the instructor, are in right echelon flying parallel to and five thousand to seven thousand feet above the towplane. They are offset to the right to provide maneuvering room. The towplane is visible below, a little behind the leader's wing. The white sleeve itself is visible about 45 degrees behind the leader's wing. (In the propeller days, the twenty-foot sleeve was not hard to find; later, with the greater distances involved with jet speeds, just finding the banner—they were to replace sleeves—could present a major problem.) Guns were charged and left on "safe." Each pilot would go to "arm" only at the beginning of his run, returning to "safe" as he came off the target; after all, one of his squadron mates was pulling that rag through the sky.

There were four classic "runs," or approaches, in which we were obliged to become proficient: low sides, flat sides, high sides, and overheads. Until the introduction of jet airplanes, that was the full bag. A couple of those runs became natural victims of the dynamics of faster but less maneuverable airplanes. Why all this attention to flying "canned" maneuvers against a towed sleeve, when it is generally accepted that over 90 percent of all aerial combat kills were accomplished from directly behind the victim? With the victor firing at close range and the victim unaware that he was under attack until the bullets started coming? There are a couple of reasons.

First, the runs were tactically valid, especially against horizontal bombers that carried self-protection swiveling and turret guns. An attacking fighter presents a difficult target to defending gunners if he properly executes a firing run. He minimizes his exposure to enemy fire while retaining a high kill probability against his enemy.

Second, the runs we practiced were an excellent tool for teaching pilots to shoot accurately at moving targets. In particular, the end game 90-degree deflection shots featured high angle rates and range rates, the most difficult problems to solve in any kind of gunnery. If one could shoot accurately out of our array of firing runs, one should be able to shoot accurately in the more benign tactical scenarios that can also occur in combat. Most of the high scorers in the two world wars, Korea, and Vietnam were demonstrably excellent shots; many fighter kills were accomplished with surprisingly few rounds of ammunition expended. Consider the significant numbers of successful pilots who, like Butch O'Hare, shot down five enemy planes in one flight, or the smaller number who may have duplicated David McCampbell's feat of nine plus two probables in one flight. Economy and efficiency in expending ammunition do count! You don't get those extra scores if you run out of ammunition early. Nor is your survivability enhanced if you run out of ammunition before you run out of enemy.

Training objective number one is to teach people to shoot. Since training time is limited—it always is—they must be taught systematically. Hence the need for some form of canned runs. Another reasonable objective might be to teach them to shoot using maneuvers, runs, that not only work but may be useful in real combat. "Useful" can include offensive effectiveness and defensive prudence.

A high-deflection shot—deflection in this case refers to the angle through which an attacker's line of flight is offset from the target's track through the air—might be one where, at the moment of shooting, that angle approaches 90 degrees. Compare it to throwing a ball to someone who is running full-speed perpendicular to your line of sight—the quarterback is trying to hit the wide receiver who is running flat out, parallel to the line of scrimmage. That problem involves range but mostly lead angle, especially if the range is short enough that the trajectory of the propelled object, bullet or football, is relatively flat. You have to hit where he will be, not where he is. If, on the other hand, he is not moving or is moving directly toward or away from you, there is no angular change. The only problem is range; there is no deflection or "lead." If you master that hardest problem, combining varying deflection angle and varying range, the lesser ones should be easy. That is the theory. That is why we did it that way in 1946, and why we still do it that way in gunnery training today, albeit with variations.

With the exception of the overhead run, all runs in plan view had essentially the same shape, a kind of asymmetrical "S". These runs were called high sides, flat sides, and low sides: "sides" because they were high-angle, high-deflection runs with 90 degrees being the goal at the commencement of firing; "high," "flat," and "low" referred to the shooter's position with respect to the sleeve. If the nose of the shooter's airplane was pointing down, below his visual horizon, when firing, he was above the target, hence "high." "Flat" was level with the banner, nose on the horizon. "Low," similarly, was below the sleeve, shooting up. Those references are to altitude and the horizon as seen from the shooter's cockpit.

"Lead angle" is something else in a different geometric plane. That plane is defined by the Hellcat's and the sleeve's velocity vectors. Confusing? The only thing that matters is that however you approach the target, try to be instantaneously approaching the sleeve in a 90-degree, or beam, aspect when you start to shoot—"instantaneously," because this is a dynamic situation. You can't stay there; you just pass through. That is what makes it tough. You have to pass through this magic point in space wherein you are approaching exactly sideways to the target—90 degrees—at a range of roughly one thousand feet, while holding the appropriate lead, which is initially 80 or 90 mils.[18] You are now in a version of a pursuit curve, holding a lead angle that, to be correct, should diminish with range and your approach flight path angle. That angle diminishes with range. It has to; that is what makes it a pursuit curve. If you start approaching a moving object from the side in another moving object and keep pointing at it, eventually you will wind up directly behind it. Or, depending on range and your rate of closure, you will run into it.

You start to shoot on arriving at that magic point until one of two things happens: you run out of range—you better start getting out of there by the time you reach five hundred to six hundred feet—or you run out of "angle-off." Angle-off is the name of that initial approach angle that we have been trying to make 90 degrees. If that angle reaches zero, you will be flying parallel to the sleeve, directly behind it and that other airplane a thousand feet or so ahead of the sleeve, the towplane. If you are still shooting when you are behind and parallel to the sleeve, the best that can happen is that the sight of tracers will induce a dramatic reaction from the tow pilot. The worst is that you will put holes in either him or his airplane, or both. It has happened.

These, then, are some of the hazards. So how do you make a good run and avoid the hazards at the same time? We can start by going back to the flight, which is just starting down the range. Imagine yourself as the flight leader. You are exactly where you should be, approximately five thousand feet above the sleeve. You can see the sleeve below and behind you, about midway between the trailing edge of your left wing and the tail of your airplane. Before you roll into this run, which is going to be a high side, consider what else you can see.

As you look straight ahead, you see, peripherally, the aft bow of the windscreen, where the sliding portion of the canopy meets it. (For this exercise, that sliding canopy will be closed.) Ahead is another metal bow, this one around a thicker, flat piece of glass. This glass is (more or less) "bulletproof." Partially obstructing your view is an object sitting on a pedestal protruding above the instrument panel. This is the gunsight—not a physical reticle, such as your basic metal "Iron Cross" surrounded by a circle, but a collimated, indirectly illuminated sight designated Mk 8. The base, which contains the optics, the reticle, and the light source, is padded against unplanned impacts with your head. You can tell that the contraption is invitingly placed to serve as a grab handle because it is neatly stenciled "NO HANDHOLD." (When a sight is out of alignment, it is almost certainly because someone did use it as a handhold.)

An image of the reticle is projected on the combining glass, a flat circular piece of glass mounted at an angle above the sight base. Among the advantages of the arrangement is that you can see the sight under varying light levels, including night. The combination of collimation and a planar reflecting surface eliminates most misalignment problems and boresight shifts that might be caused by the pilot's head position and motion. The projected image consists of two amber-colored concentric circles with a dot or "pipper" in the center; these are 50- and 100-mil circles. There are intermediate, dashed tick marks at 20-mil intervals radiating from the center, enabling more precise control of lead or lag angle. You are about to aim six .50-caliber machine guns by pointing the whole airplane, using the sight as your reference, at a moving point in space so that, when you are firing, the bullets and the target arrive at that point at the same time. Nothing to it, right?

The guns are Colt/Browning air-cooled, recoil-operated automatic weapons.[19] They are boresighted to converge in a tight pattern at about one thousand feet. That range is selected in part to utilize the flat part of the bullets' trajectory and also to keep bullet dispersion small enough to produce an effective, repeatable pattern.

Start a slow turn toward the towplane. After about 90 degrees of turn, drop the nose and steepen the bank. Let the nose drop until it is lined up with the towplane and its direction of flight. As the nose is getting there, let your sight drift back behind the towplane. While doing this, you are primarily watching the sleeve; the towplane is just a convenient reference to give you an idea of the direction of motion of the target and to serve as a rough guide for when to reverse your turn, which is about now.

Using the tow cable as a guide, stop the aft motion of your pipper and start to roll. You are going to roll through something less than 180 degrees about an imaginary point along and slightly below the tow cable so that you can start tracking an imaginary point ahead of the sleeve. That point represents not less than your best guess as to final lead angle. This way you can achieve the proper lead, which is going to be about 80 mils, by letting the pipper drift back, as opposed to having to pull more g's to gain the right lead by moving the pipper forward. Now you are going to apply increasing back stick pressure to keep the lead where you want it. Your bank angle is increasing toward 90 degrees. Your speed is increasing. It is imperative that this be smooth, ball-in-the-center, coordinated flight. Otherwise you will throw the bullets off to one side or the other—they will go above or below the target. If you have done everything right up until now, you are not quite at the 90-degree angle-off position, not yet in range but closing fast.

How do we know when we are in range? That brings us back to the mil. What makes the mil an attractive unit for gunnery is that an angle of one mil subtends a one-foot object at one thousand feet. If we are one thousand feet from and perpendicular to a twenty-foot sleeve, the sleeve will cover 20 mils in the gunsight. Using that information and making allowances for not being quite at 90 degrees when we make the decision, we fire when we think we are there. That theoretical 80 mils of lead is only good for that angle, too. As we continue to approach the target, doing the best we can to keep things stable while shooting, we let the lead decrease as the angle-off decreases. It is taking increasing g-forces to hold the lead angle because of decreasing range and increasing angular rates.

When you fire, you do not hold the trigger down. Short bursts are the way to go, for a couple of reasons. For one, in the real world you must conserve ammunition. The guns fire at about 600 rounds per minute; you can go through 400 rounds per gun (the combat load) quickly. In this training exercise only two guns are loaded, with 100 to 150 rounds each. Second, you would like to evaluate your marksmanship. Every third round is a tracer. Tracers aren't effective for precise air-to-air fire control, but they can provide an idea of gross underlead or gross overlead. Intermittent, burst shooting lets you make corrections. (In the propeller airplanes there was time for more than one burst and some effort at correction, even with the typical two-to-one speed advantage. In the jets it is different.)

That target gets very close very fast after you open fire. To avoid the ultimate, perhaps disastrous, ignominy of flying into the sleeve, you must think about getting out of there. Level your wings! With all those positive g's the airplane wants to climb over the sleeve. You better be quick, however, and a little extra back pressure on the stick will help. Once clear, fly parallel to the sleeve and start a climb back up to the original "perch" altitude, converting airspeed to altitude. I have seen patterns where, to save time, the new approach or perch position was on the side opposite the preceding one. That results in people making runs from opposite sides of the target. If the airplanes get strung out, and with live ammunition flying about, it can get dangerous. In the higher-performance machines where getting strung out was more likely—that includes all of the jets in my recollection—you turned abeam and over the towplane back to the same initial starting point.

The most significant variation from the preceding description was the overhead run, the favorite of most pilots. Its passing from the scene, a casualty of the higher closure rates and decreased turning capability of the faster airplanes, was widely lamented. The importance to propeller-era gunnery deserves some comment. The idea was to commence a split-S maneuver such that you were inverted, ahead, over, and on a heading directly opposite the sleeve. Let the nose fall through so that you are approximately in position for that hypothetical 80-mil or so lead angle when you are pointed roughly straight down. Here the whole maneuver is in the vertical plane, wings level without turning. All your corrections are in the airplane's pitch plane. Get the correct lead angle, keep the ball in the center, and fire when in range as before. From here on adjust lead angle and look for your range cues. Keep the ball in the center! The smart pilot would have trimmed the airplane for the maximum speed he expected to see, sparing him the effort of either excessive pitch forces or coping with a ball that tended to slide to one side or the other. If everything goes right, a statistical improbability on the first tries, your next problem is to get safely off the target. Obviously, you can't pull off as before. You have to go behind the target in a near-vertical dive. For the rest of it, a piece of cake! Go back and try again.

An advantage of the overhead run is that the requirements for precise coordination and control are greatly decreased. The airplane naturally wants to do exactly what you are trying to make it do. The firing g's are relatively high, helping to create a nice tight bullet pattern. If only you can center that pattern on the target, the result will be a satisfyingly high bullet count. You will do well to make one or two good runs out of ten, but that will be enough. The holes in the rag will prove it! It's an open secret about towed target gunnery that even the good guys don't do it right every time. In a typical flight there are runs where you don't even shoot, knowing you are off target. You wait for the run that looks good, and that might occur only once or twice a flight. Especially with a good high-g gunner, most hits will occur on one particular run.

As the most demanding phase of the training syllabus, gunnery came late. But before the end we had one high-altitude oxygen flight. I remember it well because my engine quit at twenty-one thousand feet. The instructor continued to climb with the rest of the flight, leaving me in my inevitable descent escorted by a wingman; that ensured a witness as to where I might eventually plant the airplane. We had been weaving around scattered, swelling cumulus clouds. I could see little on my descent from altitude, not enough ground area for me to select an emergency landing site. The airplane glided comfortably, its propeller windmilling. For the moment I was closer to bored than concerned. I couldn't rush the descent, and there were no decisions to be made until I could see the terrain better. So I started doing slow rolls. At about thirteen thousand feet the propeller stopped windmilling. The engine came to life. My wingman joined up from his trail position. We went back to Opa Locka and landed.

The problem probably lay in the automatic lean function of the complex carburetor. If I had been smart, I would have fiddled with manual lean on my way down instead of wasting time and altitude doing acrobatics. I had at least gone into the manual lean setting when the power plant quit and quickly switched tanks. Some sort of fuel/airflow problem is the culprit most often when an engine simply stops running. You can't believe how fast you can switch tanks when the engine stops. Ultimately I passed through a density altitude that corresponded to the proper mixture setting. The R-2800 engine, God bless it, decided to run again.

The next stop after Miami was Cecil Field near Jacksonville for carrier qualifications, where we did everything except actually land on a carrier. The difficulty in accessing a ship was the large postwar backlog of pilots still in training. Instead I went to Norfolk, Virginia, to join—surprise!—a Hellcat squadron, VBF-3.

Professional Recollections

Much has changed in military aviation since the Hellcat was a first-line fighter. Those weren't quite white-scarf-and-goggle days, but they were close enough. All of us were issued white scarves, although we didn't wear them flying. We had and wore goggles. One of the significant differences between then and now was the people, and their attitudes and values. Aviation, particularly carrier aviation, was only modestly inhabited by straight-arrow types, and those who were straight arrows consciously failed to advertise the fact. A saying was, "If you can't be good, be colorful." My frame of reference is primarily the junior officers—lieutenant, senior grade (Army/Marine captain equivalent), and below. As a result of the Navy's ambivalent attitude toward aviation, a regular lieutenant (senior grade) could be as much the neophyte in aviation experience as the ex–aviation cadet ensign who was four or five years his junior.

My first nontraining aviation commanding officer was Lieutenant Commander Frank L. Lawlor, USNR. (He may have been an augmented regular by then.) Frank Lawlor was a product of the naval aviation cadet program. It was said that he was an engineering graduate of the University of North Carolina. He had been a member of the real Flying Tigers, General Claire Chennault's Chinese AVG air force under Chiang Kai-shek. This organization of mercenary pilots achieved a remarkable record flying Curtiss P-40s against the best airplanes the Japanese had in China, including the Zero. Most of what they accomplished was after Pearl Harbor. The original American Volunteer Group members were approximately three-quarters naval aviators. They were recruited under the dual enticements of fighting against an "oppressor" and substantial pay, augmented by bonuses for kills.[20]

Frank Lawlor was exceptional in the AVG in that he had a four-year college education and was already married with a child. One of the first of the many books about the AVG devoted a paragraph to the soft-spoken Southerner who talked pridefully of that young son. That he got a paragraph in the book attests to the recognition he had earned even then; that he got *only* a paragraph is consistent with his character as I observed it later. It has been suggested by other sources that Lawlor was reluctant to contest disputed kill claims, even though the kill bonuses were the closest they got to real money. Lawlor represents to me the archetypical aerial gunner. No one I ever talked to knew what his score was in the Flying Tigers. I recall hearing that he got about nine kills with Air Group 9 toward the end of the war. It is not easily verifiable. Barrett Tillman's list of Hellcat aces only goes down to ten,[21] and Frank is not available for comment; he died in retirement some years ago.

I think the record shows that virtually every fighter ace was an inherently good shot. That implies more than being simply a good static marksman with a rifle or a pistol against a stationary target. What it means is being able to shoot moving and nonmoving targets with a variety of weapons. That includes being able to recognize the relationship between things like range and lead in a dynamic situation, then actually getting in position so that when the target is in range one has achieved the lead appropriate to what is going on. The result will be rounds on target, whether machine gun rounds on a sleeve, shotgun pellets destroying a clay target, or something more serious—like a live target in another airplane. The shotgun reference is not accidental. Skeet and trap shooting were used during the war to teach pilots and aircrewmen the skills I refer to. Frank Lawlor himself was good with a shotgun. As the stories went, he had hunted and was good with a rifle as well. They fit the image. I know he could shoot with a Hellcat. I saw him do it.

In those days it was common, on reporting to a squadron, to see a chart on one of the blackboards.[22] The chart, left over from the last time the squadron had shot, listed the pilots and their best scores in order. VBF-3 had such a chart. There was Lawlor at the top of the list with a score that indicated a hit rate of about 35 percent. In classic marksmanship where the good guys rarely stray outside the 10-ring, that does not sound impressive. *Au contraire, mes amis.* It is impressive indeed! Consider it. The pilot is firing two recoil-operated machine guns. This means that they reload themselves about 600 times a minute by letting the recoil slam the bolt back violently, ejecting an empty shell in the process. The bolt then slams forward just as violently, forcing a new round into the firing chamber. These guns positively locked the bolt in place just long enough to fire, whereupon the process started over. At a cyclic rate of 600 per minute, this is a dynamic, noisy exercise. The guns thrash around in their mounts, shaking the bejesus out of the whole airplane. They are not rigidly held in place within the airplane; they wiggle around a lot, causing substantial, unsystematic bullet dispersion at the target. This is one of the bigger factors degrading accuracy. There are others.

The guns are located several feet out on the wings. The gunsight is right in front of the pilot. To get guns and sight aligned so as to converge at a precise range or a segment of ranges is not easy. The total process is sometimes called harmonization. Keeping the system harmonized may be even harder than getting it harmonized to begin with. I have already talked about the "No Handhold" gunsight. Hitting a sleeve with 35 percent of all rounds fired from a moving F6F—with outboard-mounted guns—is comparable to a nice tight group in the middle of the 10X-ring in whatever demanding kind of shooting you choose to use as a comparison.

We had a gunnery training exercise shortly after I joined VBF-3. We started with gun camera flights to avoid wasting a lot of ammunition, not to mention wear and tear on guns, airplanes, and aviation ordnancemen. We had damn few of the latter. They are the men who have to load, reload, and ultimately clean all those guns. The nifty belts of ammunition you see in old movies and still pictures don't come that way. The ammunition comes in boxes, wrapped in greasy, Cosmoline-soaked packages. Somebody has to unpack the boxes, separate the rounds, and, with strange-looking hardware that comes loose in another box, assemble the material into the impressive belts of ammunition proudly displayed by the heroes in those pictures. Aviation ordnancemen perform that vital, unpleasant task. Under the postwar organization that included "streamlined squadrons" and CASUs (carrier aircraft support units), pilots also participated in the fun experience of belting ammunition. We also got to assemble our practice bombs and rockets, right out of the box. This was neither a high-tech nor an elitist Navy.

The base of the gunsight had a receptacle for a magazine of motion picture film. The spectacular motion picture gunsight sequences from the film *The Fighting Lady* and the television series *Victory at Sea* were largely from gun camera film under combat conditions. Shooting bullets and taking movies of the proceedings are not mutually exclusive. The combat reason for gun camera film is damage assessment. Gun camera film in nonfiring, "dummy" practice flight is also a great training aid for dynamic exercises like aerial gunnery. You do everything except actually shoot the guns, and when you land you have a record of your performance suitable for analysis. Ideally, you view the film with a stop-action projector. With the aid of calibrated rulers it is possible to evaluate lead, range, and angle-off. Viewing the film dynamically—in motion—gives a good idea of the smoothness of tracking or the lack thereof. In practice, the principal value of gun camera footage was as a tool for evaluating tracking performance, and perhaps an estimate of range. A primary value for most of us in 1946 was that we got much-needed practice before shooting.

Frank Lawlor characteristically showed no interest in camera gunnery. Then one day he came to work and found we were going to shoot. He put himself in the first flight and shot not the 35 percent I have advertised, but 32 percent—cold turkey, after having not been in a gunnery pattern for months. Our Flight Officer was Lieutenant (jg) Jack Harris. Jack had been Frank's wingman toward the end of the war in CAG 9. He told a story about Frank chasing a Japanese reconnaissance "Betty." (Betty was a fast twin-engine airplane, perhaps the best of the Japanese bombers.[23] Its cruise speed was not substantially inferior to the Hellcat's.) There was neither time nor fuel remaining to chase the enemy, who was retreating with what he had come for, information about the American task force. Frank did the unusual, and what should have been the ineffective. According to Jack, he honked the nose of the Hellcat up in the air and, using some variant of vertical "Kentucky windage," squirted off a couple of bursts, increasing the nominal range of his guns well beyond the flat, short-range trajectory we were taught to use. The result was one "splashed" Betty. The story must be true; Jack never lied and rarely exaggerated.

A legitimate training goal in the chaotic postwar period was to establish some kind of order with respect to rank and flying experience. There was a gaggle of neophytes like me and my peers in VBF-3. We were split between ex-cadet ensigns and equally inexperienced lieutenants (senior grade), former officer students. The ensigns were doomed to the traditional "boot ensign" role; they would work their way up in time. But what about those damn lieutenants? Well, qualify them as fast as possible and slip them into leadership roles as soon as

F6F-3s of VF-8 ready for takeoff from the USS *Intrepid* (CV-11). Three TBMs in the background and two Hellcats on the fantail show the usual Grumman wing-folding arrangement. (Grumman History Center)

safety and sanity permit; those leadership roles were revocable in case anything important should come up.

With a complement of twenty-four airplanes there were six four-plane divisions. The skipper, Exec, and Maintenance Officer, all lieutenant commanders, had three of them. There was one moderately experienced lieutenant, Naval Academy class of '43, who had the fourth division. The other two division leaders were lieutenants (junior grade). Most of the section leaders were ensigns. Within two months of my arrival there would be changes.

One day I found myself on Lieutenant Commander Lawlor's wing. I was not his normally assigned wingman. It was a squadron "group grope" on some target or other. There I was, more anxious to avoid embarrassing myself than to make a good impression. I didn't know what his standards were. To be safe I kind of stuck my wing in his cockpit and left it there. Not so tight a wing position that he couldn't turn toward me, but tight enough that no matter how hard he turned away from me it was unlikely that I would get badly out of position. Lawlor's management style was restrained, but I wasn't taking any chances on earning a reprimand. The flight involved a couple of long straight-and-level legs. I just sat there, eyes glued on my leader and his airplane.

Lawlor was about six feet tall, skinny enough to have an angular look. He had stringy, dirty-blond hair and, of course, steady, pale blue eyes. His face had gone wrinkled and leathery early, a fact I attributed to hours of sitting in an open cockpit under the sun, not to mention the ravages of surviving all that combat. (Having since observed a larger sample of pilots, I now conclude that the leathery look was probably genetic. How else to explain the occasional round-faced Celt, still smoothly baby-faced after much the same exposure?)

Lawlor was a fidgeter in the cockpit. He would stare fixedly in some direction for minutes at a time, then lean his head back, staring upwards, resting his eyes for all I know. He took off his helmet and scratched his head. The helmet stayed out of sight for a while, perhaps in his lap? He was a chain smoker in an airplane, circumstances permitting. (Many pilots were. I remember pipe and cigar smokers as well, even in single-cockpit airplanes. Some airplanes had ashtrays, occasionally even cigarette lighters.) Once, for what seemed an eternity during a helmet-off period, Lawlor ducked down below the cockpit sill. He disappeared completely. My God, he not only couldn't hear anything; now he couldn't see anything either! Suppose I had to get his attention? Maybe he had dropped his cigarettes or was looking for more matches in a flight suit pocket. After a while he came back into view. He looked toward me for the only time during the entire flight—totally expressionless, helmet on now, goggles pushed up on his forehead. Then he looked away.

We went through the tactical exercise. I apparently didn't embarrass myself. In a squadron reorganization a month later I was one of two inexperienced lieutenants to get a division. It was a not unflattering experience, but I recognized that it could quickly change.

In September of 1946, VBF-3 began phasing out the Hellcats as by ones and twos brand-new, fresh-from-the-factory Bearcats arrived.

Chapter 4
F8F Bearcat

THE TRANSITION FROM MIAMI AND HELLCATS to Norfolk and Bearcats was not direct. First there was carrier qualification training out of Cecil Field, Jacksonville, Florida. The carrier qualification training unit had all the airplanes then in the Operational Training Command. They were the F6F Hellcat, the F4U Corsair, the TBM Avenger, and the SB2C Curtiss Helldiver.

Carrier qualifications consisted of intensive training in the carrier landing pattern at short paved strips, outlying fields, under the ministrations of extroverted, generally loud-mouthed Landing Signal Officers. LSOs were quiet only while waving their "paddles." Their signal devices were two identical hand-held flags that resembled oversize ping-pong paddles, hence the nickname. Initially, they had been red flags; with time they got smaller and were mounted on rigid frames. The problem with flags was that they tended to stream with the relative wind, making them difficult for pilots to see. The rigid frames solved that problem, but the LSOs then had to hold them against a relative wind from behind, which routinely could exceeded 30 knots—tiring for a hard day on the platform. In the real carrier world—as opposed to simulated decks on fields—the "platform" was just that, a platform extending from the port side of the landing area of the carrier with a movable windbreak that could be erected behind the LSO. The platform was bounded on three sides by a net made of steel cable and cargo netting. This was to give the LSO and his talker a place to go—dive, actually—to avoid an airplane whose pilot threatened to fly through the space they normally occupied. Eventually the solid flags of the paddles were replaced by strips of high-visibility cloth on wires in a frame. The revised paddles were easy to see and relatively easy to hold.

The signals were few in number and not difficult to interpret. Execution was the problem. There were signals for low, high, fast, slow, wing leveling, skidding flight, and—most important of all—the "wave-off," a mandatory get-the-hell-out-of-there signal, a brisk, sometimes frantic waving of the paddles over the LSO's head. This differed so substantially from the ideal arms-extended, horizontally-level-flag position—the desired "Roger"—that it was rarely misunderstood. The other mandatory signal was the "cut," the LSO dropping one hand and bringing the other sharply across his chest. This meant that it was OK to land. You chopped the throttle, held the airplane attitude you had, and let the airplane land (fall?) onto the deck.

It is also necessary to get a stream of airplanes established such that they approach the blunt end of the aircraft carrier on speed, on glide slope, and at a proper interval so that they can be recovered as if they were landing on a regular airfield. This must be done regularly, consistently, repeatably, and safely. Otherwise, forget the aircraft carrier as a weapon and get into the air show business![1] There is a landing "pattern" with defined checkpoints. The pattern must be capable of being smoothly filled from above so that airplanes can flow through it. A World War II *Essex*-class carrier carried over a hundred airplanes; a "recovery" involving that many airplanes was unrealistic, but one involving a sizable fraction of that number was not.

In training they didn't just give a fast lecture to a bunch of neophyte pilots and throw them into the air to find a ship to land on. We were lectured to, yelled at, and scared half to death with horror stories of the consequences of poor performance around the ship. Those consequences, serious though they might be to the perpetrator, had the nasty potential of affecting hundreds of lives as well as millions of dollars of U.S. taxpayer investment. It is of historical interest that no U.S. first-line aircraft carrier specifically designed for World War II or later, the USS *Essex* and subsequent, has ever been sunk by enemy action or any other kind of action. But there has been substantial and spectacular damage caused by enemy action—the USS *Franklin* (CV-13) and USS *Bunker Hill* (CV-17) are examples—as well as substantial and spectacular noncombat damage. The latter can be, and has been, caused by a combination of accident, material failure, and plain human error. The most frequent and potentially correctable contributor is human error. Hence all the lecturing, yelling, and scare tactics by our friendly Landing Signal Officers.

After a suitable period of lectures and chalk talks we were considered ready to give it a go. Aboard ship? Certainly not. In flights of six or eight we flew hours of a very special version of "circuits and bumps" around an outlying field. These fields were short, single-strip affairs out in the pine trees in the Jacksonville area. We were taught to approach the field in normal cruise condition in four-plane divisions. We orbited overhead until the LSO gave us a radio signal, "Charlie." That meant, and still does, let down into the pattern and start making passes. In older days the signal was simultaneously given by signal flag and by the Morse code for the character *C*.

When given a "Charlie," we would fly alongside the runway, which simulated a carrier deck, offset to the right in right echelon. From an altitude of three hundred to six hundred feet—three hundred was common around a ship, but local conditions ashore sometimes drove us higher—we "broke" to the left by single aircraft, dropping our landing gear and flaps and accomplishing other prelanding sundries as we did so. We let down to about 100 to 150 feet above the field elevation. When it was done right, the first pilot after 180 degrees of turn would be directly opposite the LSO platform, headed downwind and ready to start his first approach, the rest of the flight stretching out behind him in trail in what would become an oval, racetrack-like pattern.

Approaching a ship, which might have 30 knots of wind across the deck, the pilot would then initiate his approach. For FCLP (field carrier landing practice) and lighter winds, he would delay the turn. The approach itself consisted of a continuous, almost flat turn with a minimal straight path right before the "cut." Approach speed was close to power-on stall speed, but not between power-off and power-off stall speeds as had been the goal with prewar biplanes.

The pilot focused his attention on the ship, or field, from the moment he left the abeam or 180-degree position—first, striving for a desired path with respect to the landing area and, second, looking for the LSO's paddles. In the props, with their small turning radius, picking up the LSO occurred after about 90 degrees of turn. Unless you were initially screwed up beyond recall, the first signal was a "Roger," then "Paddles"—that was the LSO's nickname—gave you a signal indicating what you were doing wrong. If nothing was wrong, he continued with the "Roger" until the "cut."[2] If you were low, the LSO held his paddles symmetrically low, below the horizontal "Roger" position. If you were high, the paddles were symmetrically high, well above shoulder level. If you were fast, one paddle remained horizontal and the other was held low—or agitated, depending on how fast, maybe beating against the LSO's right knee. If you were slow, the LSO brought the paddles together in front of himself and brought them out smoothly to the "Roger" position, arms again horizontally extended.

That simple description does not suggest the eloquence of the infinite variations used by different LSOs—not in the signals themselves, but in the way they were given. They could be smooth, agitated, threatening, even beseeching. The slow, or "come on," signal brought out the thespian in all of them. It could come across as a wheedling "Come on,

Baby, just squeeze on a little power, a little power," or as an attention-getting "Power! Power! Power, asshole!"

Low *or* slow could kill you; low *and* slow could kill you and maybe some other folks too, especially if you slammed into the ramp or the "spud locker." As VHF radios became common toward the end of the war and, later, UHF, the critical signals were backed up by radio transmissions from one of the assistant LSOs or from an enlisted "talker," also on the platform.

The "Roger" could also be used an as indication of bank angle, augmented by LSO arm and body English showing what he wanted. Skidding flight was indicated by the LSO energetically kicking one foot at the pilot. In time LSOs became quite acrobatic. If you, the pilot, did it right, you saw nothing but the "Roger" until you took the "cut" at the real or simulated ramp. Since you were somewhat above stall, it was prudent to initiate a rate of descent and then get back to the landing attitude that would ensure that your hook would catch a wire. In the Hellcat the technique was to ease the stick forward and then immediately pull it back to its previous position, then ease it all the way back into your lap, ensuring that the tail was well down. If you were on speed, that airplane was going to come down. These were not gentle landings. "Carrier landings are controlled crashes" is only part euphemism.[3]

In our carrier qualification training scenario, the first pilot, presuming he did not get waved off, made his landing as a touch-and-go, immediately adding power to take off and then take his place in the developing daisy chain pattern. There were no wires in FCLP, nor was there a painted diagram of a carrier deck on the runway. If you did what the LSO's signals told you, you would land somewhere close to the target landing area. He knew where it was and how close you were supposed to be. Besides, each of your passes was carefully described in LSO shorthand in a book maintained by someone on the platform. You would hear about each and every pass at the end of each FCLP period. What you were looking for was "OK, three wire."

A typical flight consisted of about eight approaches per pilot, after which the flight either landed for a between-periods debrief—if it was a double period—or rendezvoused and flew back to Cecil Field, making room for another flight, which was probably by then orbiting overhead in a different kind of airplane. After ten periods or so we were supposed to be ready to go aboard ship.

The flying was challenging but a lot of fun. Most of us carried the usual baggage of apprehension about getting through any naval aviation training program, but the washout rate was low. If elimination was to occur, it was probably going to occur at the ship. There were incidents, some more serious than others. One involved Vic Mottarella, a former cadet with whom I was to be shipmates for the next two and a half years.

Florida, through World War II, was an open-range state; that is, there were no fences. Livestock, principally cattle, were permitted to wander at will. Florida had a lot more cows than most Americans realize. At the end of one of our FCLP periods we made full-stop landings for a between-periods debrief. Vic made a final approach and landing. He had his Hellcat under control, slowing nicely, when a peripatetic, unconcerned bovine decided to insist on her open-range right-of-way—in the middle of the runway! Whatever the legality of the situation, Vic was unable to avoid the encounter. The result was disastrous for the cow. It didn't do the Hellcat much good either. No engine "sudden stoppage"; cows are tough but not that tough. However, the propeller was a mess. Vic got to ride in the truck with the LSOs back to the base. He was able to get rid of the nickname "Cowboy" in only a few weeks. In today's Navy, where personal call signs are de rigueur, he would have been "Cowboy" for the rest of his career.

On a similar flight I turned downwind after a touch-and-go landing. I saw a huge column of black smoke billowing from a fiery core just short of the approach end of the runway. I had landed and got back in the air only seconds—barely a minute—earlier; it had happened that fast. My immediate conclusion was that someone in my flight had spun in. The flight consisted mostly of guys from my permanent flight in Operational Training. The two who weren't in my Opa Locka flight were friends from Kingsville. I had lived and flown with all of them for over a year. Remembering, I can almost feel the impact in my gut, the sense of fear and dismay as I frantically scanned the pattern, counting airplanes and trying to figure out who was missing. The LSO came on the air: "Your signal, 'Dog.' " That old phonetic for the letter *D* was the signal for continuing to orbit until the "deck" was once more clear to accept aircraft. It also covered any other exigency that delayed normal flight operations.

Before I could reach orbiting altitude, I was sure that we were all there. Confirmation came when we joined up to proceed back to base and I could count airplanes with more assurance. We flew back to Cecil Field; someone else didn't get back to where he started that day. Accidents have always been a fact of life in aviation. Until then, this was the closest in real, proximate time and space I had come to one. The airplane was an SB2C Curtiss Helldiver on a training flight not connected with the carrier qualification detachment. The pilot had experienced an engine failure and attempted to glide to our "bounce" field. His decision was reasonable. Before ejection seats, bailing out of "high-performance" propeller-driven airplanes could be a chancy business,

F8F-1 Bearcat with 150-gallon tank. Note the taped-over .50-caliber machine gun ports and the single external store station under the wing. Although the typical Grumman stubbiness is evident, the airplane's overall cleanness of design is accentuated by the smoothly faired bubble canopy. (Grumman History Center)

especially from low altitude. Getting out of a cockpit and clear of the various parts of an airplane that could inflict damage on one's person was not trivial. Putting a strong carrier airplane down on a reasonably level surface was more than a viable alternative. It was an often-preferred option. In this case, the pilot had attempted to "stretch" his glide to make a real landing field, a classic and much-warned-against procedure. The result was that he stalled the airplane at an altitude too low to permit recovery. Along with the mixed emotions we carried with us on our flight home was the knowledge that each of us could have made the same error.

After successfully negotiating the carrier qualification program at "Jax," I was by the luck of the draw one of the ones who did not get a ship qualification detachment. It was on to the replacement pilot pool in Norfolk, orders to VBF-3, and in due course F8F Bearcats.

General Description

In November of 1943 the Navy ordered two prototype XF8F-1 aircraft.[4] These Bearcats were a return to the design philosophy of smaller, more agile fighters, but with a difference. The Bearcat had the 35-foot wing-span formerly typical of fighters. Its normal operating weight was about 9,000 pounds without external tanks or other stores. This compares with the Hellcat's 43-foot wingspan and over 12,000 pounds. A signifi-cant difference from older small fighters was that the Bearcat retained the R-2800 engine that powered both the Hellcat and Corsair. The -34 version of the engine as installed in the Bearcat is rated by some sources[5] at the same 2,100 hp as in the Hellcat. I know that the Bearcat had a different carburetor, and I am sure that we were told it was rated at 2,250 hp.

Performance was startling. The airplane currently holds the world land speed record for piston-powered aircraft of 483.041 statute miles per hour, about 420 knots. The record was set in the late 1960s by a well-known racer, test pilot, and all-round record setter named Green-mayer. The previous record, set in 1939, had been held by a Messer-schmidt Me-109. Bearing in mind the performance of the service ver-sions of the Me-109,[6] one must conclude that it was a very special -109. The Bearcat was specially prepared for the record attempt, but service versions, especially the F8F-1, were honest 440–50-mph aircraft at low altitudes. The F8F-2, with an additional supercharger stage, had better altitude performance—which was the reason for the supercharger change—but somewhat lower performance overall. For years one of the milestone Bearcat performance standards was from a standing start on the runway to ten thousand feet in approximately a minute and a half. That was accomplished not later than 1948. It was a long time before it was beaten by a U.S. jet fighter.[7]

There are several theories about the reason for the Bearcat. One is that it was designed to combat not only the newer Japanese fighters but also the Kamikaze threat. Considering that the first prototype Bear-cat flew in August of 1944 and that the Kamikaze threat didn't peak until early 1945, I doubt that theory. A more probable explanation, and the one cited in *The Illustrated History of Fighters*, is that it was de-signed to fill the need for better fighter performance on the smaller carriers, specifically the "Jeeps." In 1944 the small CVE escort or "Jeep" carriers carried improved Wildcat FM-2 aircraft built by General Motors. They proved surprisingly effective but were substantially outperformed by the Hellcat.

With its short, barrel-shaped fuselage and squared-off wing tips the F8F's Grumman heritage was apparent. However, the resemblance stopped there. This was very much a different approach. Great attention had been paid to aerodynamic cleanup compared with earlier Grum-mans. The skin was smooth, flush riveted. Corners were rounded, and filets were used to reduce drag through and around unavoidable corners. The engine cowling provided effective air intake and cooling with minimal drag. Except for the generally bulkier proportions, it is not difficult for a layman to see a resemblance to the German Fw-190, including the inward-folding landing gear.

Lest there be any implication that this was a derivative airplane, the F8F had a number of features that were pure Grumman. The airframe was strong, but not the brute-force kind of overkill characterizing some other products of the "Iron Works." Limit load was 8 g's. A unique feature permitted the airplane to operate at up to 12 g's, theoretically. That is, it was to be a flyable, useful airplane up to ultimate load. The feature was what might be called frangible wing tips. The rivets securing the outer panels were designed and installed so as to fail in a predictable manner; at precisely 8 sustained g's, the outer panels were supposed to break cleanly away, leaving a 12-g airplane. Turning performance was going to be pretty much shot, but the airplane would be very fast!

I asked Butch Sher, our squadron Grumman representative, about that feature, and he assured me that it really worked. It did, but not exactly as designed. Two rather large, strong individuals, one each from VF-3 and VBF-3, experienced an unanticipated anomaly. Each, on separate dive-bombing flights at different times, separated only one wing panel. Since no one is going to reinvestigate the incidents after all these years, George Veling and Bill Leonard are safe. What I think happened is that each horsed the airplane around in a high-g climbing turn off the target, trying to see where his last bomb had hit. This is not symmetrically "normal" loading (that is, perpendicular to the wing planform). The maneuver they performed constitutes a rolling pullout, for which "limit" load is not only different but smaller.

Each of these young men, confronted with the same problem, accomplished the same happy ending. It wasn't easy. The first difficulty was to regain control of the airplane. The shorter wing should stall, causing an incipient spin. Each pilot recovered. After recovery, since aerodynamic lift is proportional to wing area, the big wing was going to generate more lift than the little wing—in other words, it wanted to go up, causing the airplane to roll into the little wing. How to counter that tendency? With a lot of aileron and rudder and simple brute strength. It would be helpful if there was enough residual control authority in this newly asymmetrical flying machine to make that possible, and there was. I mentioned that these were large, even football player–size, pilots. That became important. In a simple, non-power-assisted control system, the control forces can get very high. Veling and Leonard both found out quickly that if they flew very slow and held onto the stick for bloody life with two hands, they might fly home. They did.

Grumman's first solution to this unanticipated problem was as innovative as the original idea: electrically detonated explosive rivets. When one wing tip detaches, the other wing is automatically blown off to match! There must have been a glitch or two because the next, and last, I heard on the subject was that the detonators had been disabled and the wing tips were riveted on to stay, just as on a regular airplane. The whole affair must have been a headache and an embarrassment to Grumman, but it caused no long-lasting safety or operational problems. Other, less dramatic innovations added up to a sparkling performer, an airplane that is one of my two all-time favorites.

Instead of the conventional, birdcage canopies of earlier airplanes, the Bearcat had a nicely streamlined bubble canopy. The small headrest and overturn structure did not inhibit rearward visibility, which was outstanding. I would have preferred a seat with vertical adjustment, but even at my height I could see well enough. There was no fore and aft seat adjustment either; instead, the pedals adjusted, normal for aircraft of the day. In order to save weight and complexity, the hydraulic system was of low capacity. Wing folding, outer panels only—new for Grumman—was manual.[8] Flight line personnel enabled the operation by opening locks on the underside of the wings. Folding was accomplished with a short metal bar—special support equipment—inserted into angled holes on the folding panels. Just manually push or pull the wing into the folded position; a swab handle would do in a pinch. Folding wasn't all that important except aboard ship, since these were small airplanes.

The small-scale aircraft hydraulic system was important with respect to the landing gear. The main gear fairings were actual airfoils that helped the gear achieve the full-down position on lowering. Unfortunately, they were also airfoils when retracting the gear, so it was important to get the gear up early before the fast-accelerating airplane reached a speed where the hydraulic system couldn't overcome the aerodynamic forces. Flaps were actuated by a simple handle. Flap position was determined by looking out at the wing and seeing which numbered lines (numbered for degrees of flap deflection) were visible—not sophisticated, but it saved the weight and complexity of a mechanical/electric indicating system.

The airplane was beautifully balanced in the air, but that large engine in a short fuselage called for careful ground handling. Whether a deliberate design device or simply another attempt to save weight, the brakes were small and relatively ineffective (perhaps to keep strong men like George Veling and Bill Leonard from standing the airplane on its nose). The cockpit was downright cosy compared with most other U.S. airplanes. If the Hellcat and Corsair were Indy or stock car racers, the Bearcat was a sports car. It even had a center console that housed

F8F-1B at a shore-based catapult test facility. In addition to the single external store wing stations, equipped with sway braces, the airplane carries two outboard zero-launch rocket launchers. The protruding 20-millimeter gun barrels identify the airplane as a -1B or later. The catapult crew is hooking the bridle, which is already engaging the catapult shuttle, to hooks in the wheel wells. (Grumman History Center)

a large fuel selector handle right between the pilot's legs. There were detents for wing station auxiliary tanks, but the only ones that mattered to us were for the single internal fuel tank, with a capacity of 179 gallons, and the external fuel tank that we almost always carried. (The Hellcat, by contrast, carried 250 gallons internally, distributed among three tanks.) The location and physical size of that selector handle were to become a much-appreciated design feature. The stick was short, the shortness exaggerated by a leather boot, remarkably similar to one surrounding the short-throw stick shift of a modern sports car.

Armament for the prototypes and the F8F-1 consisted of four .50-caliber machine guns mounted internally in the wings. These were replaced by four 20-millimeter cannon for the F8F-1B and subsequent F8Fs. Both installations worked. Once it was figured out how to stuff the twenties into the wings, there was no reason to suffer the loss in firepower implicit in going from six to four machine guns. In the 20-millimeter installations there is a little rounded bulge on the upper surface of the wings to make room for the feed mechanization.

In operation there was one phenomenon that I experienced in no other airplane. These were small, short-coupled airplanes with a modestly sized vertical tail. If, in the middle of a firing run, the gun(s) on one side jammed or stopped, you could suddenly find yourself trying to fly sideways. This was noticeable even when firing only a pair of fifties; when four 20-millimeter cannon were firing and you lost two on one side, the phenomenon was dramatic.

There were five external store stations: a centerline station that was usually devoted to a fuel tank, and four wing stations, two on each wing. The wing stations, when used, were devoted to bombs and rockets. For us that meant practice ordnance, usually miniature bombs and sub-caliber rockets. Part of the reason for the Bearcat's short service life was the small number of ordnance stations and their limited capacity.

Grumman produced about twelve hundred Bearcats of all types. These included F8F-1, -1B, and -2 airplanes. There were small numbers of F8F-2N night fighters, and a somewhat larger number of F8F-2P photoreconnaissance airplanes. All versions of the -2 had a larger vertical tail and the augmented supercharger. The *Midway*-class carriers retained the F4U Corsairs in their fighter and fighter-bomber squadrons. The *Essex*-class carrier air groups' fighter and fighter-bomber squadrons flew Bearcats. VBF-3 was completely equipped with F8F-1 airplanes by October of 1946. Within a year we were reequipped with F8F-1Bs. By late 1948 the fighter-bomber squadrons started reverting to Corsairs. With the advent of the first jets and the Korean War, the remaining Bearcats were removed from service and turned over to the reserves. Many of the operational pictures still extant show Bearcats in their reserve paint job, orange band around the aft fuselage. Production ended in May of 1949. By 1952 they were all gone from the active fleet.[9] A number of surplus Bearcats were sold/transferred to the Royal Thai Air Force and the French Air Force. The latter saw commendable service in the ill-fated war against the Communist Vietminh in what was then French Indochina.

How It Flew

I reported to VBF-3 in August of 1946. By late September the F8Fs started arriving, one or two at a time. The old hands got first crack at them. A number of us "nuggets" had missed carrier qualification, which made the skipper and the air group commander nervous. Accordingly, there was an attempt to get us aboard ship in Hellcats while we still had some. That entailed, first, revisiting FCLP with a vengeance, and with fleet rather than training LSOs. If there was a characteristic amelioration of attitude between fleet LSOs and their Training Command counterparts, it escaped my attention. That exercise lasted only until it became evident that we would be a Bearcat squadron before we could get a scheduled carrier deck-time in Hellcats.

We still flew a normal training schedule in Hellcats while awaiting our turn to get new airplanes. This meant mostly bombing and tactics flights. Finally came the opportunity to transition. The airplane familiarization drill as practiced then bears little resemblance to the way we were introduced to airplanes in the Training Command or to the way the Navy prepares pilots to fly the complex airplanes of today. We read the handbook, got a supervised cockpit checkout from someone who had just flown the airplane himself for the first time, and got a lot of advice on procedures and idiosyncrasies already discovered. That is about as formal as it got. We were turned loose for about nine flights of "Go out into the practice area and learn how it flies for yourself!" We didn't have chase pilots, not even on the first flight. After nine flights we were considered qualified to fly with the grownups. There was no discrimination; everyone checked himself out in the airplane the same way, starting with rank seniority followed by flight experience. One good thing was that by the time the "nuggets" got into the airplane a data bank of experience existed.

Among the pieces of advice was to taxi slowly with minimum power. The airplane was more susceptible to nosing over than most tail draggers. Although overall visibility was excellent, visibility over the nose while on the ground was not; hence a continuing requirement for S-turning while taxiing. The pretakeoff check procedure offered some concern for the neophyte. Even with full back stick, one couldn't be sure that the tail wouldn't come up with application of full power. Those weak brakes offered some safety margin in that they would start to slip as power was increased. The airplane would start to slide forward in the very direction where the pilot couldn't see much. The compromise was that we checked magnetos at about 30 inches of manifold pressure. This meant that you didn't know that the magnetos were good in the precise power regime where they were most likely to fail, at full or nearly full power. Also, you didn't know for sure until you added full power for takeoff that you could even get full power. The airplane didn't need full power for takeoff, but the most common failure or partial failure modes did not entail a simple loss of power. Instead, the engine refused to run well at all, with irregular popping, banging, and backfiring; the noise from the short exhaust stacks, in front of and below the cockpit, made it readily apparent when the engine was not operating properly.

I adjusted as best I could to these phenomena on my first flight. The little beast was somewhat intimidating, its performance already approaching the legendary; expressions like "tiger by the tail" were beginning to be heard. I got the airplane on the runway, was cleared for takeoff, and away I went. I added power smoothly. I was prepared for much more torque, the tendency to pull sharply to the left, than I experienced. One of the unsettling parts of the preflight brief had been the recommended takeoff trim settings: zero, zero, zero, neutral all round. This didn't seem to make sense, considering that the larger Hellcats and Corsairs had the same engine. I knew about the Hellcat, and I had heard what a torque monster the Corsair was. The trim settings for each of those airplanes were substantially nose-right and right-wing-down.

Except for the speed with which things happened, the Bearcat's takeoff run was docile. It ran so straight and true down the runway that the airplane might well have done it hands off. I wasn't about to try it hands off; I hung on for dear life. This was the acceleration I had anticipated for the Hellcat. Frame of reference is important: the ride was impressive, not to be compared with the first afterburner takeoff in that other "F8," the F8U Crusader, but, it was exciting. And quick. The Bearcat did not jump into the air, exactly, but close enough.

Once airborne my next problem was to get the landing gear up before exceeding the gear-down limiting airspeed. I reached for the gear handle and encountered something every Bearcat pilot faced: a safety precaution Grumman had designed to make it difficult to retract the landing gear inadvertently. The gear handle could not be simply lifted to the retracted position; there was a spring-loaded safety pin that had to be retracted first. It was integral with the gear handle and actuated by a simple flange that could be withdrawn by two fingers of the left hand—the handle was on the left side of the cockpit—before one lifted it to the "up" position. Not too difficult if one knew how; the problem was that spring pressure on the handle created enough friction that it was not easy to retract the pin. It was common for first-time Bearcat pilots to disappear over the horizon with the gear still down. Even with the gear handle finally moved to its retracted position, it was not unusual for the landing gear to hesitate in some dangling, asymmetrical position because the airloads were too great for the hydraulic system to overcome.

Adrenaline and experience solved the problem for most of us before we figured out the easy way: As soon as you break ground, push down on the gear handle with the palm of your left hand. Then the pin is easily retracted by the two middle fingers pulling back on the miniature flange. The handle can then be easily moved to the retracted position.

Exhilarated but only marginally in control, I climbed to five thousand feet and headed for the practice area. Performance was startling. At a standard fast-cruise setting for an R-2800 engine—2,200 rpm and 32 inches of manifold pressure—I found myself looking at 240 knots indicated airspeed. These were very early-production-model airplanes with no external stores, not even pylons.

I did all the routine familiarization maneuvers—first gentle, then increasingly steep banked turns; transitions from cruise to climb to straight and level cruise, controlled descents and back to cruise; slow flight at various flap settings, then stall investigation. For these airplanes not only snap maneuvers, like the snap roll, but intentional spins were prohibited. For us Hellcat pilots, impressed by the folklore associated with the "Ensign Eliminator" Corsair, that sounded ominous.

I approached slow flight and the various stalls with caution. In 1946 certain morale-building, possibly lifesaving, innovations like stall warnings and stick shakers did not exist in service airplanes. I got slower and slower, relying on lack of control authority, increasingly high control forces, a generally mushy control feel, and perhaps something that today would be described as buffet onset. Back then, we didn't know from "buffet onset"! There was no such term in our aeronautical vocabularies. Lacking those niceties, there was the possibility that when this plane went, it really went. Never mind that no one had yet come home with a hair-raising story; there is always a first time. But it turned out to be "Not to worry!" Speaking now from knowledge I didn't have at the time, I am sure that stability was poor at slow speeds, but the airplane was controllable and flyable down to low, quite inaccurately indicated airspeeds. The wing-mounted pitot tube was short and the airplane's near-stall attitude was significantly nose-high for a straight-wing airplane. This meant that the total-pressure pitot head wasn't really "seeing" all the dynamic pressure it was supposed to. The result was a remarkable 45-knot indicated airspeed with the airplane still flying and maintaining altitude.

Encouraged and relieved, I climbed another two thousand feet and had some fun. I was not entirely disappointed at being required to forgo the formerly obligatory spin exploration. First came a few tentative aileron rolls, followed by a serious attempt at a real ball-in-the-center barrel roll—no cheating, fly the helix the way it is supposed to be flown. Roll response was a new experience for a high-performance airplane. The F8F had spring tabs on the ailerons. The first inch or so of stick travel deflected the tabs such that, when the pilot actually exerted control force through the cable linkage, the ailerons were already biased in the direction of desired travel. That is a stuffy way of suggesting that, compared with a Hellcat or SBD—or an SNJ—the Bearcat rolled like crazy.[10] After that came a progression to loops, Immelmanns, and Cuban eights. With each maneuver I was more impressed with, and more confident in, this new airplane. For the first time all my expectations about flying were realized; "love at first flight" is understatement.

There may be raised eyebrows and a sense of disbelief that pilots of an older generation really did "wring out" a new airplane on the first flight. But not only did it happen, it was the rule rather than the exception. I by no means felt the master of the airplane, but I felt comfortable in it. In a short time I had sampled a significant chunk of the airplane's operational envelope and was ready to try something more immediately critical—getting the thing back on the ground. I had been pleasantly surprised at both the slow-flight and stall characteristics at altitude. At stall there was no tendency for a wing drop in either direction. Oh, if you held it deep into stall one wing might go, but it was mostly a function of how the pilot played the rudders. None of the flip-you-on-your-back left wing drop of the early Corsairs, or the full-right-rudder-trim-and-you-still-don't-have-enough of the Hellcats. How were this airplane and its novice pilot going to behave close to the ground?

With all that excess available power and agile control response, I had some apprehension about ricocheting all over the runway trying to get my spirited steed back to its barn. I sneaked up on the problem by negotiating a few touch-and-go landings first before trying to corral the machine for real.

My recollection of my first few landings is not as vivid as my memory of the first air work. It was more than a few years ago, but perhaps it is a case of not remembering pain. I am sure there was some minor trauma. Good landings came later with practice and experience, after what must have been significant bounces in that first period. Nose attitude at touchdown was more critical than with the Hellcat because of a tendency for the nose to drop on reducing power. That may have been partly a result of Hellcat conditioning, where a little nose-down-and-up, stair-step, worked just fine. One thing was apparent early: don't let the nose drop, because you may not have enough control authority to get it back! (Later on, that characteristic proved critically important aboard ship.) Approach speed was only marginally faster than in the Hellcat. Overall control harmonization was excellent. Whatever trim settings were required must have been minor. Compared with the Hellcat, they may have been neutral.[11] Wave-offs, go-arounds, were easy. Coming off the runway after a touch-and-go landing, the airplane simply leaped back into the air with no adverse tendencies. Once in the landing pattern we normally left the landing gear down for subsequent passes. We also cranked the bubble canopy open and left it open.

I have made a point of the neutral control response over a large part of the Bearcat's operational envelope. The airplane was relatively small, with a big radial engine capable of developing significant torque. Torque effects, however, were for the most part neither a problem nor detectable. Once the airplane got really slow, as we were to find out, a sudden application of power could have unfortunate results. There are always limits.

Professional Recollections

Our loosely supervised familiarization stage lasted for something over ten hours. The flights were usually a little over an hour each; I recall the target number as nine distinct flights, although it varied. From there we progressed to formation and fundamental tactics. The old hands in the squadron were uniformly good regardless of rank, the best possible environment for the new kids on the block. Weapons training was in the offing, but a couple of things got in the way.

Before there was such a thing as a Defense Department, a separate Air Force, and a characterless Armed Forces Day, the services were less ecumenical. There was, for instance, Navy Day, which appropriately coincided with Theodore Roosevelt's birthday.[12] In 1945 the Navy used the occasion for an aerial show of force, undoubtedly in anticipation of budget crunches to come. The show of force was not trivial. On the East Coast a parade of five thousand naval aircraft flew in a single formation from the Norfolk–Virginia Beach area as far north as New York City and back. The demonstration attracted enough favorable public and press attention to call for a repeat in October of 1946. And so we practiced incrementally by squadrons and air groups for a couple of weeks.

We had a dress rehearsal the weekend before the big day. It consisted of assembling a huge gaggle of different kinds of airplanes into one monstrous formation and then pointing it in one direction. It wasn't a simple task. Virtually every model and type of airplane the Navy owned, trainers excepted, was involved, with Bearcats and Consolidated PBY Catalina flying boats at the extremes, and everything from PB4Y Liberators (four-engine patrol planes, identical to the B-24 Army Air Corps heavy bombers) down to the variety of single-engine carrier airplanes in between.

The sheer range of aircraft involved immediately raised the problem of speed. It was neither fair nor accurate for the carrier pilots to allege that the PBY did everything at 90 knots; it only seemed that way. On the other hand, 115 to 120 knots was pushing it for that airplane. There were some carrier airplanes like the venerable SBD that could cruise comfortably below 130 knots, but the Bearcat was not one of them. And the example of the SBD loses relevance because SBDs were essentially all gone by then; the PBY became the pacer for the mass formation. All was not necessarily lost, however, because the carrier airplanes, especially the fighters, could do a gentle weave around the axis of the formation. Since the flight was to be a long one, the weave had to be gentle. That added up to a speed of about 135 knots for us, still far from comfortable. At slow speeds the F8F was neutrally stable, at best.

A formation flight that was going to last three hours or more with that many airplanes would translate into one fatiguing experience! And if for all that time the sun was going to be shining through the bubble canopy, the cockpit was also going to get uncomfortably warm. The solution that occurred to me, along with more than one other pilot, was to crack open the canopy a couple of inches. That increased the ventilation substantially but introduced another phenomenon: I could now hear what the engine was doing. To save fuel we were working on a power setting of about 30 inches and 1,400 rpm (this represented a wider permissible rpm range than any other R-2800 installation I ever flew). The result was that with the short Bearcat exhaust stacks, I could virtually count the revolutions, including the scattered misfires. It was a little unnerving, but the engine didn't seem to mind. The airplane was still a handful in that slow-speed formation. I found that one notch (15 degrees) of flaps made the exercise tolerable.

The rehearsal went off on schedule and, apparently, to the satisfaction of whoever was in charge. We were on for the big event! Alas, one of those big, wet, fall warm fronts moved in. It hung around for days. The Big Parade was canceled because of weather.

After that distraction the squadron got into the rhythm of a standard training syllabus. The formation and tactics flights were a revelation. We were doing the same stuff as before, but a lot faster. In these smaller airplanes, "parade" formation felt even tighter than in the Hellcats. I have mentioned that the more experienced pilots were "good," a subjective observation that bears explaining. They were to varying degrees experienced, and all their experience had been in fighters. Except for the real old hands—the two fighter skippers, their Execs, and the air group commander—virtually all that experience had been in Hellcats. They had the particular motivation and attitude that goes with the fighter mission. There was nothing to unlearn. They had no reluctance to explore the capabilities of the airplane and put them to use. This is not to imply that they didn't represent varying levels of skill and ability, or that they—who soon became *we*—weren't capable of mistakes. However, general satisfaction with my peers and growing respect for my seniors characterized the next few weeks. Frank Lawlor became a guru in my eyes. I was also convinced that Willie Williams, our Exec, was the finest acrobatic pilot alive, as well as the sternest formation taskmaster.

Next on the horizon was carrier qualification in the F8F—this time, finally, for real. The details of yet one more FCLP syllabus were familiar. Going through the exercise with a whole squadron, complete with the experienced hands, was somehow different. More professional? It felt that way. Ultimately, by squadrons we flew seaward from Naval Auxiliary Air Station Oceana to find the ready, empty deck of the USS *Franklin D. Roosevelt* (CV-42), the first aircraft carrier to be named for a person (named appropriately indeed for one who, if the claim can be made for any man, was the father of the modern U.S. Navy).

Having been through the exercise several times in three distinctly different kinds of airplanes, I confess that my memory is vague as to the details of that virginal experience. With the jets in particular, the first real CarQuals session could be time-consuming, with lots of wave-offs and, with angled deck carriers, many bolters. In 1946 it was considered no big deal to run a whole carrier air group through a straight deck, eight "traps" apiece, in one or two good days. It was, after all, merely a refresher for everybody except the two Bearcat squadrons. There was no reason to anticipate any special difficulty, and there wasn't any.

My recollection is that VBF-3 sent out a big flight, perhaps four divisions, sixteen airplanes. Emotion may color my recollection, but I place myself somewhere at the tail end of the third division: I was eager and apprehensive, and it seemed to take a long, long time for me to get into the pattern. I know I used the relief tube three different times. (My susceptibility to the proverbial nervous pee made me an expert in the use of that device in every airplane I ever flew that had one. That includes the F9F Panther, while wearing an exposure suit over Korea in the middle of winter. You had to be desperate to attempt that evolution in a Mk 4 "Poopy Suit.")

In spite of having much too much time to think about it, I made my eight traps with no wave-offs. I confirmed what I had learned on the field: don't let the nose drop after the "cut." The cumulative effect of hours of FCLP produced the desired result. For that period, at least, I was on the good side of automatic mode. My passes and landings were far from superlative—"superlative" earning a simple "OK" from our LSOs—but the comments were milder than many I had endured on the beach.

The drill each time was to make the landing. The deceleration that signifies that you have caught a wire becomes a sensual experience to a carrier aviator. It is a real high. After the runout, before you have a chance to savor your success and certainly before you have time to think, a man in a yellow shirt hurries out in front of you. He makes pushing gestures: "Release the brakes." You do. The wire that is still caught in your hook pulls you backwards as the arresting wire starts to retract. It is not a reassuring sensation. The wire stops pulling; you continue backwards. The guy in the yellow shirt now gives you the "hold brakes" signal, very impatiently. Can't he make up his mind? With most airplanes you would also get a command to raise your tail hook, but with this one some other deck sailors are busy clearing the hook from the arresting wire and manually stuffing the hook back into the tail of the airplane.

The old carriers, the straight-deck kind, had eight to ten arresting wires. In addition there were more arresting wires supported in pairs terminating in stanchions at the edge of the deck. These "barriers" looked like two-strand fences. The stanchions were hydraulically operated so that they could be lowered quickly. They were the means of stopping an airplane that failed to catch a wire before it ran into the airplanes parked on the forward two-thirds of the carrier's deck. There wasn't room for an "eight-wire" arrestment without the runout extending at least into the first barrier. An alert barrier operator would drop one or more of the barriers if he was sure that the pilot had caught a late wire. That has saved more than one pilot from embarrassment and bent metal. I know; I caught more than one eight wire in my time in Bearcats.

But not this day. The barriers and arresting wires were dropped as soon as I came to a stop.[13] When my hook was stowed—you couldn't prove it by me!—the same demanding yellow-clad figure held up two fingers and whirled them over his head. (For CarQuals the forward part of the flight deck was empty.) I held the brakes and applied power. He pointed toward the bow. I released the brakes, added the rest of the power, and was airborne about the time I passed the island. And so it went, seven more times. I was finally a carrier pilot. I kept telling myself that all the way back to Oceana.

That was in early December of 1946. Then it was business as usual back at the squadron. The next significant milestone was a seven-week deployment to Guantánamo, Cuba, for an extended shakedown for the USS *Kearsarge* (CV-33) and a workup for the air group.

There were a couple of things worthy of note in the interim. I refer to the Aeroproducts propeller and its differences from Hamilton Standard products. This fancy new propeller with its individual actuating cylinders had a nasty habit of developing seal leaks with a consequent loss of hydraulic fluid. The good news was that, without fluid, the propeller failed in the low-pitch (that is, high-rpm) position. The bad news is that turned the Bearcat into a very fast, fixed-pitch-propeller airplane. Confronted with a failure, a pilot might be impatient to get the airplane down quickly and point the nose toward the ground. Carried to an extreme this could result in engine failure due to over-revving or an even more dramatic propeller failure—like maybe blades starting to come off. A further complication was the phenomenon of "compressibility," a mysterious new term first associated with late–World War II airplanes. The myths surrounding the "sound barrier," though not yet in full bloom, were off to a resounding start. At least one Hellcat pilot, and more than one Corsair and Thunderbolt pilot, had encountered severe control difficulties in terminal—ominous term—airspeed dives. The essential difficulty was that these old-fashioned airplanes were flying faster and faster and, more important, higher and higher. Get one of those big, round-engined hummers high enough, point it down, especially with significant power, and it would really accelerate. At speeds in excess of those designed for, with their sharp corners and various protrusions these contemporary airplanes could experience local shock-wave effects well below the speed of sound; a Mach number of 0.6–0.65 could make things downright interesting. Compressibility effects might not be symmetrical. An incipient shock wave on the top of a control surface without a counteracting companion on the bottom might freeze the control to where the pilot couldn't hold it. It might even move the control surface in the "wrong" direction. In an extreme example, control movement might produce an airplane reaction exactly opposite to the intended one. (That phenomenon is an important plot device in the old Ralph Richardson movie *Breaking the Sound Barrier*.)

What we did know made us apprehensive. Grumman tried to help by installing an emergency "speed brake." The device was supposed to enable you to regain control of the airplane in a steep dive. Unlike other dive brakes, it consisted of a small hinged plate on the bottom of the airplane. The location was selected to create or spoil a shock wave. The principal effect was to remind us that someone thought there was a way to get into trouble that we didn't know about. I never knew anyone to activate one of those brakes, so I don't know if it worked or not. It may be because the Bearcat usually didn't fly as high as some of its contemporaries.

None of our folks got into any significant difficulty with the propeller problem, but there were some uncomfortable moments. It was a major fuss to get two squadrons' worth of propellers fixed. Every propeller had to be removed and run through O&R[14] Norfolk for new seals and a fix Aeroproducts had designed. The process was a nuisance while it went on, and our training syllabus was slowed down. But the solution worked. There were occasional propeller failures over the next couple of years, but the epidemic was over.

Another happening proved a harbinger of things to come, indicating a potentially lethal characteristic of the generally docile Bearcat. The emphasis on the carrier environment increased as our state of readiness improved and as the first deployment neared. This included striving for a tight landing pattern and a short interval between landing airplanes. A misjudgment by a following aircraft could lead to an unplanned "foul deck" wave-off even on a field. There came a time when several of us were on the flight line observing a returning flight. We watched them break. The leader was visible on the downwind leg until he started his approach. He disappeared behind the trees, a normal event. (This was the old NAAS Oceana. The runways, north and west of the present field, were relatively short and were thickly bordered by pine trees.) We saw the wingman follow his leader. His rate of descent was significantly greater when he turned off the downwind leg. As he disappeared behind the same trees, apprehension became alarm. We almost expected to see a column of black smoke.

Over the intervening distance we heard the application of power. That could be good or bad. The next thing we saw was Ensign Klobucar—the pilot—climbing up over the pine trees at a high-pitch angle, *inverted*. At a safe altitude, he rolled right side up. From there he took interval on the plane ahead of him and proceeded to land. Very scary.

On the other side of the obscuring pine trees, Klobucar had been initially high and fast. He solved the first part by diving off excess altitude on the downwind leg. That was the high rate of descent that had first got our attention. Anticipating the inevitable increase in airspeed, he whacked off all the power. As he approached the correct glide slope, still decelerating, he honked the nose up to stop his rate of descent. He had converted from high and fast to low and slow. Then he jammed on full power. Already at full high rpm, full low pitch, where he was supposed to be for landing, he called for all the torque the R-2800 engine could produce. At sea level, that was a lot of torque.

In most contemporary airplanes that would have been the end. Not so in the F8F. At that combination of low airspeed—approaching stall—and high torque, the airplane started a slow torque roll to the left. The roll continued in spite of full opposite aileron deflection. Approaching the inverted position, Klobucar lowered the nose of the airplane, either on purpose or inadvertently. Airspeed increased; some control effectiveness returned; the roll stopped; the airplane was still flying. With oncoming pine trees in his face, Klobucar pushed stick forward, raising the nose (he was now inverted). That is when we saw him climbing over the trees. We had just been exposed to a darker side of the Bearcat's otherwise benign nature.

The Guantánamo deployment went as scheduled. In seven weeks of intensive training—which included the dreaded ORI, Operational

Readiness Inspection—a loose collection of airplanes, the USS *Kearsarge*, and a bunch of people developed into an effective weapon system. Along the way we made more than casual acquaintance with honest-to-God Cuban Bacardi rum and a certain one-eyed Indian named Hatuey.[15]

An otherwise productive experience, the deployment was marred by tragedy: Ensign Klobucar did it again on a landing approach to the ship, but this time he failed to recover. He went into the water inverted, opposite the LSO's platform. There was no possibility of survival. It was the same maneuver he had gone through back at Oceana, minus the spectacular recovery. It would be unrealistic to overemphasize the hazards of the flying we were doing or the frequency of serious accidents. In context, the early postwar Naval Air Forces were numerically much larger than they are today. The people and the machinery were less sophisticated. Accident rates were higher, and there were more accidents. Dealing with them was a fact of life.

The next major event on our horizon was the Midshipmen Cruise of 1947. The midshipmen training squadron consisted of the USS *New Jersey* (BB-62), USS *Randolph* (CV-15), USS *Kearsarge* (CV-33), USS *St. Paul* (CA-73), and several destroyers. A formidable force indeed, and all to provide summer training for a bunch of midshipmen? Not really. This show of force was a precursor to a permanent Sixth Fleet in the Mediterranean.

It was a great cruise. We visited Göteborg, Sweden, Edinburgh, Scotland, and southern England (the battleship and the cruiser went to Denmark, while the carriers were in Sweden). We got in a lot of flying, for a couple of reasons: One, our presence was supposed to be noticed; and two, the air group was augmented by the bomber and torpedo squadrons from Air Group 9 to provide extra seats for the midshipmen to fly. Our fighter squadron were split, with us in the *Kearsarge* and VF-3 in the *Randolph*.

The cruise was largely uneventful except for the loss of Lieutenant Reggie Lamb in an accident virtually identical to that of Ensign Klobucar. In aviation, learning can cost dearly. That was the last such accident I recall.

When we got back to the States, the Navy sent us to Naval Air Station Quonset Point, Rhode Island. As a base it was palatial compared with the boondocks of Oceana. Our training routine frequently involved flying out to Cape Cod Bay where an old ship anchored in the bay served as a bombing target. Otis Army Air Field had ranges for rockets and bombing. Our commonest route to this training area was to seaward of

Newport, Rhode Island. Six to eight airplanes in formation would fly close to the cliffs on which sat the magnificent "cottages" of the rich. They made an impressive sight. We flew at such an altitude that we looked *up* at these structures. In spite of our large side numbers and the block K on the tails of our airplanes, nobody ever reported us.

We were sent to Quonset Point in time for one of the snowiest winters in years. One afternoon George Veling, Assistant Maintenance Officer, was flying back from the practice area alone. He had had a minor problem with his airplane at Otis. The afternoon had started out sunny, but barely off the ground, he found himself flying through snow flurries that quickly reached blizzard intensity. It was soon evident he couldn't get back into Quonset Point. He headed north to outrun the storm, knowing that there were several fields between where he was and Boston. The storm got worse. Visibility was close to zero when he spotted a small grass field with a half dozen light planes on it. He dragged the field one time, barely keeping it in sight; it looked about two thousand feet long. He landed successfully and taxied up to the only building, a small line shack next to a road. Then it snowed in earnest, all night long. The proprietor of the field let him use the phone and then took him into North Attleboro, Massachusetts, the nearest town. We told George to stay put until the weather got better.

The next day was bright and clear, but there was a problem. The skipper, now Commander Robert W. "Duke" Windsor, Lieutenant Bob Hoppe, and I drove an hour and a half to investigate. The problem was clear: Our airplane sat up to its knees in two and a half feet of snow in an otherwise unbroken expanse of white, a pristine New England winter wonderland. The field was surrounded by snow-covered trees, and I noticed power lines at one end. Lined up in a neat row in front of the line shack were five small airplanes, all on skis! As we surveyed the situation, a huge snowplow appeared. The roads had been in pretty good shape on the way from Quonset Point; this field was on a secondary highway that had already been plowed. The snowplow driver stopped his appointed rounds out of curiosity. After we gave him a guided tour of our marooned machine and explained our predicament, he had a solution: when he got through earning his state paycheck, he would bring back his magic vehicle and make us a runway. We borrowed the field manager's telephone one more time. The skipper arranged for a stake truck to bring a plane captain, a couple of mechanics just in case, and a starter unit; the Bearcat's tiny battery—after cold soaking, with no oil dilution[16]—couldn't be counted on for even one start.

The FBO[17]/field owner heard our end of the conversation. "Not so fast, there!" The snow and those ski-planes were his source of winter revenue; he wasn't about to let us ruin his landing surface just to recover one blue airplane! Besides, it looked kind of nice sitting there. It'll be a great monument, I thought; maybe until spring. Duke Windsor tried persuasion: "How about we let him plow on the edge, over to the fence, and then just enough on the far side of the field to get us out? The field will still be useful. You'll hardly notice." Nice try, Skipper. Who indeed will notice a big, ugly ditch of a taxiway covering a third of the field boundary and a makeshift runway in all that white stuff?

But the guy agreed to let us do it! Duke and Bob Hoppe drove off. I sat in the line shack, drinking the owner's coffee and trying to be inconspicuous. In a couple of hours three of our finest showed up in the stake truck. They hauled the starter unit and a couple of toolboxes out to the Bearcat. The starter unit consisted of a "handy Billy"–type motor generator on a cart with a couple of batteries. It could augment an airplane's installed battery, and that was about it. The four of us fiddled around with preflight, pulling the prop through and doing everything else we could think of without the benefit of a proper preheater. We wanted to get the engine fired up so that we could check it out. A second objective was to warm up the engine. Then we could dilute the oil on shutdown so that the next start, the critical one, would occur on demand.

With much attention-getting popping and banging, accompanied by frightening but predictable torching—visible flame—out of the short exhaust stacks, we coaxed the engine to life. I ran through every check that I, the two mechanics, and the plane captain could think of. Finally, I performed the oil dilution procedure and with reluctance shut down. At that point, sitting in the cockpit with the machine performing like the ever-loving jewel I had hoped for, I wished that the other necessities had been taken care of, like having a clear path to something that would serve as a runway. By now it was the middle of the afternoon, the shadows lengthening; where was our friendly snowplow? Feeling like a suspicious ingrate, I permitted myself to wonder about the integrity of a (by definition) underpaid and overworked employee of the Commonwealth of Massachusetts. About then he arrived. He took that big state-owned piece of machinery onto private property and went to work.

It became a race against darkness. The field was not lighted, and tactical aircraft had neither taxi nor landing lights. Recognizing that time was important, the driver worked with a will. He got advice from me and my cohorts, interrupted by an occasional admonition from the field owner. The first problem was to ensure a plowed track wide enough for the airplane's main landing gear. The second was to make the "runway" wide enough that I wouldn't run into the snowbanks he was throwing up on the sides. An additional concern was that those snowbanks extended almost up to the trailing edge of the lowered flaps; I certainly wanted full flaps for this takeoff.

It was dusk when I started the engine. My loyal plane captain stumbled, walking backwards in the deep snow giving me taxi signals; he was in the snowbanks off to the side so that I could see him. We had trouble with the first corner. Following it was a moderately long straightaway to another corner, a sharp left that would take me parallel to the fence down to the "runway," but we never got that far. In the interest of speed in getting the job done, my road builder had given me a taxiway barely wider than the track of the airplane, so in trying to negotiate that first square corner, I got one wheel thoroughly stuck in the snow. By now it was almost dark; dusk doesn't last long in the winter. I went through the oil dilution procedure again and shut down. The taxiing had been a bitch! It had been a lumpy ride, and I was sweating like a pig from trying to taxi straight enough not to get stuck. It did not build confidence for the takeoff to follow. My new friend the plow driver left. Anticipating something like what had happened, he promised to swing by at first light in case we needed him again.

Through all of this we attracted interested onlookers. There were volunteers to take care of my three-man ground crew for the night. The field proprietor drove me to a small hotel—small was the only kind of hotel in North Attleboro. It was a short but interesting evening. The hotel was hosting a dinner meeting of the local Kiwanis Club, whose members wanted me to sing for my supper. I didn't, but they fed me anyway. The bartender in the hotel bar fixed me up with a date. At a roadhouse on the outskirts of town, we encountered her steady boyfriend, who manifested an instantaneous, overpowering impulse to punch my lights out. With some help from her friends we dissuaded him. When the place closed and we were asked to leave, the same friends drove me back to the hotel. On the way into town, we skidded on the snow and slammed into the back of a parked truck. Fortunately, we were almost stopped at impact, doing minimal damage to the car, but in concern for the driver's pregnant wife, we spent some anxious moments in the local police station debating whether she was all right. Apparently she was. Finally, I got back to my room for what was left of a night's sleep, just your basic RON[18] in a strange town.

The next morning the snowplow tidied things. The taxiway was now a track and a half wide with rounded corners. I had perhaps eight hundred feet of "runway." The F8F had been known to get airborne in 114 feet, albeit under more favorable conditions. The snow under the wheels was reasonably well packed but a bit rough. The power lines were of concern but would not necessarily be a problem. I got the engine started with no difficulty. My taxi director had better footing this time, thanks to the additional width. The runway too had been widened, with a little turnaround area at the end; when I finally got in position for takeoff, I could see a sliver of runway on either side of the fuselage as I looked forward. The lines of plow-thrown snowbanks on either side were to be my primary directional reference on takeoff.

I had no fear of getting airborne in timely fashion, provided that I could keep the airplane going straight. It occurred to me that I might not be able to do that, and the mental picture of being upside down in the snow presented itself. I wondered if the few people around would be able to lift the tail high enough to get me out of the cockpit before I smothered. I decided not to think about it.

I went through the pretakeoff checklist. To my relief everything checked out within prescribed limits; this was no time for a rough-running engine. The plane captain gave me a thumbs-up. He trudged into the snow off the runway to get out of the way, and just before turning his back to avoid a faceful of blowing snow, he crossed himself. I chose to regard the act as a gesture of concern rather than a lack of confidence.

Adding as much power as I could without sliding forward, I released the brakes and added the rest of the power. That little rascal virtually leaped into the air; I must have cleared the power lines by a couple of hundred feet, easily. Hot damn! That I only had about half a load of fuel and no belly tank didn't hurt. In a climbing left turn I looked down at the field I had just left. It looked tiny. Standing by the line shack were the rest of my ground crew and the owner. There were also a couple of dozen cars lined alongside the road, early risers come to see what these crazy Navy folks were up to. Might as well give them a show! I climbed to about five thousand feet and dove toward the field, crossing it on the deck, perking along at full power. I pulled up into an Immel-mann turn, emphasizing the vertical climb portion. The maneuver is easy to do in a Bearcat, not at all dangerous, and it looks great. I made one more low pass, terminating in a climbing roll.

A few minutes later, as I turned onto final approach at Quonset, I saw a couple of Bearcats taxiing out. Hearing Duke Windsor's voice on the radio, I picked up my own microphone: "Skipper, if you're coming to get me, don't bother. I'm back."

After Christmas they moved us from Quonset Point to the old night-fighter base at Charlestown, Rhode Island. It was not a welcome change. While Quonset Point was a big, well-equipped, permanent Naval Air Station, "Charleytown" was a typical World War II "temporary" Naval Auxiliary Air Station, with the usual temporary frame buildings, poor insulation and heating systems, and black-painted cast-iron plumbing.

It made an awkward commute for the married men from their rental housing, and it removed the bachelors from easy access to such local attractions as the Kingston Inn.

Charlestown had some interesting operational attributes. For the sake of night-vision adaptation for night-fighter pilots, all the airfield lighting was red. Red lighting does not destroy the night adaptation that takes about thirty minutes for the human eye to develop in total darkness. In a relatively rural area of New England in the 1940s where things were pretty dark, red lighting made sense. The bad thing was that one could be right on top of NAAS Charlestown at night and have trouble seeing the place; red lights are hard to see, especially dim ones. (In the northeast corridor of the 1990s United States, night vision would be a joke. There are so many lights on the ground, one city after another connected by interstate highways, that night-vision adaptation doesn't stand a chance.)

We went through the motions of instrument training but generally without enough dedication to maintain proficiency with the one navigational aid we had, a low-frequency range receiver.[19] We were serious about GCA (ground-controlled approach). This is the system, developed by the Navy, of literally "talking down" a pilot with the use of precision azimuth and elevation radars. GCA provided the only electronic glide slope before the invention of ILS (instrument landing system). For GCA all that is needed, provided that PAR (precision approach radar) is available on the field, is an operating two-way radio. GCA can save your life, so we practiced a lot. It is a great emergency backup today, since it is available at most big civilian airfields and virtually all Navy and Air Force fields. We had to make at least six "hooded" or actual GCA approaches every six months to maintain minimum proficiency. Usually we made more. We never made approaches under actual instrument conditions, so our practice flights were "hooded" with a chase pilot in another airplane. The chase pilot was supposed to yell at you, over the radio of course, to get your head out of the cockpit if you were in imminent danger of running into something.

In order to avoid interfering with the normal working-day flight operations of an entire air group, the custom was to schedule GCA flights in off hours before the beginning of the working day. This meant that a two-plane launch was scheduled for somebody every working day at about six-thirty in the morning. Back that up by whatever time was required for tearing oneself out of bed, getting dressed, transporting oneself to the flight line, manning airplanes, and so on, and it is understandable that early-morning GCA flights were not everybody's favorite thing. Most of those early flights fell to the bachelor officers living on base. That was not difficult for the scheduling officer to arrange, since we Bachelor Officers' Quarters dwellers were also the junior members of the squadron in both rank and experience. Those frequent, mandatory early reveilles generated a level of disgruntlement that might manifest itself in boyish enthusiasm.

One cold, gray day, Ensigns Frank Posch and Vic Mottarella drew the GCA duty. In a mild break with custom Vic, who was to make the first approaches, requested individual rather than the more usual formation takeoffs. He held his airplane on the runway past normal takeoff airspeed, pulled the nose up, and, as he passed over the snow-covered runway overrun, did two slow rolls. Then he entered the GCA pattern, and he and Frank flew the required approaches. The tower operators were not amused. They worked for the air station, not the air group, and there was no bond of loyalty between the two organizations. When he and Frank landed, Vic found himself on report.

Duke Windsor got him off the hook with the air station by promising to take appropriate disciplinary action, a usual procedure in such instances. The skipper, as it happened, was mostly amused by the incident. The rule violation itself, with the attendant safety ramifications, was not funny, of course, and other pilots were to be discouraged from doing the same thing. Fortunately for Vic, his reputation as a generally cool head and an almost precociously good pilot saved him. He got a verbal reprimand and a short period of restriction to quarters.

Vic had arrived in the squadron at the same time as his good friend, Vote Votolato. Vote once demonstrated one of the Bearcat's less endearing qualities. Before shoulder harnesses were invented, running into a "fence" (barrier) would usually result in the pilot's face striking the instrument panel. The shoulder harnesses used throughout World War II and beyond reduced but did not completely solve the problem. Bigger cockpits helped; you simply didn't sit as close to the instruments in later airplanes. There was some concern as to how real that hazard might be in the small F8F.

The actual hazard turned out to be something quite different. If one hit the deck in a carrier landing, main landing gear first, the F8F bounced—usually not high enough to clear the barriers, but high enough to ensure that the landing gear struts would impact the top strand of a barrier above the wheels. The resulting moment flipped the airplane over on its back in a rotation so fast that the eye could barely follow it. The maneuver ended with the airplane slamming down onto the deck inverted. Remember, the pilot's head would have been sticking up on top of the fuselage under a bubble canopy, protected only by a light, flimsy-looking overturn structure and a cloth helmet.

When Vote demonstrated the maneuver, the sheer violence left us "Vultures' Row" observers in near-shock. There was no doubt for most

Brand-new Bearcat pilot. NAAS Oceana, Virginia. September of 1946. (Author's collection)

of us that the best of consequences was going to be bad. He was certainly unconscious, if not dead. With a massed effort the flight deck crew raised the tail of the airplane. The crash rescue medics eased him out of the cockpit and put him on a stretcher. By the time they reached the island structure we could see him moving. Wonder of wonders, he had suffered only a mild concussion!

Personal Recollections

I spent over twenty-eight months in VBF-3 after reporting aboard NAAS Oceana in August of 1946. During that time we made four deployments to Guantánamo for training, many shorter periods of training and refresher operations off various parts of the East Coast, and two long cruises to Europe and the Mediterranean—long by East Coast but not West Coast standards. Shortly before my detachment we made a three-week cruise to the Davis Strait between Greenland and Labrador. That took place in November of 1948 and was informally referred to as Operation Cold Balls.

During the entire tour, bachelors lived in relatively spare Bachelor Officers' Quarters, starting with NAAS Oceana. Oceana offered quarters that were typical for the time. The BOQ consisted of three World War II "temporary" buildings arranged in a quadrangle. They had red brick shells and looked presentable from the outside. In general we were two to a room, with a head and a shower room on each floor. Some lieutenants had single rooms; the three lieutenant commanders in the squadron, the skipper, Exec, and Maintenance Officer Bob Drewelow, were all married and lived off base. Our accommodations were about on a par with a good modern prison cell. The furniture, badly marked and scarred, was plain maple—two dressers, one night table, another table that doubled as a desk, two wooden chairs; there were two metal beds with the obligatory thin mattresses, and a freestanding lamp. Each room had a washbasin against one wall and a small closet. The room and corridor walls were made out of an ancestor of modern dry wall. It was less durable, though, subject to marring and peeling paint, and, as we discovered, it was easily penetrated by a vigorously applied clenched fist. There was at least one base telephone in the entranceway on the first floor and a couple of pay telephones, one on each floor.

The wonder of the BOQ set was Howard Houser. When one of the outside telephones rang, whoever happened to be near answered it. If the person called was not in the immediate vicinity, the answerer would shout, bellow, holler—whatever, "Telephone for So-and-So!" It seemed that about seven times out of ten the call was for Howard Houser. The caller was always female, and seldom the same female twice in a row. There was this whole gaggle of different girls calling the BOQ for Howard! All in all, Howard marched to a different drummer.

Our Sixth Fleet Med cruise from June through September of 1948 is memorable because it is the only Med cruise I ever made; afterwards I was to be a Pac Rat (Pacific Ocean sailor). Among the highlights of the cruise were eighteen consecutive days anchored in Golfe de Juan near Cannes and twenty-one days in Naples divided into two more or less equal chunks. The longest single port stay and by far the most enjoyable was the eighteen days in Golfe de Juan. Nearby Cannes was great, but it would be misleading to emphasize that city at the expense of Cap d'Antibes and one of its principal attractions, Eden Roc. The bikini bathing suit was fresh on the scene—French style, not the expurgated version that was first exported to us in the colonies.

The idea of visiting the French Riviera in the summer conjured up notions of glamorous, hedonistic sophistication among the rich and famous. Actually, that is not too far off the mark. At sea we worked hard and did some great flying; in port things were pretty loose. How loose depended in part on how far you were prepared to go. I tended to be a rule follower, for fear of retribution more than from any inherent respect for whatever system was controlling my life. Some people are not instinctive rule followers. Howard was one of those.

Life aboard the *Kearsarge* was not a free ride for members of the air group; the ship's Executive Officer saw to that. Pilots were assigned time-consuming collateral jobs. The junior officers were assigned "boat officer" duties, riding shotgun in liberty launches in port. Because I was more senior and had prior ship's officer experience, I stood Officer of the Deck watches. We always anchored out; I don't remember being at a dock anywhere during the entire cruise. That made us prisoners of the liberty boat schedule. Wherever we were, it was customary for the last boat to leave the dock for the ship at midnight, the usual termination of authorized liberty. But there were other ways to get back to a ship. Back in the States, a whole informal commercial support system existed. There were scheduled "water taxis" in places like San Diego and Long Beach. There were on-demand "nickel snatcher" waterborne jitneys, in various sizes and levels of comfort. And then there were the "bum boats." A bum boat was any casual vessel that made itself available to meet the unscheduled needs of sailors confined to the ships. The Mediterranean had no such indigenous support structure, but the locals soon caught on. In most ports, there were boatmen who learned that midnight availability could be a source of revenue.

By the time we got to Cannes, acceptable versus unacceptable behavior was pretty well defined. Discretion was indeed the better part of professional and personal behavior. Complying with liberty hours and maintaining professional behavior while on the job, as well as reasonable and generally image-enhancing behavior off the job, were part of the overall scheme. Enforcement of liberty hours, however, was flexible. A time came when awareness grew, first in the bomber squadron and then throughout the air group, that Howard Houser had not been seen for about five days. There was concern, although in those innocent times there was no thought of anti-American terrorism. The principal fear was that when Howard finally showed up, he was going to be in deep administrative yogurt.

I had the midwatch as Officer of the Deck of the USS *Kearsarge* on an otherwise uneventful night. The weather was clear and calm. A rhythmic, slightly asthmatic *put-put-put* heralded the advance of a craft before the quarterdeck watch gang could see it; the sound was unmistakably neither American nor naval. A small civilian boat came alongside the platform at the bottom of the accommodation ladder. A white-clad figure emerged and climbed the ladder, clinging unsteadily to the railing for support—Howard Houser, arriving. He was all together, cap on, more or less squared, uniform intact, all buttoned up, including the choke collar. Beyond that he was pretty messy—rumpled, soiled, and unshaven. Shaking off apparent fatigue, he came to attention and saluted aft, where the ensign would have flown in daylight. He saluted me smartly as well. Then he committed a minor protocol offense.

The procedure for arriving dignitaries—and the procedure extended to all commissioned officers and their equivalents—was to address the Officer of the Deck or the senior officer on the quarterdeck. A visiting admiral, for instance, might be greeted by his host admiral but more probably by the ship's Command Duty Officer or a staff Duty Officer. A typical communication to the OOD might be, "Have my barge lie off. I sha'n't be long.[20] But instead of properly addressing me, the official functionary, Howard directed his remarks to the boatswain's mate of the watch: "Have my bum boat lie off. I gotta take a shower and change clothes. Then I'm going back ashore."

So much for protocol.

A two-year-plus period in VBF-3 flying Bearcats was not an unbroken string of stimulating professional and enjoyable social experiences, but there were many of those during that cruise. Some remain fresh in my mind. One experience I missed was an eight-on-eight gaggle with the Royal Air Force Spitfires out of Malta; that nobody got killed is a minor miracle. But I didn't miss the two twin-tail jet Vampires that the RAF sent out the same day. We were forewarned. Frank Posch and I were waiting at ten thousand feet, about to conclude an uneventful combat air patrol. Anticipating a high-altitude engagement, we were in high blower at precisely the altitude threshold for the supercharger. I caught a glimpse of silver out of the corner of my eye. About three miles distant the first of the subsonic Vampires rolled in on the *Kearsarge*. Our CIC (combat information center) never saw them on radar—perhaps the jets had come in low and popped up. We fire-walled our throttles and started down. Having a good angle on them, we actually closed the distance. We crossed the flight deck at an attention-getting low altitude—Vampire-Bearcat-Vampire-Bearcat. As long as we were headed down, I continued to close even in trail. Pretty impressive for a piston slapper, I thought. Then the British flight leader pulled his nose up and climbed away. Bye, bye! He really opened the distance.

This was the only cruise I ever made in which we made an attempt to consistently fly our own airplanes, that is, the ones on which our names were painted (organizing that can make a Flight Deck Officer's life a nightmare). This cruise, I must have flown "205K" 90 percent of the time. I have no idea what my manifold pressure reached in pursuit of the Vampires. Overboost was not a question; it was a fact. Observers' reports of black exhaust smoke were not encouraging. Oh well, the engine seemed to run all right afterwards. With that, like Scarlett O'Hara, I deferred the subject to an undefined tomorrow.

Our designated bombing target was a small island—a big rock, actually—just south of the main island of Malta. One day Lieutenant (jg) Art Kreutz had a problem in the bombing pattern. Nothing serious, possibly not worse than loose dzuz fittings in his engine cowling. As a precaution, the flight leader sent him in to the RAF base on Malta for repairs. He was scheduled to return to the ship for a late-afternoon recovery. That allowed plenty of time to troubleshoot the airplane, fix it if needed, and have lunch. The Brits had never seen a Bearcat before, and Art had never seen a Spitfire, at least not close up. In the way of aviators a spirited discussion developed about the relative merits of the two airplanes. There was only one way to resolve the debate: fly them against each other. As his story goes, Art made the Rules of Engagement easy with the assertion to his host, "From a standing start—we both go together—I can make a run on you before you get that thing off the ground."

Over lunch a rule modification was agreed to. It was decided that some means of equalizing pilot experience in model was necessary to make sure that the contest was about airplanes, not people. To neutralize the human factor, Art was to fly the Spit; the selected Brit would fly the F8F. Since neither pilot had so much as sat on his steed before, that made it fair. I have no reason to believe that they actually tried to get Art drunk in that RAF mess, but he did have at least one therapeutic mild English beer. At a critical juncture Duke Windsor flew in with a wingman. With the injection of Command Authority, not to mention good sense, the contest was canceled.

After a stormy crossing of the Atlantic back to the States, we didn't go directly to Quonset. On the fly-off from the carrier, we conducted a simulated strike on Oceana and then flew up the coast to Rhode Island. The strike was in marginal weather. We didn't much care about the strike, but we wanted to fly-off, a lot. Riding a ship into port, any port, was not desirable. As we joined up after our runs on the airfield, our simulated target, the weather improved. Get-home-itis was rampant, an almost palpable thing leaping from cockpit to cockpit, and not just among the married guys either.

I was leading our second division in "205K." By the time we were abeam of Atlantic City, it was clear that my engine was not happy. My mind flashed back to high blower at low altitude and the British Vampires. I didn't have to declare an emergency, but I played with every combination of mixture, rpm, and manifold pressure consistent with keeping me and my division on station in the formation. The R-2800 didn't run right, but it got me there. (The mechanics changed the engine the next week. Afterwards, the power plants chief gave me a short lecture about engine operation and maintenance.)

There was one more short deployment in November of 1948, a three-week cruise to the Davis Straight between Greenland and Labrador—Operation Cold Balls, not the official name. As a cold-weather test of carrier operations it was a fizzle, which was fine with us. The weather at Quonset Point was worse the whole time we were in the Davis Strait.

There were other excitements. Jim Holloway,[21] the Exec of VB-3, conducted an unplanned test of the current exposure suit. That was the one with the Doctor Denton booties on the feet and the drawstring neck. Some of us, in the interests of comfort if not watertightness, wrapped terrycloth towels around our necks before tightening the drawstring. Unfortunately, that design modification acted like a large wick. Anyway, whether it was a cold catapult shot or a faulty engine is immaterial—Jim and his crewman wound up in the water, ditching their SB2C in front of the oncoming bow. They managed to avoid getting run down and were picked up in good time by the plane guard helicopter, but their exposure suits were filled to the waist with icy, arctic water. With those enclosed exposure-suit feet, they couldn't drain themselves. The solution was to take off their flight boots and cut out the toes of the exposure suits, thereby flooding the bilges of the Sikorsky with yellow-dyed seawater. They were cold as hell but all right.

On my last flight of that cruise I was leading a division assigned as combat air patrol to a "Jeep" carrier with a Marine air group aboard. Our planned Aggressor airplanes didn't make it that day. They were supposed to be new P2Vs from Argentia, Newfoundland. The usual default practice would have been to separate us into two-plane sections and run practice intercepts, but the Marines in CIC chose not to. We spent the next hour or so in a left-hand turn. When they finally turned us loose, I decided to protest their failure to exercise us. We got down on the deck and accelerated, preparatory to giving them a low, loud wake-up call.

Suddenly, there was a loud bang. Three Bearcats passed me as if I were standing still; I had run my 150-gallon belly tank dry. I was back up to five hundred feet before I got the handle between my legs switched to internal tank. You wouldn't believe how fast I turned that handle. The nice thing about those large engines was that they would restart with no pilot action other than giving them some fuel. Feeling chagrined and stupid, I headed back toward the *Kearsarge*. There was nothing wrong with running the tank dry; that was the only way you could be sure you had used all the fuel. But doing it at essentially zero altitude with three other people trying to fly formation on you was another matter. The engine might have taken too long to get started, leaving me to take an icy bath a long way from home. It was enough to get one's adrenaline going. I had already observed how effective our exposure suits were, and I remembered bits and pieces of a report, mandatory reading before this cruise, about a similar cruise made by the USS *Midway*. The report listed a variety of things that could happen to machinery when exposed to severe cold. Included was an item inserted by some well-meaning scientist: conventional greases and lubricants could assume the consistency and behavior of Magic Glue.

Thanks to our Marine friends, we arrived overhead early. We es-

F8F-2 at the Naval Aviation Museum, Pensacola, Florida, illustrates the departure from Grumman's usual wing-folding design. The little bulges on top of the wings cover the 20-millimeter cannon feed mechanism. A large chord rudder trim tab extends beyond the trailing edge of the rudder. (Grumman History Center)

tablished an orbit, awaiting recovery time. Finally, we got our signal, "Charlie." Common practice was to drop our tail hooks before starting down, allowing plenty of time to deal with a possible malfunction. There were many simple, weight-saving design features in the F8F, including the tail hook mechanism. It consisted of a cable, pulley, and ratchet assembly, terminating in a tee handle on the floor of the cockpit. One simply pulled the handle and kept pulling it, until there was only an inch or so of remaining slack. At that point the hook was supposedly down, and your wingman confirmed that with a thumbs-up signal.

I reached for the handle. It came up about an inch. I tried again. Same thing. "Oh, shit!" Visions of the *Midway* cruise, of frozen, congealed grease, and of icy water danced through my head. I looked out at my wingman. Frank Posch was holding up a gloved thumb. I had already lowered the hook, a reflexive, subconscious act while my brain was who knows where. It's a good thing this cruise is almost over, I told myself. I don't seem to be safe in this airplane!

I concentrated as never before on what was to be my final arrested landing in a Bearcat. It was the last operating day of the cruise.

Leaving VBF-3[22] was not the end of the F8F for me. I went to Texas to instruct in F6Fs and F8Fs. Later, in Postgraduate School, we did extensive performance analyses on the Bearcat, starting with a wind-tunnel model followed by alternate analytical methods. In Test Pilot Training my project airplane was the F8F. We conducted performance and stability and control determination using actual, in-air measurements. I flew the airplane for the last time in the late spring of 1951 at Patuxent River, Maryland.

Chapter 5
F4U Corsair

AFTER A LEAVE PERIOD that included Christmas of 1948 and New Year's Day of 1949, it was back to my old Basic-Instruments Training base, Cabaniss Field, Corpus Christi, Texas. At first glance the place seemed unchanged, just noticeably older. At second glance it was different. Cabaniss was now the training field for all carrier Advanced Training. There were F6Fs, F4Us, and SB2Cs, soon to be replaced by ADs. I was assigned to Advanced Training Unit Two, the Hellcat squadron, shortly to receive its first Bearcats. There was another, less obvious difference in Cabaniss: to accommodate the heavier service airplanes the runways, originally designed for trainer aircraft, were in the process of being redone by a Texas road contractor—the low bidder, of course. That should get the attention of anyone who remembers what Texas roads used to be like.

There was a detour on my way to the flight line: I had to go through the Instructor Advanced Training Unit (IATU) at Mainside first. The course consisted of a ground school and a two-phase flight syllabus, one of your basic good deals. The ground school was interesting and its concept exciting. During the war the Navy had hired a group of psychologists and educators to set up and administer a program of teaching theory and practice for flight training. This was one of the first scientific approaches to that field of instruction. By the time I saw the course, the founders were long gone back to civilian life, but the concept was alive and well in the hands of the succeeding military instructors. The course was divided into teaching theory, with a strong psychology base, communication and presentation techniques, and teaching practice—a breakdown that is familiar today. Whoever had set it up had a sense of humor, and the military instructors retained the "how not to" demonstrations, even those that required the skills and timing of sitcom comedians.

The flight phase of the IATU was divided between instruments in the SNJ and fighter tactics in the most demanding airplane in the command, the F4U Corsair. We students in the IATU were learning to be the instructors. In the "J," for instance, we sat in the front seat and pretended that we knew everything there was to know about flying while IATU instructors sat in the back seat and played student for us. The student/instructor relationship is especially difficult to pull off that way. In the Corsair we went through all the maneuvers of the fighter training syllabus, which also included almost everything in the attack syllabus, with an instructor chase pilot. Our job was to learn the maneuvers and evolutions in a student role and then switch around to lead and teach the same maneuvers to the flight.

Two of the four Advanced Training Units flew Corsairs,[1] which was one of the reasons for the selection of that airplane for the IATU. The Corsair was also perceived to be the most difficult airplane to fly, for Advanced students as well as for their instructors-to-be. The latter problem was eased by the quality of our instruction, for the nucleus of the IATU instructor corps were Blue Angels of the Navy's flight demonstration team.

The "Blues"[2] were home based in Corpus Christi. This was during their Bearcat period; there are those who maintain that the show in the F8Fs is still the best ever for the team.[3] At the time it wasn't believed, with good reason, that the Navy could convince congressional budgeteers to support a full-time flight demonstration team. The "demonstration" pilots had to have a primary job, and teaching Advanced Training flight instructors seemed a natural assignment. There was nothing phony about the concept or its implementation; when those guys were not on the road, they were indeed on the job, and they were good instructors. Their dual flying role was possible only because of a flight demonstration schedule less demanding than today's.

There were certain qualifications required for selection to the Blues. These weren't advertised, because the selection process was informal. The team was maintained primarily to make the Navy's flight training program, particularly the naval aviation cadet program, attractive to potential candidates. For the Blue Angels the Navy wanted officers who were good pilots, could represent the program in a positive way, and were unencumbered by responsibilities off the job, such as wives; I believe that the flight leader, Lieutenant Commander Dusty Rhodes, was the only married member at the time.[4] It also appeared that the Navy didn't want Naval Academy graduates or Marines for the team. This was not prejudice: Naval Academy people had never been naval aviation cadets, the program being specifically promoted. Marine aviators of the day went through the same flight training program as the other cadets, and for the most part they selected the Marine Corps only while in training sometime before getting their wings. (In that respect the process was similar to what goes on in the Naval Academy today on Service Selection Night. That event is a midshipman's first formal opportunity to "go Marine.") Today's more ecumenical Blue Angels seem always to include at least one Naval Academy graduate and one Marine.

I remember Dusty from the ready room, mostly passing through; he surely took some instructional flights, but my guess is that it was not many. The pilots I remember best include Jake Robcke, Ray Hawkins, George Hoskins, Mac MacKnight, and Fritz Roth. Fritz was a jaygee at the time and the youngest of the team. He had a dachshund, also named Fritz, that he took with him almost everywhere. The dog was no stranger to the ready room. The two Fritzes may not have been totally inseparable, but the larger Fritz was known to take the smaller one with him, lying in his lap in the cockpit, on road trips (though never, to my knowledge or according to hearsay, during an actual air show).

The Bearcats the Blues flew were no better equipped for instrument flying than those in VBF-3. Keeping the schedule sometimes forced the team to fly through weather demonstrably messier than visual meteorological conditions. There were rumors of a phenomenon called Blue Angels' VFR, or Visual Flight Rules. I had a mental picture of an exploration of that phenomenon: the two-legged Fritz dealing with the stress of flying through marginal weather; the four-legged Fritz in his lap sensing the tension or, quite on his own, deciding to feel scared witless. If it ever happened, it went unreported.

The instrument training syllabus was in some ways more demanding, and had more instructional content in terms of required technique and student/instructor communication, than the Corsair fighter syllabus. That and a need for more flight-to-flight continuity in the fighter/attack syllabus may explain why the Blues seemed to fly more often in the SNJ. Ray Hawkins was my instructor on an instrument flight I remember. Ray was tall and handsome, Central Casting's idea of what a fighter pilot should look like. He was also a bona fide war hero, with a Navy Cross to prove it. In the spring of 1949, he was a lieutenant (senior grade); as a lieutenant commander, he returned to lead the Blue Angels in 1952 and 1953.

None of that is why I remember flying with Ray. I was impressed partly by a quality that Tom Wolfe attributes to Chuck Yeager in *The Right Stuff*. Wolfe jokes about it in his account of airline captains' laid-back manner of communicating with their passengers. Wolfe's description leaves room for the illusion that Yeager invented the style, all the rest being emulators—an impression Yeager does nothing to dispel in his autobiography. But Ray had a quality other than the Right Stuff, something I might call the Real Thing. This *thing* includes a manifestation of the true aviator,[5] the ultimate professional: a quality of quiet confidence, unshakable in the face of adversity. The greater the stress, the calmer and more unflappable the possessor of this quality becomes. Now we have all known people who can handle stress just fine—up to a point. Faking it when you don't feel it is a recognized leadership tool, and that pretty much describes Wolfe's Right Stuff. The Real Thing I'm thinking about involves something else: a combination of confidence and ability that lets the possessor automatically attribute his own qualities to his professional peers. If things get hairy, he feels no need to intrude into any situation short of unmistakable, impending catastrophe. He trusts the other guy until the other guy demonstrates that he is not worthy of trust. I do not have in store a dramatic example, but I was first made aware of that quality by Ray Hawkins.

Ray was my instructor on one of those SNJ instrument flights. I was in the front seat. He was in the back, in turn my "student" and my instructor. The flight went well. I learned some good stuff from him, a mixture of technical content, pacing of instruction, and manner of delivery. He had helpful ideas on how to transmit needed information without either overloading a student or contributing to the student's anxiety. Every flight student in the world has some anxiety, however well it might be concealed; sometimes the hardest students to deal with are those whose apparent confidence is so strong that they don't even recognize that they are anxious. Ray did his job without putting any unnecessary pressure on me. With my aversion to noisy, excited instruction, that alone was enough to make me love his style.

At the end of the flight we arrived back at Mainside, Corpus, in a virtual dead heat with a late-afternoon Texas thunderstorm. We just beat it, but its advance party of strong gusty winds was there to greet us. For added excitement the wind was 45 degrees off the most favorable runway. If we made it in time, we were going to be the last plane into the field before the storm passed. If the storm was part of a squall line, as it appeared, it could be quite a while before we could land there. We wanted to get down while we still had the chance.

I was not by any means your current, hot-shot SNJ pilot; before returning to Corpus, I hadn't flown an SNJ since a night flight to pick up Mack "Whiskey" Maison at Otis Field in 1948. Ray Hawkins knew from my student flight jacket that I was a relatively low-time pilot, at just a thousand hours at the time.[6] Other than that he didn't really know me from Adam. He could deduce that somebody in the Navy Department thought I wasn't totally dangerous, otherwise they wouldn't have sent me to the Training Command to instruct; but what do aviation detailers know? As we approached the field, I fully expected a calm, low, well-modulated "I've got the airplane" just before he took over the controls. But the words didn't come. By the time we turned onto final approach, I stopped anticipating and started concentrating on a landing.

The weather had become downright interesting. Debris was blowing around, and there was an ominous cloud, brightened by lightning flashes, moving toward the field. From the wind sock, swinging errat-ically but strung out as if it contained starch, I guessed that we were getting gust crosswind components of 20 knots or so, undoubtedly greater than the airplane contractor's demonstrated limit. I was almost too busy to note the absence of something, another anticipated phe-nomenon: I could not feel Ray "helping" me on the controls. That, I thought, takes real guts! (Myself, I would have been riding them all the way down.) Then I got busy; not flailing, just busy. I got help from the wind just before touchdown. From a classic full-stall landing attitude— the only kind of landing I knew how to make, tail down, left wing down into the wind—during a fortuitous lull in the crosswind the airplane sighed onto the runway with barely a tremor. Skill had little to do with it; blind, dumb-ass luck is more likely.

I taxied in and parked the airplane. As we walked away from the flight line, Ray started debriefing the instrument training portion of the flight in his matter-of-fact way. Before we stepped into the shelter of the line shack, he glanced over his shoulder; the black cloud raced across the field, the wind now blowing like bloody hell. "That was an OK landing."

After the instrument training syllabus, the serious stuff began. I was about to meet the Corsair—the "Hog," "Hose Nose," "Bent-wing Bird," "Ensign Eliminator." An airplane with that many horrific nicknames is not a trivial machine.

General Description

In the 1941 edition of his series of pamphlet-style publications, *The Ships and Aircraft of the U.S. Fleet*,[7] James Fahey describes the Vought-Sikorsky XF4U-1: "A heavy long range fighter, 'The fastest airplane in the U.S. today.' Designed for high-altitude operation, the new Vought outspeeds other models on the upper levels at 35,000 feet and above. Her 18-cylinder 'Double Wasp' develops 2,000 H.P. on take-off though normally rated at 1,850. Performance figures are restricted." The Corsair may be the archetypical example of the U.S. versus European approach to fighter design. Like the Hellcat and Republic Thunderbolt, it was a comparatively large airplane with a wingspan of 41 feet and a nominal gross weight of about 14,000 pounds. The "Double Wasp" was our old friend, the Pratt & Whitney R-2800 double-row eighteen-cylinder radial engine, which also powered the Hellcat, Bearcat, and Thunderbolt. The Vought part of Vought-Sikorsky had started as Chance Vought Aircraft. The first Vought Corsair was a fabric-covered, stick-and-wire carrier biplane scout bomber built in the 1930s. The amalgamation of Vought and Sikorsky was a corporate move concurrent with or preceding the pseudo-conglomerate that was United Aircraft.

Vought was awarded a contract for the XF4U in 1938. According to Barrett Tillman,[8] the prototype first flew in May of 1940. The first Corsair crash occurred in July of 1940. It is not nastiness that prompts me to put those two events together. There is an unfortunate correlation connecting Vought's two most successful airplanes, the F4U and the jet-powered F8U. Each represented a performance breakthrough compared with its contemporaries. Each had a distinguished combat record; between them they had spectacular kill ratios in at least three different wars and in who knows how many theaters and subtheaters and sub-wars. However, in the U.S. experience alone the Corsair was, one way or the other, operationally "destroyed" by U.S. pilots in numbers close to the numbers of enemy aircraft destroyed. The F8U's operational record is comparable. In the early versions especially, both were demanding airplanes.

Some thirty-eight years after that first flight the last active-duty Corsair flew its final flight for the Honduran Air Force. In between there were almost too many versions to count. There were over twelve thousand Corsairs produced during World War II, principally by Vought and Goodyear, with over seven hundred produced by the beleaguered, sometimes maligned, Brewster company.[9]

The design features that make the F4U so recognizable served a purpose. The inverted gull wing made possible a short landing gear that could be folded backwards into the wing. The big barrel-shaped cowling housed a large radial engine. The long nose, which moved the cockpit further aft, held additional fuel. The powerful radial engine needed a large-diameter propeller, further justification for the inverted gull wing for ground clearance. The oversize vertical fin and rudder compensated for the considerable engine/propeller torque developed.

There were changes through time, many of them corrective. Barrett Tillman's book contains a picture of Vought test pilot Lyman Bullard flying the prototype. He is sitting well down in the cockpit—you see him at about shoulder level—beneath a birdcage canopy that appears designed to restrain rather than to protect; the cockpit itself is located comfortably forward; in flight the short tail wheel is not visible. In later versions the cockpit was raised and rotated for improved visibility to compensate for added fuselage length (to provide room for additional fuel). From an eye-level vantage point, as from another Corsair, you could see the knees of a taxiing pilot above the cockpit sill. The birdcage evolved by stages into a modified bubble canopy. The tail-wheel gear became an articulated contraption that raised the tail to provide better visibility on the ground. Not so easily visible, a spoiler was added to the leading edge of the right wing. This addition tamed the stall, until then characterized by a vicious left wing drop, decidedly discomfitting when attempting full-stall landings. Not visible at all are modifications to the main landing gear oleo system to remove the "bounce," a main contributor to early aircraft carrier suitability problems.

Vought engineers paid considerable attention to detailed filleting, smoothing, and other drag-reducing techniques. This extended to necessarily movable stuff like cowl flaps. These flaps must be open for full-power operation at takeoff and under some conditions of low-speed, full-power climb. The original design contained individual actuators for the many segments. I remember listening to a frustrated Maintenance Officer at Lee Field near Jacksonville, Florida, in the summer of 1943. He had two different models of airplanes to keep running, the Grumman F4F Wildcat and the first F4Us to enter the Operational Training Command. (At this time Hellcats were not in the Training Command; they hadn't even been heard of in the Training Command.) That Maintenance Officer had no difficulty at all keeping a high operational availability with the Wildcats, but the Corsairs were his personal twenty-four-hour-a-day nightmare. Among other things, the airplane was a hydraulic monster, and for whatever reason it was not uncommon to see a Corsair at rest with the flaps hanging limply and the business end of the tail hook sagging to the ground. Vought airplanes on the ground could really look ugly! In the case of the Corsair, however, the result of all the pragmatic design decisions was a machine that looked great in the air. The cartoonist and author Bill Mauldin, creator of "Willie" and "Joe," the disreputable G.I.'s of World War II, spent part of a cruise in Task Force 77 during the Korean War. From his seat in the turret of a TBM converted to COD[10] use, he watched an F4U-4 join up for the trip out to the carrier. Having expounded on the sleekness of the new carrier jets, he nevertheless comments on the "old fashioned 'classiness' of the Corsair."[11]

A popular taunt leveled at us Hellcat drivers by our Corsair colleagues in Operational Training was, "Three-bladed pilots are peasants!"—an obvious reference to the four-bladed propellers of the Training Command Corsairs, which I remember as mostly FGs. With that reminder of perceived inferiority still ringing in my ears, lo these years later I was surprised to see that one of the Corsairs in the short-lived television series *Baa, Baa Black Sheep* sported a three-bladed propeller.

Bill Mauldin's comment about the "old-fashioned classiness" of the Corsair design is supported by this photograph of the prototype F4U-4. (USNI Photo Library)

Actually, that airplane is a truer representative of what VMF-214 actually flew in the Solomons. The Vought-built Corsairs apparently had three-bladed propellers until the F4U-4 and its Goodyear equivalent, the FG-4. Because of my lateness in joining the Corsair community I still regard the F4U-4 as the definitive Corsair. In terms of the ultimate general purpose Corsair—as opposed to specialties like night fighters—my evaluation is correct. With respect to the actual numbers of World War II airplanes in service, I am wrong, as is evident from Barrett Tillman's book and other sources.[12] Three-bladed-propeller Corsairs were in service on CVE "Jeep" carriers as well as large carriers in the Pacific well into 1945.

The F4U-5 with its big supercharger was too late for general squadron service, competing as it did with the early jets. It saw extensive service as a night fighter, configured as F4U-5N, through the Korean War. Barrett Tillman has an interesting comparative performance table.[13] With no intention of commenting on Mr. Tillman's research, I have a little trouble with the F4U-5N numbers as compared with the F4U-4. The whole idea of the big supercharger was to improve performance at altitude, yet the service ceilings of the two airplanes are listed as essentially identical. (That the figures are for the -5N night fighter instead of a straight -5 doesn't explain it. The -5N might be expected to be marginally slower than the -5 because of extra drag caused by a radar pod on one wing, but altitude performance should not be significantly affected. Top speed is given as 469 mph at 26,800 feet for the

-5N and 446 mph at 26,200 feet for the -4. The speed difference, although not tactically significant, is consistent with the more powerful supercharger in the -5N. Yet the service ceilings are cited as 41,400 feet and 41,500 feet, respectively, which is *not* consistent with the effects of the big supercharger. It is possible that we are dealing with a practical limit for propeller-driven airplanes. For another high-performance propeller airplane, also with a large turbo supercharger, Bill Gunston quotes the "operational" ceiling of the P-47N as 43,000 feet. Similarly, William Newby Grant gives the P-51B a maximum ceiling of 42,000 feet, the P-51D 41,900 feet.[14]

It is more than logic and aerodynamic theory that gives me pause. In the late 1940s there were events affecting the U.S. military establishment vastly more important than quibbling over performance figures of military airplanes, especially propeller airplanes. The National Security Act of 1947 created a Defense Department umbrella over the previously separate War and Navy Departments and the new Department of the Air Force. The newly separate U.S. Air Force in general and the Strategic Air Command (SAC)[15] in particular were to carry the major postwar defense load, with the other services relegated to peripheral, support roles. Not surprisingly, there was objection to this notion in some military circles; one manifestation was something called the Revolt of the Admirals. That the first Secretary of Defense was James V. Forrestal,[16] former Secretary of the Navy, is a tribute to the bitterness of a fight in which naval aviation, both Navy and Marine, was fighting for survival, and to the efforts of the proponents of the naval service. Significantly, the Marine Corps as a whole had to justify its existence as a service entity—again and again, as it turns out.[17] For the moment they had survived; the 1947 legislation was a battle, not the war.

Our second Secretary of Defense was a Harry Truman appointee named Louis Johnson. Our ex-artilleryman president had little love for the Navy; Louis Johnson had even less. Truman and Johnson tried to accomplish through the budget what had not been accomplished through legislation. With the help of a 1949 modification to the law, they very nearly did. The Marine Corps and naval aviation were effectively to be starved out where they could not be legislated out.

Among the manifestations of all this were the cancellation of a proposed supercarrier, the USS *United States*—the first carrier to be ordered since the war—and greatly increased funding for the Air Force. A key factor was the presumed invulnerability of the B-36 bomber, our principal pre-ICBM and pre-*Polaris* submarine strategic weapon. In typical fashion the performance figures for this airplane—speed, range, load-carrying capability, and altitude—were cited as if they could all occur simultaneously. The claim—can you believe it?—was that it flew so high and so fast that ordinary airplanes couldn't catch it. In this fantasyland, the Air Force's Tactical Air Command (TAC), poor country cousin to the more powerful SAC and ADC (Air Defense Command), didn't fare much better than the Navy. Things got so tough that the Chief of Naval Operations, Admiral Louis Denfield, and Secretary of the Navy Sullivan both resigned in protest.

The early jet airplanes could reach the forty thousand feet at which the jet/turboprop B-36 could fly. Most of them, however, had fuel control and aerodynamic problems that made them ineffective as weapons at that altitude; they couldn't maneuver very well, and the fire was apt to go out! It was believed in some circles that a good propeller airplane, specifically the F4U-5, could not only get up there but could fight there—albeit with reduced effectiveness—without either losing its engine or stalling out. But in this era of claim and counterclaim, of course, nobody wanted to take responsibility for denigrating the new jet fighters by publicizing the performance capability of a propeller-driven airplane. Since "service ceiling" is usually defined as the altitude at which rate of climb has decreased to 100 feet per minute, the F4U-5's service ceiling must have been somewhat higher than advertised for the notion of using it to intercept B-36s to have any credibility.

Toward the end of this stormy period, sometime in late 1949 or early 1950 I attended a lecture at the Naval Postgraduate School, then in Annapolis. The speaker was an ordnance specialist, Captain William S. Parsons, USN. He was a special kind of ordnance specialist, having ridden along in the *Enola Gay* for the purpose of arming a new kind of bomb. He later became a member of WSEG (the Weapon System Evaluation Group), a Department of Defense watchdog committee that evaluated major weapon systems like the submarine Navy, carrier aviation, and SAC. In answer to a question that had little to do with his lecture subject for the day, Captain (later Rear Admiral) Parsons related this anecdote: He and his WSEG colleagues were riding a B-36 at close to the advertised forty thousand feet. One of his colleagues was a TAC fighter pilot colonel who wasn't any more thrilled with SAC in general and the B-36 in particular than the Navy was. "Hey, Bill," he called. "Come over here. I want you to see something. Must be a goddam optical illusion!" Parsons joined him at the Plexiglas window in time to see an F-80 slide by on completion of its run—maybe not the most lethal-looking run ever, but a gunnery pass nonetheless. The F-80 was perhaps the least likely of the early jet airplanes to be considered a threat to the Marvelous Machine, the B-36, but it still got up there.

If even one of the new jets could burst the bubble of B-36 invincibility, there was no need for the Navy or anyone else to offer the aging

Dirtied up in landing configuration, an F4U-4 lets it all hang out before landing aboard the USS *Tarawa* (CV-40). (USNI Photo Library)

Corsair as a solution. There must have been sighs of relief all around.[18] As the fuss was subsiding, the Corsair went off to yet another war.

How It Flew

By the time I first sat in a Corsair with specific intent to fly it, the airplane had become a very honest machine. It was never exactly docile; there were some built-in characteristics that would not go away. Considering what the F4U-4—my frame of reference—had to offer, a pilot would have to be either dead inside or in the wrong business not to appreciate that the airplane was a special kind of flying machine. It was a large airplane, and it felt large, especially on the ground. I found it surprisingly easy to taxi, but that is probably because of what I had heard about its unsavory past; the instructors at IATU did their best to overcome the Corsair's sometimes frightening reputation before we ever got into the airplane. Ground visibility was certainly not as good as in either the Hellcat or the Bearcat, but standard tail-wheel-airplane taxi techniques worked just fine. With the tall, full-swiveling tail wheel, maneuvering with brakes, rudder and throttle was easier than expected, except in strong winds. In the cockpit, the pilot felt like he was sitting more on top of the airplane than in it, particularly compared with the Bearcat. The cockpit felt huge. There was nothing exceptional about the layout or the location of the various controls. Cockpit ergonomics of the time were fairly consistent from airplane to airplane, at least for most American airplanes, especially the Navy fighters.

The pretakeoff check procedure was nearly identical to the Hellcat's. There was no problem of either keeping the tail down or sliding forward as in the Bearcat, making it possible to use full power for magneto checks. It was nice to know that you could get full power before commencing the takeoff roll. This airplane was different from my previous experience with "full power," particularly other R-2800 installations. In the Hellcat the pilot was fairly close to a thrashing monster of a power plant; on the ground especially, it shook and rattled like crazy. The Bearcat felt more solid, more held together, but it was noisy too, and the pilot sat close to short exhaust stacks. Sitting behind the long nose of the Corsair, separated and insulated from the engine by fuel tanks, the pilot experienced a comparatively Cadillac-like smoothness and sound level. By no means approaching the coarsely percussive *hmmmm* of the in-line Rolls Merlins in the Spits and Mustangs, the Corsair sounded different from other radial-engine piston bangers.

If the correct trim settings were correctly dialed in, the takeoff was unremarkable. The critical setting was rudder trim. Even so, if you recognized that you were dealing with an incorrect setting, you could handle it. You might not overpower the rudder forces, but you might at least avoid dashing off the side of the runway, exploring new terrain en route. The Corsair was a torque monster, but rumor has it that there were worse. (The AD Skyraider comes to mind; and George Veling, my former squadron mate from VBF-3, reported after an exchange tour with the Air Force that the P-51 was a real handful without proper takeoff trim.) As with other piston fighters, Corsair takeoffs were normally without flaps. Acceleration was somewhere between that of the Hellcat and the Bearcat—closer to the Bearcat, but without the excitement and agility of that airplane. That may be an unfair comparison. The Corsair in the air was a jewel. All those big propeller-driven airplanes had significant control forces; the important thing was how heavy and under what circumstances.

Maneuverability is a function of controllability. Controllability is the natural enemy of stability; stability and control are among the pilot's best friends, but they are by nature in opposition. The aircraft designer is a kind of referee between them when he conceives an airplane, and the operational pilot is stuck with the result. (Not so the test pilot, as we shall see. The test pilot's job is to scream, moan, bitch, and complain to the designer.) What stability means in essence is the inertial quality that makes an airplane—or any other object, for that matter—want to keep doing what it is doing, to resist change. A stable airplane, perturbed in pitch by a vertical gust, will try to resume its former level attitude. A stable airplane will initially resist a turn, as is manifested by what is called adverse yaw: when the pilot initiates a turn, the nose may initially appear to move opposite the direction of turn. In the same way, a stable airplane perturbed in roll will attempt to return to a wings-level attitude.

A consequence of stability is that when a pilot wants to maneuver, he must overcome increasing forces proportional to how fast and how far he wants to change attitude and direction. For instance, the control forces in a *positively* stable airplane for a 6-g pull-up are substantially higher than for a 3-g pull-up. Similarly, the pilot encounters higher control forces, in both pitch and roll, in a 60-degree bank turn than in a 20-degree bank turn. That is fine for long-haul, straight-and-level flight with a minimal requirement for maneuvering; it makes the airplane easy to fly. A *neutrally* stable airplane, on the other hand, would be a figurative and perhaps physical pain in the butt just to keep on altitude, pointed in a desired direction and with the wings reasonably level, but if it is a fighter, it might save that same pilot's butt by offering minimum resistance to abrupt, violent maneuvering. Obviously, in fighter design it is always trade-off time.

U.S. fighters are always stable—occasionally, according to some, excessively so. There has been speculation that some European fighters, particularly the British, were deliberately designed to be close to neutrally stable; the Spitfire has been cited as an example.[19] The Corsair was a stable airplane with reasonable, not objectionable, control forces. It had a comforting, solid feel in cruise configuration, yet maneuver response was quick and relatively easy. It was not as quick as the Bearcat, but it some ways it was more controllable. My subjective impression is of better "control harmony" in the Corsair than in either of the Grummans. That expression refers to a desirable state in which stability and control responses are similar about all three axes.

I have already complained about right rudder and right rudder trim deficiencies in the Hellcat. The Bearcat was neutrally stable in pitch at best-rate-of-climb speed at the low altitudes at which we usually flew. I didn't find that objectionable, because I could see no requirement to spend long periods of time at best-rate-of-climb speed. The verification of that "deficiency" was greeted with look-at-what-I-found glee by more than one of my Test Pilot School colleagues. Someone with more clout than a bunch of students must have felt the same way about directional stability, because the F8F-2 showed up with a bigger vertical fin and rudder. It may be that the airplane's behavior deteriorated at altitudes higher than I was accustomed to.

The F4U was a fine acrobatic airplane. It wasn't capable of the F8F's air show level of performance, but all the usual maneuvers were easy. With the horror stories of the Corsair Legend fresh in my mind I cautiously explored the slow-flight and stall characteristics before I had the temerity to get really slow or upside down. I was pleased to discover that stalls, especially what would now be called approach-to-landing stalls, were straightforward—mostly that means no left wing drop— with sufficient warning, mushy control response, and the need for lots of back stick. Reassured but still wary, I was careful not to approach a stall, let alone a spin, in the maneuvers that followed.

When it came time to land the "Ensign Eliminator," my apprehension was gone. Landing the Corsair was a piece of cake. The airplane's attitude on the ground with that raised tail wheel took a little getting used to, but the visibility on roll-out was good for a tail-wheel airplane. I shot half a dozen or so touch-and-go landings followed by a final. By the end of the flight I didn't feel the airplane's master, but I was comfortable in it. Even better than comfortable, I liked it.

The instructor course in the Corsairs was enjoyable. My strongest memories are of the gunnery portion of the syllabus. The Corsair was the most comfortable airplane I had yet flown in a gunnery pattern. Both the Hellcat and Bearcat had taken a fair amount of constant monitoring and adjustment in firing runs, although each got better as speed increased during a run, as long as you were properly trimmed; in each of those airplanes you had to actually "fly" the run more than the F4U. That was partly because I was still learning to be an air-to-air gunner in the Grummans. In the Corsair, for the first time I learned to let the airplane do most of the work, correcting only as necessary. I think control harmonization made that possible. In the F4U I became a respectable, reasonably consistent gunner for the first time. The key is consistency. Almost anyone can have a good day; the good gunners do it repeatably and on demand.

Before one of our training flights, I was number three in the run-up area waiting for takeoff clearance. There was an 18- to 20-knot wind coming right down the runway. We were sitting in a row in echelon, cocked about 45 degrees out of the wind toward the runway. The wind component perpendicular to my airplane's big rudder was about 14 knots. I found that if I held the rudder neutral against the force, my leg fatigued and started to shake, more than in my description of coping with the Hellcat's right rudder forces. I took the path of least resistance: I let the rudder go to the end of its travel, my right foot of course moving with the rudder pedal. That drove my right knee up so that it poked above the cockpit sill. It felt like it was right under my chin. I could find no position that was comfortable, and the wait for takeoff clearance seemed interminable. I wondered, if the force caused by 14 knots of wind against that barn door of a rudder was that hard to handle on the ground, what would it be like with substantially higher winds? Or their aerodynamic equivalent—in a spin, for instance? In a spin the rudder would be stalled. Full rudder applied against the spin would stop the autorotation, but not by "flying" it to a stop. The rudder initially would be acting as a speed brake, creating drag to yaw the airplane against the spin. I wondered if the inability of a pilot, simply not strong enough, to get the rudder against the stops and hold it there explained some of the Corsair stall/spin fatalities.

Professional Recollections

On completing IATU I went back to Cabaniss, where the runway problem had been mostly solved. Occasionally someone found a soft spot and broke a wheel through the pavement, usually on a taxiway, but the field was at least operational. I reported to ATU-2 (Advanced Training Unit Two) about the time the first F8Fs arrived. After an area familiarization in an F6F, flying with a former night-fighter pilot named Sludge Segerbloom, I was ready to start instructing.

I remember the familiarization flight with Sludge for two reasons. The first was that we spent some time chasing cows on the Chapman Ranch. The second involved a fuel management problem. In accordance with a custom that says "once checked out, always checked out," I was supposed to look around the cockpit, remember where everything was, and go! I recall reminding myself, It may say Grumman on the rudder pedals, but this is not a Bearcat. There are three internal fuel tanks in this airplane, not one. That, I told myself, is important. Sure enough, at about thirty feet AGL (above-ground level), while hot on the tail of a particularly energetic steer, I heard a loud bang followed by silence. Sludge moved rapidly away in the direction of the horizon. It was the same exercise as running the belly tank dry over the Davis Strait, except that the fuel selector was a lot harder to reach. In this airplane I only got up to about two hundred feet before getting the engine restarted. When I rejoined Sludge, he gave me one of those special grins and picked up his microphone. Over the squadron tactical frequency I heard, "Just learning?"

Under change-of-duty orders similar to mine, Mack Maison arrived at Cabaniss before I did. Because he had prior Corsair experience, he was assigned to ATU-1, the Corsair fighter training squadron. There was another Corsair squadron, ATU-4, an attack training squadron, most of whose instructors were former TBM pilots. For whatever reason, per-haps a lack of experience in the airplane or a desire to play it safe, ATU-4 pilots made a lot of on-the-wheels main-gear-only landings. They also had a landing accident rate twice that of ATU-1.

I had time to take only one F8F flight of students through training before I got orders to Postgraduate School. (It was to be over two years before I was again on a field with F4Us.) My flight consisted of seven recently recalled reserve ensigns. I started as the assistant instructor. The senior instructor was a high-flight-time jaygee. In one of the early flights, on a join-up, one of the students managed to fly through the instructor's airspace, essentially through the instructor's airplane. The student survived the midair collision; the instructor did not, and so I inherited the flight. The Aircraft Accident Board did not find any cul-pability or negligence on the part of either pilot, so the student continued in the program. Blameless or not, you can bet I watched that student like a hawk, especially on join-ups. In spite of that inauspicious begin-ning, it was an enjoyable experience. They were all good pilots, highly motivated and easy to teach. It was a busy time.

We flew seventy hours in about three weeks of that June of 1949. By the end I was really dragging. One of the last syllabus flights was a formation cross-country to Dallas and back; on the return leg I was so tired I had to fight to stay awake. The command thought that these retread pilots' experience made them good candidates for an acceler-ated program. Because of the runway and taxiway problems, the whole program was badly behind schedule.

Meanwhile, there was a diversion. A training movie was being made that took a real-live student through the program, with the Advanced Training phase to be in Bearcats. The role was played by a real-live jaygee, Billy Phillips, who later commanded one of the last F8U squad-rons. He didn't do any actual Bearcat flying for the movie; my student flight did, me included, of course. The photographic platform was a P2V from the patrol plane ATU based at Mainside. Depending on what kind of pictures they wanted, the photographer would sit at a waist hatch or in the tail turret.

We were briefed on what was wanted for each flight. These flights took place about two-thirds of the way through our syllabus, so the students had a fair amount of F8F time. They had also flown a lot at low altitude under the hot Texas sun. I remember walking down the passageway on the Mainside hangar's upper deck on sparkling, polished linoleum. The eight of us shambled along in our crummy flight boots, dirty flight suits worn out at the knees, undried sweat still on our backs from the flight from Cabaniss, white sweat stains rotting holes in flight suit armpits, and carrying torn leather flight gloves. We looked like every caricature of the raggedy-ass Marines or Bill Mauldin's "Willie" and "Joe." Everything around us was clean, and quiet. I looked at the sterile, pristine surroundings and thought, So this is the patrol plane Navy!

The name of the film was *The Naval Aviator*. In almost twenty more years in the Navy I never did see the damn thing!

I heard about Bob Hoppe's accident before I left Cabaniss for Postgraduate School. It was a near thing. Somehow his Bearcat and a VF-31 Bearcat piloted by a former Blue Angel, Lieutenant (jg) Billy May, tried to occupy the same airspace. May got out with no trouble. According to the story, Hoppe had some difficulty. The gyrations of the damaged airplane kept him pinned in the cockpit until it was almost too late. On about the third or fourth try, the last available, he finally clawed his way out in time to open his parachute. He survived with bruises. It was not a good season for Bearcat midair collisions.

After I arrived in Annapolis I heard that Mack Maison had been killed. He was on a one-versus-one air combat ("dogfight") training flight with a student. He spun the Corsair and failed to recover. He rode it all the way into the ground. That big rudder again? It was not a good season for good friends, either.

I spent a little over two good years in school, including the equivalent of a semester in what was then called Test Pilot Training at Patuxent. There were some interesting airplanes involved. In June of 1952 I received orders to ComAirPac (Commander, [Naval] Air Forces, Pacific Fleet) for further orders to a fighter squadron—VF-821, a recalled New Orleans reserve outfit flying out of Naval Air Station North Island in San Diego. Typically, they had been called up as a unit. When I reported aboard, they had just returned from a Korean tour aboard the *Princeton*. They were operating F4U-4 Corsairs. This was a transition period in which many Navy fighter squadrons were converting to jets; VF-821 was scheduled for brand-new F9F-5 Panthers before deployment. The prospect of flying Corsairs in a squadron for a few months and then transitioning to the latest Navy jet airplane was outstanding!

The squadron was in a postdeployment period of personnel transition when I arrived. A bare handful of the original squadron personnel were remaining for a second deployment; of those, only two were genuine "plank owners" from New Orleans. Most of the other pilots were returning to inactive duty. The vacancies were filling up with regular Navy and other reserve pilots who had been recalled individually. The old guys didn't leave all at once, of course, so I knew many of them as well as the second-timers with whom I was to deploy. The Korean War became a test for the whole "weekend warrior" concept. The test was

Generating a morning halo, an F4U-4 launches from the USS *Boxer* (CV-21) for a strike against North Korea, July 1951. (USNI Photo Library)

passed spectacularly. The reserve squadrons did a fine job, jumping back into fleet operations without missing a beat.

Notions come to mind about the dedication and patriotism of young men who devote one or two weekends a month to the service of their country in a period of peace and prosperity. Before the notions get out of hand, one might consider what kind of folks willingly, even gladly, give up their families and other weekend diversions to fly old airplanes and tell war stories in the Bachelor Officers' Quarters bar on Saturday night. These guys were not all your basic straight-arrow types; they tended to be colorful, at the very least. In New Orleans VF-821 had flown FGs left over from the war. According to the pilots and their maintenance crews, these airplanes may have been old, but they were kept in good shape. On activation, the squadron received regular Navy

F4U-4s. According to those same pilots and maintenance crews, the "new" airplanes were trash. There may have been a grain of truth to the assertion. Some of those airplanes might well have come out of long-term preservation in a desert boneyard like the one at Litchfield Park, Arizona, or more probably from Weeksville, South Carolina. (Edward T. Maloney's book *Chance Vought F4U Corsair* shows a picture of a blimp hangar in Weeksville in which are stored over three hundred Corsairs.[20] He identifies this hangar as a principal source of Korean War Corsairs.)

By the time I saw them, the "trash" airplanes were flying just fine. They looked good too, although some had aluminum skin patches in interesting places. One of them had over 120 such patches, not all that skillfully applied. A fresh coat of paint did little to disguise repaired battle damage. The little bombs, signifying combat missions, painted on the fuselage removed any possibility of ambiguity. Naturally, the airplane was favored transportation for weekend cross-country flights; land that thing anywhere, and you were an instant hero! Most of those holes probably resulted from a low pullout after dropping a fragmentation bomb, but what lay observer at a strange airfield knew that?

One of the first orders of business after I reported into the squadron was the obligatory area familiarization flight. As always, area familiarization actually had little to do with it; the real purpose of familiarization flights was to assure the new command that you could in fact fly the airplane without unduly endangering yourself or others. I got a thorough cockpit checkout from the Maintenance Officer, a lieutenant from the original New Orleans group. My chase pilot was Lieutenant Hal Crumbo, USNR. We flew offshore west and south of San Diego. For a while I had the lead with him in a loose, trail position. I reexplored the slow-speed end of the Corsair's flight regime, then joined up for formation work. We spent most of the flight chasing seals off small rocky islands off the coast of northern Mexico and looking for surfaced submarines. The idea was to sneak up on a submarine at high speed at low, very low, altitude so that we could scare the socks off a surprised bridge crew. An altogether adult and professional pursuit, of course. It was good hunting. We got five.

When I joined the squadron, the old skipper, Lieutenant Commander R. F. Edmondson, USNR, was on leave. He returned only long enough to be relieved by Commander Damon W. Cooper, USN, who was to be our skipper through the entire cycle of training in Corsairs, transition and training in Panthers, and a Korean War deployment aboard the USS *Essex* (CV-9). "Hutch" Cooper was tall and lean and resembled a younger, less craggy Gary Cooper. He was a mid-1941 graduate of the Naval Academy. A fine pilot and even finer naval officer, he was to serve with distinction in three wars and retire with the three stars of a vice admiral. Our Executive Officer was Lieutenant Commander E. G. Loughridge, USNR, who was slated to stay on for a second tour. Gene Loughridge was a retread bachelor who had nothing going on in his life to compete with this current war. In many ways he typified the raunchier segment of the reserve population. An excellent pilot and all-round good guy, he was not much for paperwork or conventional discipline, and he was known to take a drink.

The tempo of flight operations was low through September. As people returned from leave and new people checked into the squadron, activity picked up. When Hutch Cooper arrived in October, we started to fly in earnest. Hutch had commanded a TBM Avenger torpedo squadron on a CVE toward the end of World War II. He had commanded ATU-4, formerly the torpedo training squadron, at Cabaniss Field when they were flying Corsairs. He was no stranger to the airplane; as Air Intelligence Officer on a carrier division commander's staff, he had flown occasional see-it-for-myself flights over Korea on a tour just completed, and those flights were in Corsairs.

In part because I had a brand-new aeronautical engineering degree, Hutch Cooper made me the squadron Maintenance Officer. Whether that made any sense or not, the idea was just fine as far as I was concerned. Corsairs were a known quantity where keeping them running was concerned, and the quality of the sailors who maintained them, still built around a solid nucleus of the New Orleans "volunteers," was high. As Maintenance Officer I got to work with the largest number of enlisted men assigned to any squadron department. Particularly in a fighter squadron, the officer-to-enlisted ratio is high. It was not too difficult to fall into just being an airplane driver and lose sight of that other thing you are supposed to be, a commissioned officer in the U.S. Navy. Working close to the hardware is stimulating by itself. Working close to bright, young, eager enlisted aviation types was its own reward. If you can work with and around the American sailor without learning something every day, you just aren't paying attention. He is equally impressive at working miracles on the job and contributing to improbable mischief at other times. There was another advantage: as Maintenance Officer, I got first crack at the required "maintenance test flights" after major aircraft inspections.

We operated out of hangar 525 at North Island. Like most of the hangars it fronted on a macadam mat, which was bordered on two sides by concrete runways for the transports and higher-performance (jet) airplanes. In keeping with long tradition, the propeller-driven aircraft used the irregular macadam patch for landings and takeoffs, sometimes—just like the old days—several abreast. The number and variety of airplanes ruled out a standard over-the-field, carrier-style break. Instead, incoming tactical airplanes performed the same exercise offshore, breaking into individual elements and then proceeding in daisy chain trail to the field. Often that brought the airplanes over the amphibious base, then almost over the Hotel Del Coronado to a landing on the mat. Individual airplanes did the same thing, acting like a formation of one.

That was me in my Corsair on a post-100-hour-maintenance-check test flight. I "broke" just as if I had a whole squadron behind me and proceeded single file—easy to do in only one airplane—toward the amphib base. Still offshore, I went through the prelanding checklist. After dirtying up for landing, I took a precautionary glance over my left shoulder. I saw another Corsair in plain view, hell-bent on flying right through me. I racked the airplane into a hard 90-degree right bank to avoid him, wildly flipping activating handles, mixture and propeller controls, anything else that seemed appropriate. After appreciating that I wasn't dead, I was mad as hell. I trailed my oblivious adversary into the field. I was going to follow him to his flight line where there would be a discussion!

Passing through about five hundred feet on long final I called the tower. With so many airplanes constantly flying, it was more of an announcement than a request for permission to land. I became aware of background noise that turned into a coherent transmission: "Corsair in the groove, check your landing gear."

The words barely penetrated my rage-clogged brain. Some jerk forgot to put his wheels down, I thought.

"Corsair in the groove, your wheels are up! Put down your landing gear or wave off."

Jee-zus! How stupid can people be? I glanced at my own landing gear indicator. It read, "up," "up," and "up." Oh, shit! I should be seeing symbols for wheels in the three windows, not the word *up*. I slapped the gear handle down barely in time to land the airplane.

This was a classic case of breaking a habit pattern. I had instinctively, unconsciously retracted the landing gear in my evading maneuver; my emotional reaction to the incident interfered with rational thought. Having once made sure that the gear was down, I failed to recheck it. The moral: Especially after an interruption, start an uncompleted checklist all over again. All it costs is a little time. Without it, the consequences could vary from embarrassment to disaster.

In early November we had a weapons deployment to Naval Auxiliary Air Station El Centro, California, over the hills from San Diego in the (mostly) desert that was the Imperial Valley. Weapons deployments

A night fighter/bomber F4U prepares for a launch against Korean targets as ordnancemen complete and check electrical connections to rockets. Note the muzzle flash suppressors of the 20-millimeter cannon in the wing. (USNI Photo Library)

for training are a staple of carrier aviation. Traditionally, Naval Air Stations were in coastal cities, usually large coastal cities, with adequate port facilities for ships of the fleet. As time went on, the number of cities that would tolerate lots of ships full of liberty-seeking sailors diminished. Smaller or more specialized port cities like Long Beach and San Diego on the West Coast and Norfolk, Virginia, and Charleston, South Carolina, on the East Coast became "home ports" for the fleet; major airfields were located at San Diego, San Francisco, and Norfolk. But airplanes wear out their welcome even faster than ships, especially when their pilots are looking for places to shoot bullets and drop bombs. Thus, places like El Centro and NAAS Fallon, Nevada, became established as training sites; their use for that purpose continues, along with Yuma, Arizona. Today the operational pace at those fields is accelerating, since it is increasingly difficult to accomplish meaningful training near the older coastal airfields. As our growing population surrounds and threatens to devour airfields, there are plenty of objections to airplanes and airplane operations. That the airfields may have been there first is irrelevant.

My first El Centro deployment ended almost before it began. I had barely had time to learn that the two principal bombing targets were north and west of the field, and that the gunnery range was east, when I was summoned elsewhere. VF-821 was scheduled to be one of the first two Pacific Fleet squadrons to get the new, larger-engined F9F-5s that were to replace the F9F-2 Panthers then in the fleet; the East Coast had preceded us in acquiring the new airplanes. But there were problems with the F9F-5's new J48 engines. Since the Pacific Fleet was going to war in those machines, ComAirPac in the person of the Force Materiel Officer decided to send representatives to an investigation of the problems. As the designated Maintenance Officer of what was scheduled to be the first AirPac F9F-5 squadron, I was selected to accompany the staff Engines Officer to Quonset Point, Rhode Island, and then to the Bureau of Aeronautics in Washington.

I was informed of this development in the Bachelor Officers' Quarters bar shortly after I was taught to decipher one of the signs behind the bar, "IITYWYBMAD" (If I tell you, will you buy me a drink?). By magic, so it seemed, I was presented with TAD (temporary additional duty) orders almost simultaneously with the information. No big deal. I threw some gear into a green Navy-issue flight bag and prepared to fly a squadron airplane over the hills to San Diego in time to catch a commercial flight east. That, fortunately, could await the dawn, but the dawn proved uncooperative. The coast from San Diego to Los Angeles had fifteen hundred feet or so of ceiling with good visibility underneath. The desert, El Centro included, was CAVU (ceiling and visibility unlimited) to the moon. The hills between El Centro and San Diego were covered with a stratus layer at about the same fifteen hundred feet (referred to "mean sea level," that is, not "above-ground level"—meaning that the tops of the hills were in the clouds). This is an example of the benign Instrument Flight Rules conditions where you get to take off in the clear and land in the clear and pretend to be a hero because you flew straight and level for a while in the soup.

I had a critical problem: I didn't have a valid instrument card. Both fleets were in the process of rectifying this common lack among day-mission carrier pilots by mandatory courses of instruction in Instrument Training Units. I had completed everything in the North Island ITU but the long cross-country flight, which was a kind of graduation exercise. I couldn't fly over the mountains without flying instruments; I couldn't legally fly instruments unless I was on an instrument flight plan, and I couldn't file an instrument flight plan without a valid instrument rating. The solution to my problem was easy, albeit time-consuming. The topography of California helped. I simply flew up the valley to Riverside, through the pass to the Los Angeles basin, and down the coast to San Diego. Instead of a direct, 100-nautical-mile trip to San Diego, I flew over 250 nautical miles over the ground, staying under the cloud deck all the way by not flying over any mountains.

I carried one wing tank on the airplane, a rather special wing tank, not for fuel; the Corsair's 225 gallons of internal fuel was certainly enough for my trip. Mechanics had sawed off the nose of the tank and welded matching lugs around the periphery of the two pieces. That made it possible to open the tank for loading and bolt it together for carrying under the wing of the airplane. Presto, one luggage carrier! This was a neater approach than most to the recurring problem of how to carry stuff in a single-seat fighter. We had several such modified tanks in the squadron.

The technically professional part of that trip properly belongs in a later chapter. The first stop was my old stomping grounds, NAS Quonset Point, Rhode Island, to consult with the members of an Air Group 7 fighter squadron commanded by Commander John Starr Hill. (They had had the most time and experience in the new F9F-5s of any squadron. They had been the first to operate them; some of their experiences had been downright unpleasant.) Eventually, the daylong conferences, the examinations of material and records, and the hands-on briefings of installed and uninstalled engines by the mechanics who worked on them came to an end. My traveling companion, the AEDO (aeronautical engineering duty only) commander who was the AirPac Engines Officer, had plans for the evening, leaving me free to get into trouble by myself. I managed a ride to the Kingston Inn, a popular and sometimes storied hangout from my F8F days. Back when we were all bachelors, the place was a home away from the squadron, if not exactly a home away from home. The proprietors were an attractive sister-and-brother team who were contemporaries of some of us junior officers. In that November of 1951 I had not been in the "K.I." for three years. The joint had not changed much. Predictably, there were no familiar faces among the customers, but it was a lively Wednesday night of the sort I knew. The sister, now married, was as attractive as I remembered.

Personal Recollections

When I joined VF-821 in the chaotic postdeployment period, most of the married pilots from the old squadron were on leave. Replacement pilots were trickling in, and Hutch Cooper had not yet appeared. My introduction to that squadron's way of life was largely in the hands of the bachelors. They were a colorful bunch. Several of them lived in a large house right outside the main gate of NAS North Island. I don't know how the house was for living, but it was great for partying. The permanent inhabitants included Gene Loughridge, Lieutenant H. H. "Hal" Caserta, Lieutenant Frank L. "Free Love" Brown, and Ensign (soon to be Jaygee) James O. "Jimbo" Ball. The last three augmented into the regular Navy and/or had extended active-duty careers as reserve officers.

Our base of operations became the Mexican Village bar and restaurant at the foot of Orange Avenue, near the landing of the Coronado Ferry. The Mexican Village was an institution among Navy ship and aviation folks long before I was introduced to it; my Navy Junior wife remembers, as a teenager, picking up Mexican carryout food for her parents—entering by the back door to avoid the gauntlet of junior officers sitting at the bar. My own introduction was an early lunch that extended into most of an afternoon. It became evident that Gene, in particular, did virtually everything but sleep there. He ate there; drank there, of course; cashed checks and performed other banking chores there; conducted most of his other personal business there too, all from a favorite stool at the end of the bar. He didn't have to go more than a couple of doors down to buy other necessities like packaged booze, groceries—when he actually bought groceries, which was seldom—or "sundries," whatever that means. Gene may not have been beloved by the proprietor and staff, but he was more than tolerated, especially by the bartenders.

The decor of the Mexican Village at that time might be described as Early Tijuana. As an eastern boy, I can't vouch for the authenticity, but it sure had a great Mexican look to me! The furniture was a reedy material resembling rattan. There was a phony wishing well inside the entrance. Baskets of plants and other exotica hung here and there. There were hangings and table coverings with Mexican patterns, and an occasional serape hung between the bullfight pictures on the wall. The place was dimly lit except for breakfast or brunch. The focus of attention was well lighted, a mural that covered the entire wall behind the bar. The mural featured at one end a furious, shotgun-carrying, poor Mexican farmer, complete with white beard and militant moustache. He is standing next to an obviously pregnant, patently flirtatious, flagrantly sexy girl in a see-through blouse. The rest of the picture was a succession of stereotypical Mexican characters, each with a broad grin, pointing to the next in line: the Grandee, the Bandit, the Matador, the Caballero, and so on, down to the end of the line where the peasant Born Loser, hands upturned, shrugged helplessly.

I frequented the place off and on, except for a three-year sojourn at the Bureau of Aeronautics, until the summer of 1964. Over the unspoken but palpable objections of members of my family, I performed a walk-through inspection in January of 1987. By 1964 the decor had already seen several changes and a major expansion; by 1987 they had expanded again to occupy a space that I remember from 1951 as a beer-only taproom next door. (The owner of that establishment had been a large, borderline-blowsy person in her late thirties; I may give her the benefit of the doubt on her age. I remember her because she seemed to be around a lot. I think she had a thing for Gene Loughridge.) After walking through the entrance—*that* had not been relocated—I looked for the mural behind the bar. Where it should have been was a gaping rectangular hole that provided visibility into the new addition. Adjusting to my family's lack of enthusiasm for a nostalgic drink—my nostalgia, not theirs—I turned to leave. On impulse I asked the bartender what had happened to the mural.

"Check the other room. Hell, we wouldn't get rid of that."

I checked the other room. There was the mural, in tacky, partially restored splendor. I wandered around the otherwise undistinguished room. On a portion of a back wall near a corner there were half a dozen squadron patches; this was an establishment that once had displayed dozens. One of them was the triangular patch of the original VF-821. The patch represented the original New Orleans squadron members, not second-tour latecomers like me. On a dark, purplish field was a golden cutlass; the blade was crescent shaped, for the Crescent City of New Orleans. Across the face of the patch was a partial mask representing Mardi Gras. Above the mask were eighteen small red crowns, each representing one of the "plank-owner" pilots who had been called to active duty with the squadron.

This was my first visit to Coronado since the completion of the bridge and the restoration of the old Hotel Del Coronado. The bridge must have changed the whole orientation of the island. One of the reasons places like the Mexican Village prospered was proximity to the ferry, the only viable link to San Diego; the alternative was a long trip down the silver strand. A standard excuse was to stop in the Mex Village for a drink while waiting for the ferry line to get short. (The North Island Naval Air Station comes by its name legitimately, having at one time been literally an island, narrowly separated from Coronado as well as from San Diego by San Diego Bay.)

In January of 1951 we traded in our Corsairs for used—sometimes overhauled—F9F-2 Panthers, instead of the brand-new F9F-5s we had been promised. It was farewell to the F4U but not to the environs or people of Coronado and VF-821.

It was more au revoir than final farewell to the Corsair. I was to fly a version of the airplane one last time, an F4U-5N just before the Korean War ended in 1953. FASRON-8 at NAS Alameda, characteristically short of available pilots, called the Commander, Fleet Air Alameda staff: Fleet Air Support Squadron Eight needed a flight test on a night-fighter Corsair before transfer to VC-3[21] at NAS Moffett Field. I was available, and based on my experience I was a qualified Corsair pilot.

That I hadn't flown an F4U for almost two years and had never been in a -5 didn't seem to matter.

This airplane had just completed a major periodic inspection, the reason for the test flight. It was also fresh out of the paint shop, its night-fighter paint job an intentionally flat, nonreflecting black; side numbers were the normal size but a dull red color, difficult to read even in daylight. But how it flew was more important to me than how it looked. I knew of no reason for flying qualities to be significantly different from those of a -4. The major difference of which I was aware was important primarily aboard ship: the -5 had a big supercharger that could not be checked at rest; the airplane had to be moving with full power before the supercharger cut in. Off Korea a night-fighter detachment's role was usually that of night interdiction bombing.[22] Day or night, deck-run takeoffs with a full load of bombs could prove interesting, and the pilot wouldn't know until well into his takeoff run whether the supercharger was going to engage. If it didn't come on line, he was probably going to test the water temperature of the Sea of Japan. With the long runways at NAS Alameda, however, that was going to be no problem for me. Supercharger or no, the airplane would probably get airborne; if it didn't, there would be plenty of room in which to abort the takeoff.

I performed the usual walk-around preflight inspection, relying heavily on the extensive preflight already accomplished by the line crew. I was mostly concerned with things like tie-downs removed and no installed external control locks or engine intake plugs. I verified the absence of a red-flagged cover on the pitot tube. I checked the wheel wells for foreign objects as well as the front of the engine cowling for rags, tools, or anything else that might not belong there.

Taxi and pretakeoff run-up were unremarkable, as was the takeoff. When that supercharger decided to engage, it really meant business, but prior to that, takeoff had been pedestrian, more like a Hellcat than a Corsair. By the time I got the gear retracted, the airplane was moving out and climbing nicely. I checked the airspeed indicator preparatory to establishing normal climb speed. What airspeed indicator? The instrument was there all right, but the needle sat motionless on zero.

I said to myself something like "Oh, golly," or perhaps "Gee whiz!"

Flying the airplane without an airspeed indicator presented no major difficulty; setting power appropriate for the R-2800 engine and letting the speed take care of itself would do the trick. However, flying the evolutions prescribed on the test flight card, my mission for the day, was out of the question. Landing the airplane might prove even more difficult. Of all the things one might like to have for landing, such as altitude, vertical speed indication (rate of climb/descent), airspeed, or angle-of-attack indication, airspeed indication was the least dispensable. (Angle-of-attack indication would have been a more than suitable alternative, but in 1953 most of our jets did not yet have angle-of-attack indicators. The propeller planes never did get them.)

I barely remembered the numbers for a Corsair landing approach. After two years in jets, I didn't remember what a Corsair was supposed to feel and sound like on final approach—reasonable alternatives to valid airspeed indication. I switched on the pitot tube heat. This feature heated the tube so as to prevent or get rid of an accumulation of ice. Perhaps the device, designed for winter or cold-weather use, might have some beneficial effect. Burn up a piece of foreign matter? Fry an errant bug? I didn't know, but I was willing to try.

I thought back to the preflight. How well had I inspected the pitot tube? I know there had been no cover or dangling red flag. But had I touched it, actually looked into the hole to see if it was plugged? The answer, sadly, was no.

While awaiting the unlikely possibility of getting help from pitot heat, I climbed to altitude over the field. I slowed the airplane down, clean configuration, to the point of incipient stall. Then I dirtied up the airplane (to landing configuration). With landing flaps and gear down I sneaked up on an approach-to-landing stall. When it broke cleanly, I accelerated back to slow flight and sampled the maneuverability in a series of shallow turns. I established a 500-foot-per-minute descent at the same slow-flight speed—I could do this by noting the nose position with respect to the horizon. Nose position is a direct function of angle of attack. Dropping the nose a little further and readjusting rate of descent, I decided, That ought to be about 10 extra knots for the wife and kid!

I went back to the field, entered the landing pattern, told the tower of my problem, and landed the airplane, using the technique just described until it was time to flare. It worked like a charm—one of my better landings.

Back on the flight line, the plane captain and a waiting mechanic went to the pitot tube, located under the right wing as I recall, before I could get out of the cockpit. When I joined them, the mechanic shook his head at me; he wore an accusatory expression for both me and the plane captain.

The airplane, remember, had just come out of the paint shop after the major airframe and engine inspection. What the mechanic now saw was that the dull gray metal of the pitot tube was tightly wrapped with ordnance tape of almost exactly the same gray color. It was a good wrapping job, contour tight; from even a few feet away the tape was undetectable. The painters had wanted to ensure that no paint could get into or clog the orifice, and in that they succeeded. However, anyone who performed a satisfactory visual inspection would have discovered the tape. At least six people before me *should* have caught it, starting with the paint crew. But every aviation organization is unambiguous in asserting that the ultimate responsibility for the operation and safety of an airplane is the pilot in command. It is written in the U.S. Federal Aviation Regulations, as clearly as those regulations ever get, as well as in governing Navy directives. The responsibility was mine for the lack of a professional preflight inspection.

It was neither an ennobling nor a confidence-inspiring experience for the last flight I was ever to make in that great airplane, the F4U Corsair.

Chapter 6
F9F Panther

*I*N JUNE OF 1950 I was assigned to temporary duty—a six-week extended "field trip"—at the Naval Air Test Center (NATC) at Patuxent River, Maryland, along with a dozen of my peers from the Naval Postgraduate School. The rest of my Postgraduate School class were assigned to other Bureau of Aeronautics activities such as the BAR (Bureau of Aeoronautics Representative) offices of various U.S. Navy airframe contractors. Then, as now, contractors were assigned Department of Defense representatives in accordance with their primary customer, Air Force or Navy. The Navy had the primary office with such companies as Grumman, McDonnell, Vought, Martin, and Convair (later General Dynamics). Assignment to a BAR office consisted mostly of paper shuffling, with little opportunity to get close to airplanes; temporary assignment to the Bureau of Aeronautics[1] itself was even less fun.

The major test divisions at NATC were Flight Test, Tactical Test, Service Test, Electronics Test, and Armament Test. Flight Test and Tactical Test were the glamour divisions; they had their "stars," people like Major Marion Carl, a leading Marine ace, and Lieutenant Commander Bob Elder. (With a combination of respect and irreverence these two were known—behind their backs, of course—as "Fab 1" and "Fab 2," for "Fabulous 1" and "Fabulous 2"; I am not sure in what order.) Pilots in the Electronics Test and Armament Test divisions, meanwhile, could point with engineering pride to their mastery of the technical esoterica inherent in those increasingly sophisticated black boxes and weapons. Then there was Service Test, the least glamorous division of the five. Its mission could be summarized as "run 'em til they break, then fix 'em"; this division investigated all the different models[2] of aircraft in the fleet that pilots were required to operate and round-hat sailors were required to maintain. Of all the divisions, it required the least formal

155

training in flight test procedures and techniques and the least special knowledge of electronics and weapons. One result was that Service Test was often called Service Rest, an unflattering nickname that persisted until the test divisions were reorganized into mission-oriented test directorates. Another result was that the four of us from the Postgraduate School who were assigned to Service Test were permitted to fly the new airplanes.[3]

The Service Test "Jet Section" was run by Lieutenant Commander Paul Durand, Exec of VF-3 during my Air Group 3 Bearcat tour. His assistant was Lieutenant Jim Ellis, also from VF-3. The third major player was Lieutenant Benny Sevilla, who had flown Corsairs in the *Midway* air group at Oceana. The Jet Section owned two airplanes, an F2H-1 McDonnell Banshee and an F9F-2 Panther. The Banshee was such an early version that it didn't even have wing tip tanks.

A by-product of the Service Test mission was that it was desirable for as many different pilots as possible to fly the airplanes undergoing test; it made for a larger statistical base. Thus, Service Test routinely indoctrinated and checked out visiting pilots. We four from the Postgraduate School fit the category, with the added advantage of being around for six weeks. The question was not, Could we fly?—rather, How soon and how often? The answers were yes, we could; but not very soon and not very often, at least for the jets. There were, however, a couple of jewels of aircraft around to which we were granted virtually unlimited access, like two versions of the big Grumman propeller-driven AF Guardian antisubmarine airplane. Those were going through "accelerated service trials," which meant much off-hours flying in an effort to accumulate many hours in a short time. The Service Test pilots were more than happy to share that work load.

The important thing for me was that I flew both the jet airplanes assigned to the division. By chance I flew the Banshee first, then the Panther. But the Banshee solo was not actually my first jet flight; a two-seat indoctrination ride was a desirable but not a necessary prelude to leaping off into the blue in a radically different kind of flying machine.

One day Jim Ellis had a T-33 for an essential trip to Naval Air Station Mustin Field, Philadelphia. He invited me to ride along in the back seat of that training version of the Lockheed F-80 Shooting Star. Virtually everything on the outside of the T-33 was new and different to me, including the shiny aluminum finish. Inside, many of the differences were omissions; the early jet airplanes were simple. Instrumentation was essentially the same as for the props, except for higher numbers on the airspeed indicator and a "barber pole" hand indicating limiting Mach number. The throttle had become a thrust control. It still looked like a throttle, except that there was an around-the-horn starting and shut-down detent at the low end of the quadrant. There were no mixture or propeller-pitch controls for the engine, an Allison J33 single-stage centrifugal-flow turbojet.

Much of what went on before takeoff was a mystery to me. Jim had business to conduct, so there was no time for a tutorial. The takeoff ground run seemed excessively long. Compared with what I was used to, the T-33 jet plane was incredibly quiet. The long alligator canopy was closed for takeoff. I could feel and hear the whine of the engine behind me, but the sound level and quality were far different from the roaring and banging of the big radials that were my standard. Acceleration after takeoff was impressive, as were the rate of climb and the high indicated airspeed that produced best rate of climb. As we passed through twenty thousand feet, the world below took on a different aspect. I had been to altitudes as high, but never before in a position to sightsee. Visual detail was lost, to be replaced by major topographical features; I saw below a multi-hued three-dimensional relief map of the eastern and western shores of Maryland and the Chesapeake Bay, all in decreasing scale as we continued our climb past thirty thousand feet.

At cruising altitude I was aware of wind noise dominating the muted whine of the engine. As I became acclimated to the new sensations, I noticed the gentle beginnings of Dutch roll, an undamped low-frequency low-amplitude wallow characteristic of the F-80 series and many other early jets. A small price to pay for such an exhilarating experience; this was a different kind of flying! Jim let me fly the airplane for most of the trip back. It felt wonderfully responsive, communicating a new dimension of performance and agility. The combination of relatively low drag and substantially higher speed compared with the fastest propeller airplanes gave even the early jets some ability for vertical maneuvering. That capability was to have a drastic impact on fighter tactics.

Jim Ellis's generosity did not extend to letting me land the airplane back at Patuxent—a prudent decision, since the landing would have been my first in a jet, compounded by the lack of visibility typical of the back seat of an airplane with tandem seating. That ride, however, and especially my first "pilot-in-command" solo flight in a Banshee were my preparation for the Grumman Panther.

General Description

The genesis of the F9F Panther was an outline specification by Grumman (then still GAEC, Grumman Aircraft Engineering Corporation). The specification was a response, in June of 1945, to a Navy requirement for a high-performance night fighter. The configuration was to include two engines, a crew of two with side-by-side seating, and tricycle landing gear. This led to Grumman design 75 in September of the same year.[4] Design 75 featured four small Westinghouse turbojet engines instead of the specified two, probably because of the unavailability of larger engines with sufficient thrust. Design 75 was designated XF9F-1 in October of 1945.

The Navy subsequently changed its requirement to a day fighter. Grumman's response was design 79, actually four different "studies." Versions A and B had composite power plants, a propeller in the nose driven by either a conventional reciprocating engine (79A) or a geared turbine engine (79B) with a jet engine in the tail. The basic configuration was similar to the Ryan Fireball, which was already flying. The 79C had two turbojet engines, while the 79D featured one. Design 79C appeared to be the preferred choice, mostly because of doubt as to the availability of the engine on which 79D was predicated, the Rolls-Royce Nene. But the Navy thought otherwise. In June of 1946 a go-ahead was given for two XF9F-2 and one XF9F-3 prototypes. The -2 was to employ a Pratt & Whitney–manufactured Nene, designated J42; the -3 was to use the Allison J33-A-8, a similar engine that was in the F-80 and T-33 (not necessarily the same version or dash number).

The decision was in keeping with the Navy's practice of providing a backup in a major procurement. In this example it was a backup engine. The F2H Banshee and F9F Panther were contemporaries. Neither was a designated backup, but the Navy only needed one of them to work to ensure that there would be at least one viable jet carrier fighter. (There are other examples of backups in the carrier fighter program. Before the Banshee and the Panther, there had been the FH Phantom and the North American FJ Fury; both of those first-generation jet airplanes saw limited squadron service, the FJ in VF-5 at North Island, and the FH in VF-17 at Quonset Point. Before that there had been the Hellcat and Corsair.) The Navy's initial bias in favor of the Nene engine was reflected in the two-to-one ratio of the prototypes. History has validated the engine decision with respect to the F9F-2 and -3. The decision became more complicated with the F9F-4 and -5.

Jet engines are simple in concept. They come in two fundamental varieties, having either axial-flow compressors or centrifugal-flow compressors. In either case, a compressor at the front end squeezes intake air into a tight package. The compressed air is then fed into a combustion chamber where it is combined with fuel, and the mixture is ignited. The resulting heated gases expand like crazy. The only place they can go is out the tail pipe, which has been conveniently shaped into a nozzle. In their rush to escape through the only available hole, the gases produce the thrust that makes the whole contraption go. On the way out they pass through, and turn, a turbine wheel. The turbine wheel is connected to the compressor by a shaft so as to power the compressor, which by now is busy compressing the next batch of air— except that it is not a batch but a continuous flow. Ignition takes place only one time, unlike a reciprocating engine where ignition is periodic and its timing critical. Once a jet engine is operating, it is self-sustaining in that the fire stays lit until either fuel or air is cut off.

The differences between these two jet engine types dictated airplane design even more than the categories of "in-line" versus "radial" had for reciprocating engine. Still, there were similarities. The Nene, J42, Tay (basically a big Nene), J33, and J48 (a Pratt & Whitney–built for Rolls-Royce Tay) all had centrifugal-flow compressors. The compressor wheel looks like a big vacuum cleaner blower wheel. Incoming air is compressed by vanes that essentially direct the air outward, utilizing centrifugal force to aid in the compression; the bigger the diameter of the wheel and the faster it turns, the more the compression. If the air were not contained, all that would result would be a change of air direction and velocity. But the compressed air is contained and redirected by a collection ring to which are attached artfully designed elbows. These redirect the flow into an array of peripherally disposed burner cans. Such a compressor produces a high compression ratio per stage (the compressor wheel constitutes a "stage"). The centrifugal compressor tends to have a large diameter, a feature somewhat analogous to the radial engine. Air going through the engine has to make several changes of direction on the way. That means losses. There is no effective way of cascading or stacking multiple centrifugal-flow stages so as to improve the overall, total engine compression ratio. That is a limitation.

The axial-flow compressors, on the other hand, are analogous to steam power plant and ship propulsion turbines, except turned around. That is, the front-end row has the big blades and the back-end row has the little blades. Each row, or "stage," of blades produces a relatively low pressure increase or ratio. However, within other constraints one can build as many rows, stages, as there is room for.

As this description suggests, centrifugal-flow engines were simpler to design, develop, and build than axial-flow engines. That is why single-engine jets of the period, like the Panther, F-80, and MiG-15[5] had centrifugal-flow engines, and twin-engine fighters like the Banshee tended to have axial-flow engines.[6] The axial-flow people initially had trouble building high-thrust engines but, as aviation history has shown, there was virtually limitless opportunity for expansion, innovation, and invention within the axial-flow concept.

The F9F-2 that Grumman rolled out in November of 1947 was a

These F9F-2s on the port bow of an *Essex*-class carrier show the outboard-leaning folded wings of the Panther. The ingenious ladders made possible refueling tip tanks with wings folded, but they turned the gas gang into mountain climbers. Also visible is a corner of the forward elevator and the track of the port catapult. (Grumman History Center)

smallish airplane by today's standards, grossing less than 10,000 pounds empty, with a maximum gross weight of under 20,000 pounds. Wingspan with tip tanks was just under 38 feet. Wingspan folded was a nominal 23 feet 6 inches; wingspan folded with tip tanks was 25 feet 6 inches.

But those numbers don't tell the whole story about the wings. The Panther had initially been designed with vertically folding wings. With wings folded there must be vertical clearance between the wing tips and the aircraft carrier's hangar deck overhead. The Grumman engineers optimized this one; the airplane fit, but just barely. Then it became evident that tip tanks would be standard in order to meet mission requirements. F9F tip tanks were bolted on rather permanently. (Banshee tanks, however, could still be jettisoned in flight.)[7] With tip tanks, Grumman now had to modify the wing-fold system to regain hangar deck clearance. As modified, the wings when folded leaned about 35 degrees away from the vertical—outboard, that is, not inboard. This meant that any time more than a couple of Panthers were parked close together, the deck spot was locked, à la children's Lego blocks, and a whole generation of aircraft-handling officers on *Essex*-class carriers went gray or simply tore their hair out over it. Suppose side number 205A is sitting at the forward edge of the flight deck on the port bow, nested in front of fifteen other Panthers. The aircraft-handling officer gets a call: "205A is overdue for a sixty-hour check. Strike it below." He must move fourteen of the fifteen F9Fs just to get at 205A, let alone move it down to bay 3 of the hangar deck where the maintenance will actually be performed.

Longtime Grumman test pilot Corky Meyer made the first flight of the XF9F-2 on 24 November 1947, seventeen months after the initial design studies. The first F9F deliveries to fleet squadrons, F9F-3s, commenced in May of 1949. The J42 engine's demonstrated superiority over the J33 skewed production in favor of the F9F-2; there were 569 F9F-2s built, compared with only 55 F9F-3s.

The F9F-2 had a top speed of 525 statute miles per hour and a range in excess of 1,100 miles. Time to ten thousand feet was less than seventy seconds (but not from a standing start; the Bearcat record was safe for a while). The later F9F-5 was credited with 604 mph and 1,300 miles' range. Service ceiling for all versions was about forty-three thousand feet.

A total of 1,351 Panthers of all kinds were produced—F9F-2, -3, -4, and -5. The Panther was the first Navy jet to see combat; those first jet combat airplanes were VF-51 aircraft, flying over Korea as part of a strike group from the USS *Valley Forge* (CV-45) on 3 July 1950.[8] The first Navy jet-to-jet, air-to-air combat kill was a Panther victory over a MiG-15. There were 826 Navy and Marine jet fighters in the Korean War, 715 of them F9Fs; they flew 78,000 missions for an overall ratio of 110 missions per aircraft.

How It Flew

When I first strapped myself into the cockpit of a Panther, I had help. Jim Ellis balanced himself on the foot wells on the left side; the Service Test line chief stood on a portable platform on the other side. At a minimum, they were going to be sure that I didn't damage anything before leaving their flight line. Jim went over the whole cockpit and the various flight and system controls, covering everything at least twice. In preparation for this day I had studied the pilot's handbook at great length, but I had not committed the volume to memory; there was too much to absorb and remember. I scribbled away on my knee pad, jotting down the items that seemed most important or easiest to forget.

We took new-model checkouts seriously, especially with jets; it was true in spades for propeller-to-jet-transition pilots like me. In the rear seat of the T-33, everything had been a mystery, especially before the engine got fired up, but I had been essentially a passenger that time. My next time up, in the Banshee, I had been more than an observer; I had been required to understand what was going on, and I did—except for that starting procedure. Having two engines to start, with flaky fuel controls to boot, had been intimidating. After that one flight in the Banshee, I wanted an experienced plane captain looking over my shoulder for this starting attempt in the Panther!

Starting airplane engines can be a trial for the neophyte. All engine installations are not alike, even when the basic engine is familiar. I have seen more than one Corsair or Hellcat pilot look like a fool because he couldn't start the familiar R-2800 engine in a Bearcat. It makes a bad impression when you can't even get the machine going. (One of the ways in which old-hand pilots demonstrate their prowess is to start engines that other people can't, especially under adverse conditions, like when the engine has been cold-soaking in subzero weather.) What was true for the reciprocators was doubly true for the new jets, where the whole starting process smacked of black magic. I have seen pilots who never did quite get the hang of it, including squadron skippers and the occasional air group commander. You can burn up a lot of starters that way.

Burning out a starter was one hazard. It was, however, preferable to a "hung start" or the dreaded "hot start." The latter was grounds for a hot-section inspection that required removing the engine; at worst, a hot start could require an engine change, a consequence substantially more serious than the pilot's simply looking foolish. A hung start could become a hot start, with the same results. In the F9F the hazard was largely in the pilot's head; the starting procedure wasn't really that difficult, just a little complicated.

To start a jet engine, the turbine and compressor must be brought up to sufficient speed[9] to produce airflow through the engine. Fuel must be introduced and then brought to combustion temperature (in other words, ignited). The first step was taken care of by an integral electric starter motor that needed a substantial external power source, a starter cart. The rotating part of the jet engine must be brought to 8 to 10 percent of rated rpm. In the early Panthers the "throttle" in the closed position sat at the bottom, aft end, of a long slot in the quadrant, consistent with the usual reciprocating-engine arrangement. Fuel was introduced and the starter was engaged by a whole array of toggle switches. The procedure went like this:[10]

Engine fuel system selector switch—	NORM
Battery and generator switch—	BATTERY & GEN
Fuel master switch—	ON (After a few seconds, fuel boost warning light should go out.)
Starting master switch—	ON
Ground start cranking switch—	START (Hold for two seconds.)
High pressure cock (at 8–10% rpm)—	ON

The engine should then come up to idle speed (28 ± 5%, 3,500 rpm). If it didn't, there was a strong temptation to help it along by throttle manipulation. That never worked; the inevitable result was a hung start, at best. The pilot monitored the process by watching rpm and engine temperature. A sharp temperature rise to 400 degrees C (752 degrees F) indicated ignition. Although it was not always audible in the cockpit, the pilot might hear a *thoomph* as the fuel ignited.

The F9F had small engine intakes. In order to meet transient engine demands for more air, especially on the ground, Grumman installed rectangular spring-loaded blow-in doors on the aft fuselage. It was common for the doors to slam open momentarily on ignition. Ignition was not continuous in normal operation. There were two igniters, one each in two of the lower burner cans, reminiscent of oversize spark plugs. They worked in much the same way as spark plugs, but they operated only during the starting cycle. They were noisy devils; a mechanic could determine that they were functioning simply by putting his ear close to the fuselage and listening.

The desired result on starting was for rpm and temperature to rise together; if rpm stabilized and temperature continued to rise, things were not going well. Again, the common mistake was for the pilot to get impatient with the engine acceleration rate and open the throttle too far, too soon. A predictable result was that hot-section temperature would go through the roof while engine rpm hung up at 15 percent or so. If the pilot stop-cocked the engine—that is, if he cut off the fuel flow below about 900 indicated degrees—he wouldn't damage anything. He wouldn't get a start, but he wouldn't hurt the engine.

The starting mechanization was made simpler in later airplanes; around-the-horn throttle quadrants with built-in micro switches replaced some of the toggles. The effect of the change was to ease the pilot further out of the loop. In the setup I just described, there were too many separate things for the pilot to do in a specific order. In VF-821 with the older mechanization, we burned up more than a few starters, although we rarely damaged an engine. Colleagues in VF-23 and VF-721—VF-821's closest jet squadron neighbors at sea and on the beach, respectively—had similar problems.

When Jim Ellis and the line chief decided that they had done all they could for me, they climbed down. After removing the portable stand the line chief had used, the plane captain taxied me out of the chocks. I was on my way. With a complement of different airplanes in ones and twos, the Service Test flight line was sparsely populated. I didn't need to bother with the Panther's two-stage wing spread and lock procedure; the F9F had been parked with its wings already spread and locked.

Unlike propeller airplanes, the early jets did not require an extensive pretakeoff run-up; the aircraft systems, such as they were, could be verified during taxi. Even in later airplanes most of the complicated items were accomplished before leaving the flight line.

I knew I had a good radio and good hydraulic pressure. Hydraulics were important for more than flaps and landing gear. The Panther had a hydraulically operated aileron boost. The 1,500-pound pressure system powered a cylinder that drove the ailerons through a mechanical linkage. The rudder and elevator controls were still mechanical. It was important, and easy, to verify that hydraulic pressure was up and that the ailerons worked. If conditions were not nominal, the flight would be aborted. In the event of failure in the air, a manually operated switch activated a solenoid that disengaged the boost, leaving the pilot with effective, all-mechanical ailerons; the all-mechanical mode was characterized by much higher control forces, but it worked.

The most common failure modes were a loss of primary aircraft hydraulic pressure or a failure of the aileron boost cylinder. Each problem was normally easy to deal with. There was a lower-capacity backup hydraulic system that could be engaged with the flick of a switch. If the aileron boost cylinder itself failed, usually because of an internal hydraulic leak, it could be taken off line by a disengage lever located on the cockpit's right console, right above the auxiliary hydraulic pump switch. The airplane was flyable, if not very maneuverable, without aileron boost.

There was an insidious, secondary failure mode that was to get my attention later. The aileron boost disengage activated an electromechanical system that could also fail, and failure somewhere in that system chain could leave a sick aileron boost cylinder on line, one the pilot could not get rid of. The resulting configuration could be flown successfully under some conditions, but not all. The commonest symptom of aileron boost failure was that the control stick would move easily, almost normally, to the left, but the pilot needed both hands and a lot of muscle to move it to the right—or even to hold it in a neutral, wings-level position. A compound failure—aileron boost and disengage system—occurring suddenly at low altitude could have serious consequences.

Although I had been duly briefed on emergency procedures, I had not been briefed on this dual aileron problem; that early in the airplane's history, no one had ever experienced it. But as it turned out, nothing like that marred my first Panther flight. The tricycle landing gear and absence of torque made taxiing ridiculously easy. For the first time I could actually see where I was going and taxi in a straight line unbroken by constant S-turning. It took substantial throttle movement to get the airplane moving because of the slow acceleration characteristic of jet engines, although once the engine started to wind up, one had to retard the throttle so as to hold down the speed. A common temptation was to taxi too fast—much too fast, on occasion.

After takeoff clearance was received from the tower, it was permissible to make a rolling takeoff, applying full power once on the runway, checking only for 100 percent rpm and proper engine temperature. With my vast experience of two prior jet rides—three, if I count the return trip from Philadelphia with Jim Ellis—I was prepared for a long takeoff roll. The relatively underpowered jet airplanes of the day required long takeoff runs; the F9F-2 was about average in that respect.

Controlling heading on takeoff was easy. Once elevator authority was available, a little back pressure broke the nose wheel clear of the pavement. When the airplane reached flying speed, four thousand feet or so down the runway, it flew off as docilely as you please. I retracted the landing gear and the flaps, in that order. While accelerating to climb speed, I closed the sliding cockpit canopy. One of the surprising characteristics was the high indicated airspeed for best rate of climb compared with propeller airplanes; indicated airspeed for best rate of climb at sea level for the F9F-2 was about 300 knots, compared with the F8F's 110 to 130 knots. In the early jet years it could be maddening to fly behind some newly transitioned senior officer who hadn't processed that speed difference. In a jet airplane, 180 to 200 knots not only wouldn't do it for climb speed; jet airplanes didn't fly worth sour beans that slow. Best endurance airspeed for the F9F, for example, was about 210 knots, and it was noticeably uncomfortable flying that slow.

In spite of substantial preflight briefings, I failed to compensate for something else. The ailerons, the only power-boosted control, were very sensitive. The aileron stick-neutral position was about an inch to an inch and a half wide, and within this control-centered range there was no discernible stick force; the stick could sort of flop without accomplishing anything. The pilot must move the stick until he feels resistance and then apply the control in normal fashion. But if he has never done it before, he doesn't know how far. He pushes. Not enough. He pushes harder. This time the airplane banks more than he wants. Too far! He corrects. But now he must traverse the infernal inch-wide dead zone before opposite aileron can be applied. That almost guarantees over-control in the opposite direction until, ultimately, the pilot learns the feel of the arrangement.

For the first few flights it was actually easier to turn the airplane than to fly straight and level. The F9F's relatively poor lateral stability required occasional aileron inputs in wings-level flight. Some pilots, including me, disappeared over the horizon on a first flight, wagging the wings merrily up and down like a drunken buzzard with a bad gyro.

In the absence of propeller- and engine-induced torque, the rudder control was almost unnecessary. For the most part one could fly with feet on the floor while the "ball" remained steadily centered. The straight-wing jets had good directional stability—good compared with the swept-wing jets, which customarily require directional stability augmentation in the form of yaw dampers.

The F9F had a high, conventional horizontal tail—that is, a fixed stabilizer with a trailing-edge elevator. The linkage was mechanical all the way. This meant significant pitch control forces and a resultant requirement for judicious use of elevator trim. The trim controls for all three axes were rotatable wheels, clustered on the stepped left cockpit console, just behind the throttle quadrant.

The pitch control forces were not excessive compared with the high-performance props, and maneuverability was good. The major new maneuvering phenomenon was a simple consequence of speed: for a given g-loading, a fast airplane flies through a bigger turning circle (vertically or horizontally) than a slow airplane. Radius of turn is proportional to the square of the velocity (speed). Also, turn rate is lower for a faster airplane than a slower airplane. Since ability to turn is bounded by stall speed and structural strength, turning maneuvers in jet airplanes, whether in a horizontal or a vertical plane, require more space and more time than the same maneuvers performed in propeller-driven airplanes.[11] That is why the Blue Angels in Bearcats were in view within the airfield boundaries for their entire show and why the Blue Angels in F/A-18s disappear for minutes at a time between maneuvers. (It also is the reason for the two solo airplanes; they fill in the gaps while the four-plane diamond is returning for the next evolution.)

The ease with which a jet airplane slips through the air, as opposed to bulling through the air in the manner of even the best propeller airplanes, makes jet flight an entirely different sensation. Collection of sensations is more accurate, affecting all the senses. In the Panther the sound level was low. There was audible air (slipstream) noise. The engine's sound was a muted whine. The cockpit pressurization system contributed a barely perceptible background roar as cabin air was forced through vents. If he listened carefully, the pilot became aware of the rasping huff and puff of his own breathing through the diluter-demand oxygen mask. The dry air/oxygen mixture smelled faintly of rubber, sealant, and paint.[12]

Visually, there was the sky overhead, bluer, cleaner, sharper than as seen from earth. The bubble canopy sat well forward of the wings. Without the encumbrances of engines, wings, and other protuberances the pilot could see almost as well as the nonflying earthling assumes he can. Without even craning his neck, he could see the earth below laid out as if by some celestial Rand McNally. Colors were muted by intervening, dust-laden dispersive atmosphere. The coarse prop-plane airplane vibrations were absent. Somewhere below the pilot's level of consciousness a different kind of vibration, incredibly smooth, seemed to soothe away cares and tribulations. *They actually pay people to do this?*

A movement of the stick to the left required minimal effort. Response was virtually instantaneous as the airplane banked and commenced a left turn. Roll-out and on into the opposite bank were equally easy, although stopping at a desired bank angle required practice. There was little back stick required up to 30 degrees of bank, but there wasn't much turn rate either. Appreciable turn rates required 45-degree banks or greater; real maneuvering meant 60 degrees of bank or more (those are 1.4-g and 2-g turns, respectively).

Pitch response was neither as quick nor as exhilarating as roll response, but the control forces and response were consistent with my experience. Performance was not. Even with the most ferociously high-powered propeller airplanes, once the nose was poked significantly above the horizon, airspeed bled off rapidly. "Poking the nose above the horizon" implies an increase of angle of attack, which increases lift. If significant turning is also involved—that equates to g-forces (acceleration due to gravity), where g's are a convenient means of describing multiples of lift—airspeed can go to hell in a hand basket. Induced drag is the culprit; induced drag is the part of total aerodynamic drag that results from the production of lift.

What makes induced drag nasty for maneuvering is that it is a function of the lift coefficient, whether that lift coefficient is geometrically, permanently, built into an airfoil (such as a wing) by virtue of its shape or transiently increased by the pilot's increasing the angle of attack by pulling back on the stick. However it is created, induced drag is proportional to the square of the lift coefficient. That means that a little old 60-degree banked, level turn, which trigonometry tells us is a 2-g turn, does not double the induced drag from 1-g wings-level flight; rather, the induced drag increases by a factor of 4, or 2 squared. How about a 6-g limit load turn? Induced drag increases by a factor of 6 squared, or 36 times that of level, nonturning flight. You can slow down in a hurry that way, maybe even stall the airplane.

The jet airplanes introduced a new dimension, the vertical. The jets' aerodynamic shape featured much lower drag coefficients than their predecessors. Since jet engine power, as opposed to thrust, is a direct function of velocity or speed, the designers had to make it easy for the jet airplanes, which initially had inherently low-thrust engines, to accelerate to speeds that would generate enough power to let them fly at all. That is an oversimplification, but it was essential to reduce the kinds of drag—like form and parasite drag—that do not contribute to lift. Once the smooth, low-drag jet airplane's profile got moving, it would accelerate to a speed where thrust equals drag, in accordance with the laws of physics, just as for every other airplane (for airplanes of comparable weight, lift and induced drag will be about equal—airplane to airplane). Because the other contributors to the total drag of the jets were designed to be significantly smaller, the jets were inherently faster than the props; and because of lower total drag, they also would decelerate slower, even under high-lift conditions.

The beneficial consequences were immediately obvious to me in the F9F. When I first pulled back on the stick from high-speed cruise, the initial climb rate was startling. Moreover, both speed and climb rate stayed high for a period during which I gained significant altitude with only a gradual decay in speed. I had just experienced my first zoom climb; never mind that it barely qualified as a zoom climb. I found that if I did the same thing when recovering from a high-speed dive, my altitude gain was spectacular before I slowed back to cruise speed. This and other phenomena were revealed to me as I felt out the airplane and went through the obligatory complement of maneuvers. The altitude gain for vertical maneuvers like the loop and Immelmann was awesome. The complementary altitude loss for a split-S, the other common vertical maneuver was sobering. Better have plenty of altitude underneath before trying that one!

The ability to trade off altitude for airspeed was one of the first discoveries made in the history of flight. The trade-off consists of converting potential energy to kinetic energy. Potential energy can be explained as energy due to position, such as height above the earth within the earth's gravitational field; kinetic energy can be described as energy due to velocity. Kinetic energy is proportional to the square of velocity. The basic idea can be illustrated by dropping a rock off a tall building. Before the rock is dropped it isn't moving at all, zero kinetic energy; just before it hits it's going like hell, with a great deal of kinetic energy. According to the physicists there is no energy transfer in the process— just a change in state, except for some minor dissipation of energy as heat due to friction during the rock's fall through the air.

What early pilots figured out was that velocity generated by a rapid loss in altitude could be in a direction other than straight down. They found that if they pointed an airplane down, it would accelerate rapidly. After leveling off, excess speed decayed relatively slowly, especially when accompanied by application of full power. From this phenomenon evolved one of the first air combat tactics: get high and dive onto the enemy's tail before he can maneuver out of the way. In the propeller airplanes this was a one-way street, and that way was down; this was because of the rapidity with which airspeed fell off in steep angles of climb. The inherently lower-drag jet airplanes, however, made it possible to convert excess speed to a positive gain in altitude and still retain enough speed, or energy, for further maneuvering. Fighter tactics based on energy management were developed from this newly available performance that featured vertical as well as horizontal maneuvering.

The differences between propeller and jet flight was heightened in the older, low-powered jets. The only things the jet pilot had to worry about in normal flight were the throttle (the "go handle") and the flight controls. Jet aircraft systems were simple, and the lower-thrust engines were quiet. Later airplanes were different. The F3H Demon had an engine that was a real screamer. The high-performance F-4 Phantom II (originally F4H) presented brute-force solutions to most problems and wore its external design compromises like egg on its face. Its two J79 engines were raucously loud. As if noise and in-air vibration were not enough, the available thrust in that airplane made the pilot aware that he had some kind of tiger by the tail, especially in afterburner. The F-4's handling qualities also told the man in the front seat that he was up there for business, not fun. But the undemanding straight-wing jets, by contrast, felt as if they were just there to be enjoyed. Enjoy we did.

In exploring the flying qualities of the F9F, I did not bypass the low-speed characteristics. My first encounter with the zoom climb phenomenon was inadvertent, resulting from a desire to see what happened to climb performance at the "wrong" airspeed, one well below that for best rate of climb. I tried to slow down by pulling back on the stick quickly—too quickly. I did slow down, eventually, but not before learning something of dynamic versus static performance. Wary of other, less pleasant surprises, I progressed through minimal controllable airspeeds and stalls with care. The slow-flight and stall characteristics were honest and straightforward, typically Grumman.

Power-off glide was another pleasant surprise. The airplane seemed to want to glide forever, even though I was carrying a substantial fuel load. Best glide speed was close to best endurance speed at about 210 knots, indicated.[13] I learned later that a Panther could glide well over a hundred nautical miles from an altitude of thirty-five thousand feet. One report claimed 120 miles. There was an apocryphal tale that someone once found himself at thirty thousand feet, low fuel state and miles away from his San Diego destination. According to the story, he deliberately shut down his engine. He glided eighty miles. Then, over North Island, he relit and landed with an ample fuel reserve.[14]

Regardless of any basis in fact, the yarn got my attention because the last thing for me to do on purpose would be to shut down the only engine I had. With a windmilling engine—and the centrifugal-flow engine would windmill—a pilot still had to depend on what he hoped was a full battery for fuel pressure and, especially, to power the igniters. The start procedure was to achieve a recommended engine rpm, about 15 percent, and hit the air start switch. The switch was conveniently located on the stepped portion of the left cockpit console, right behind the throttle and outboard of the rudder trim knob. It was not difficult to adjust airspeed (with airplane pitch attitude) so as to achieve the recommended engine rpm, but there was a string of possible electrical failure modes, any one of which could prevent either or both igniters from firing. No igniters, no ignition, no start!

A reciprocating engine can be thought of as having two "igniters" (spark plugs) per cylinder. As long as the engine turns, the plugs will fire every other revolution, each bank of plugs powered by its own magneto. Get one or two cylinders to fire, and the engine will start, maybe even spring into life with a satisfying roar. That is why running tanks dry in propeller airplanes was no big deal as long as the pilot had a little altitude and a reasonably high airspeed. In the J42 engine, by contrast, the two spark plug–equivalents in flight just sat there, idle, surrounded by a lot of heat and flame. It was not unheard of for igniters to foul or burn up, not to mention ceramic cracks, bad contacts, poor connections, broken wires, and so on.

Apprehensive at the very thought of needing an air start, I never had a jet engine fail in flight, not in my whole flying experience. The only air start I ever attempted was years later in the twin-engine F-4. That was occasioned by shutting down one engine on purpose, part of a test flight procedure at Patuxent; I had another perfectly good engine to take me home. After hitting my test point, I used ten thousand feet of altitude getting the dead engine fired up and back on line! I decided I was not emotionally suited for air starts.

The Banshee and Panther were my introduction to tricycle landing gear. After years of high-torque tail draggers, landing these airplanes was easy. (Landing a tail-wheel airplane is not all that difficult, but the process requires a level of attention.) The Panther almost landed itself. It was possible to full-stall the airplane, which could produce a discernible thump at touchdown. The easy way was to fly it down to a roll-on landing. Even we ham-handed types found it difficult to avoid consistently smooth landings. Still, approach-to-landing speeds were 30 to 35 knots faster than the speediest props, and getting stopped once on the ground could be a problem on the short runways that were the norm. It paid to land on speed and "on the numbers"; landing "hot and long" was not recommended.

The Panther was docile on approach. Power control took some getting used to, because of the jet engine's slow response time. At worst, it was possible to bracket the appropriate throttle setting by making minor adjustments. The airplane was reasonably stable in pitch, less so in yaw, and almost twitchy in roll until the pilot learned to minimize aileron inputs. A common mistake was to overcontrol with aileron so as to stimulate the infernal Dutch roll; once it started, the pilot could find himself wallowing down the glide slope all the way to touchdown.

The landing roll presented no challenges beyond high speed. A desirable attribute of any tricycle is that it wants to continue to roll straight ahead with the third wheel in front, and no tendency to swap ends. However, an aerodynamically clean vehicle with relatively small wheels and hard tires is not easy to slow down and stop. Brakes were effective, but premature hard application could blow tires; a high-speed skid on one or more blown tires could be disastrous. Repeated brake application could cause brake fade or enough heat to set a wheel on fire. Fortunately, someone discovered a compensatory technique that was widely emulated. The Panther's high horizontal tail retained control effectiveness down to quite low speeds. Once on the ground it was possible to raise the nose to a high angle of attack; the limit was reached when the tail skag dragged along the pavement. It looked weird to see an F9F with its nose up in the air, rolling along the runway, but the aerodynamic drag was an effective speed brake. (It looked even weirder to see sparks flying from a dragged tail skag; tail skag shoes were a frequent replacement item.) If you saw the airplane early on roll-out, so that you couldn't tell if you were looking at a landing or takeoff attempt, a reasonable reaction might be, "My God, he'll never get in the air that way." A first-time Banshee pilot did in fact over-rotate on takeoff one day. Not recognizing his problem, he kept the stick back, nose high in the air. The Banshee's upsloping aft fuselage geometry permitted a much higher angle of attack on the ground than a Panther. The pilot used every inch of the short, six-thousand-foot runway at Patuxent. He never did get airborne. He wound up in the dirt off the end of the runway.

Professional Recollections

In my six weeks at Service Test that summer I flew the Panther several more times. After the first flight I flew relatively unsupervised. That, plus my lack of familiarity with the subtleties of the machine, was potential for trouble.

For one thing, the oxygen system had a new wrinkle compared with other diluter-demand systems common in the Navy. With increases in altitude the old diluter-demand systems enriched the oxygen content of the air/oxygen mixture the pilot was breathing until the mixture reached 100 percent oxygen. But at cockpit altitudes in excess of thirty thousand feet, gaseous expansion at high altitudes is such that human lungs do not have the volumetric capacity to process enough oxygen to ward off hypoxia.[15] The Navy's solution to the problem in 1950 was pressure breathing. At around thirty-six thousand feet, this new system switched to a mode that forced oxygen into the pilot's lungs through his oxygen mask. The pressure-breathing technique compressed the oxygen in the lungs so as to make it possible for the blood to absorb adequate oxygen, which is the purpose of breathing in the first place. In other words, the technique reversed the normal breathing sequence: instead of expanding the chest cavity to let air into the lungs, the pilot had to contract the chest cavity to force the air out. Because it was an unnatural act that had to be consciously directed, the process was mildly fatiguing.

There was another consequence. We speak during exhale cycles, when extended chest muscles restore themselves to the normal unextended condition. The effort required is minimal, therefore easily controllable; it is not inherently different with more exertive forms of vocalization like shouting or singing. However, speaking while pressure breathing is different. It is hard enough to expel the oxygen that is constantly flowing into one's lungs without also having to force it through vocal cords. The output becomes a series of short, vocal grunts. Communication at extreme altitudes was difficult and therefore as laconic as aircrews could manage.

Only rarely did Panther pilots have to utilize pressure breathing. For one thing, the F9F-2's service ceiling was only about forty-three thousand feet. A colloquial definition of *service ceiling* might be an altitude at which an airplane can barely fly at all without falling out of the sky. There is little reason to fly close to service ceiling except to verify that an airplane really can achieve that altitude. I did it only once, on my second Panther flight, to see if I could get there. I experienced the pressure-breathing phenomenon, but since I was all alone in my piece of sky, I had no need to communicate.[16] There is another reason why pressure breathing was rarely encountered except for test purposes: cockpit pressurization. What is important is the pilot's immediate environment, not outside-the-airplane ambient pressure. That is why we don't need oxygen masks in airliners. It is not generally deemed feasible to pressurize military airplane cockpits to where oxygen is not needed at all, but extreme cockpit altitudes are not encountered if everything is working properly—unless the pilot has a case of the stupids.

Exploring the service ceiling, I reached forty-three thousand feet that day. I huffed and puffed against positive oxygen pressure but hardly noticed because I was uncomfortable for another reason: my life vest had expanded with altitude. There wasn't much give to my shoulder harness, so most of the force was taken by my chest, already working hard enough simply to breathe. In the Navy almost all flights are at least partially over water, so we customarily wore life jackets. Our life jackets, a successor to the Mae West horse collars of World War II, could properly be described as vests. In many ways superior to the predecessor, the vest incorporated important differences. The back hung down further, almost to shoulder blade level when uninflated, the better to hold an incapacitated crewman's head out of the water. The front was a true vest, with pockets and hangers for items like emergency flares, flashlights, survival knives, shark repellent, and dye marker. The snap closures in front made it more difficult to put on or get out of than the Mae West–type vest. Normal inflation, as in the old one, was accomplished by pulling individual toggle switches that punctured two built-in CO_2 cartridges. There were backup oral inflation tubes in case of CO_2 malfunction or if necessary to reinflate. And therein lay the immediately significant difference. In the old Mae West jackets, the oral tubes were two-way: they could be used to let air in or out. In the new vests, the oral inflation tubes could be used only to inflate, presumably as a safety factor for an incapacitated man. Deflation required a special tool that pilots did not normally carry.

The higher I flew the more uncomfortable the life vest became. I could not release any air to stop or relieve the expansion of a thing that seemed bent on self-inflation. Poking holes in the jacket never occurred to me. Destruction of government property would be unseemly, and besides, I might yet need the jacket; NAS Patuxent has a lot of water around it. Unable to discover any rational explanation for my problem, or a solution, I sought in my mind for someone to blame. That damn Jim Ellis! He knew I was going to fly this airplane and go to altitude. He must have blown just enough air into the jacket that I wouldn't notice on the ground but would still have trouble in flight. Benny Sevilla would be more likely to pull something like that, but he wasn't around. Paul Durand? Naah, he was too straight-arrow for that, and such action would be unbecoming for a senior lieutenant commander. It had to be Ellis.

When I descended into denser air, the problem solved itself: the life jacket magically deflated. On reaching lower altitudes, I had a mental breakthrough. Pressurization! I had forgotten to turn on the cockpit pressurization switch. Problem completely solved? Not quite. I couldn't find the damn switch; I couldn't find it for the remainder of the flight. I had discovered the culprit, and he was me. After I landed, I didn't say a word about my difficulty to anyone.

During the following Postgraduate School semester, I sniveled a couple more flights in the Panther on an occasional Saturday morning. They were made possible through the kind offices of Lieutenant Gordon A. Snyder, then new to the Service Test Jet Section, later to be my boss at ComFAir (Commander, Fleet Air) Alameda.

Next spring the Test Pilot Training stable of aircraft included one F9F-3. As one of a kind, the airplane was in demand by the staff as well as the students. The Marine major who controlled the flight schedule had small regard for the eight of us who had come from the Postgraduate School. More than once his assistant, Lieutenant (jg) Dave Williams, put one of us on the schedule only to find the name erased by the major. I got one ride in the F9F-3. On a Saturday. The Marine was out of town. When he found out about it, he gave Dave Williams hell.

The next time I sat in the cockpit of an F9F was in January of 1952 when VF-821 transitioned from Corsairs to Panthers. The airplane was a combat-worn F9F-2, not one of the brand-new F9F-5s we had been promised. Pratt & Whitney had not yet cured the early ills of the J48 engine. We were to deploy in June and so couldn't afford the down time or the hazards associated with a less-than-fleet-ready airplane; our training cycle was already marginally short. Or so ComAirPac decided. VF-

721, our neighbors in the adjacent hangar at North Island who were a couple of months behind us in the cycle, would receive the first F9F-5s.

The problems with the J48 were solvable, but they were serious. On the East Coast there had been several accidents, two of them fatal. There was one catastrophic bearing failure. There were some instances of hot gas leaks from an exhaust weldment. There was one disastrous human error whereby a fuel nozzle was improperly installed. (The business end of the nozzle wound up between the burner basket and the burner can case; it made a great cutting torch, but it didn't do the engine or the pilot much good.) There were also turbine blade problems, the final solutions for which were to take a while. It was a real mess, but the J48 engine in its various configurations became a very successful, reliable engine. As well as the F9F Panther, J48s powered the swept-wing F9F-6, F9F-8, and F9F-8T Cougars. The latter was an outstanding two-seat jet trainer that survived well into the 1960s as an instrument training airplane for fleet pilots.

The J48 was an American-built Rolls-Royce Tay. There are inevitable difficulties any time a complex piece of machinery is produced by a "second source." Part of the problem is that no company's engineering drawings, however good, are immediately transferable to another company without a certain amount of trial and error and detailed indoctrination. The difficulties are compounded when production is moved from country to country, especially when the normal production methods of one country are substantially different from those of the other. The J48 had been significantly reengineered for American production. Pratt & Whitney was not unique in this regard. The Curtiss-Wright J65 engine was much different from its British Sapphire original, as was the Martin-built B-57 bomber from its progenitor, Canberra. Some of Pratt & Whitney's changes were innovative; virtually all of them contributed to the long production life of what would prove to be an outstanding engine.

The upshot of the J48 problems was no F9F-5s for VF-821. As Maintenance Officer I was soon to encounter difficulties with our incompletely overhauled F9F-2s wholly different from what had been experienced with our departing Corsairs. Some airplanes came to us as transfers from returning Korean-tour squadrons without benefit of overhaul.

It is possible to categorize airplane part and material failures. There are, for instance, infantile failures; these occur within the first few hours of operation after production and seem especially common in electronic products. Then there are recurring, sometimes chronic, failures resulting from a fault or weakness in an overall design or a single part; these tend to get fixed by dedicated changes and design modifications over the service life of the product. There is at least one more category, associated with what I call the Old Airplane Syndrome (cousin to the Old Automobile Syndrome). Entirely different stuff breaks, gives out, and wears out in old airplanes than in new ones; things go wrong that never went wrong before, and this is what we were beginning to see in the Panthers. The dual failure affecting aileron boost described earlier is a good example. A necessary element for that to occur was a simultaneous failure of the aileron boost and the aileron boost solenoid, the latter failure usually caused by corrosion that took a couple of extended sea tours to generate. The Panther also had an attention-grabbing failure involving an aneroid bellows shaft in the fuel control. The shaft and bellows were part of an altitude compensation device. When it failed, the shaft would hang up in its bushing and wouldn't turn. The symptom of failure was that the engine would quit as the airplane climbed through about twenty-seven thousand feet. Air start, here we come!

Lieutenant (jg) Val Schaeffer had that happen to him one day over Majon-ni in Korea. Majon-ni, at the head of reconnaissance route Green 3, featured a singularly active anti-aircraft battery. We made it a point to avoid overflying when in the vicinity. One minute Val was sitting on my wing, the next he was drifting rapidly aft and losing altitude.

"Lead, I've got a flameout!"

He restarted in short order and rejoined the flight, hardly missing a beat. I would have been petrified if it had been me.

"You OK? Want to go back to the ship?"

"I'm fine. How about we keep it under twenty grand, though."

We stayed under twenty thousand feet, and there was no further problem. By then we knew the nature of the failure. We just didn't know how to fix it. Nor did the Pratt & Whitney representative who was with us aboard the *Essex*. That failure mode was one of many exciting discoveries that awaited us in the months ahead.

There was at North Island no coherent, organized program to prepare us for airplane transition. There were briefing sessions of varying depth and duration, frequently ad hoc, dealing with specific subjects. There was a dedicated maintenance training detachment, rudimentary by current standards, that covered aircraft systems—nothing like the sophisticated NMTDs (Naval Maintenance Training Detachments) that came later. As the airplanes arrived, we simply began to fly 'em and fix 'em, just as if we knew what we were doing.

Most of the enlisted men in a fighter squadron are assigned to the maintenance department. The men from the New Orleans area who were called up with VF-821 were a well-qualified, motivated bunch. Unfortunately, many of the experienced petty officers were either returning to civilian life or being transferred. Those who remained were skilled enough, but for the most part they had the wrong skills. They had to adapt to power plants and complex airplanes much different from the familiar Corsairs. (Fortunately, even though the change to jet propulsion was dramatic, the first jet engines were relatively simple and generally reliable; they were in fact less labor intensive and less skill intensive than the big radials they replaced, such the R-2800 and especially the Curtiss-Wright R-3300. Probably the most challenging item for the mechanics was learning about fuel controls instead of carburetors.) ComAirPac did the best they could for us, but it wasn't much. They sent us a couple of experienced junior petty officer ADs (aviation mechanics). There were a few short courses available locally on different jet engine subjects. By ones and twos we cycled people through when we could.

My big maintenance problems involved the F9F's hydraulic systems. The Panther's aircraft systems were an order of magnitude more sophisticated than the Corsair's, and our airplanes were not new. Old hydraulic systems leak a lot. There was something else: The most common aircraft hydraulic fluid was a red petroleum-based liquid. If heated to a high enough temperature, it would burn. If atomized under pressure, it was readily ignitable and would then behave much like an acetylene torch, which could be nasty in an airplane. In order to make airplanes less susceptible to in-flight fires, the Navy went to a less flammable fluid called Hydrolube, essentially a mixture of water and ethylene glycol. A lot like automobile antifreeze and with some of the same characteristics, Hydrolube made a great paint remover, and without effective anticorrosion additives, it proved substantially corrosive.

We experienced hydraulic failures in numbers and varieties that overwhelmed us. This was particularly true in those first weeks. We operated and maintained the airplanes for a full training program at the same time we were learning what we needed to know about them.

Aviation mechanics used to be jacks-of-all-trades who did everything there was to do on an airplane, where "everything" includes both engine and airframe. In time, skills were segregated into specialties. The ADs (aviation mechanics)[17] were "power plants" people. Airframes were the province of the AMs (aviation structural mechanics). In VF-821 they were in short supply, as to both numbers and specific training. Increasingly sophisticated airplanes had caused a split in the AM ranks. There were AMSs, where the *S* referred to "structural" or "sheet," as in sheet metal. AMSs were called metal benders, after one of the characteristic implements of their trade, a pressing machine–like contraption. The squadron didn't have enough AMs, and the ones who were aboard were almost all AMSs. What I needed most was that other variety, AMH, where *H* signified "hydraulic."

The old New Orleans hands were willing, and they were good. Initially they didn't have the knowledge, however fast learners they might be. I remember in particular a petty officer first class AMS. He was a Navy Department civilian in Overhaul & Repair Facility when he wasn't going to war. He, AMH1 A. Boutte, and three "A" school graduate strikers[18] were the ones who kept us flying in those early months when we were trying to come up to speed. The AMS1 went back to his real life before we deployed, but by then ComAirPac had shored us up with people with the right qualifications. There were some anxious months in between.

The squadron had a nominal complement of sixteen airplanes. In the beginning our in-service airplane availability hovered around 30 percent, not enough to maintain a rigorous training schedule. After we got the hang of things and the airplanes were in better shape, availability improved to 50 percent and climbing. We leveled off at 60 to 62 percent while ashore. Once at sea, availability reached 90 percent and higher. There were two reasons. One was the captive audience; everybody was there aboard ship and could be called to work in extremis. The other reason was that the highest priority for replacement airplane parts was, and is, reserved for deployed forces; anything shore based automatically has a lower priority. (I believe there is a pattern that extends through time and different airplanes. Ten years later I experienced almost identical availability figures ashore and afloat in a squadron of one-time overhauled F8U Crusaders.)

ComAirPac couldn't do anything about our parts priority, nor could they provide parts that didn't exist. So they did the next best thing: they gave us more airplanes. At one time we had twenty-two airplanes sitting on the line. That approach can backfire; if you can't maintain a small number, having to take care of a larger number can be overpowering. This time, however, it helped us acquire more operable airplanes, especially after we stooped to "cannibalizing," robbing an already down airplane of a vital part in order to fix another. That is how Hangar Queens are born. Everybody in the airplane business openly deplores cannibalizing, yet almost everybody practices it at some time or other.

Take the case of 205A; even today I am embarrassed about it. The airplane went down for a leaking nose strut. After several unsuccessful repair efforts, it was determined that the oleo strut itself was out of round; we would need a new part. Unfortunately, the only way to replace it was to order an entire nose strut assembly. The order turned into a back order—four weeks' minimum delay—and so 205A sat in hangar

525 and began to acquire dust. After a day or so a different part, also not immediately available, was needed for another airplane. With my permission it was dutifully tagged and "borrowed" from 205A. Then another. And another. After a while the requests for permission stopped, and "See if you can pull it off 205" became the norm. When the nose strut finally arrived, not four but six weeks later, there were twenty-six parts deficiencies on the airplane.

One early afternoon, Lieutenant Jerauld D. "Barney" Barnes, who was Power Plants Officer and Assistant Maintenance Officer, walked into the maintenance office."Guess what? We got twenty goddam airplanes up."

"Surely you jest," I said.

"Hell, no. Not only that, they are preflighted and ready to go. All twenty."

Flying had been intentionally light for a few days as we prepared for a weapons deployment to El Centro. I went up to the mezzanine deck of the hangar to report this miracle of airplane availability. The skipper was at a meeting at AirPac headquarters, but I found the Exec. Gene Loughridge gave me his sly grin at the news. "Let's go fly!"

"All twenty?"

"All twenty."

It was easy to find twenty pilots ready to drop whatever important stuff they were doing; word spread to the shops and offices and the ready room. Within twenty minutes Gene was briefing the flight for an Important Parade Flight Rehearsal. He worked out an arrangement of a five-division formation for a fly-by, to be followed by a tail chase over the Pacific. Within forty-five minutes of my announcement to Gene we were manning airplanes.

The airplanes all started. They all made it to the run-up area. They all flew. Gene rendezvoused the squadron offshore, and we made our low pass in formation over the field—with the tower's permission and concurrence, of course. In ensemble we constituted a large, dark blue aluminum cloud. We flew as tightly as we could, by four-plane divisions and within the divisions as well. It was downright exhilarating.

After the low pass we turned seaward and climbed to altitude, where the leader put us in a close—very close—tail chase. This was the classic arrangement for formation acrobatics. Each pilot puts the tail of the plane ahead in the middle of his windscreen, virtually filling the windscreen. The interval between planes is just a few feet, comparable to that for any tight formation. From then on the leader flies through any evolution he desires. Each succeeding pilot duplicates the wing and nose position of the airplane just ahead so as to emulate his maneuver. Other than stall maneuvers, there are few limitations to what is possible.

Shortly after I joined VBF-3 in 1946, the two Air Group 3 fighter squadrons were part of a flight demonstration at the Cleveland Air Races. As part of the air show they flew two eight-plane tail chase loops side by side. They were still in Hellcats then.[19] That exercise would have been a little ambitious for twenty Panthers. Gene gave us a good workout but nothing extreme. Mostly climbs, dives, and tight turns with a couple of gentle barrel rolls thrown in. It doesn't sound like much, but it was great fun. He signaled us back into parade formation. We returned to North Island where we made a simulated carrier "break" for landing, again with the tower's permission.

After the flight four airplanes were reported in down status, but the discrepancies were all minor. Hutch Cooper was waiting for us. He had seen the fly-by as he was leaving his meeting. He feigned indignation—not at the flight, but because we had gone without him.

That exercise in morale building was to be Gene Loughridge's swan song with the squadron. Like a ship's Executive Officer, a squadron Exec is responsible for the routine operation of the organization. He is supposed to be a model of good order and discipline. When necessary, he plays bad guy to the skipper's good guy. Gene didn't quite fit the mold. His laissez-faire management style, punctuated by sometimes erratic personal behavior, ultimately got him cross-wired with Hutch Cooper. Hutch could be incredibly loose and relaxed, all in all a great guy to work for. However, as is common with good commanding officers, Hutch wanted things done his way in his squadron; he arranged for Gene Loughridge to be transferred to another squadron. His replacement was Lieutenant Commander William G. "Bill" Coulter.

Bill Coulter was a different type altogether. He was a good Exec, effectively complementing Hutch at the head of the squadron—not surprising, since Hutch had picked him. Coulter, like Hutch, had a laid-back personality. With a wry sense of humor, his angular, lined face seemed always to reflect a secret amusement. Bill Coulter arrived in the squadron with an ulcer and an aviation background heavy on multi-engine transport experience. Strike one and strike two, I thought. He will never deploy. If the medics don't get him, the aircraft carrier will. It didn't seem reasonable to me that, however talented, a pilot could successfully leap into carrier aviation that late in his career, especially carrier jet aviation. In fact he did great. He was a fine pilot.

When the time came, we got our airplanes over the hills to El Centro. The previous visit to the Imperial Valley had been in Corsairs. Some of what I had earlier observed in a neighboring Panther squadron began to make sense. The runways at Naval Auxiliary Air Station El Centro were about seven-thousand feet long, not much by today's standards, especially for jet airplanes with small engines; six thousand feet of runway was considered a workable minimum. I observed pilots routinely using almost every inch of the runway on takeoff. I wasn't sure at the time whether it was by choice or if the airplanes really were barely staggering into the air, as it appeared. It was by choice, a choice not really necessary for them in November or, later, for us in February; in that same desert in hot July, however, the technique prevented getting prematurely airborne in a mushing attitude from which one could not accelerate.

Another phenomenon was the infernal racket. The F9F required periodic fuel control adjustments. Lacking the sophisticated instruments of today, the mechanics would fire up the machine and fiddle with adjustments for what seemed an eternity because it was done at full power. You wouldn't believe a smallish engine could make such a racket for such a long time. After a minute or so the sound became fiercely irritating. The disinterested bystander could find himself getting angry. Why do they keep it up so long? That can't be necessary! They must be incompetent or worse. They're doing it on purpose, just to be annoying. *Incompetent* is too strong, but *inefficient* may not be. In time, as our people filtered through fuel control school and learned to fabricate their own test gauge manifolds—they didn't exist in the supply system—the process became closer to science than to the black art it resembled initially. Meanwhile it was noisy. It got so bad at North Island that our across-the-street neighbors in Officers' Quarters got the air station to make us stop night turnups. I couldn't blame them, even though our night-check crew maintenance operation was what kept us going.

I have a cartoon of the Panther era that illustrates a quaint aspect of the pesky fuel control adjustment. The cartoon shows a front view of an F9F. In one of the two bifurcated engine inlets the only visible sign of a mechanic is the soles of his shoes; he is head first inside the engine as far as he can get without disappearing completely from view. Incredible as it may seem, this was the preferred position for the fellow adjusting the fuel control. It was also the preferred position for a plane captain stealing an unauthorized nap—in the latter case, of course, with the engine not running. A straight-through, axial-flow engine can suck off a man's hat from a considerable distance, or suck up the whole man if he gets too close. That is why there are all those big yellow signs aboard ship, the ones that say "Beware of Jet Intakes." That danger did not exist to the same extent in the F9F because the two intakes and the blow-in doors on the turtleback of the fuselage provided alternate paths for inlet air. A man might lose his hat, but there was little danger to his person lying lengthwise deep in an intake. Not that there weren't other hazards. The decibel level could cause hearing loss with repeated exposure, something the aviation physiologists were quick to discover; hence the "Mickey Mouse" ear protectors worn by today's carrier flight deck crews. I am not sure there weren't other deleterious physical effects to a man lying next to an engine at full power; the amplitude of the sound, especially at low frequencies, could have produced other effects.

The weapons deployment to El Centro differed from our previous trip in Corsairs more in degree than in kind. We still flew mostly bombing, rocket, strafing, and gunnery flights. Air-to-ground interdiction was to be our primary mission in Korea. The gunnery was because we were, after all, a fighter squadron, although the arbitrary division of service responsibility on the Korean peninsula made it unlikely that we would be committed to the aerial circus over the Yalu River. That was Air Force F-86 country.

In preparation for our initial carrier qualification in jet airplanes, we added a lot of FCLP (field carrier landing practice) to the syllabus. We flew the same carrier landing pattern as the propeller aircraft. Even with the docility of the straight-wing jets, the operation was not without excitement. The modestly higher approach speed made the pattern of greater dimensions, compared with the pylon-turn-around-the-LSO approach I remembered from the Bearcats. It's all relative.

The airplanes whose approach pattern really did resemble pylon turns were the biplane F3Fs of the late 1930s. That was the machine in which the "Flying Chiefs" reputedly achieved a phenomenal ten seconds between landing aircraft for an entire recovery. What makes that remarkable is that most of that time is used in getting the preceding airplane out of the arresting gear and at least one barrier raised in time for the next aircraft. In the Bearcats we tried for a landing interval of less than thirty seconds, although I recall George Veling on one occasion getting down onto the deck in ten seconds. It took a lot of luck and a Landing Signal Officer with great faith in the Bearcat's late wave-off capability, not to mention confidence in the pilot. We managed twenty seconds between aircraft for an eight-plane recovery one day; that was as good as it got.

Thirty seconds was optimum as a goal for the Panthers. Forty-five seconds was more reasonable to expect for jet aircraft, and a minute between airplanes was not going to make anyone mad. At El Centro we were a long way from worrying about landing interval. First, we had to learn how to do it *at all* in this new airplane. The carrier approach flight path was wider and deeper than for the props but did not provide additional time "in the groove" because of higher speed. The problem became one of acquiring sight of the LSO's flags early enough to respond to his signals. High-visibility color notwithstanding, one could see the paddles only from a certain maximum distance. Just as with the propeller airplanes, the LSO picked up an oncoming plane with a "Roger" signal, followed by a corrective signal if needed—that is, if the pilot were not so screwed up initially that the LSO needed to wave him off right then.

That brought up another problem. In response time the Panther was the opposite of the Bearcat. The Bearcat reacted to application of power nearly instantaneously; there was no discernible lag between opening the throttle and the R-2800 engine pushing you back in the seat. In the Panther, the J42's windup time was leisurely at best. This created a time constraint for the LSO. He had to anticipate that a pilot was getting into trouble before it happened,while there was still room for the pilot to respond successfully. The alternatives were not pleasant. Flying into the water was not desirable; flying into the blunt end of the boat was disaster. The upshot was that an approaching pilot could count on seeing, processing, and responding to only one or two signals before either getting waved off or being committed to a landing. The best solution was to fly a correct approach all the way. That meant a lot of practice, grinding around a hundred feet or so above the desert floor. We flew the oblate, semicircular path to a short straight final just before touchdown. It was head-out-of-the-cockpit except for an occasional quick peek to verify airspeed and altitude—an exercise in selective concentration.

I remember one of our lieutenants on a particular FCLP flight. He had been having difficulty in the pattern but finally seemed to catch on. Unfortunately, his concentration was overly selective and lacked flexibility. When he landed back at El Centro after the FCLP period, we discovered an array of mesquite branches in the left intake duct of the engine. It seemed that he had flown into and bounced back into the air off a sand dune. He didn't even remember doing it, though he had a vague recollection of an unexplained bump sometime during the flight. Thank God for the Grumman Iron Works! Not to mention alternate air paths to the engine. It was not reassuring that the LSO hadn't seen it happen, but the interval between airplanes could have been such that he was still working the previous airplane. That pilot did not deploy with us.

We spent considerable time dropping bombs and shooting rockets at targets 103A and 103B. That was appropriate because bombing, strafing, and shooting rockets were to be our mission in Korea. The bombs were mostly the familiar miniature Mk 76 with shotgun shell marker charges. Occasionally we dropped water-filled bombs. The rockets were subcaliber rockets whose flight paths tended to be erratic.

We flew bombing runs similar to those we had learned in propeller airplanes, except for dive angle. Something in excess of 60 degrees had been preferred in those airplanes, because the steeper the dive angle the less the required lead angle and, consequently, the smaller the errors. At the 90-degree dive angles that had been feasible for the World War II Stukas and Dauntlesses there is essentially no lead required; all corrections are made with aileron, and remarkable accuracies are possible.[20] In the Panthers we found 60 degrees to be a workable maximum but not very useful. A safe recovery had to be initiated at such a high altitude that accuracy was degraded; 30- to 45-degree dive angles were common choices with, in the combat world, 15-degree dive angles used for particularly difficult approach paths.

Safe recovery means, first, not flying into the ground and, second, not flying through one's own bomb blast. A released bomb has the nasty characteristic of flying along right under the airplane until impact. If one has released too low, shrapnel can hole one's airplane. Low bomb releases were a recurring factor in the Korean War. More than one pilot blew himself out of the sky. A couple did it more than once. One individual was celebrated in the press for persistence and heroism for having been shot down five times and coming back for more,[21] a closer look might have shown the distinct possibility that a couple of those times the damage was self-inflicted.

Accuracy on the bomb and rocket ranges was roughly determined by the participating pilots. If a pilot on a particular run couldn't determine his own hit, the next guy behind would be sure to spot it for him, with some glee if the drop resulted in a bad miss. The real scoring was done by observers at the range. They scored hits and evaluated patterns and dive angles. Dive angle was determined by viewing runs through a crude device called a "harp," which it resembled. The harp was calibrated in angles, designated by radial lines, to facilitate estimating dive angle for each observed run. There were concentric arcs to assist in estimating range at release altitude. With practice, pilots learned to fly specified dive angles accurately and repeatably.

We approached aerial gunnery with the usual fighter pilots' enthusiasm, but we were psychologically adjusted to the notion that we were going to war as "attack pilots." Some of the firing runs that provided the most fun, and the best accuracies, in the propeller airplanes were eliminated by jet aircraft characteristics. The overheads and steep high side runs were the first to go. We concentrated instead on flat side and low side runs. The latter provided the best combination of flyability and optimal firing time. Even so, we were fighting a losing battle with the laws of physics. Without lead-computing gunsights or a valid indication of range to target, our firing accuracies were low. The ComAirPac standard for qualifying in aerial gunnery was only about 3 percent hits on target, but not all of us met even that modest standard. For a time the squadron owned one later-model airplane that had both a lead-computing sight and an APG-30 range-only radar; unfortunately, we didn't know how to use the system or maintain it.

What I believe to be my best gunnery day in an F9F went unacknowledged. When it came time to count holes in the sleeve after the flight, there were a number of red ones, my color. But because of a foulup, another pilot was also shooting red, and he claimed that all, or most, of the holes were his. There weren't quite enough hits to qualify both of us by equally sharing what was there. Close, but no cigar; we were both screwed. I was a little grumpy about it. It seems that the bulb was burned out in the other guy's gunsight; he had made all his runs with nothing in front of him but a clear windshield. Difficult as it was to score with a fixed sight, I thought it unlikely that a pilot could hit anything without even the apocryphal piece of chewing gum stuck to the glass.

As with most of our training, the squadron was largely on its own, although for the gunnery phase we had some help. ComAirPac had selected a nucleus of pilots to constitute a kind of traveling road show. One of these experts joined us for a few days to impart what knowledge was available on how to shoot in these new airplanes. Our squadron gunnery performance was less than sterling but, in part because of our visitor, it wasn't bad either. (This early ComAirPac effort to provide coaching in weapons training was a legitimate ancestor of "Top Gun," the Fighter Weapons School celebrated in the movie of the same name.)

There was a lack in our training that bothers me more in retrospect than it did then. We devoted almost no time in our training to one-on-one fighter tactics and not much more on multiplane section and division fighter tactics. If challenged by enemy fighters, we would have needed to ad lib and be damn lucky as well. As it happened we were to experience no air-to-air action in Korea, although a couple of times it was close. The enemy had a good airplane in the MiG-15. Fortunately it didn't have much range and couldn't carry weapons capable of threatening ships or ground targets. Moreover, the record shows that no Panther was ever shot down by a MiG-15; but there was a generous handful of MiG kills by Panthers before the Korean fighting was over.

After El Centro there was still much to be done before deployment. Significant was carrier qualification aboard the USS *Bonhomme Richard* (CVA-31). (This was my introduction to a ship to which I would keep returning.) Our LSOs, led by Lieutenant Commander Mike Terrell, did a good job during CarQuals; we didn't break any hardware or damage any people. We still used the classic straight-deck arrangement of multiple arresting wires backed up by stanchion-mounted barriers— pairs of arresting wires that could be raised, fencelike, from the deck during landing operations.

It was possible for jet airplanes to go either through or over the barriers into the airplanes parked on the bow; the USS *Princeton* within the year had had a bad accident and fire when an F2H Banshee did just that. A new device, called a barricade, had just been installed on the Bonnie Dick. The barricade consisted of a web of nylon straps, most oriented vertically, that could be raised behind the barriers to snag an airplane that managed to get through them. The barricade was higher than the barriers and was much more effective at stopping the newer airplanes. The problem was that at first it was only rigged for known emergencies, and that took about twenty minutes. By the time we went to sea, however, the barricade would be rigged for flight operations and kept at the ready for raising, much in the manner of the barriers. We were hardly home free with the barricade, but it was a step in the right direction.

The prebarricade problem is dramatically shown in the motion picture *The Bridges at Toko-ri*, based on James Michener's novel. The solution to the hero's emergency landing problem is to park the largest object aboard ship right behind the last barrier. That object was the mobile crane,[22] which effectively barred the landing airplane's path to the pack of airplanes parked forward on the flight deck. In the movie William Holden catches a late wire; his F9F stops just inches shy of disaster.

James Michener's short novel captures the flavor of the Navy's air war in Korea, including its frustrations; the motion picture retains much of that flavor. Michener's protagonist survives the big strike on the primary target, the bridges of the title, then goes after a secondary target to get rid of his remaining ordnance. He takes what appears to be a minor hit. Unfortunately, it is to his fuel system. Unable to reach the Sea of Japan and safety, he crash-lands. After a failed rescue attempt he is killed by North Korean ground troops, shot in the behind in a Korean irrigation ditch.

In June of 1952 we deployed. The *Essex* would be our home for the eight-month cruise. The Bonnie Dick and *Essex* were indistinguishable except in detail. They were both *Essex* class and had been modified to the same configuration. The 5-inch 38-caliber flight deck gun mounts had been removed. Neither ship had fully enclosed hurricane bows. Both had updated hydraulic catapults, but not the same configuration: the

Two VF-721 Panthers break for landing aboard the USS *Boxer* (CV-21). Two F4U Corsairs are on the ready deck. (Grumman History Center)

Bonnie Dick had the newer Mk 8; the *Essex* had the older Mk 4B. The Mk 8 had higher weight capacity, which translates to higher catapult end speeds, which in turn translates to a better margin above stall speed on takeoff. Our F9Fs, lacking the hard points for heavier ordnance loads that came later, did not test the capability of the Mk 4B, but there were other considerations. A modification to the Mk 4, the 4B increased performance by virtue of a two-step impulse. If one did not have one's head planted firmly against the headrest, a catapult launch consisted of a violent acceleration punctuated by two sharp raps on the back of the noggin, raps such as might be administered by the business end of a ball peen hammer.

We departed San Diego on 16 June 1952 for the Far East via Hawaii. The two weeks in transit seemed interminable, broken up by a series of lectures on what was in store for us and how to deal with it once encountered. For the pilots, there was heavy emphasis on "escape and evasion." Our "instructors" were survivors of various shootdowns who had managed one way or another to get out of North Korea without being captured. After the second or third tale of a downed pilot, armed with a puny .38-caliber Smith and Wesson revolver, challenging professional soldiers armed with businesslike service rifles, I concluded that my pistol was to be loaded with tracers, a personal here-I-am signal to the nearest rescue helicopter. By definition, a downed pilot was an amateur in professional-foot-soldier land.

We entered Tokyo Bay on 25 July. Overcast skies accentuated the harsh, volcanic reality of the land. A moderate breeze blew down the bay, ripping the dark water into occasional whitecaps. To seagoing aviators, that translates to 10 to 12 knots of real wind. The ship's motion increased the relative wind to a damp 26 knots, blowing right into the faces of those standing on the flight deck. As contiguous land became more visible, first on one side of the ship and then on the other, the unfamiliar terrain became defined. The step-function angularity of the hills was real, not the artistic imaginings of Edo-era printmakers. Patches of deep green contrasted with the somber gray of the sky.

As the *Essex* proceeded up the bay, leading its handful of trailing "Small Boys"(destroyers), we saw our first Japanese vessels. They were lone fishing sampans that appeared occasionally along our path, each occupied by one or two crewmen. I didn't know what to expect, the shaking of fists or perhaps more overt gestures of disapproval, like urinating in our direction. (My generation's perception of prewar Japan was a strange mix of myth, ignorance, suspicion, and prejudice; the insular, isolationist, and expansionist Japanese hadn't done much to correct such perceptions.) Instead, each occupant stood at our approach and bowed respectfully in formal Japanese style. They would have done the same at the passage of one of their own men-of-war; we, as recent conquerors of those men-of-war, were accorded equal respect. There were no signs of anger or resentment.

We saw increasing numbers of other craft on our approach to Yokosuka, larger than sampans but nothing approaching in size even a small coastal steamer. Our bombing of Japanese home waters had been effective; it was too soon for evidence of rebuilding. Yokosuka had been a major Japanese naval base. It has a good harbor, although small by our standards. The dock and shop areas were carved out of volcanic rock hills. The few relatively flat areas were connected by an elaborate network of small vehicular tunnels that doubled as efficient bomb shelters. Amply defended by anti-aircraft batteries, the base must have presented a tough target for attacking American bombers.

As we entered the harbor, I saw activity against the shoreline. The activity became a mass of small craft approaching us at high speed; if they weren't making an attack, it was a great simulation. What the hell is going on? I wondered. Torpedo boats? Not torpedo boats at all, but small landing craft—American landing craft, LCMs and LCVPs. Approaching the ship, the group split, passing down either side. Some continued as far as the destroyers astern. They reversed course smartly and by preassigned groups took station on our individual ships. Each craft had heavily bumpered and fendered sides and bows. All Japanese manned, these were our push boats. They took the place of harbor tugs, making up in numbers and maneuverability what they lacked in horsepower. The technique worked surprisingly well in all but extreme wind conditions.

We left Yokosuka on 28 July and began operating on station in the Sea of Japan three days later. We first-tour people were about to see the Korean Unpleasantness[23] firsthand. We were to have four separate on-line tours in the Sea of Japan: thirty-four days, forty-one days, eight days, and forty-two days. The last ended in January of 1953 and included both Christmas of 1952 and New Year's of 1953. (The short eight-day period happened when the *Essex* had a casualty to the port catapult requiring navy yard work.)

As always, our war was dictated by circumstances beyond our control. After American forces were almost pushed off the Korean peninsula in the summer of 1950, MacArthur's brilliantly conceived and executed Inchon landing regained the southern half of the country. By November of 1950 we were almost to the Yalu River. After 120,000 Chinese crossed the river, splitting the U.S. forces, came the affair of the Chosin Reservoir, where not more than 14,000 U.S. Marines took the brunt of the attack. Following a withdrawal under fire all the way to the coast, the Marines made an assault landing in reverse at Hungnam. There followed a period of months of maneuvering for position before the North Koreans suggested negotiations in the summer of 1951. General Matthew Ridgway, the second Eighth Army commander after MacArthur was fired by Harry Truman, continued offensive maneuvering through October before, history suggests, he accepted the notion of a defensive strategy. At least one Marine Corps source states that the First Marine Division learned in the spring of 1952 that the war had moved to a diplomatic and strategic standoff.[24] The Chinese continued to seek tactical gains along the Main Line of Resistance for propaganda and operational advantages.

So-called peace talks continued for two years until the armistice of 27 July 1953. During that period of negotiations there were 18 million words written and over 150,000 additional casualties. The conferees spent fifteen months alone arguing about the exchange of prisoners. The allies—that is, the United Nations—wanted only voluntary repatriation of prisoners; the North Koreans and Chinese wanted their people back whether they wanted to come home or not.

That was the war we inherited. Nobody told us that the folks on the ground were no longer going to be allowed to win. On the previous tour in the *Princeton* as part of Air Group 19 Xray, ending in the summer of 1951, VF-821 had flown mostly interdiction-of-supply-lines strikes when it still appeared that U.S. forces were regrouping for another try.

Riding aloft in my 500-knot foxhole, I had little reason to carp. Not so the ground troops who had to counter the Chinese while they "continued to seek tactical gains." The ground troops were seriously uncomfortable and at continuous risk of becoming seriously dead. Some of the worst exposure we encountered was in support of them in places with romantic names like the Punch Bowl. On a major ground support mission a frequent tactic was to make a coordinated strike, much like an air group "group grope" on a ship or a Vietnam "alpha strike"—one run only, in which everybody dropped all ordnance. One element of fighters, eight to twelve airplanes, led off with a flak suppression run, rockets, strafing, and fragmentation bombs. Then came the Corsairs and ADs, the latter with incredible loads of ordnance hanging on up to fifteen separate bomb stations. Then another element of fighters, similar to the first, made a follow-up flak suppression run to make sure that everybody's head was still down.

Going in first was a piece of cake; the enemy might not know that we were even in the vicinity until the jets came streaking in. Going in last was different. At best we flew through the remnants of all the garbage thrown up at the preceding attack airplanes (I particularly remember the lingering white puffs of 37-millimeter rounds). It was not altogether easy to tell the old stuff from the new, the new possibly being directed specifically at you. Also, you didn't know if the fellow firing on the ground understood about lead angle; you might very well fly into something intended for that AD Skyraider just ahead.

We didn't leap into the fray without some indoctrination. Since much of our flying was to be road reconnaissance in two- or four-plane elements, an old hand, somebody from the first tour, would lead three or four of us on a route—routes were given color-coded sequential names like Green 3—that was known to be benign. H. H. "Cass" Caserta, our Schedules Officer, led my first flight. He took us over Wonsan Bay, showed us Yo-do Island where the rescue helicopter lived, and led us around the known anti-aircraft sites. Taking us down the route south of Wonsan itself, Cass spotted something in a small village. He led four of us on two attack runs, keeping up a running commentary that would have done justice to John Madden describing an NFL football game. I dutifully made my two runs, dropping a 250-pound GP (general purpose) bomb on each run near Cass's designated point of aim. I never saw a thing that looked like a target. I presume Cass did; he talked about a truck that disappeared under an overhang on a side street.

That was the same route that was to cause Lieutenant Commander Maury Yerger, the Exec of VF-23, some embarrassment. He took a flight down the route on a road recce. Either he went a little too far south or a South Korean jeep from"I" Corps headquarters came too far north. Maury and his cohorts strafed them off the road without, fortunately, any wounds to themselves other than skinned elbows, knees, and pride.

Maury was to have worse luck. He was shot down on 17 October 1952 and captured by the North Koreans. He was released on 6 September 1953 in the prisoner exchange, six weeks after the armistice was signed. The North Koreans, like the North Vietnamese, ran their prisons in the manner of the Chinese Communists, with a heavy emphasis on confession, self-incrimination, and conversion to the true faith, communism. What we called brainwashing apparently took precedence over eliciting either information or a denunciation of one's own country. In the later conflict the North Vietnamese seem to have been more interested in the latter.

The air group's familiarization and hand-off strike was a two-carrier attack on the city of Chongjin. The strike leader was the *Princeton*'s CAG (Commander, Air Group). Chongjin was, or had been, a large North Korean city with a population approaching two hundred thousand. It lay on a strip of coast that ran almost perfectly north-south, considerably north of an easily identifiable cape. The other leg of the coast led southwest from the cape, in the general direction of a coastal Korean town with similar spelling, *S*ongjin. Landfall for the two-air-group strike was that cape. But instead of hanging a right for Chongjin, the strike leader hung a left and began to follow the southwest leg.

From my second-division position I was pretty sure what the problem was. I eased my division a little wide in the formation while I fumbled for my target maps; they were in a hardbound notebook, close to standard 8½-by-11-inch letter size, cumbersome to handle in a fighter cockpit. I satisfied myself that we were not on the way to Chongjin, but who was going to tell the emperor about his new clothes? With CAG Air Task Group Two Commander J.G. "Jim" Daniels leading the *Essex* strike group and Hutch Cooper leading the VF-821 contingent, it wasn't going to be me. Then I heard a soft, Kentucky-accented voice on the radio ask an innocent-sounding question; after a moment, without further conversation, the strike leader started a slow turn to the right. Hutch Cooper was a cool one.

We were not the first to visit Chongjin. The place was heavily damaged. Most of the large buildings had been holed at least once, and what rolling stock remained in the railroad yards looked uninviting as targets, mostly boxcars and no locomotives. There were numerous anti-aircraft sites on hills and other high ground around the city; these were our assigned targets. We plastered Chongjin effectively. There were newly holed structures when we finished, but no fires and no secondary explosions. My site—easy to find, just as in the briefing material—appeared to be empty; there was no apparent return fire from the position. Overall anti-aircraft fire was sporadic and inaccurate.[25]

Chongjin had been selected as an indoctrination target because it was a relatively "safe" first attempt. We now felt as competent to help win the war as anybody; at least we could find Chongjin as reliably as the people we were relieving.

We settled into a routine of flying one or two flights a day. About two-thirds of those were flights "over the beach," and one-third were combat air patrols over the carrier task group or barrier CAPs between the carrier and the land. Theoretically, enemy aircraft could come at any time.

Every time we crossed the coast, "feet dry," we could expect to be under fire part of the time. In recognition of that fact, we were awarded Air Medals, colloquially known as box-tops, in a ratio of one for every twenty missions over the beach. Combat air patrols didn't count. Crossing the coastline also had to be preplanned; that is, you couldn't stretch the patrol area of a barrier CAP so that part of your orbit was over land and thereby get credit for a combat flight. (That was the rule for most of the Korean conflict. Less than a year later, the rule was changed to one box-top for every ten flights over the peninsula and one for every twenty CAP flights, the same as our awards for combat flights. CAPs were only *potentially* combat flights; live rounds over the beach were something else! From our disengaged position safely back in the States when the new rule went into effect, some of us were less than pleased. We knew we weren't heroes, but they could at least keep the merit badge system consistent.) Higher awards like Distinguished Flying Crosses and Bronze Stars were awarded on the strength of individual citations based on a single mission or sustained accomplishment. The Legion of Merit was a command award that went to a ship or ship/air group leader—like an aircraft carrier skipper—when his command had done a noteworthy job; over the course of a full combat tour, that meant most of them.

One day I led the second VF-821 division of Panthers in a two-carrier strike on the North Korean capital of Pyongyang.[26] The attack was part of a full day of coordinated U.S. Navy and U.S. Air Force air strikes against the city. For the two carrier air groups it was a major effort. A large number of airplanes was to cross the waist of Korea from Wonsan to Pyongyang. The target city lay slightly inland, halfway between the Yalu River and what was later the Demilitarized Zone. The direct route brought us over the supporting elements of the front line where North Korean and Chinese troops were arrayed along the Main Line of Resistance. With no reason to regard us as harmless transients, the enemy anti-aircraft units would be sure to greet us if we came within range.

With injudicious disregard of the familiar, we didn't quite get everyone high enough as we went past our acquaintances at Majon-ni; an AD Skyraider caught shrapnel from a near burst, which chewed up the airplane enough to warrant sending it back to the ship with an escort. The rest of the exercise went almost as planned. The "almost" part had to do with our intended Air Force companions. The Navy had most of the flak suppression and anti-aircraft targets, but the real damage was supposed to be done by the Wild Blue Yonder folks in light blue. I am sure they got there, sometime, but they weren't around when we were, which guaranteed us the undivided attention of our North Korean hosts. My division was assigned an emplacement that contained a couple of larger-caliber guns supported by four 20-millimeter anti-aircraft guns. Even though we daisy-chained around, confirming that we had the right target, the bigger guns weren't shooting as I rolled in.

There is something about automatic weapons fire that the movies and television never seem to get right in their special effects. Tracers from your own weapons form a smooth line or arc, especially if you are turning while shooting (that last is no way to hit anything on the ground, by the way), but stuff coming the other way zigzags all over the place, higgledy-piggledy. I saw a fair amount of higgledy-piggledy on the way down. It seemed to me that one of their guns stopped firing. Out of reflex more than hope of doing further damage, I shifted my aim point before getting out of there. My number four on pulling off the target behind me said that only one gun was still firing when he rolled in. He thought it might have stopped firing before he recovered from his run. We always think something like that. We may have done some damage, but maybe not; almost certainly not as much as we thought we did. That's the way it goes.

My division was back together almost as soon as we came off target. The rest of the squadron and then the strike group rendezvoused outside the target area. The return trip was uneventful; this time we gave Majon-ni a wider berth. I was written up for a Distinguished Flying Cross for that one run. By the time I saw the result, it had been downgraded by the Seventh Fleet Medals and Awards Board to a Green Weenie (a Navy Commendation Medal) with Combat "V"; I couldn't quarrel with the decision.

Two- to four-plane road recce flights were our bread-and-butter missions, but there was in fact very little bread or butter. The enemy had learned to move his people and supplies mostly by night. The day operations had the effect of patrols to ensure the absence of activity, like a cop on a beat: as long as he is visible, there is no crime. The air group's night-fighter and night-attack detachments, flying Corsair -5Ns and night-configured ADs, reported an entirely different war from the one we saw. At night, truck convoys with or without headlights and real-live trains pulled by locomotives were the rule rather than the exception. The night-fighter detachment Officer in Charge for most of the cruise was Lieutenant Clyde W. Chapman; his excited accounts of night missions, spiced with comments like "They were shooting real bullets out there!" earned him the lasting title of "Real Bullets" Chapman. Flying about 10 percent of the total air group hours, the night flyers, according to some reports, inflicted 90 percent of the damage to enemy vehicles and people on the move.

For us day people it was a real highlight to get a radio call on the way to the beach, like "Undermine[27] So-and-So, stand by. We have a divert target for you." That usually occurred on the first daylight flight of the day. We didn't launch quite at first light, more like at pale dawn. The land mass would still be in shadows as we were vectored toward a stretch of railroad track where a train was stopped. The night people had cut the tracks in front of the locomotive and behind the boxcars. The presence of the locomotive was a tribute to the effectiveness of the track cuts, for most of the time the enemy was able to get a whole train into a tunnel before daybreak; rail cuts were usually repaired quickly with track segments and replacement ties pre-positioned along the routes.

As the four of us strung out to make individual bombing runs, an arc of 20-millimeter tracers reached into the sky. Rolling in for my first run, I saw rounds falling short, probing ineffectively in my direction. In the early light, a single 20-millimeter tracer looked the size of a basketball. I pressed on with the first of a series of bomb drops. No one-run-and-out this time; we were going to take our time and get this hummer! My first drop—we were carrying a mix of 250-pound GPs and 260-pound fragmentation bombs, three on each side—was short and ineffective. Lieutenant (jg) Shorty Keefe's drop was short too but closer; a welcome burst of steam from the locomotive followed the hit. Fragmentation damage? Maybe. Or perhaps the engineer had merely opened a valve to make us think we had done damage. That was a common ploy, especially when a locomotive was able to duck into one of the many mountain tunnels. In order to discourage repeated efforts to skip bombs into the tunnel opening, a train crew might vent all the steam they had, the intended message being "Sure kill! Go home, Yankee."

Numbers three and four of the flight straddled the target without visible effect. That was the section leader, Lieutenant (jg) Jack Wolfe, and his wingman, Ensign Hal Clark. We made our runs perpendicular to the train. It would have been easier to hit some part of the train if we were to track the long dimension, along the railroad tracks themselves; most dive or glide bombing errors are in range, not deflection. But we were after the locomotive. As a target, it was worth more than all the cars and their contents put together. The vertical side elevation of the locomotive would partially compensate for range—along the run-in line—error. Besides, if one were lucky enough to skip or throw a bomb into that inviting engine boiler, the results would be spectacular.

I saw no more 20-millimeter tracers after my first run, although I heard the sporadic popcorn popping of small-arms fire and the occasional rattle of small-caliber anti-aircraft artillery. (With pressurization turned off, we could hear the ground fire.) Methodically, we expended all our ordnance. We never got the big bang, but there were more than a couple of good hits that meant the locomotive wasn't going anywhere soon. Either because of cumulative damage or a decision of the train crew to vent steam pressure gradually, we didn't get the big geyser either. We were relieved on station by a division of Panthers from the other carrier; later reports said that they had expended most of their ordnance chewing up the boxcars.

I remember Hal Clark in another incident. He was number four in the first division of an eight-plane flight. Two divisions of F9Fs meant a specially assigned target, not a catch-as-catch-can road recce. Hutch Cooper had the lead.[28] On the way home Hal had a hung 250-pound GP. If he couldn't release it, he and an escort would fly to "King-50," an auxiliary strip down the coast, to have the bomb off-loaded. (Bombs and rockets could come off an airplane on an arrested landing; no one wanted loose ordnance flying down a crowded flight deck.) Hutch directed him to try once more to release the bomb. Hal did, in level flight from his position at the back end of the division. Ensign Clark was lucky—doubly so, it turned out.

We were over Wonsan. Wonsan was a small city at the head of the valley marking the beginning of one of our road recce routes. It sat at the southern end of a coastal plain that included Hungnam and, further inland, Hamhung, both well known as part of the Marines' evacuation route from the Chosin Reservoir. A convenient point of entry from the carriers, Wonsan had had the bejesus knocked out of it over the previous two years. It was accepted that there was nothing there worth further effort.

From my position in the second division I saw the bomb separate from the airplane. "Bombs away!" I announced over the radio—superfluously; Hal could feel and see the release (in an F9F the nose of a bomb hanging on an outboard station was visible from the cockpit).

The shape disappeared from view. Peripherally, I saw a flash. I looked down. What I saw was no puny 250-pound bomb explosion but a roaring fire capped by a pillar of expanding black smoke. He had hit an ammunition dump or a fuel storage site where no one had reason to suspect there was one. Ensign Clark was written up for a Distinguished Flying Cross, and he got the award. Damage is damage!

Hal was part of still another incident, this one commemorated in a series of pictures in the cruise book: he lost an essential part of his tail hook on landing. In the old days, an arresting hook was a single forging, a straight shaft flared and rounded at the end into a grooved shape designed to grab and retain an arresting wire. The Panthers were among the first carrier airplanes to have the new two-piece hook. Here, the tail hook shaft terminated in a small, cylindrically shaped, perpendicular stub. The stub was inserted into a matching cylindrical hole in a separate, large, hook point. The hook point had a single circumferential groove for the arresting wire. The two pieces were held together by a high-tensile-strength through-bolt. Shear loads along the hook shaft were absorbed by the stub. At least that is the way it is supposed to work. This time, on an otherwise normal landing attempt, Hal landed and grabbed the three wire—but not for long. Following what began as a normal arrestment, he found himself still moving down the flight deck until he was enveloped by the nylon straps of the barricade.

I knew how he felt; I had pioneered that very exercise in the air group. In my case I caught the two wire, leaving plenty of room for what followed. I felt a satisfying deceleration. Then something let go; the airplane was still moving. There was another slight tug, then a release. And again. And one more time. By now I was almost stopped, about to try the brakes, when I saw the towering nylon straps of the barricade looming ahead. I recognized the inevitable. I barely had time for the obligatory "Oh, shit!" when the nylon embraced the nose and wings of the airplane. The reinforced top strap virtually fell into the open cockpit on top of me.

Our CAG, Jim Daniels, had observed the proceedings. He rushed to the plane and climbed up to the cockpit, the first to arrive. "Are you all right?"

All I could think to say was, "What the hell happened?"

What had happened was this. I had caught not just the two wire but the three wire. Because the groove in the hook point was already occupied by the two wire, the three wire engaged the bottom, the toe, of the point, causing a substantial rotational moment. There was enough play in the matching pieces, the stub and the interior cylindrical hole in the hook point, to permit them to try to separate, to "stretch" the attaching bolt. The bolt stretched enough to fail. After the point separated, the stub tripped two more wires. That is why I was moving so slowly when I finally engaged the barricade. The flight deck crew found a piece of the bolt, a classic failure. It was necked down at the break just as if it had come out of a tensile load tester in a strength-of-materials laboratory. The failure was not unique, but neither was it common.

It was always entertaining for other pilots when something vital broke on an airplane the Maintenance Officer was flying. It was "Physician, heal thyself," played sideways. My counterpart in VF-23 was a nonflying mustang LDO,[29] Lieutenant Paul Lewis. Typical of the breed, Paul was a gruff, hard-bitten type who really knew his job. Fortunately for me, he was not reluctant to share his expertise. I was doubly blessed with the people I had working for me in VF-821. The maintenance crew worked hard all the time, but never harder than on replenishment days and the nights before replenishment.

Replenish meant to restock the carriers with the necessaries of fighting a war. Replenishment is self-explanatory except for the techniques involved. The ships were floating around in the middle of the Sea of Japan; there were no docks to come alongside. At an appointed day and time Task Force 77 rendezvoused with ships of the "train," a separate task group consisting of tankers for black oil and aviation fuel, ammunition ships, and stores ships. In turn the combat ships went alongside the individual replenishment ships, connected themselves with overhead transfer lines and fuel hoses, as at your friendly neighborhood gas station, and filler 'er up.

Our usual routine on the line was to fly three days and replenish on the fourth. Formidable as *Essex* ships seemed in their time, they were small compared with their modern counterparts; high-intensity flight operations could empty them of "beans, bombs, and bullets" in a couple of days. Especially critical was aviation fuel. Fuel was AvGas, grade 115/145,[30] which was required for the big radial engines. Since there wasn't the capacity aboard those ships to store two different kinds of fuel, at sea the jets burned 115/145 too.

There were penalties: Every time we switched from one kind of fuel to the other—on the beach the jets normally burned JP-4 and later JP-5, both of which were mostly kerosene—we had to reset all the fuel controls. Also, jet fuel was almost a full pound per gallon heavier; we could actually carry more pounds of jet fuel in the airplanes' fuel tanks. Then there was lead. To achieve that high "octane"[31] rating, 115/145 contained a lot of lead, and everything in the engines downstream of the burner cans became liberally coated with residue. That included the insides of the tail pipes and, especially, the turbine wheels. The blades became coated with a thick, sick-looking layer of multi-hued junk—predominantly yellow, but containing blues, purples, and reds as well. The thickness and irregularity of the coating must have disrupted the airflow through the turbines so as to decrease efficiency. The material must also have been highly toxic, although there were no specific attributions of illness, then or since. About one hour of JP operation would clean the blades off good as new. Aboard ship we just put up with the mess.

We tried to schedule periodic maintenance inspections, major and minor "checks," for replenishment days so as to minimize aircraft downtime. For each level of check, we pulled the tails off, literally. The F9F was built that way for maintenance access; the entire tail section was bolted to the rest of the airplane just aft of the wing root by a number of oversize studs held on by locking nuts. For the minor checks the engine's tail pipe stayed on. The minor inspection was relatively superficial for major engine parts. The major checks required removal of the tail pipes and even a teardown of burner cans.

A predictable pattern evolved for replenishment eves. Flight operations stopped just before sunset. The decks were "spotted" with a best guess as to the next launch. The sick birds and those scheduled for maintenance were stashed on the hangar deck; aircraft-handling officers had to be lucky magicians with a talent for working complex puzzles, especially with the awkward wing-folding arrangement of the two Panther squadrons. Maintenance work started immediately after operations ceased and continued through the night. Barney Barnes, the Power Plants Officer, and I oversaw what was going on closely until about eight at night. We always hoped that major decisions could be made by then on the one or two airplanes undergoing checks. Do we change this now or wait until next time? Is this part serviceable for another sixty hours? Is that a cracked turbine blade or just a harmless nick? Ultimately we retired to my room or Barney's for an hourlong "consultation"; on a legally dry naval vessel in the middle of a war zone, we were occasionally joined by an unauthorized third party, Jack Daniels or Jim Beam. Along about midnight there would be a call from Chief Hieldbrandt with a question. Barney and I then joined the night-check crew gathered around an airplane in hangar bay 3.

Typically there would be something to look at on an engine. More often than not the problem would involve a minor check, on an airplane with the tail pipe still installed. In the finest scientific fashion, an engine mech striker would stick a long swab handle lewdly up the tail pipe. Under the direction of Chief Hieldbrandt, he would slowly rotate the turbine wheel.

"There. Stop right there! See, that's the one. What do you think?"

The three of us would peer up the tail pipe, illuminated by flashlights and a high-intensity trouble light, and attempt a diagnosis. If there was any doubt, first the tail pipe came off. Then, if the diagnosis was bad, we were stuck with an engine change, not desirable at all. Sometimes the question was easier. It might involve a burner basket on an already disassembled can. Hydraulic problems were more frequently encountered but required fewer judgment calls. Hydraulics either work or they don't work; they leak or they don't leak.

Because of the deck spotting problems peculiar to Panthers—those outboard-folding wings again—VF-23 and VF-821 ultimately came to use each other's airplanes interchangeably. We got to know their airplanes'—and their pilots'—idiosyncrasies as well as our own. It was common to schedule one or two backup "spare" aircraft for each launch. The spares briefed the assigned missions for each squadron, then launched as needed, joining whichever squadron was short in order of takeoff rather than in accordance with squadron affiliation. The two squadrons worked well together. What's more important, we appeared to like each other. No other time have I known two embarked carrier squadrons, especially fighter squadrons, to be so close to each other for so long and still part as friends.

On the first cruise in Corsairs, VF-821's main effort had been directed toward supply-line interdiction. They had the damage assessment photos to show that they had done something useful—not just simple rail cuts, but substantial bridge drops and road damage that could not easily be repaired by an unsophisticated enemy. But by the time we got there, the enemy was smarter, and he was not as dependent on some of those supply routes. General Ridgway accepted a defensive strategy in the fall of 1951; by the spring of 1952 even the Marines recognized that although their tactics were generically offensive, their role had become defensive.

For the aviators it was not hard to get shot at, but it was hard to do something useful while being shot at. Shorty Keefe and I risked our necks one day flying up a North Korean recce route that followed a twisting riverbed; that was the easiest place to build the road. The further north we went, the steeper and more potentially entrapping became the snow-capped hills on either side of the narrow valley. In the lead, with Shorty in loose trail behind me, I racked the airplane up on a wing to negotiate a sharp turn, and there at a bend in the road was an honest-to-God tank, just sitting there.

I leveled my wings, dropped the nose, and added full power. Recognizing that the approach was poor, I armed already selected rocket stations. Yelling at Shorty on the radio, I pickled one off and arced around for another approach. I was surprisingly close. Shorty was even

F9F-2 Panther of VF-721 returning from a strike over North Korea. The rough terrain is typical. (Grumman History Center)

closer. On the second run I actually hit the damn thing; there was a smallish plume of black smoke after the rocket explosion. Shorty's next hit was also very close. Significantly, we saw neither signs of life nor hostile return fire. Jubilant nonetheless, we headed back to the ship, satisfied for once to have found a suitable target. Our excited debriefing of the Air Intelligence Officer in the back of the ready room got Hutch Cooper's attention. He joined us. After hearing our story and consulting the map, the skipper treated us to a smile. "That thing has been there since the winter of the Reservoir."

Toward the end, anything that moved north of the 38th parallel was fair game, the idea being that all the folks up there were engaged in helping the enemy. We in our airplanes were all over the place. Therefore, only something that someone considered important would be on the move during the daytime. Even a lowly oxcart was a desirable target. That is not a wild invention. Oxcarts often did carry material for enemy troops. They had quick-release harnesses; the moment a driver detected an approaching airplane, he would cut the ox loose from the cart and dive over the side, frequently into the nearest ditch.

On a coastal road east and north of Songjin, I endeavored to destroy just such a vital enemy supply link. I made my run in a shallow glide from seaward perpendicular to the road with the hills rising behind. With my four 20-millimeter cannon armed I found the target in my gunsight. My elusive enemy wasted no time in releasing his fifteen-dollar ox from his five-dollar cart and summarily abandoned ship onto the side of the road. Frankly, I felt better chasing an ox down the road than some anonymous man who may or may not have been carrying anything harmful to the United Nations. Besides that, the ox was a more important target. By now I am really concentrating, scattering tracers all around, but not into, this speedy bovine critter. I am deliberately flying slow so as to prolong firing time, when something enters my peripheral vision. Those damn hills! They are steeper than I thought. I bring up the speed brakes, add full power, and hope I can clear the first hill. It wasn't in a class with James Michener's hero, shot in the butt in a ditch full of Korean night soil, but I was trying very hard to bust a half-million-dollar Navy airplane, and my million-dollar ass, all for a target optimistically valued at less than twenty-five American dollars on anybody's open Korean market.

Air Task Group Two was more fortunate than most air groups. Our pilots suffered some burn casualties from the consequences of enemy fire, a small number of other wounds, and a handful of shootdowns. Lieutenant (jg) John Lavra of VA-55 got some bad facial burns when his AD was hit by flak. The wounds ultimately healed, but it was a long, painful process. Lieutenant (jg) Joe Kanevsky of VF-23 took a round of 20-millimeter fire that did even more damage to his elbow than to the inside of his cockpit. He spent the better part of a line period in the Yokosuka Naval Hospital; he liked his nurse so much that he later married her. An aggressive young jaygee from VF-23, Dan Musetti, was shot down on a road recce. The rest of the flight never even saw him go down. A particularly tough loss was Lieutenant Al Nauman, Operations Officer of VF-871, the Corsair squadron. Al was considered one of the real cool hands of the whole air group. He was smart, experienced, well liked, and a fine pilot. Outside of the immediate target area at about ten thousand feet, normally a fairly safe altitude, he got bagged by a round of heavy anti-aircraft fire that shouldn't have been there.

We had our close calls. There is a spectacular color photograph of an AD Skyraider sitting in the arresting gear of the USS *Essex*, burning furiously. That was Lieutenant Roger Nelson, one of the more solid citizens of VA-55. Roger took a 37-millimeter hit in the accessory section of the big R-3350 engine. It took out one cylinder completely and most of a second; that the engine continued to run at all was miraculous. His remaining problem wasn't so much the loss of power from two cylinders as the potential for fire, not to mention two large new holes through which essential lubricating oil could escape. Somehow he nursed the airplane from the beach to the task force, anticipating the need to ditch at any time. "I got it this far. Might as well try to land," he figured.

He had a large, interested audience as he approached the groove. The aircraft was trailing white smoke and a visible mist of leaking fuel. Oil was streaming down the left side of the fuselage as the Skyraider neared the ramp. No nervous-Nelly twitching and Dutch rolling on final for Roger; he came down the groove steady as a rock, just like always. OK, three wire! When the airplane jerked to a stop, the whole thing burst into flames. Rog was out of the cockpit instantaneously, racing along the wing like a quarter horse out of the chute. He didn't even get singed.

The flight deck fire crew put out the fire in short order. The aluminum skin had not burned through, but it was papyrus thin and shrunk onto the stringers and bulkheads. It was almost transparent; you could see the details of the underlying strength members. The airplane was a "strike,"[32] not even good for parts. It was pushed over the side.

Lieutenant (jg) L. T. Freitas was our only noncombat pilot fatality. The accident was puzzling, although there appears to be a logical explanation. Freitas was a quiet, studious type, whose manner contrasted with the ebullience and raucousness of most of VF-23's other junior officers. I remember his extraordinary helmet. An issue of *Esquire* magazine had featured a centerfold, not the kind associated with *Playboy*: a wonderfully detailed color reproduction of a golden eagle–like bird, wings spread. The original of the design had been important in an older culture, perhaps Mayan or Aztec. Freitas painstakingly copied the fierce, beautiful piece of heraldry onto his own golden-yellow Navy hard hat. He did it with great care. It took a long time; he wore another helmet in the meantime. When finished, it was beautiful. For the Navy of that period it was unique; our helmets were ribbed objects so essentially unattractive that it didn't occur to anyone else to decorate one.

That day I stood next to Freitas on the escalator up to the flight deck. He had his new helmet; it must have been the first or second flight he had worn it. On the escalator and walking across the flight deck we talked. Not anything about the mission, just talk. We were in different flights. I admired the helmet. Then it was time to man airplanes. Our airplanes were parked together just forward of the port deck edge elevator, tails angled out over the water. As the VF-23 airplanes alternated on the two catapults, the deck emptied in front of us. Angled as I was, I had a clear view of the port catapult when Freitas positioned for launch. The cat fired. The takeoff started normally. He cleared the deck with plenty of end speed and started the usual clearing turn; from the port cat the turn was to the left. The angle of bank hesitated, then increased—greater than normal, but still all right. Then his turn tightened, and before I could process what I was seeing the Panther plunged into the sea. At 25-plus knots of ship speed I lost sight of the impact point almost immediately. Then a yellow-clad figure appeared in front of my airplane, energetically directing me to the same catapult. I had a job to do. I would think about Freitas later.

Within a week Lieutenant Hal Crumbo was launched from the starboard catapult in one of our airplanes. Once airborne, he sucked up his landing gear and started his clearing turn to the right. The stick was so stiff it would hardly move. In testing the feel he moved the stick to the left; it moved easily and too far, and the aircraft bank shifted toward the left. It looked like Freitas all over again. He grabbed the stick with both hands and got enough right deflection to level the wings. He climbed out of the pattern, still hanging on for dear life. At a couple of thousand feet he sneaked his left hand off the stick long enough to hit the mike button and declare an emergency. At altitude he entered a racetrack orbit, a racetrack with l-o-n-g legs so as to minimize the turns. He found he could fly wings-level with one hand for short intervals by bracing an elbow against his knee. That way he could manipulate the throttle and talk on the radio while flying the airplane. Turns to the right still took two hands. He awaited completion of the launch. He couldn't land or head for an abort field—he was going to need an escort—until the other aircraft had cleared the flight deck.

What Crumbo had experienced was a classic example of the aileron boost cylinder failure described earlier. Once he recovered from the left bank and started a climb, satisfied that he wasn't going to die immediately, he reached quickly toward the right console and turned off the aileron boost switch. Nothing happened! The bad aileron boost was still on line. Now he was stuck with his two-handed monster. Electing to recover aboard ship rather than go to the beach, he made a surprisingly good approach and landing.

Aileron boost failure had probably been Freitas's problem as well, with or without a concurrent boost switch solenoid failure. That Hal's intended first turn had been to the right might have given him just the extra time he needed to stay out of the water. If our diagnosis was correct, each failure was essentially instantaneous. Both airplanes had checked out on preflight. The double-whammy acceleration impacts of the Mk 4B catapults may have contributed. Not that it mattered for Freitas. We couldn't change the results.

One time toward the end of the cruise it felt as if we were going to get serious about our war. The normal complement of Task Force

77 was two carriers, augmented to three during changeovers. For this exercise, we had four. The targets ranged from Hyesanjin on the Manchurian border, some sixty miles from the coast, to the northeastern tip where North Korea, Manchuria, and the USSR come together close to Vladivostok. For once there were targets of apparent value, in particular the oil refinery at Aoji. The rail yards and roundhouse at Rashin were worthwhile but showed the results of prior visits—not very accurate prior visits, judging from the dispersion of old bomb craters. There were other targets as well. After our daylong series of strikes was over, assessment photos showed substantial damage by our four attack carrier air groups.

I was scheduled for two TARCAPs (target combat air patrols), one in the morning and one in the afternoon. I made the morning flight, leading a four-plane division in a buffer zone between the Hyesanjin target area and the three-way border. We were in a loose two-section spread, flying a typical lazy CAP racetrack. In accordance with conditioning and doctrine, we scanned constantly, everywhere. These were eyeball scans; there were no radars in our airplanes and no fighter director net this far from the ships of the task force.

Our visual search was not ecumenical; the Russian border received special attention, and we were not disappointed. Four MiG-15s appeared just on the other side of the border. Their orbiting rectangle emulated the movements of our oblate oval. Once every orbit, we headed directly toward each other. Was someone going to cross this time? The question must have been the same on each side. This is the story that wasn't; nothing happened. After most of an hour on station we returned to the task force and landed uneventfully.

The prevailing winds in the Sea of Japan were out of the north. The carriers, constantly at Flight Quarters, spent most of the day steaming into the wind, launching and recovering aircraft. Inexorably, the whole task force moved north, toward China and Russia. The unaccustomed offensive activity and the constant northward movement of the carriers did not go unnoticed by our northern neighbors. Vice Admiral J. J. "Jocko" Clark, of "Fighting Lady" fame, was intent on completing his mission; if there was a "no cross" line of demarcation in the Sea of Japan, Jocko ignored it.

A flight of F9F-5s from another carrier was assigned a BARCAP (barrier combat air patrol). One airplane never made it to station for some reason; another did not actively participate because of a mechanical problem. The two remaining airplanes encountered a flight of seven Russian MiGs. The lead wore a different paint scheme, as if he were from a different unit; maybe it was a training flight suddenly involved in a war. With higher speed and more maneuverability, they began to make runs on the Panthers. Before it was over, the two F9Fs had claimed two kills and a probable. Both made it back to their carrier; both had been shot up, one severely. According to secondhand briefings that filtered through the task force most of the U.S. effective hits were made as the MiG's recovered from their runs, some of which were made with open speed brakes to prolong firing time. I spent that late afternoon in the ready room, as did most of other fighter squadrons' pilots, in anticipation of the need for a full-blown fighter sweep. That didn't happen either.

Throughout all of this our base, our home away from home, had been Naval Station Yokosuka, Japan. We saw it only in ten- to sixteen-day chunks. The Land of the Rising Sun, home of the God Emperor, had been defeated by a Barbarian Western Nation. What could the people's attitude be to these foreigners who now ruled their homeland? The answer was neither apparent nor what some of us expected. For outward behavior at least, the answer may lie somewhere in the strength of the Japanese character, their essential civilization and a centuries-old tradition of politeness and respect in human intercourse. Here was this Japanese naval base supporting American men-of-war, fighting a war in Asia; it felt strange. The workmen were good. When they finished repairing the wooden planks of our beat-up flight deck, it looked like cabinet work compared with what an American navy yard would have done. I was among those to be enchanted by the country and the people.

We left Yokosuka for the last time on 25 January 1953. We arrived in San Diego on 6 February 1953. I had orders to a development squadron, VX-4, at Point Mugu, California. I would detach from VF-821, redesignated VF-143, on my return from leave.

Chapter 7
F9F-6/8T Cougar

HE KOREAN WAR was partly a developmental laboratory for jet fighter combat. Concentrated over the northwestern quadrant of the Korean peninsula and south of the Yalu River, "MiG Alley" featured swarms of U.S. Air Force F-86 Sabres and Russian-built Chinese MiG-15s. The northern border of Korea, following the contours of the Yalu and Tumen rivers, runs roughly northeast to southwest. That places the western end of the Korean-Chinese border substantially closer to the Main Line of Resistance and the South Korean capital of Seoul than the eastern end; if one is to invade or strike South Korea by air, the trip is shorter from the west. Military responsibility of the U.S. forces was split by a vertical administrative boundary down the middle of the peninsula. This arbitrary division was a substantial contributor to the disaster of the winter of the Chosin Reservoir, and in addition to not being based on topography, it inhibited cross-boundary communication and liaison. Cumbersome for the ground forces, the division had merit for the two U.S. air forces (U.S. Air Force and Navy; three, if you treat the Marines separately).

The aircraft carriers of Task Force 77 needed the sea room and deep water of the Sea of Japan to operate effectively; the narrow, largely shoal-draft, Yellow Sea off the west coast of Korea was suitable only for smaller "Jeep" carriers (a CVE manned by U.S. Marine Corps pilots and a small Royal Navy carrier with embarked Fleet Air Arm squadrons operated propeller-driven airplanes in the Yellow Sea for most of the war). The international waters of the Sea of Japan led north all the way to the three-way Korean-Manchurian-Russian border. The range and load-carrying ability of the carrier-based tactical aircraft made it possible for the ships of the task force to operate routinely east and south of Wonsan.

Thus, when MiG-15s crossed the Yalu from their western bases they encountered Air Force F-86s, not Navy/Marine Panthers or Banshees. This may have been fortunate, because despite their good record in engagements with the MiG-15, the straight-wing Navy jets were not a performance match for it. And even the spectacular number of MiG kills by the F-86 is attributed more to the skill and training of the American pilots than to the superiority of the F-86; a common evaluation is that the MiG-15 was marginally superior to the F-86, especially in acceleration and maneuverability.[1]

At close to the same thrust-to-weight ratio as their straight-wing cousins, the swept-wing airplanes achieved level-flight speeds on the order of Mach 0.9; contemporary straight-wing airplanes were Mach-number limited[2] to speeds in the range of Mach 0.82 to Mach 0.86, depending on the particular airplane. More important, the swept-wing airplanes were transonic in a dive, albeit just barely. The difference was made possible by the swept wings.

The reason lay in aerodynamic and compressibility theory explored by the Germans toward the end of World War II.[3] In air, a moving body compresses or squeezes the molecules together as it accelerates. The resistance to acceleration, drag, increases relatively slowly until a limit is approached. At that limit (the speed of sound), the molecules of the fluid (air) have been pushed so close together that the normally compressible gas behaves like an incompressible liquid. The precipitous drag rise in the region near the speed of sound is responsible for early belief that the speed of sound represented an insurmountable barrier.

The movement of a boat through water may help illustrate the phenomenon. A boat with a sharp, thin bow will produce a smaller bow wave—a visible "piling up" of water in front—than a boat with a blunt bow (the analogy is incomplete because part of what makes a boat's bow wave visible is the foam, a feature of turbulence rather than compressibility). Similarly, an accelerating airplane with thin wings can get closer to the speed of sound than one with blunter, fatter wings before the "piling up" of air immediately ahead produces noticeable compressibility effects. These effects include local shock waves that can form on various parts and protuberances of an airplane. Some higher-performance propeller fighters, less aerodynamically clean than the early jets, encountered these effects at speeds as low as Mach 0.6. Depending on where the local shock waves formed, such an airplane with mechanical, unboosted controls could become uncontrollable, adding to the myth of the killer "sound barrier."

That myth was destroyed by Chuck Yeager's supersonic flight in a rocket-powered airplane in 1947, but it was a while before conventionally powered turbojet airplanes routinely duplicated his feat of "breaking the sound barrier." In the meantime we approached it incrementally with design features like swept wings.

It is the perpendicular component of the relative airstream (the air the airplane is flying through) that determines compressibility effects. An airplane with a straight-wing leading edge presents essentially its entire leading edge perpendicular, or "normal," to the airflow. This perpendicular component can be reduced by sweeping the wings back through some angle; one way of putting it is that this fools the compressible air into thinking that the airplane is flying slower than it is. Theory stipulates that the wings must be swept back at least 30 to 35 degrees to be effective. When an airplane so designed is flying at close to Mach 1.0, the perpendicular component of the free airstream is impacting the wings at only about Mach 0.83. It is not a coincidence that the wings of the F-86, MiG-15, and Grumman Cougar are all swept back almost exactly 35 degrees.[4]

The first flights of the F-86, MiG-15, and F9F Panther all took place in 1947. The first flight of the Cougar was in September of 1951. Grumman was not guilty of heel dragging; indeed, work on a swept-wing version had started almost as soon as the first Panther started flying. Instead, it might be said that Mikoyan and North American acted boldly in embarking on swept-wing designs as early as they did. The MiG-15, made possible by the availability of the British Rolls-Royce Nene engine, flew six years before the first British swept-wing aircraft.[5]

North American Aviation was working on the design that became the U.S. Navy FJ Fury when the U.S. Army Air Corps submitted a request for a somewhat larger airplane. The Fury, which saw only limited production, was the Navy's second operational jet airplane (the first was the McDonnell FH Phantom). It has been reported that in an effort to compete with the oncoming second-generation Panthers and Banshees, North American proposed a number of design changes to the Fury, including swept wings. The Navy chose the newer airplanes instead. Meanwhile, North American delayed response to the Army request for a full year in order to propose a swept-wing design.[6] The result was the F-86. Notwithstanding the Navy's rejection of a swept-wing Fury, when that service finally ordered Navy F-86s in 1951, they were called FJ-2s, implying a follow-on to the Fury rather than a new design, even though they were substantially different airplanes.[7] The Grumman Cougar was the Navy's first swept-wing fighter.

General Description

It was more than naval service conservatism that delayed sweeping the wings of carrier fighters; there was apprehension that the aerodynamics

F9F-6 Cougar taxiing forward on an *Essex*-class carrier. The partially extended tail hook suggests that the airplane has just landed. Note the partially open fuselage blow-in doors, typical of the F9F series. (Grumman History Center)

of swept wings might not be compatible with carrier aviation. An extreme view was that the emergence of swept-wing fighters would ultimately make aircraft carriers obsolete.[8] Spurred on by swirling contrails south of the Yalu, in the early 1950s the Navy examined several design proposals for swept-wing fighters. Among the most attractive was the simple expedient of putting swept wings and tail surfaces on the existing Panther airframe. Grumman's design G-93 came into being almost as soon as Panthers started flying; the first three Cougars, based on that design, were built from standard F9F-5 airframes.[9]

The Cougar incorporated other new design features in addition to the 35-degree wing sweep. The vertical tail was split at the horizontal stabilizer into two separately controllable pieces; the bottom portion was controlled conventionally by the rudder pedals, the top portion driven by a yaw damper. One of the nastier characteristics of swept lifting surfaces is directional, or yaw, instability. Virtually all airplanes with swept or delta planforms have yaw dampers. The lack of a yaw damper can be simply annoying over much of the flight regime in that an airplane may constantly hunt directionally—the pilot can feel the airplane wandering around under his butt. At the extremes of the airplane's operational envelope, yaw instability can be disastrous; an airplane that suddenly decides to fly sideways at high indicated airspeeds might break apart. Perhaps the best known of the North American Aviation test pilots, George Welsh, was killed when that happened to an F-100 that had been equipped for test purposes with a short vertical tail.

One Grumman test pilot had a more benign experience in the XF9F-6: the top portion of the vertical tail simply came off in flight. In true Grumman Iron Works fashion the airplane flew home just as if nothing had happened. It flew so well that the configuration was further evaluated in two subsequent flights. Stability and handling qualities were judged to be fine for all usual phases of flight (except carrier landing approaches).

Instead of conventional ailerons the Cougar had hydraulically operated spoilers on the top surfaces of the wings. Spoilers could kill lift, and thus be effective, over a wider flight envelope than ailerons. The usual trailing-edge ailerons operate by physically changing the camber of the wing, selectively controlling lift on each wing, thereby controlling roll or bank. For that to work properly, the airflow over the wing must be well behaved over the airplane's useful flight envelope. For swept wings, spanwise flow—that is, airflow along the wings toward the tips—is much increased over that of straight wings. The further the air travels over an airfoil, the fatter the boundary layer of dead air immediately adjacent to the surface becomes. The width of that boundary layer and accompanying turbulence can be significant toward the wing tips, near which ailerons are normally placed for maximum effectiveness. For any wing, stall tends to occur first at the tips. One of the first things to go is aileron effectiveness. It is worse for swept wings.

Wing spoilers, similar to those seen on sailplanes today, were an intriguing solution. These devices were normally flush with the wings. When the stick was moved laterally, as for a conventional aileron control input, a small fencelike device came up out of one wing, disrupting the airflow. Reacting to the resulting loss of lift, that wing would drop into the bank the pilot was commanding. For the most part the pilot felt no difference compared with conventional ailerons.

Unlike the sailplane versions, which are mechanically operated, the Cougar spoilers were hydraulically driven—and hydraulic controls bring problems. What happens in the event of loss of hydraulic pressure? That is what backup hydraulics are for. How about another kind of failure that causes one spoiler to open and *stay* open? Or simply not to open at all? Those are nasty problems indeed, which fortunately did not occur often.

As a breed, pilots are inherently more conservative than they like to appear. The aura of derring-do and exploration of the unknown has a strong foundation in fact, but aviators prefer to be absolutely sure of everything, except perhaps that one new area or frontier they may be exploring on purpose. They are mistrustful of new devices and gadgets that contribute only incrementally to the whole. Thus it was with wing spoilers, "flying tails," and other innovations of the swept-wing airplanes.

Take spoilers, for instance. Airplanes with ailerons roll/bank about the longitudinal axis of the airplane. They respond to an increase in lift of one wing and a decrease in lift of the other, and the rotating fuselage remains right where it is. A spoiler airplane, by contrast, rolls or banks by simply decreasing lift in one wing. Theoretically, then, its center of rotation is the center of lift of the unspoiled wing; the fuselage (the center of mass of the airplane) and the spoiled wing both descend a foot or so, depending on the size of the airplane and the steepness of the bank. Some hangar flyers concluded from this that the new spoilers would present problems in tight formation flying, especially in a mixed formation of aileron and spoiler airplanes.[10] Others were afraid that a low turn in a landing approach would cause unintended contact with the ground. But those and other fears generally stayed where they belonged, firmly in the heads of the concluders. There were other concerns more worthy of attention.

The Cougar's horizontal tail was also swept. The stabilizer/elevator combination had two operating modes. One mode was conventional in that the entire stabilizer could be moved in response to longitudinal trim control. Pitch control was input through the usual trailing-edge elevator. The arrangement is similar to that of some 1930s biplanes where trim was exercised by moving the leading edge of the horizontal stabilizer up and down instead of by elevator trailing-edge tabs. The Cougar's other pilot-selectable mode incorporated a power-boosted "flying tail" with linked elevators and artificial feel. Pitch control inputs, by conventional fore and aft movement of the stick, moved the whole horizontal tail. In this configuration the elevator followed stabilizer motion through a mechanical linkage similar to a linked tab. The design feature was similar to an arrangement in the F-86E, which had entered production in December of 1950 after over five hundred F-86s had already been built.[11] The purpose of the flying tail was to provide additional pitch control authority, particularly during transonic flight. The F-86E modification was a result of research experience with Yeager's Bell X-1 and the XP-86.

F9F-6 deliveries commenced in November of 1952. In the rush to get airplanes to the fleet—the Korean War was still in progress—early airplanes were delivered to squadrons with some desirable features not yet activated; these included yaw dampers and the flying tails. When the Korean "Police Action" ended in July of 1953, VF-191 at Naval Air Station Moffett Field and VF-24 at NAS Alameda, California, already had airplanes. The squadrons were commanded by Lieutenant Commander Robert "Bob" Elder and my former Bearcat skipper, Commander Robert W. "Duke" Windsor, respectively. The impatience was understandable. It is safe to assume that these naval aviators had visions of establishing a Navy "Mig Alley" as soon as they could get to Korea.

The first thirty F9F-6s—including the three prototype or "X" models, which had been built from F9F-5 airframes—had the same Pratt & Whitney J48-P-6 engine as the F9F-5; the rest of the F9F-6s used the P-8 version of the same engine. The F9F-7 airplanes were equipped with the Allison J33 engine. (In this the Navy followed the precedent established with the F9F-2 and -3 and the F9F-4 and -5, alternating between Pratt & Whitney and Allison engines for backup purposes.) By now the J33 was recognized as not really competitive, with about 1,000 pounds less thrust than the J48. For that reason the Navy and Grumman probably would have preferred to have all F9F-6s, but contract commitments undoubtedly influenced the total F9F-7 production buy of 168.

Maximum speed of the F9F-6 was 650 mph at sea level, 590 mph at thirty-five thousand feet, at a combat weight of 16,244 pounds. Maximum aircraft carrier weight was 18,450 pounds.[12]

A total of 649 F9F-6s were produced, including the three X models. There were sixty F9F-6P photo planes. Many F9F-6s were later converted to F9F-6D drones. (These were the Navy's first full-size, high-performance maneuverable target drones; VX-4 and the Naval Missile Center, Point Mugu, California, were energetically shooting AIM-7E and AIM-9C and -D air-to-air missiles at some of those surviving drones as late as 1967.)

The final development of the F9F series was the F9F-8. Grumman's design G-99 featured many changes over the previous aircraft in the series, and the F9F-8 finally wore in one package many of the features that are today considered standard for high-performance jet fighters. Among the changes over the -6 were a sawtooth leading edge in which the chord of the outer wing panel is greater than the inner. (Sound familiar? Check the wing planforms of the F-8 Crusader, the F-4 Phantom II, the Israeli Kfir, the French Mirage, and the McDonnell-Douglas F-18 Hornet, among others.) That notch, along with other benefits, inhibits the spanwise airflow that can be troublesome for swept wings. The F9F-8 continued the use of thin, longitudinal "stall fences" on top of the wings to address the same problem by physically interrupting spanwise flow (similar fences are evident on F-86s, MiG-15s, and other contemporary airplanes). The increased outer chord also provided greater lift, particularly at high angles of attack, which improved low-speed handling. The wing trailing-edge fillet was extended back to the end of the fuselage. Later F9F-8s had boundary layer splitter plates between the engine air intakes and the fuselage; the purpose was to prevent the static air of the boundary layer from choking the flow of air into the engine under some conditions of flight. Variations on this theme are evident in virtually all of today's aircraft that have engine air intakes adjacent to the fuselage. Grumman engineers did not invent all of these features, but they recognized their value.

The basic armament and mission of the various Cougars remained essentially constant except for the F9F-8B variants, which had a nuclear-weapon-delivery capability. The F9F-8 was the only U.S. airplane for which I ever heard postulated an "X-mission"; this great idea was conceived during the period when U.S. Navy carrier aviation and the U.S. Air Force Tactical Air Command were both part of the preplanned nuclear deterrent force. This was the plan: Launched from its aircraft carrier base, the Cougar could get all the way to its planned target and *most* of the way back. At a precisely planned moment, the returning pilot was expected to eject from his fuel-exhausted airplane and land in the waiting arms of a destroyer, sitting in exactly the right place at the right time; this was supposed to happen without benefit of radio communications, forbidden for tactical reasons. When the nuclear mission was turned over to airplanes with greater range, there were many relieved Cougar pilots.

There were 601 F9F-8 airplanes and 110 F9F-8P photoreconnaissance airplanes; the Cougars the Blue Angels flew were F9F-8s.[13] The last of the Cougars was the F9F-8T, which first flew in 1956. This tandem-seat trainer had its fuselage extended for a second seat, two fewer 20-millimeter cannon, and a reduced armament load. Otherwise it was representative of the single-seat F9F-8s that were then still-active fleet airplanes; it even retained the F9F-8's in-flight refueling probe. The last of the four hundred Cougar F9F-8Ts was retired from service by the training squadron VT-4 in February of 1974. Its replacement was another long-lived Navy airplane, the TA-4 Skyhawk.

There was a time when I though the F9F-8T might be the Airplane That Never Was. When the Twogar, as some wag called it, first flew in 1956, I was in the Airframe Design Division of the Bureau of Aeronautics, responsible for collecting and maintaining operating flight restrictions for all Navy airplanes. A Marine major named John Glenn, assigned to the Aircraft Division, had program management responsibility for Grum-

Prototype F9F-8T in gray paint. Most F9F-8Ts, including this airplane in later photographs, were orange and white. The long boom is a test pitot tube. The wing root fillet extends the length of the fuselage to the tail pipe. (Grumman History Center)

man airplanes.[14] Grumman had by then followed an interesting failure called the F10F Jaguar[15] with the all-new F9F-9 Tiger. By no stretch of the imagination an "F9F," the Tiger pioneered a number of innovations, including extensive use of complex forgings and implementation of the so-called area rule.[16] The F9F designation was an effort to circumvent a current congressional edict against development of a *new* fighter. (So far as I know, no member of the naval service was subjected to the ministrations of a special prosecutor or went to trial for this blatant disregard of congressional intent.) The designation was later changed to F11F.

The Tiger was a good high-performance airplane, but it had short-comings, notably short range and low endurance. Endurance was so low as to bring into question the airplane's ability to meet Navy aircraft carrier cycle time requirements. Worse, the extent of these shortcomings came to light late in the airplane's development—so late, it was believed by some in the Bureau of Aeronautics, as to indicate intent to mislead by the airframe contractor. Some senior folks in BuAer were downright irritated with Grumman. This occurred at the very time a decision was to be made on a new trainer. It did not look good for the F9F-8T.

There was an alternative available in the Lockheed T2V. The T2V, essentially a new airplane, was based on the older T-33, which in turn was a two-seat version of the original P-80 Shooting Star. The T2V bore a strong family resemblance to its earlier cousins and to the F-94. The F-94 was a Lockheed all-weather fighter with basically the same configuration as its predecessors, including straight wings; the F-94C, which had wings of a new design, was reported to be marginally transonic.

Despite the family resemblance, the T2V was cosmetically and structurally different from those airplanes. Among the differences was that it met the Navy requirement for carrier suitability, beefed-up structure, tail hook, and all. The airplane's development history, however, ensured other limitations. The Navy wanted an advanced trainer, one as close to current and future fleet airplanes as possible. The T2V, however, did not have the available higher-speed wing of the F-94C, which would have facilitated flight close to the transonic region; it was not a gunnery airplane; and its straight wings could not provide training and experience with the sometimes spooky aerodynamic characteristics of swept-wing airplanes, fast becoming the new standard. To more than one of us in BuAer, the advantages of the F9F-8T were so overwhelming that it seemed that only excessive cost could tip the decision toward Lockheed. That did not seem likely, since Lockheed was perceived to be a more expensive supplier than Grumman.

It came as a surprise, then, when rumors spread through the rickety wooden halls of the "W" building that Lockheed was to be selected. It was more than a surprise to future astronaut and senator John Glenn; he sensed a substantial injustice in the making. What was going on may not have been a collective Navy fit of pique with Grumman, but it felt like it. He called a meeting, not in his own shop, the Fighter Branch, where insurrection in the making may have been apparent, but in the Transport and Trainer Branch, the home of the T2V. I was invited, as was the Class Desk Officer for the T2V, Lieutenant Commander Glenn Lambert. There were other attendees, including Navy civilian engineers. Singly and together we were to come up with documented justification as to why the F9F-8T was the logical choice. That could be a risky business if we were to be in the position of fighting City Hall in BuAer— a very senior City Hall.

It would make a better story if our collective wisdom had prevailed over that of our superiors, but that isn't the way it happened. Common sense prevailed with us—we decided to lay low and see what developed—and with the decision makers. There was a small production run of T2Vs but nothing approaching the four hundred F9F-8Ts that were to serve the Navy well for almost twenty years.

How It Flew

Although I flew the airplane only once, I had a close association with the F9F-6 shortly after the first deliveries to VF-191 and VF-24 in the spring of 1953. Later, in 1960, I flew the F9F-8T for a back-in-the-saddle-again refresher in the F8U Crusader RAG (replacement air group) squadron VF-124. With that small data base, much of what I have to say about the flying qualities of the Cougar comes not from personal experience in the cockpit. I was, however, forced to become familiar with the difficulties associated with the early Cougars.

My orders to the development squadron VX-4 after the Korean cruise in VF-821 got derailed along the way. I was one of two former Panther Maintenance Officers selected to oversee a pilot "top overhaul" program. The standard periodic airplane overhaul in one of the Navy's Overhaul & Repair facilities took as long as two years. At the rate at which we were banging up, abusing, and otherwise prematurely aging airplanes in the Korean War, the Navy was going to run out of flying machines before it ran out of war. An experimental selective aircraft rework program was the brainchild of Rear Admiral John B. "Jack" Pearson. (I was not thrilled at losing a good flying job in VX-4.) Pearson was an engineering-duty-only aviator and the ComAirPac Force Materiel Officer; he was responsible for keeping all Pacific Fleet airplanes in service and flying.

His quickie overhaul program involved three F9F-2s at O&R Alameda. The object was to evaluate the precise condition of each airplane and then fix only what needed fixing; this contrasted with the normal approach, which entailed arbitrarily disassembling an airplane and then putting it back together again, much like an aircraft factory building airplanes out of overhauled rather than new parts. The new program worked. We processed the three airplanes in three months instead of twenty-four. Then we tracked the airplanes through their next service tour. One suffered some damage after about six months; the other two went through full-service tours with maintenance histories indistinguishable from their more completely overhauled peers.

To put me on scene in Alameda, ComAirPac gave me permanent instead of temporary duty orders to the closest AirPac activity, the staff of ComFAir (Commander, Fleet Air) Alameda. After we pushed the Panthers out of the O&R hangar doors I found myself the ComFAir Airframes and Ordnance Officer, working for Lieutenant Commander Gordon A. Snyder, who was Engines Officer as well as Aircraft and Engines Assignment Officer. In this capacity I was to learn more than I wanted to know about the ills that could befall Cougars.

The first and most important new thing a pilot should know about swept-wing airplanes is that maximum lift—essential for slow-speed flight, as in landing approaches—occurs at much higher angles of attack and pitch angles than for straight-wing airplanes. Furthermore, aerodynamic stall can occur so subtly that a pilot may inadvertently exceed

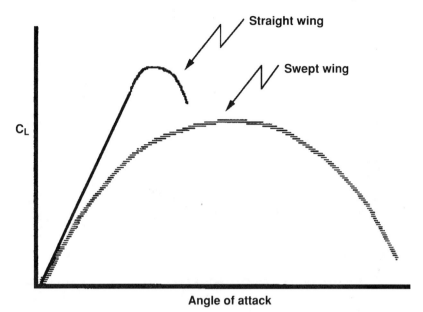

Figure 1: Lift Curve.

maximum lift to the point where lift decreases substantially at the same time that drag is increasing precipitously. A possible result is that the airplane may fall smartly and catastrophically out of the sky. It is an unfortunate part of aviation history that such an occurrence was not infrequent with early swept-wing airplanes; it happened more than once to F9F-6s, usually only once per airplane.

The different world of swept-wing aviation starts with the shape of the lift curve. (See figure 1.) Lift, specifically the lift coefficient, of a straight-leading-edge airfoil increases steeply in a straight line as angle of attack increases. (Angle of attack is the angle the wing chord makes with free stream air.) At some point, the straight line starts to curve or neck over as it approaches a maximum. For most of the Navy straight-wing airplanes I have flown, measured lift curves became jagged and irregular after the maximum—which represents aerodynamic stall—was reached. That irregularity means that post-stall flight was both uncontrollable and unpredictable. There could be no doubt in the pilot's mind when stall occurred: the airplane would enter a noticeable gyration—the nose would fall through, sometimes accompanied by a wing drop—to be followed almost immediately by a spin unless recovery was initiated.

The lift curve for a swept wing, on the other hand, is shallower, the

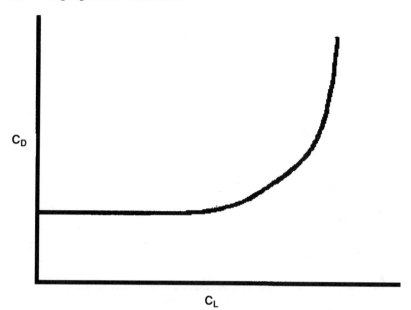

Figure 2: Drag vs. Lift.

maximum value is smaller, and the angle of attack at which the maximum value of the lift coefficient ($C_L$max) is reached is significantly larger. The symmetry of the swept-wing curve and the lack of a noticeable break at nominal stall make it possible to increase angle of attack to where lift *decreases* with increases in pitch/angle of attack. What that means is that the pilot's fundamental reaction, to pull back on the stick to slow or stop rate of descent, can have the opposite effect at high angles of attack. Worse, there are no sensory or instrument cues to tell him that that is what is happening; at least there weren't until angle-of-attack indicators were invented.

In cruise or high-speed flight, airplanes are flying in a region of low lift (or low lift coefficient) and low drag coefficient. In that region, significant increases in lift can be achieved with only minor increases in pitch/angle of attack and with little penalty in the form of increased drag. As maximum lift coefficient is approached, however, drag begins to rise steeply.[17] In somewhat idealized form this is shown in figure 2. In the region of maximum lift—the section of figure 2 where the graph's curvature increases sharply—a greater angle of attack can cause drag to increase faster than lift. That phenomenon is responsible for one of aviation's hoary admonitions: "Stick controls airspeed; throttle controls rate of descent or altitude." This is in opposition to its equally hoary partner: "Stick controls altitude; throttle controls airspeed." The contradiction is the basis for much disagreement among pilots and more than one barroom argument.

The right answer is that both are correct, more or less—each, however, only in its appropriate flight regime. Cruising at altitude, a contemporary airplane is flying at the flat part of figure 2. If a pilot gets, for instance, fifty or sixty feet low, he eases back on the stick, smoothly correcting to his desired altitude. The airspeed indicator hardly budges. If, however, in making an approach to landing at or below recommended approach airspeed, gear and full flaps down, a pilot has a high sink rate and attempts to slow his rate of descent solely by application of back stick, one of two things may happen, probably both: sink rate will increase; airspeed will decrease. He is flying in the high-curvature region of figure 2. The proper solution to his problem is more power, to be *followed* by enough back stick to regain the proper angle of attack.

The back-stick-only solution applied to a modern general aviation airplane flying close to stall might cause a somewhat bumpier landing than intended. For a swept-wing jet, the result may be extreme. At the knuckle of the curve of figure 2,[18] the swept-wing airplane can undergo something more dramatic than drag increasing faster than lift. Lift may actually *decrease*. "Falling out of the sky" can be more than euphemism.

That happened to one of Duke Windsor's VF-24 pilots. On his approach to NAS Alameda, he came in a little slow with a high sink rate. He tried to "flare" the airplane by pulling back on the stick, a technique that worked well with the forgiving Panther. It didn't work here; the airplane continued to descend at an even faster rate. In apparent desperation, the pilot yanked back on the stick. The Cougar continued to descend almost vertically in a nose-high, wings-level attitude to impact on the runway. The airplane stayed in one piece, but the entire structure was bent, torn, crushed, and otherwise deformed. The pilot suffered massive, fatal internal injuries.

A short time later I flew the F9F-6. The ComFAir staff Operations Officer received a familiar call from FASRON-8 (Fleet Air Support Squadron Eight): they needed a test pilot for a Cougar just out of a major inspection. On the theory that an F9F was an F9F, I jumped at the opportunity. I was familiar with the aerodynamic principles involved from Postgraduate School and Test Pilot School; I knew about the VF-24 accident as well as other experiences of VF-24 and VF191; in fact I considered myself rather an expert on the airplane, even though I had never flown a Cougar.

I performed a more thorough preflight inspection than usual, paying particular attention to the pitot tube (the taped-over pitot tube in the Corsair at FASRON-8 was still fresh in my mind—I did not want to find myself in the air in *this* airplane without an airspeed indicator). The configuration of the airplane was similar to that of the VF-24 and VF-191 squadron airplanes; it was in fact destined for VF-24.

Start, taxi, and pretakeoff procedures were nearly identical to the F9F-5. There were a couple of extra features to be noted, if not actually exercised. The all-hydraulic control system of this spoiler airplane had no backup mechanical control system in the event of failure of both hydraulic pumps. Instead, there was an emergency backup system to provide a number of control cycles. How many cycles was a variable that depended on how energetic the pilot's control inputs were. When the emergency system was exhausted, the pilot was left riding a projectile. The idea was to provide controllability long enough to make a safe emergency landing, or at least to fly the airplane to an area where it was acceptable to let it fall to the ground, presumably after the pilot had safely ejected.

On takeoff roll the somewhat higher-thrust version of the J48 provided noticeably better acceleration than the F9F-5, certainly more than the J42-engined F9F-2. Even though I was mentally prepared for it, the amount of control movement and the control force to achieve takeoff pitch angle were more than I expected. Once airborne, I held the nose down to accelerate to best-rate-of-climb speed, about 330 knots for the existing conditions. Then I eased into the climb.

Performance was better than I had expected, not dazzling but certainly exhilarating. There was a substantial amount of roll instability. Without quite the twitchy feel of the Panther, the F9F-6 was sensitive to lateral control inputs. There was no difference in roll response or feel that I could attribute to spoiler as opposed to aileron control. Nor was the advertised yaw instability evident at altitudes up to thirty-five thousand feet. (It was reported that yaw instability coupled with nasty spin characteristics could be a problem above forty thousand feet. Hutch Cooper's successor as skipper of VF-143 stalled and spun a Cougar while trying to top a line of thunderstorms above forty-five thousand feet. He failed to recover from the spin. For some reason he stayed with the airplane too long and was killed.)

I remember that the airplane felt solid rather than agile. My recollection may be influenced by impressions gained in the F9F-8T seven years later. The extended outer-panel wing chord of that later airplane and other aerodynamic changes helped cure the stability and handling problems that afflicted the early ones.

There were problems with the F9F-6. There were new and different flight qualities to be learned and adjusted to. The combination of swept-wing stall characteristics and yaw instability made the airplane "diverge" or "depart" dramatically in accelerated stalls.[19] That was characteristic of the swept-wing breed, not of Grumman's design. A typical sequence would be an uncontrollable pitch-up followed by a half-turn autorotation. What that means is that the nose would start to rise sharply toward the sky, and then the airplane would flip over on its back! A spin was almost certain to follow. VF-191 lost an airplane when that happened to a pilot at low altitude.

A normal, 1-g stall was less exciting. After climbing to altitude and exercising all the aircraft systems—that was the purpose of this post-major-inspection test flight—I explored the airplane's handling qualities and control response. The high angle of attack before stall occurred and the lack of stall warning were equally impressive. This was an airplane I did *not* wring out on the first flight with a series of acrobatics; I knew what to expect, but I had never experienced it before.

Prior training and experience kept me from making radical control inputs as I got into the slow-flight, pre-stall regime; such inputs are a sure way to bring on a stall and, if made as part of stall recovery, to turn a simple stall into a fully developed spin. I slowed the airplane, dropped gear and flaps into landing configuration, and flew as slow as I could without stalling. There was little aerodynamic warning of approaching stall—no noticeable buffeting or shaking. Satisfied that I was flying as slow as I could without losing altitude or continuing to lose airspeed, I decreased power—not all the way—and eased the stick back. I found myself in a nose-high attitude with a high rate of descent. I could increase the latter alarmingly by pulling back on the stick even further. Somewhere in the evolution, the airplane stalled. When stall occurred was not apparent; I had only instruments, primarily the airspeed indicator and the vertical speed (rate of climb/descent) indicator, plus visual cues like a ridiculously high pitch angle, to verify stall. Most contemporary straight-wing airplanes did everything but hit the pilot over the head at the approach of stall by manifesting buffet, vibration, and aerodynamically induced stick shaking. Even those that did not give natural warnings were beginning to be equipped with different kinds of artificial stall-warning devices: buzzers, horns, lights, and mechanical shakers. This beauty, however, was prepared to lead me unwitting into a flight regime where disaster lurked.

The rest of the flight was routine. I liked the airplane. I landed on runway 25, coming in over the approach road to the main gate of NAS Alameda. One of the longer runways, 25 was a little over seven thousand feet long. Pattern entry and the approach were normal, but the landing was not routine. I adapted fairly well to the unfamiliar nose-high attitude. I adjusted nose position and throttle adequately enough for the desired glide slope. Just before touchdown, I attempted to decrease my sink rate, to flare the airplane for landing—with back stick, just as I was used to; as the psychologists say, "Early learning is strong learning."

My attempt to flare was not a success. Sink rate increased. As I contacted the runway, I heard a bang—there went a tire. The ride was bumpy. I was desperate to slow down and get off the runway. Only partially successful in the former, I executed the latter. Still too fast, I was rewarded with a second bang as the other main gear tire blew. At least I got all the way off the runway onto a taxiway and was spared the embarrassment of forcing the duty runway to close. There was embarrassment enough as it was: I barely had time to shut the engine down when I was greeted by the vanguard of the alert crash and rescue crew. A parade of brightly painted emergency vehicles led by a fire truck and an ambulance roared up to my stopped flying machine. Lights flashed; sirens blared. Before I could get unstrapped, fire-retardant foam was being sprayed onto what was left of my smoking main landing gear wheels. The now D-shaped wheels were flat on the bottom and the tires were mostly gone, but there was no other damage except to my pride. I don't know what the FASRON-8 Maintenance Officer had to say about staff pukes who couldn't take care of his airplanes; I preferred not to find out.

There was no developed ComAirPac training syllabus for the F9F-6. Individual squadrons modified existing syllabi as they saw fit in order to accommodate the features of their new airplanes. More than one Cougar skipper decided to include a supersonic dive in order to familiarize his pilots with the phenomenon of transonic flight. The maneuver was not tactically useful, except possibly as an escape maneuver against a subsonic opponent, but it could build confidence and remove the mystery attending an unknown flight regime.

The maneuver was performed by simply pointing the nose down from forty thousand feet or more with full power. The relatively fat-winged, relatively underpowered Cougar used up a lot of altitude to achieve supersonic flight. The supersonic transition, I have been told, was unremarkable. There was a pitch-up on acceleration and a more noticeable pitch-up on deceleration back to subsonic. That deceleration could present a problem. The conventional trailing-edge elevator provided marginal control authority in that flight regime. The control forces became almost too great for pilots to handle. Trim effectiveness was reduced. There was the possibility of a violent pitch-up into a spin on deceleration if too much back trim was used. One of Bob Elder's VF-191 pilots had so much difficulty recovering from a supersonic dive that he had decided to eject before he finally got his Cougar back under control. It was one of a series of incidents that convinced folks that the flying tail and other improvements were necessary.

Professional Recollections

At about the same time as these horror stories, our old friend Hydrolube reared its ugly head. The ethylene glycol–based hydraulic fluid's tendency literally to gum up the works became critical, especially for the Cougar with its hydraulically operated wing spoiler controls and soon-to-be-activated flying tail. Hydrolube had to go, to be replaced by the old standard petroleum-based red fluid, flammability considerations aside.

A modification line was set up in hangar 20 at NAS Alameda to change the hydraulic fluid in the Cougars. It was decided to incorporate concurrently a number of Grumman "service bulletins" that addressed various ills. In fairness to Grumman, the airplane had been rushed into the fleet, perhaps prematurely; and with several squadrons conducting intensive training at the same time, phenomena that cropped up gradually in other developing swept-wing airplanes were encountered all at once in the Cougars. Prominent among the changes to be made were activation of yaw dampers, flying tails, and a feature designed to prevent wing spoilers from sticking in either the housed or extended position.

Changing hydraulic fluid proved substantially more complicated than an automotive oil change. The two different hydraulic fluids were immiscible; like the proverbial oil and water, they simply wouldn't mix. It was mind-boggling how many nooks, crannies, crevices, dead ends, and dead pools existed in an F9F-6 hydraulic system, arguably the most sophisticated hydraulic system around at the time—certainly the most sophisticated in naval aviation. So it was flush, flush, flush, all day long. Even so it proved almost impossible to prevent the formation of a gooey pink emulsion, at its worst resembling wallpaper paste. The stuff was like pink cholesterol clogging the machine's arteries, and what it did to the innards of various actuators was even worse. Persistence ultimately triumphed, but it was not an easy task. Big hydraulic workstands pumped away, recirculating hydraulic fluid like oversize heart machines.

Grumman rushed a field team to Alameda to accomplish the multi-headed task. The team was on site for weeks. Their first order of business was the hydraulic fluid, then the service bulletins implementing the needed hardware changes. This constituted a remarkably quick response even for those days, characteristically less administratively doctrinaire than today. It was very much "Here's the job, let's get on with it!"

The field modifications were at the instigation of ComAirPac, a fleet operational command. They were accomplished with the knowledge and consent of the Bureau of Aeronautics. BuAer was responsible for procuring and delivering to the fleet operationally suitable airplanes. Every change to an operating airplane, be it under the jurisdiction of the Federal Aviation Administration or the military, must be formally identified and certified in the aircraft logbook, a permanent record that stays with every airplane, civilian or military, as long as it is in service. The requirement is that the logbook accurately represent the true condition and configuration of the airplane: a mechanic or aircrewman must be able to approach a strange airplane, one he has never seen before, and, logbook or operating handbook in hand, satisfy himself that he can safely maintain and operate it. The logbook contains every authorized change since the machine was first put in service. The key word is *authorized*. For civil aircraft the authorizing device is an FAA Airworthiness Directive; the comparable documents in the Navy are Aircraft Service Changes and Aircraft Service Bulletins generated by BuAer.

What was being done to the F9F-6s in hangar 20 at NAS Alameda needed to be both authorized and made a matter of record, but we didn't wait for formal authorization to do the work. Things moved so quickly that informal, verbal authorization was the rule; there were many telephone calls for this purpose to the home of BuAer, Main Navy on Constitution Avenue in Washington and the ramshackle "W" and "N" buildings behind it. Commonly, a Grumman field engineer would just show up with some new airplane parts and a sheaf of papers, a service bulletin that described a particular change—not a duly authorized Navy Aircraft Service Change, but a Grumman service bulletin.

Much of that long-distance telephone time to Washington was to determine after the fact how to document what had been done; it ain't legal to enter a Grumman service bulletin in a Navy airplane's logbook! We at Alameda knew the changes by their names and identifying descriptive phrases, as well as by their Grumman numbers. But in the conversations with Washington I was surprised to learn that my colleague in BuAer's Airframe Design Division could not produce even tentatively assigned Navy numbers for some of the changes, let alone completed Aircraft Service Changes. The big surprise was to learn that they had never even heard of some of what we were doing! As this interesting fact came to light, I sensed alarm in the voice at the other end of the line; I felt apprehension that we might be told to stop until the paperwork caught up; I failed to mention some minor changes I knew to be really brand-new.

The job got done; in time the paperwork was tidied up too. I don't believe it could happen in today's world, where suspicions and recrim-

inations run rampant amid fears of contractor fraud, corrupt government officials, and litigation. Certainly it could not happen as it did then.

The benefits were not immediately evident, but the Cougar beast
was tamed. The rising accident/incident rate assumed normal proportions, and the F9F-6 assumed its place in the fleet with no further
trauma. There were, of course, carrier landings still to come. Landing
that first swept-wing fighter on a straight-deck *Essex*-class carrier ranks
with the more challenging feats in carrier aviation, especially before
airplanes were equipped with angle-of-attack indicators—and, more important, before the triad contributed by our British cousins: the mirror
landing system, the angled deck, and steam catapults.

Personal Recollections

I learned a lot during that tour in ComFAir from people like Lieutenant
Commander Gordon Snyder, for whom I worked directly, and Commander Red Schultz, who headed the ComFAir maintenance division.
Red Schultz was one of the rare Limited Duty Officers to achieve the
rank of commander. His knowledge, technical expertise, and long experience were matched by a quiet, gentlemanly demeanor and a sense
of humor that could be by turns wry or downright devastating. His
perception of the ways of the Navy was reflected in one line: "The horse
faces east." In other words the horse's head, the part that eats, was in
Washington, leaving the other part poised threateningly over the Pacific
Coast. The statement reinforced the latent paranoia in many of us that
suggested the Washington naval establishment, and indeed the whole
Atlantic Fleet, experienced favored treatment compared with the Pacific Fleet.

Around the corner from Gordon's and my offices was an office
reserved for the field service representatives of various aircraft companies. The F9F-6 modification program epitomized the special status
of the service reps and the relationship that commonly existed between
them and the squadrons they supported. It was the team from the Grumman factory that performed the major work, but it was on-the-scene
people like Cy Brown and George Watkins[20] who identified the need
and laid the groundwork.

Cy and George were more or less permanent occupants of that
office, along with Bob LaCombe and Milo Price from Douglas. Their
continuing presence was dictated by their companies' airplanes being
based at Alameda, as well as by the proximity of the O&R facility and
ComFAir. We at Alameda only occasionally came face to face with the
Vought and McDonnell reps, because the Corsairs and Banshees were
based at Moffett. There was limited desk space at Alameda for them

and other as-needed visitors like the Curtiss-Wright and Pratt & Whitney representatives.

The airplanes I had the greatest exposure to in the Navy were built by Grumman and Chance Vought. Therefore, my closest and most frequent contacts were with Grumman and Vought representatives. They were like shipmates and even family, a squadron itself being a kind of extended family. That these civilians weren't part of the Navy or might have interests other than our welfare never occurred to me; certainly their customary behavior and work habits did not indicate otherwise. We worked long hours; they worked long hours. We went to sea; they went to sea. We baked under a summer sun in Yuma, Arizona; they were there in the oven with us. It wasn't until my tour in BuAer as a lieutenant commander that I began to appreciate that contractors and their service reps really weren't in the Navy; they were in business, a very competitive business, as is evidenced by the diminished number of airplane builders.

Among many examples of effort above and beyond reasonable requirements, I have a favorite. It happened in VF-821, where I frequently found myself drowning in pools of the contaminated hydraulic fluid that dripped inexorably from Panthers with poor circulatory systems and crippled actuators. One Saturday afternoon I turned loose my exhausted hydraulic gang for the weekend. I walked out onto the hangar floor for a look at what still needed to be done. There was a lone figure next to the folded wing of an F9F-2. It was Tom Connors, the senior Grumman service rep in the San Diego area. He wasn't normally attached to a particular squadron or squadrons.

Too busy to notice my approach, Tom was straining, both arms extended through an access hole into the innards of the wing. The sleeves of his white shirt were soiled; hydraulic fluid hemorrhaged down one arm. Tossed onto a workstand was a sports coat—apparently new and expensive—marked by a large, wet stain.

He was trying to get at the wing fold cylinder, an actuating cylinder with a shaft that resembled an oversize German "potato masher" hand grenade. The cylinder had developed a circumferential crack under load, rendering it useless for its intended purpose as well as providing an escape route for hydraulic fluid. A replacement cylinder had arrived from supply that day, too late for our mechanics to install, and Tom Connors had elected to attack the normally two-man job on his own. It should have been a three-man job, but the cumbersome cylinder was a tight fit, having been designed with as large a diameter as the wing would accommodate; there wasn't room for a third person's hands, or even a second person's. The cylinder end of the actuator assembly was secured at its top to a strength member inside the wing outer panel, above the access hole. It was a long, awkward reach to the attaching bolt. The shaft end, which attached to the fixed part of the wing, did not present a problem.

Tom had observed and participated in all of VF-821's difficulties in learning to maintain the newly acquired Panthers. He provided advice and training when he could. Hands-on participation wasn't his normal mode; it wasn't supposed to be, because he had assigned two of his people to us on a rotating basis, one of whom was almost always available or on call—and this, of course, when we were by no means the only Panther squadron in the area. Two service reps was not a trivial commitment; I think there were only four Grumman reps, counting Tom, in the San Diego area. This weekend neither of the other two was available. Tom had dropped by to see how we were doing, and once there he couldn't resist becoming involved, offering information and instruction as needed.

He backed away when I dismissed the men. After they left, he had returned to the airplane to do the job alone. I tried to dissuade him, arguing that it wasn't productive: doing a two-man job alone was going to take more than twice as long; it wasn't efficient. Besides, I felt bad about his ruined clothes.

"Well, maybe you're right. But let me at least get the thing out of there. I almost have the bolt loose."

He got it out of there, and I was of some minimal help at the end— I helped grab the cylinder and pull it out of the hole—after he had done the hard part.

I don't know how folks get motivated to behave that way. It certainly wasn't the pay; in the low-paying airplane industry, Grumman's guys weren't much better off than we were. For many years Grumman has been an object of respect in the Navy, sometimes even an object of affection, as I could attest at that moment. You tend to feel that way about an organization whose people seem to be continually trying to save your neck. My association with Grumman was special because of my close association with Grumman airplanes. But the dedication and enthusiasm were characteristic of all the field people who worked and traveled with the squadrons. It was much the same in the Army Air Corps and then the U.S. Air Force. Later, some Air Force tactical squadrons had field service representatives in platoon strength, but in the Navy we always seemed to have help by ones and twos, usually one each from an airplane and an engine contractor. They slaved away in the salt mines alongside us, sharing the same conditions and experiences.

Over a career I had good experiences with many, including field service engineers from Grumman, Chance Vought, Douglas, Martin, Lockheed, Pratt & Whitney, Curtiss Wright, Kaman, Westinghouse,[21]

North American, and Convair. I had no bad experiences with any of them, although my limited experience with representatives of one airframe contractor was different. It happened more than once, but the first association involved infrequent contact with an individual who worked out of Moffett Field, where his company's airplanes were. At ComFAir Alameda, my contact with a contractor's rep usually involved a specific difficulty or problem with an airplane or engine. Sometimes the solution lay in procedures, sometimes with actual hardware, either quality control or design; whatever the problem, we always got right to it, strictly business. But at Moffett Field, I could never get this particular rep focused. After an interview I would realize that I was no closer to a solution than before, though I might be better informed about the overall quality of Company X and its products. The guy was a great salesman but not much of a field service engineer.

In January of 1954 I was transferred from Alameda to the Structures Branch of the Airframe Design Division at BuAer. I had been unsuccessful in my attempts for assignment either to a VX development squadron or to the Naval Air Test Center at Patuxent River, Maryland; the Washington tour of duty was a payback for my Postgraduate School education, which was under a BuAer-sponsored program.

During that Washington tour of duty the F9F-8 completed its final development phase. That phase included demonstrating contract compliance by in-flight demonstration of the airplane's structural envelope. A Grumman test pilot named Ernie von der Heyden flew the final high-g, high-q demonstration point.[22] Because of a problem with the test instrumentation—at least that's what Ernie said—he missed the desired point badly, on the *high* side. The actual point was closer to ultimate load (the load at which so-called permanent deformation can occur) than to limit load (the repeatable OK-to-use service loading). The actual combination of parameters—q, g-loading, airspeed, and Mach number—received considerable attention in BuAer, and added to the legend of the Iron Works.

In the early 1960s I was trying to remember those numbers. My recollection of "normal" load was 9 g's. I described the incident as I remembered it to Ralph Clark, then still the senior Grumman employee on site at Patuxent. He duly consulted Grumman's flight test facility at Calverton, Long Island, and came up empty. Then a few years ago, I attended a dinner meeting of the Society of Engineering Test Pilots at the Naval Gun Factory in Washington.[23] Also present was Ernie von der Heyden. I asked him to recall the magic F9F-8 structural demonstration numbers, and he couldn't do it either. So much, I thought, for corporate memory; Grumman's was apparently no better than Westinghouse's, with which I was by then becoming familiar.

At the end of an evening filled with aviation talk and nostalgic reminiscences, Ernie left me and the others with a thought: "When you're in your late forties, still test flying these damn airplanes for a living, you know you've gone wrong somewhere."[24]

Chapter 8
AD Skyraider

NICKNAMES TELL WHAT PILOTS REALLY THINK about an airplane. The longer and more varied the list of unofficial names, the more certain it is that aviators feel strongly about a particular aircraft; whether these feelings are favorable or unfavorable is another matter. There are no rules governing informal nomenclature, but a common denominator is respect, coupled with acknowledgment that the official name is inadequate to describe the machine.

Sometimes an official name is rejected because pilots don't like the way it sounds. Maybe it doesn't reflect the way pilots talk; maybe it sounds pretentious, even downright phony. The handles given to an airplane by pilots are never phony. They highlight attributes too significant, too dominant, to be ignored: Beast, Hog, Hose Nose, Clunk (as in "Pilots, man your clunks!"), Bent-wing Bird, The Washing Machine (or, simply, The Bendix), Torpecker, Whale, Drut (that's *turd* spelled backwards), Vibrator, and so on.

Airplanes earn attention for bad characteristics as well as good ones, although an unpopular machine seems to generate fewer nicknames than an aircraft viewed more favorably. For a bad airplane, one really rotten nickname is generally enough. Good ones get better treatment. It is not surprising that three of the names above belong to the F4U Corsair. Fear always increases the length of a list; the Corsair was also the "Ensign Eliminator."

I cannot think of any airplane that acquired more names, or that carried a more extensive and varied unofficial nomenclature, than Ed Heinemann's long-lived AD Skyraider; some of the descriptive terms tied to the airplane are too long and cumbersome even to be called names. A short list includes Spad, Flying Dump Truck, Single-engine B-17, Workhorse, Ugly Old Bird, Relic, and Able Dog.[1] For the Skyraider, the phenomenon is a manifestation of both respect and affection. Of all the titles, the one most commonly associated with the AD is Spad. There is a whole generation of pilots, not a young generation, to whom Spad *is* the AD, not the French World War I fighter from which the name was borrowed.

In a discussion of airplanes' flying qualities, I once referred in writing to the "S.P.A.D.," correctly using periods in the acronym. I received the query, "Do you mean the A-1?"[2] No, I didn't. What I meant was the "Société anonyme *pour l'aviation et ses dérivés*" fighter flown by Eddie Rickenbacker and other successful Allied pilots in the Great War. (The phrase is roughly translatable as Anonymous, or Unnamed, Society for Aviation and Its Derivatives.)

Considered one of the supreme aerial weapons of World War I,[3] the S.P.A.D.'s success was surprising to some because of its descent from a line of undistinguished, sometimes outlandish predecessors. Not one of the more esthetically attractive World War I fighters, nor one of the more inherently glamorous—the Red Baron's Fokker triplane and the British Sopwith Camel seem to have won that championship—the S.P.A.D. was a good performer with a top speed reported to be over 130 mph. It seemed destined from the beginning to be the stuff of legend and mystique.

The second S.P.A.D. (model version VII) to see operational service went, in September of 1916, to twenty-one-year-old Lieutenant Georges Guynemer, the most famous of the French World War I fighter aces. The tubercular Guynemer accumulated fifty-four victories, most of them in S.P.A.D.'s, before simply disappearing on a fighter patrol. No trace of him was ever found; he was twenty-three. The S.P.A.D. was flown by virtually all of the World War I combatants on the Allied side: France, Great Britain, the United States, Belgium, Italy, Poland, Czechoslovakia—even Japan. The best-known version is the S.P.A.D. XIII as flown by René Fonck, Guynemer (including the day of his disappearance), and such American aces as Frank Luke and Eddie Rickenbacker. There were 8,472 S.P.A.D. XIII's produced.[4] The second greatest user of the model after the French were the American pilots of the American Expeditionary Force.

The elements that make for an aircraft of legend are clearly there. The S.P.A.D. was more numerous, more nearly ubiquitous, but it was not as long-lived as our AD. Also, the original S.P.A.D. served only in that one war. By comparison, there were 3,180 ADs produced. They were operated by the U.S. Air Force, U.S. Navy, U.S. Marine Corps, Vietnam Air Force, Great Britain, and Sweden in peacetime and during the Korean and Vietnam wars.

The S.P.A.D. is a fitting source for the AD's given name, but the name was originally applied to the AD not by Skyraider pilots, but by

Table 1 Vital Statistics, S.P.A.D. vs. Skyraider

	S.P.A.D.	Skyraider
Power plant	Hispano-Suiza	Curtiss-Wright R-3350
Horsepower	180, 200, 220, 235	2,700
Weight	1,773 lbs	18,029 lbs gross weight; 13,923 lbs combat weight[a]
Wingspan	29 feet	50 feet
Maximum speed	132 mph (slightly faster as 235 hp)	305 to 318 mph
Combat range	not available	1,100 + nautical miles[b]
Armament	1 or 2 Vickers machine guns	2 or 4 20mm cannon

Source: For S.P.A.D., J. M. Bruce, comp., *Spad Scouts SVII–SXIII*, Arco-Aircam Series no. 9 (New York: Arco Publishing Company, 1969); for Skyraider, Rosario Rausa, *Skyraider— The Douglas A-1 "Flying Dump Truck"* (Annapolis, Md.: Nautical and Aviation Publishing Company of America, 1982).

[a] These weight figures are from Edward H. Heinemann and Rosario Rausa, *Ed Heinemann—Combat Aircraft Designer* (Annapolis, Md.: Naval Institute Press, 1980). They are coupled with an armament load of one 2,000-pound bomb. They don't tell the whole story. Another source, as well as legend, speaks of an external bomb load, of 15,000 pounds. That load, flown at least once, is literally thousands of pounds greater than the empty weight of the airplane.

[b] This seems low to me, although it is consistent with other sources that cite figures as high as a 1,300-nautical-mile *range*. I remember nuclear weapon delivery profiles, for planning and practice purposes, with 1,000-nautical-mile *radii*. These were not just on paper; they were flown. Other sources cite "specification" bomb loads between 6,000 and 8,000 pounds. They may all be correct, merely reflecting performance variations that go with different Navy-required configurations.

other pilots as an act of derision. The venerable piston slapper was, after all, born in the beginning of the jet age. "Spad" was applied to emphasize its status as a relic, an antique. AD pilots turned the name into a symbol of pride and affection. The performance of the Skyraider and especially its combat record made believers of the rest of us. (See table 1.)

My introduction to *our* Spad was from the cockpit of a different airplane. The dive-bomber squadron of Air Group 3, VB-3, had flown Curtiss SB2C airplanes. They were replaced by the long-awaited AD-2 in the fall of 1948. The pilots of VB-3 were understandably anxious to get rid of their "Beasts." The U.S. Navy had entered World War II with obsolescent SBD Dauntless scout bombers.[5] The SBD refused to die and, apparently with equal stubbornness, the SB2C Helldiver refused to get ready to fight until late in the war. When it was finally ready, the new Helldiver[6] failed to live up to expectations in spite of such stream-lining niceties as internal fuselage bomb carriage. In performance only

AD-2 at the Naval Air Test Center, Patuxent River, Maryland. "TT" forward of the cockpit suggests a Tactical Test Division airplane. (USNI Photo Library)

marginally superior to the Dauntless and not as effective a bombing platform, the SB2C was big, heavy, and a challenge to land aboard an aircraft carrier. It soon earned the nickname The Beast; I never, ever, heard anyone call it Helldiver out loud.

The dive-bomber pilots had been relatively passive in their in-air performance around the fighter pilots; there wasn't much basis for aggressive bar talk either, as long as they were flying Beasts. In turn, the Bearcat pilots harassed them unmercifully in the air and, with sometimes overly loud mouths, on the ground. When the ADs arrived, things changed. For single-engine airplanes, those new AD-2s were large. Of course, so was the SB2C, but the early-model Skyraider was also light and surprisingly agile. Besides that, its big R-3350 engine produced more horsepower than the SB2C's Wright R-2600 even displaced cubic inches. A different kind of flying opened up for the bomber pilots, and a shift in their attitude became noticeable; as observed by the fighter pilots, their behavior became downright aberrant.

One sunny afternoon over Narragansett Bay, south of Naval Air Station Quonset Point, I was leading the second division of a flight of eight F8F-1Bs. The sky was suddenly filled with big, blue airplanes— not actually filled, perhaps, but eight shiny new Skyraiders were swarming all over us. After the shock of that surprise attack, a melee ensued. I accelerated after an airplane that had just made a successful run on me. I was closing nicely, almost in gunsight tracking range, when he pulled a hard turn—just what he was supposed to do. I followed suit, confident as always that my trusty Bearcat could out-turn anything in the sky.

Then I saw a glimmer of red, followed by a lot of red, and found myself looking at the plan view of a big airplane that seemed to have come to a complete stop in midair. Closing like hell, all I could do was to level my wings and fly over him; collision avoidance was paramount. I badly overshot my intended target. Once past him, I rolled into a steep bank and pulled nearly 8 g's ("limit load" in the Bearcat). Too late! Over the radio I heard, "Rat-tat-a-tat. You're dead." My opponent had reversed his turn and slid onto my tail as I went by, achieving a classic "six o'clock" firing position.

My word, I said to myself, (or words to that effect), that's some kind of airplane!

And so it was.

What had made the difference in the maneuver was the huge barn-door-like dive brakes on the sides and bottom of the aft fuselage of the AD. In those days the undersides of the brakes were painted a vivid red, probably to make it easy for other airplanes in a flight to adjust speed so as to maintain proper interval, as when making coordinated bombing runs. I can attest to the brakes' effectiveness.

General Description

The Skyraider was not, as legend has it, conceived and born all in one night in a Washington hotel room. However, the facts are consistent with that idea. As early as 1941 it was evident that a successor to both the SBD and its follow-on, the SB2C, was needed. By 1943 two prototype SB2D dive/torpedo-bombers were flying. The airplane featured two crewmen, internal bomb stowage, and such weight-producing items of GFE (government-furnished equipment) specified by the Navy as *two* remotely operated gun turrets.[7] Only two of these unsuccessful airplanes were built. They were followed by the BTD, of which eight were built. Without the turrets and with only one crewman, this airplane was better but still barely competitive with the Martin Mauler and the Kaiser Fleetwing then flying at the Naval Air Test Center, Patuxent.

In June of 1944 Ed Heinemann and several of his engineers attended a conference in the old Main Navy Building on Constitution Avenue in Washington. The subject was the status and future of the BTD. In the course of the meeting it became clear to Mr. Heinemann that the BTD was not the Navy's preferred candidate. Its future was in jeopardy. His radical solution was an entirely new proposal to the Navy; he promised a new design within thirty days. Admiral L. B. Richardson responded, in effect, "Try 0900 tomorrow morning!" They did. It wasn't easy. Ed Heinemann and his cohorts burned the midnight oil in Ed's hotel room until three o'clock the next morning. When finished, they had produced sketches and the preliminary design of the BT2D Dauntless II, which in due course became the AD Skyraider. The first flight took place nine months later on 18 March 1945. The Navy ordered five hundred.[8] The Able Dog was on its way, though there were awesome challenges to be met.

Two major problems with the SB2D and BTD designs that preceded the AD were weight and complexity. The BTD was a step in the right direction but not enough. Ed Heinemann and his designers were aware of the problem, but, especially in the SB2D, there had been those Navy-required items of GFE, adding significant weight and complexity. This time things would be different. Although tricycle landing gear was increasingly in vogue, they received permission from the Navy to build a tail-wheel airplane—nose landing gear is big and heavy compared with a tail wheel. That alone resulted in appreciable weight saving, as did the decision to go with one rather than multiple fuel tanks. Both decisions make sense to my generation of pilots. If you have grown up with tail-wheel airplanes they are not scary; and the single tank was a blessing to forgetful types like me who never got over the habit of running a tank dry at uncomfortable combinations of altitude and airspeed.

The Navy directed the use of the R-3350 engine. Ed Heinemann's preference was the dependable, proven Pratt & Whitney R-2800, which powered such airplanes as the Bearcat, Hellcat, Corsair, and P-47 Thunderbolt. He concluded, correctly, that he could meet the specification requirements with that engine. The larger engine complicated his design problem, although he and his team obviously met that challenge. In retrospect, the choice of engine contributed to the airplane's versatility and long life. A source of confusion in airplane performance is the difference between specification performance and performance achieved in flight with real airplanes. The AD outperformed specifications[9] across the board, with the possible exception of speed in later, heavier models. For example, we have reported bomb loads actually flown of up to 15,000 pounds; specification bomb load is only 6,000 pounds. The bigger, more powerful engine was certainly responsible for at least part of the difference. Big engines don't necessarily make you go faster, but they always enable you to carry a heavier load.

There were seven major versions of the Skyraider subsequent to the prototype B2TD:AD-1 through AD-7. Each differed from the others by virtue of one or more major modifications. There were also dedicated mission equipment subdesignations such as AD-4*W* for airborne early

A transport-configured AD-5 in uncharacteristically hostile raiment. (USNI Photo Library)

warning. (This was the "guppy" version with the big overgrown bulge under the forward fuselage. The bulge housed a large radar antenna.) Others—the nomenclature was standard for all Navy airplanes—were Q, electronic countermeasure; P, photoreconnaissance; S and E, antisubmarine search and attack; N, night attack; L, the N stripped for day attack; and B, low-level bombing capability.[10] The most numerous model was the AD-4, which existed in more different versions than any of the others. In all, 1,051 AD-4s were built.

All the ADs looked more or less alike, except for the AD-5. I recall the AD-5 being first described as a multirole "kit" airplane that the Navy could modify, or have modified, into any one of several mission-dedicated roles, such as antisubmarine hunter-killer, transport, ambulance, photoreconnaissance, and target towing. In practice, I believe they essentially stayed in the configuration in which the factory delivered them. A total of 670 AD-5s were built.

This different AD featured side-by-side seating (only one set of controls, however, a Douglas trademark in side-by-side airplanes that was repeated in the A-26, F3D, and A3D); widened forward fuselage; overall length increased by two feet; and deletion of the dive brakes on the sides of the fuselage (the bottom-of-the-fuselage brake was retained). In some configurations, notably the transport configuration with which I am most familiar, the AD-5 had an extended greenhouse canopy over a passenger compartment. It opened to the side in a manner Navy aviation mechanics described as a "Buick door," after the long, side-opening hoods on straight-eight Buick automobiles. Up to six passengers could be accommodated under the blue-tinted greenhouse on aft-facing seats bolted to a platform that sat over the fuel tank. Aft of the seats and the tank the interior of the fuselage was exposed to view. Some avionics, like the ADF (automatic direction-finder radio), sat in the bottom of the fuselage, accessible for maintenance from either the passenger compartment or an under-the-fuselage "hellhole" access door.

The ungainly-looking AD-5 was the ugly duckling of the Skyraiders. Surprisingly, it flew and handled about like the rest, although the extra drag caused by the big greenhouse canopy, the width of the side-by-side pilot's cockpit, and the increased weight and wetted area of the long fuselage lowered performance. Although for in-service reliability and maintainability the AD-5 was generally comparable to its more tactically oriented siblings, the airplane suffered from a number of idiosyncratic problems. The most dramatic of these was manifested in a series of engine fires in the 1956–57 time frame. In more than one of these incidents, either the control cables adjacent to the fire wall burned through or the pulley's supporting structure gave way; whatever the failure, the pilot was left with an airplane that became a projectile. Several accidents resulted in both fatalities and successful bailouts.

Overall, in keeping with the Skyraider tradition, it was a successful airplane. The AD-5 was a favorite with pilots for its versatility, particularly with deskbound Navy and Marine "proficiency" pilots endeavoring to maintain their qualifications. It served with distinction in Vietnam, flown by U.S. Navy, U.S. Air Force, and Vietnam Air Force pilots.

How It Flew

My real introduction to the AD was in the spring of 1951 at Patuxent. The stable of airplanes that belonged to TPT (Test Pilot *Training*, as it was called then) included one AD-2. The one-of-a-kind airplanes in the school were retained as demonstration vehicles for airplanes' performance and handling characteristics. (Students' "project" airplanes, like the Bearcat, existed in the school in greater numbers.) I had been eager to fly the Skyraider ever since that unprovoked attack by VB-3 (shortly thereafter designated VA-34) at Quonset Point. I was not disappointed.

Right from the start, which included the usual preflight walk-around, the airplane was impressive. As has been noted, it was big for a single-engine aircraft, especially for a single-*seat* plane; For someone accustomed to the tiny Bearcat, it could be outright intimidating. The cockpit perched high on the fuselage, its forward position somehow diminishing the apparent bulk of the mighty R-3350 power plant. One had to look w-a-y up to talk to a pilot occupant from the tarmac. As is common with any good design feature, the cockpit's location and position had a purpose. The pilot's visibility over the nose was better than in any other tail-wheel airplane I have flown, more than 15 degrees below the pilot's eyeball horizon. That extra viewing angle was helpful in taxiing and other ground-handling maneuvers. It also made it possible to keep an airborne or surface target in view over a greater visual search volume, as well as facilitating target tracking with large lead angles.

The landing gear appeared integrated with the fuselage, masked as it was by wide fairings that partially covered the assembly when in the retracted position. The diameter of the main landing gear wheels looked excessively large, a feature I came to regard as a Douglas trademark. In a "clean"—no external stores—configuration the nose seemed to point arrogantly skyward. When even one big external fuel tank was installed underneath, masking further the extent of the landing gear, with the fuselage sloping aft toward the ground, tail dragger style, the AD seemed crouched like a runner in the blocks awaiting the starting gun. That was the Able Dog. Lacking the sleekness of its more glamorous jet contemporaries, it was always ready for business.

In keeping with the scale of the rest of the airplane, the cockpit was roomy. The AD is one of the first airplanes I remember in which ergonomics were given serious attention. The simplest manifestation was that control handles and knobs were constructed in the shape of what they activated: the landing gear actuating lever terminated in a small wheel; the flap handle was in the form of a miniature flap; the end of the arresting hook control was a small replica of a tail hook. The design practice continues, a welcome change over the sometimes confusing control arrangements in earlier airplanes. (I refer especially to the SBD Dauntless, which had three levers in the same quadrant on the *right* side of the cockpit. Distinguished only by the shape of the knobs on the end, these controls operated landing gear, flaps, and dive brakes.) The control stick was massive compared with the Bearcat's, bulkier and more businesslike than the sticks in the Corsair and Hellcat.

There was a standard three-axis trim system. According to Walter Roach, who flew both the AD-2 and the AM-1 Martin Mauler in the Navy's Board of Inspection and Survey (BIS) acceptance trials at Patuxent, the AD-2 had a conventional manual rudder trim. I recall the electric rudder trim control in the AD-5, activated by a knob on the left cockpit console. Electric rudder trim was not a total plus. The torque produced by the R-3350 engine as it drove four huge propeller blades through the air at takeoff power was formidable. A lot of right rudder trim was required for directional control.

In true Murphy's Law fashion, it was possible to wire the electric rudder trim control backwards. Somebody once did. It happened in an airplane flown by a friend and classmate, L. W. "Charlie" Meshier. Charlie flew an AD-5 one day on a proficiency flight out of NAS Anacostia, Maryland. After other preliminaries, he dutifully dialed in the recommended trim settings as part of his pretakeoff checklist. When he added full power, the airplane lurched sharply to the left and accelerated diagonally across the runway, directly toward the flight line, which was adjacent to the operations building. Charlie stood on the right rudder pedal to no avail; it was like pushing against concrete. Rather than participate in a multiple-airplane ground accident, he yanked back on the stick, and the Skyraider dutifully popped into the air, this time boresighted at the control tower—whereupon the tower crew inside hit the deck, just like a 1930s aviation movie. As his airspeed increased and control returned, Charlie avoided flying through the tower, or anything else.

Safely at altitude and seriously confused as to what had happened, Charlie located the problem with enlightened trial and error. He verified that the rudder trim control produced a response opposite to what it was designed for. He might have had a fighting chance if he had taken off with neutral trim. There was no way he could counter the torque forces with significant left trim.

That flight lasted just long enough for Charlie to get back into the pattern and land. It is reported that he had an informal discussion with the Anacostia Maintenance Officer afterwards.

I had no such problem on my maiden voyage in the AD; everything went fine. I immediately liked the airplane. This AD-2 out of Patuxent was absolutely clean, with no bomb racks or rocket launchers, not even the pylons to which such devices attached. With the resultingly low aerodynamic drag and the lightness of an early model, the machine was a real performer. It was surprisingly agile.

As might be expected with a mechanical control system, pitch forces were not light, but they were manageable—as long as the pilot stayed ahead of the airplane with timely application of longitudinal trim. It behaved similarly in yaw, where forces are a function of power and airspeed. Since an airplane's rudder is essentially a trim rather than control device, it was easy to anticipate trim requirements for ball-in-the-center flight. Aileron response and control force provided a pleasant surprise—not quite up to Bearcat standards, but comparable to the Corsair's and superior to the Hellcat's. No wonder my dive-bomber pilot opponent that afternoon at Quonset had reversed his turn so quickly!

My first AD flight was over the Chesapeake Bay. The afternoon weather was hazy, with increasingly evident cumulus clouds, but not too hazy and not too many clouds to prevent me from giving the AD the usual first-flight workout. With the available restricted and warning areas near NATC Patuxent, finding a legal practice area for aerobatics was no problem. (That was not a common circumstance in naval aviation. Finding an area was always easy; finding a legal one could be another matter.)

Before the fun of wringing out the airplane came the usual slow-flight and stall series. The Skyraider must be one of the most honest airplanes ever built, completely lacking in the dirty tricks department. All forms of stall occurred cleanly and conventionally—the actual stalls, that is. In a clean configuration, straight-ahead stall, the nose fell through sharply, but the wings remained level; there was no tendency to yaw or roll—certainly nothing like throwing you on your back *right now*, as in some other airplanes I have known. There was, however, no discernible warning; it happened all at once.

Most airplanes of the period provided warning of impending stall in ways such as decreasing control effectiveness, generally sloppy-feeling controls, and different forms of aerodynamic buffet. Even those with nasty stall characteristics, like the early Corsairs, let you know something was going to happen before it happened. Such characteristics extend beyond desirable; some form of stall warning is mandatory. If it doesn't exist naturally, a way must found to simulate it. The lack of stall warning in the AD was duly written up as a deficiency early in testing. I seem to recall a mechanical stick shaker in the AD-5s that I flew in the middle and late 1950s, but Walter Roach assures me that the AD-2s he flew in BIS trials didn't have them. Some form of artificial stall warning is installed in most of today's high-performance airplanes. This is a good example of accommodating to pilots' conditioning— implementing historically evolved conclusions as to what constitutes "good" rather than "bad" characteristics—from one generation of airplanes to the next.

Whatever design decisions are made to implement preferences in a particular airplane, there is more than an element of truth in the statement "All airplanes fly alike." They are designed and built that way. The flying qualities of a modern Mach-busting fighter, with its immovable side-stick controller[11] and fly-by-wire stability augmentation and control system, relate to and resemble the flying qualities of the DC-3, the Stearman, and that original S.P.A.D. But the devices and electronics used to synthesize "desirable" characteristics in a contemporary airplane, where they might not evolve naturally, are sometimes exotic and esoteric.

All the above was not on my mind when I first stalled the AD. I was, however, looking for the lack of stall warning about which I had been briefed. I found and demonstrated the phenomenon to my satisfaction. That is the sort of thing I was supposed to be learning to recognize by flying this Test Pilot Training Division airplane.

Then came the fun part, the aerobatics. I went through a typical sequence of rolls, loops, split-S maneuvers, Immelmanns, and Cuban eights. The rolls were barrel rolls, slow rolls, and aileron rolls (no snap roll in this airplane). The aileron rolls were especially enjoyable because the roll rate was fast enough to keep the nose from wandering or requiring difficult, slow roll–type corrections.

It was an exhilarating experience. I was pleased and impressed with the airplane. There was just a hint of the down side in that I found myself thinking, ". . . for such a large airplane." For the most part it was as good an acrobatic airplane as the Hellcat, or better, especially in roll. It lacked the top-end performance of that older airplane, and, I suspect, for serious g-pulling, kick-it-around-as-needed hassling a good Hellcat pilot could at worst hold his own against a good AD pilot. In my view, there was certainly no clear advantage to the AD over the Bearcat or Corsair either—and a lot of disadvantages—except for the AD's remarkable ability to slow down in a hurry.[12]

I had been aware of cumulus clouds increasing to the west for some time. When I switched to the control tower radio frequency for my return to the field, the first thing I heard was a thunderstorm warning. In my ignorance of late-afternoon spring and summer weather over the Chesapeake Bay, I established an orbit east and north of Patuxent. I settled down for an anticipated wait of perhaps thirty minutes; that seemed a reasonable time for an isolated thunderstorm to pass. With what I now know about the weather in that region, I would have started looking for somewhere else to go. A truly isolated thunderstorm is rare; once that first one appears, others sometimes start popping up like mushrooms, and then you may be faced with a squall line, a more significant problem.

This time I was lucky, except that I was impatient. I kept listening to the radio traffic. Before long it sounded as if the worst of the storm was over, and I headed for the field. The visibility wasn't bad, and I could maintain a good idea of the extent and position of the storm. There was even enough ceiling and visibility for a conventional "break" over the field. As I entered the downwind leg in moderate rain, the tower warned of variable and gusty winds. I think the controller was trying to tell me something, short of actually suggesting that I get out of there; when I rolled out on short final approach, I was sure of it. Even though the airplane felt solidly stable, I was bouncing around in the gusts. At one point I found myself holding the nose more than 30 degrees off the runway in order to keep my flight path aligned with the runway centerline. Just before I reached the runway threshold, the offset had grown to about 45 degrees. I kicked the nose around to parallel the centerline, dropping my upwind wing as I did so to counteract the inevitable drift from the crosswind. I had been able to control my airspeed and sink rate on the way down, so all I had to do was stall the airplane onto the runway, quickly, before the wind changed its mind. It wasn't graceful, but I managed. The airplane didn't just plop down onto the runway as I might have deserved, but sort of eased down, tail wheel first, just as if I knew what I was doing. That was my first and only landing in an AD-2.

I was told later that at the instant of touchdown I had a crosswind component of about 30 knots. Close to that on final, maybe, but I got lucky at the end and actually touched down in a lull. No amount of wing-down would have handled that much component! Based on that experience alone, I liked the airplane a lot. It had a wonderful characteristic that cannot be specified because no one knows how to design it into an airplane on purpose: the apparent willingness of a piece of inanimate machinery to protect a pilot's butt in spite of him.

Professional Recollections

During the next few years I was close to and sometimes flew near Skyraiders, but I didn't actually get into one again until 1956, when the AD-5s began to arrive at NAS Anacostia. They were to serve as proficiency airplanes for deskbound Navy and Marine aviators in the Washington area.

Since July of 1954, when I reported to the Bureau of Aeronautics, the airplanes available for that purpose had been limited to a small number of SNJs, a few aging Hellcats, and a couple of dozen SNBs/JRBs (military versions of the Beechcraft prewar Model 18). That was a small number of airplanes to take care of a large pilot population. All aviators were required to fly four hours per month to qualify for flight pay, and about twice that amount to meet annual minimum requirements for instrument proficiency and night flying. Scheduling was a problem. There was a designated time and day of the week after which it was permitted to reserve an airplane for the next week, and when that magic moment arrived, all the telephone lines to Anacostia were immediately saturated.

The period between the departure of the Hellcats and the arrival of the Skyraiders was frustrating for middle-rank pilots hoping to get back into fleet aviation. We did a lot of Beechcraft flying, which wasn't all bad; many of us developed our instrument flying skills beyond what we had ever accomplished in single-seat day fighters. But it wasn't all good either, certainly no substitute for what our peers were doing in a carrier Navy increasingly populated by new, swept-wing jet airplanes. As still-active carrier airplanes, the AD-5s were welcomed with enthusiasm.

NAS Anacostia was not staffed to provide training or instruction; those functions fell to the user population. There was no formal checkout syllabus, but there was a procedure to be followed: a detailed pilot briefing followed by a check flight given by a pilot already qualified in the airplane. The checkout was documented in a qualification jacket. My check pilot was Lieutenant Commander Thomas Wilbur "Willie" Budd, who had been in my training squadron flights in SNJs and Hellcats. Willie Budd was a good friend who was always willing to help.

I have less than total recall of that long-ago check ride and briefing, but a couple of things stand out in my memory. One of them was a description of the fire hazard, cause unknown, referred to previously, which by then had resulted in at least two fatal accidents. The other had to do with the speed brake. Only one of the fuselage dive brakes had been retained on the AD-5, the one underneath. It was a big brake, long enough to extend well below an extended main landing gear, and there was no helpful warning signal if the brake was open when you dropped the landing gear and reduced power for landing. If it was not retracted before landing, when you finally ground to a halt that brake was going to be significantly shorter than it was when you took off; more than one pilot taxied back to the flight line after landing with a red face and a short speed brake.

In due course it was my turn to check out other pilots in the airplane. One was Charlie Meshier, some time before the innovative takeoff I described earlier. Another was Lieutenant Commander Burr Turner, my immediate boss in the Airframe Design Division of BuAer. Burr's recent experience was in multi-engine airplanes, but he had no trouble adapting to this big tail-dragging single. The preflight briefing and ensuing checkout flight proceeded uneventfully.

NAS Anacostia and adjacent USAF Bowling Field were in the middle of a fast-growing metropolitan area; hills to the east sloped sharply upward toward St. Elizabeth's Hospital. A standard box or racetrack landing pattern was not feasible for either field. The usual approach to landing was either up or down the Anacostia River, depending on wind direction, with a long final approach. This particular afternoon was bright and sunny.

After Burr had properly gone through the landing cockpit checklist and I was satisfied that he knew what he was doing, I looked idly out my right-side canopy at the view below. For the nth time I speculated on the inappropriateness of having two military airfields so close together. As we flew low over the upwind end of Bowling's long runway—en route to the *downwind* end of Anacostia's long runway—I saw a large shadow flying formation with us along the ground. I marveled at the clarity and definition: there was our fuselage in recognizable detail, the square wing tips, the dive brake hanging down below the fuselage. . . . The dive brake?!

I jumped up and down in my seat as far as my restraining straps permitted and yelled at Burr, "Dive brake! Dive brake! Pull up the dive brake!" To no avail; our sound-attenuating hard hats and the noise of the engine took care of that. I punched his right arm. He was staring straight ahead, frowning in concentration on the critical part of his approach to landing. Undoubtedly believing that I was harassing him on purpose, as part of the checkout to test his concentration, he permitted himself a small smile but wouldn't look at me.

In mounting desperation I grabbed at the hand microphone, nestled in its bracket on my right console. In one violent motion I snatched it away, dragged it toward my waiting lips—and in my haste dropped it. The generous length of spring-coiled wire was hardly tested as the microphone fell out of sight into the fuselage bilge below. Now frantic, I hand-over-handed the wire until, finally, I had the precious communications device back in my hand.

"Wave off! Wave off, goddammit! The brake's still down!"

Burr looked at me in surprised alarm. Fortunately, he could do two things at once: even as he reacted to my outburst, his left hand on the throttle was hitting the brake switch—located there on purpose, so that the pilot wouldn't have to move his throttle hand. The brake eased itself safely out of the way in time for, as I recall, an exceptionally smooth landing.

When I got his attention, we were less than fifty feet over the runway and descending rapidly. My attempts at salvaging a threatening situation had been so flagrantly inept that Burr didn't even have to feel bad about forgetting the brake in the first place!

The three-brake configuration of the single-seat ADs represented a design compromise. The dive-bombers most admired for their accuracy were machines like the SBD and the German Stukas. Part of the secret was a vertical flight path to the bomb release point. In that ideal case the only correction is for wind drift, and that can be largely compensated for by corrections applied by rolling the aircraft so as to get the relative wind ahead of you—the remaining correction, then, is an adjustment in steepness of dive angle.

Another critical factor is release altitude. You would like to release as low as possible to minimize the effects of wind and lead angle error.

The SBDs and Stukas were good in part because their terminal dive speed, brakes extended, was low—in the case of the SBD about 250 knots. That translates to a low release altitude, from which the bombing pilot can pull out in time to avoid both his own bomb blast and flying chunks of enemy real estate.

The design problems in retaining similar performance for a cleaner, heavier, more powerful airplane were significant. In order to avoid the drag and weight-producing elements of large-span wing-mounted dive brakes, Mr. Heinemann received permission to design for 70- rather than 90-degree dive angles. That automatically placed an additional burden on the bomber pilot. His weapon delivery solution was no longer "Put the pipper on the target!" A precise lead angle was required, however small.

This brings me to a story told to me by Walter Roach. It hinges on the difference between 70- and 90-degree dive-bombing.

Walter found himself on the staff of the Commander Air Group, of Air Task Group 105 at Cecil Field near Jacksonville, Florida. There were pros and cons about being on the CAG's staff instead of in one of the squadrons—probably more cons than pros. One of the pros was getting to fly the air group's various airplanes. As an experienced dive-bomber pilot, Walter was a logical choice to spend a week of intensive bombing training with the AD squadron. It didn't occur to Walter, or to anyone else, that there was anything anomalous about his jumping into an airplane he hadn't flown since the BIS trials at Patuxent and immediately participating in advanced tactical exercises. That's the way things were done then.

This squadron spent a lot of time bombing. That was their job. They held a weekly bombing pool; awards time customarily was a late-Friday-afternoon Happy Hour at a nearby saloon, where serious debriefing was adequately lubricated with quantities of beer. This particular Friday the winner—one more time—was "Bunky," the skipper.

A constant in aviation is the combination of frustration and disbelief on the part of younger pilots when a squadron's "old men," especially *the* Old Man, outperform the young guys in activities that are not unlike athletic performances—like bombing, gunnery, and ACM (air combat maneuvering, "dogfighting").

One of the ensigns, already earning his own reputation as a "good stick," could stand it no more.

"All right, Skipper. How do you do it? What's the secret?"

"Nothing to it," Bunky replied. "The trick is proper lead angle. Just a cunt hair will do it."

"What do you mean, a cunt hair?" The ensign's impatience was mounting. "How do you measure that?"

Bunky surveyed his interrogator. Glances were exchanged around the table. Just then the waitress arrived with a fresh round of beer.

"Lou," he addressed her, "let me have a cunt hair." He extended a hand in her direction.

Setting the full tray down on the table, she stared at him. With the back of one hand she wiped a drop of perspiration off her forehead. Then she shrugged her shoulders, reached down into her shorts, and, wincing slightly, withdrew her hand and extended toward Bunky a black, curly pubic hair.

"Now," he said, "this is the way it goes."

He set his beer glass on the table and then removed it, leaving a wet ring. "That's the 50-mil ring." He broke off the head of a match and put it in the center of the circle. "That's the pipper."

He held the hair up to the light and carefully straightened it, then placed it adjacent to the match head "pipper."

"What you do is roll into the target at 8,500 to 9,000 feet. Set up a 50-degree dive. Steepen to 70 degrees as you start to track."

He squinted in concentration on his "target," flying an imaginary bombing run with his hand.

"Put the pipper above the target, just far enough for that cunt hair to fit between it and the target. Release in time to start your pull-out at 3,000 feet. You'll get a good hit every time!"

Bunky drained his beer and leaned back in his chair, satisfied with the clarity of his explanation.

Proficiency flying was not so colorful, nor as much fun. The airplanes we flew had a minimal transport capability, and since the object of the proficiency exercise was to accomplish training, destination was usually of secondary importance. Accordingly, military people with places to go and thin wallets—a common condition—not only rode with us but often influenced where we flew. We were especially sympathetic to requests from fellow proficiency-status aviators. It was not unusual to get a telephone call that started like this: "This is So-and-So. I see you're on the schedule. I couldn't get an airplane myself, but I have this———[close relative, old friend, retired/ailing parent] who because of———[something desperate] needs to get to———[some place east of the Mississippi River].[13]

I received such a telephone call the morning of a day on which I was planning a night flight. I had planned to leave work early so as to get started by five o'clock. It was late fall. The days were getting short, and daylight savings had ended—a good time of year to get in some needed night flying. The request had to do with "an officer friend" trying to take maximum advantage of a short leave. Would I take him to Memphis tonight? My knee-jerk reaction proceeded on the assumption that a fellow aviator would not make an unreasonable request. "But of course," I said. I gave him a time for the prospective passenger to meet me at Anacostia.

Although I had flown over substantial chunks of the coastal United States, my knowledge of the inland southeast was incomplete. When I agreed to the flight, I had in mind something on the order of 300, perhaps 350 miles one way, a round trip of a bit over four hours. That was acceptable, especially in view of the state of my personal life at the time; I didn't have anything better to do. And, as any self-respecting aviator can be quoted as saying about *any* flight, "It beats working for a living."

Memphis, Tennessee, is in fact seven hundred nautical miles from Washington, D.C., as I discovered when I pulled my trusty planning chart out of the desk drawer. It wasn't quite time for "Oh, shit!" and cancel, but I seriously considered it. It dawned on me that I was signing up for almost eight hours of flying. However, I saw a chance to meet most of my night requirements in one flight. It was pushing things a bit, legal but not prudent; the FFA permits commercial pilots and flight instructors as much flying time, or more, in one day.

The "officer friend" turned out to be a midshipman from the Naval Academy. The faceless requester had obviously feared that I might decline if the friend were not a commissioned officer. He need not have worried; having negotiated the Naval Academy mill myself, I felt empathy toward those suffering the experience. And there was another passenger, a sailor on emergency leave; that began to make the flight worthwhile. The plane captain and I briefed the passengers on the intricacies of the two different kinds of parachutes and harnesses and loaded them aboard. The sailor was in back; the midshipman sat next to me in front. It was still daylight when we took off.

It was a beautiful clear evening, moonless, but with hardly a cloud in the sky. Initially, I could back up my radio navigation with eyeball verification of landmarks, especially towns and cities. When it got really dark, it was strictly ADF (automatic direction-finder) navigation. That device was a multiband radio receiver, in operation much like today's solid-state descendants. Band selection was by click stops; you tuned within a band with a little "coffee-grinder" hand crank. Selectable frequency bands ranged from low—to accommodate the LFR (low-frequency range) stations still in use[14] and the NDBs (nondirectional radio beacons)—to a high band that included the commercial AM radio stations.

The least preferable navigation technique was to track, audio only, the solid tone of the low-frequency ranges. The next best alternative was to follow the pointing ADF needle from beacon to beacon (beacons were located at the larger airfields and at the intersections of some airways). But the preferred method was to dial in a succession of commercial radio stations and be entertained while one proceeded through a series of selected checkpoints. To make that easier, there was a government-issued navigation publication that listed all the radio stations in the country, giving their locations, call letters, and rated power.

There was another navigation aid, this one dating back almost to the old airmail days. When all cockpits were open, before voice communication radios and certainly before navigation radios, all navigation depended on what used to be called "contact" flying; pilots flew by eyeball contact with the ground, proceeding from one recognizable landmark to another, correlating what they saw with symbols on a map. Hardly an arcane process, this is how we teach student pilots to fly cross-country today in civil aviation. Of course, today's students in modern light airplanes have a lot of equipment going for them; for the airmail pilots, contact flying was the only navigation technique available. The competition among airmail contractors and the strict delivery requirements of the U.S. Postal Service meant that airmail pilots flew day and night, in any kind of weather in which they could find some way to navigate.[15] As air routes became established and more frequently traveled, a simple but effective aid was introduced to lessen navigation difficulties at night: a series of lighted beacons mounted on towers, spaced at regular intervals along a route. In 1956 such lighted pathways on the ground still existed along some colored (LFR, as opposed to the new VOR "Victor") airways.

My flight to Tennessee that night was uneventful but long. Although I was flying by ADF, I amused myself by pretending that I really had to rely on those beacons. At six thousand feet on this clear night, I always had several in sight. I speculated on how it would be at lower altitudes, in reduced visibility. How would it feel if I could see only two beacons? Or one? I could imagine an earlier pilot's apprehension as he approached the last of one or two visible lights. Would he be able to find the next one? And the next? I was glad I didn't have to navigate that way.

As we proceeded to Memphis, there was a light to moderate wind on the nose. If it held, it would be on my tail on the trip back; that would help. The sailor dozed under the canopy in back. The midshipman was quiet beside me, perhaps too timid to use the intercom.

My passengers came back to life when we landed. They promptly disembarked and returned to their own lives. I wasn't going to be alone on the way back, however. One USAF airman, a nonaviator naval officer, and two soldiers, one of them female, were patiently waiting for transportation to Washington. After filing a flight plan and arranging for fuel, I took my little group out to the ramp, briefed them, and loaded them aboard the airplane.

There was a minor commotion with one of the soldiers. The transient ramp at Memphis was lighted, but it was still dark and shadowy in the passenger compartment of the AD-5, even with the assistance of the plane captain's flashlight. In getting to his seat, the soldier stumbled, took a step aft, and promptly fell into the unlighted bilge. Fortunately, he didn't hurt himself or, as far as I could tell, anything else.

After we got everybody strapped in, there was another hitch. The walk-around portion of my preflight was interrupted by a member of the line crew: they hadn't yet fueled the airplane, "but it will only be a few minutes!" Beginning to recognize fatigue, I sat down on the left main landing gear tire, which was as far as I had progressed in my preflight inspection. (In typical Douglas fashion, the diameter of the wheel was large enough for it to serve as a seat.) This, I thought, is not one of my better ideas; I would just as soon not be doing this right now. It was well after nine o'clock. It would be after one o'clock when I reached Anacostia, probably after two in the morning before I got home. And I had to work the next day!

The gas crew were quicker than they had promised. They apologized for the delay, and I was on my way. As part of my pretakeoff procedure, I tuned in the ADF to the Memphis NDB I intended to track outbound for my first leg. No reception. I concluded that I was shielded from the station by some obstruction on the ground. It would be OK in the air; after all, the receiver had worked on the trip down.

After taking off to the west—the wind was still from that direction—I executed a downwind departure and tried the ADF again. Nothing. Not on the Memphis NDB, not on the commercial station I had listened to on my approach to Memphis, not on any other station I could think to try. Not even, using the receive-only function, on the low-frequency radio range. Stone dead!

I looked into the darkness ahead, past the lighted airfield, past the lights of the city and suburbs of Memphis, and past the little diamond clusters that marked smaller towns and communities in the distance. I saw with difficulty the lights of three, four—maybe five?—rotating beacons stretching in an uncertain line eastward, into the blackness. Damn, this was not going to be any fun. I would have to fly all the way to the Shenandoah Valley and the Blue Ridge mountains of Virginia before I could anticipate recognizing familiar points on the ground. In the meantime, there was going to be much looking at the chart with my red flashlight and flying the beacons. It would be a long, tedious four hours. The more I thought about it, the more unacceptable the idea became.

"Sorry folks," I announced to my companions over the intercom, "we've got a radio problem. We're not going to make it tonight."

I returned to Memphis and landed. The night-check crew promised to look at my ADF radio; with luck it would be ready in the morning. (As they would discover, it was on that particular piece of avionics that the soldier had landed when he fell into the aft fuselage.) While my enlisted passengers were accommodated in a transient barracks, the naval officer and I got a room in the Bachelor Officers' Quarters. I had the Operations Duty Officer send the obligatory "RON, mechanical" to NAS Anacostia.[16] Then I telephoned my wife—soon to be former wife—and described my predicament. As soon as I could manage, I crawled into bed. I fell asleep instantly.

The next morning featured high clouds but good visibility. There was good news and bad news with my navigation receiver. The good news was that they had found the trouble; the bad news was that they couldn't fix it. My passenger had landed on a connecting cable and broken the attaching connector, and the Memphis radio shop didn't have a replacement. But that didn't present a problem as long as I didn't have to file an instrument flight plan. Being able to see where I was going made all the difference.[17] The return flight was routine. Even the weather improved as I headed east.

Personal Recollections

I left Washington in August of 1957 after almost exactly three years in BuAer. It was by no means my tour of choice—not enough flying and not enough airplanes—but I learned a lot. I also met and worked with some marvelous people, civilian and military, in government and in industry.

The Navy employed a large number of engineers. At all levels they were capable of toe-to-toeing with their industry counterparts in discussions of even the most esoteric technical matters. The Navy's civilian engineers were not only good, they were good to work with. I remember indefatigable Ed Ryan, who was a GS-13 section head. The younger ones were mostly GS-11s and -12s. People like Chuck Troha, Bob Weinberg, and Ed Griffin, who made GS-13 while I was there, did good work for what were low salaries even for that time; a Navy lieutenant commander on flight pay earned more than they did.

BuAer's Airframe Design Division included the Structures Branch, where my section head was an outstanding AEDO (aeronautical engineering duty only) officer, Commander Ed La Roe. Ed had been a World

War II dive-bomber pilot. Indirectly, I worked for a GS-14 civilian, Ralph Creel. In those days a GS-14 was damn near God. Ralph was a sometimes irascible, extroverted type who had an industrywide reputation for being competent and tough with airframe contractors. He had a ready smile and a normally good disposition, but it didn't pay to try to fool him. Like any engineer, he wasn't always right; but he was right often enough, and he got people's attention. Some of his more colorful expressions of discontent with design practices were, appropriately, reserved for his co-workers.

I remember Ralph's response to the "design understrength" theory for carrier aircraft espoused by a particular airframe contractor. The theory said that you should design to a minimum rather than maximum level of strength—in essence, you should bias structural design decisions toward the low rather than the high side. Then, based on results of the repeated load and fatigue tests that are part of any design verification, you should locally beef up only those structural areas where weakness becomes apparent. This was different from the more usual design practice, which could produce excess strength in areas where it was not needed. (Grumman was occasionally cited as an example of how the usual approach could result in excess weight; however, I never heard a pilot complain about a Grumman airplane being *too* strong.)

Ralph Creel thought that "design understrength" was a terrible idea, and he was certain that his opinion had been vindicated when he saw the results of repeated load tests on the main spar of a new airplane. Load tests are always impressive; I saw the film of this particular test. The wing assembly—the real thing, no model, no simulation—sat in a massive, instrumented test jig where it was systematically pounded by hydraulic rams—*wham, wham, wham*—at about one-second intervals. Up to a particular *wham*, there was no mark on the spar where the camera was focused. On the next *wham*, there was just the suggestion of a tiny fatigue crack. On the next, the spar failed catastrophically. It broke into two pieces.

"Hah!" Ralph exploded. "I told them. You design understrength, you design an understrength airplane!"

In fairness to that contractor—one of our most successful manufacturers of military airplanes—there is substantial merit to the "design understrength" approach when applied prudently. I suspect that all modern aircraft manufacturers have at least vestiges of the idea in their approach to structural design. Certainly none of them deliberately designs overweight.

Starting with the Korean War and the impetus of a growing cold war, the U.S. military aviation industry was again dynamic and exciting.

Some wonderful airplanes were in various stages of development—the F4D Skyray, F5D Skylance, A4D Skyhawk, A3D Skywarrior, F3H Demon, F11F Tiger, F9F-8 Cougar, and F8U Crusader, with the F4H Phantom II not far behind. And those were just the carrier airplanes. With that many airplanes undergoing development at the same time there was a constant stream of engineers from the various airframe contractors. Part of the function of a technical bureau was to review and approve design and then to monitor contractor performance against the milestones of development schedules. Contacts with our industrial colleagues were generally amicable, sometimes intense, usually good humored, and almost never adversarial.

The list of airplanes in the previous paragraph includes an almost inordinate number of Douglas airplanes. This was in Mr. Ed Heinemann's heyday as chief engineer for the Douglas Aircraft plant at El Segundo. His series of high-performance swept-wing jet airplanes came along when the carrier Navy most needed them, just as it was moving into the era of steam catapults, mirror landing systems, and angled flight decks. One of my regrets is that during that period of intense Douglas activity I never met the man—perhaps not a realistic regret, since he was unlikely to have been wandering the back halls of the "W" building, solving detailed structural, aerodynamic, or flight-restrictions problems. More likely he would have been in the front office of the Main Navy Building, describing his next airplane to the admiral who was the BuAer chief.

The whole period assumes a sense of unreality for me when I drive along Constitution Avenue today. Between 17th Street and 21st Street, where Main Navy and the Munitions Buildings once stood with their shabby "W" and "N" building cousins huddled behind them, is a parklike extension of the Mall. One can now see the reflecting pool from the street, no longer shielded from passing view by the temporary buildings of World War I and World War II.[18]

In July of 1957 I received orders back to sea. It had been over four years since I had been assigned to a fleet carrier squadron; I worried that my active flying career might have been permanently short-circuited. These new orders were a shock: Special Weapons Officer on the staff of ComCarDiv-3 (Commander, Carrier Division Three). Another nonflying job!

In desperation I called my aviation detailer (the order-writer). Not to worry, he said. (You can bet your sweet elbow that you're in trouble when a detailer says "not to worry.") It's just the first half of a three-year sea tour, he continued. Then we'll take care of you. (I didn't find "we'll take care of you" reassuring either.) He went on to remind me

VA-54 ADs to seaward of Point Loma. NAS North Island and San Diego are visible in the background. (USNI Photo Library)

that I had had two tours in fighter squadrons plus that short stint as a fighter instructor. My career needed rounding out. (That's another favorite ploy of detailers. About then my career felt so round that it could roll down the street all by itself.)

It was to be a while yet before I crawled back into a squadron airplane. In the interim, a number of ADs helped to remind me that I was still alive as an aviator. I found them and flew them in various places: Alameda; Barber's Point, Hawaii; Atsugi, Japan; and Cubi Point, the Philippines.

Chapter 9
F8U Crusader

ON A MARCH AFTERNOON IN 1987 I sat in a hangar of the Naval Air Facility, Andrews Air Force Base, Washington, D.C. I was part of a crowd of interested spectators, friends, and well-wishers gathered to witness a significant event, the disestablishment ceremony of Light Photographic Squadron 206 (VFP-206). Outside the open hangar doors, facing each other under the brilliant sun of a cloudless sky, were two airplanes. Very special airplanes, they were the first Chance Vought F8U Crusader to fly and the last Crusader in active service in the U.S. Navy.

The XF8U-1, first flown by Vought test pilot John Konrad at Edwards AFB on 25 March 1955, had been lovingly restored by VFP-206 to a convincing semblance of its original, pristine appearance. It was all shiny aluminum and magnesium with bright accents of high-visibility red. The airplane had been loaned to the squadron for the occasion by the Smithsonian Institution.

Its companion, dowdy looking by comparison in the Navy's latest low-visibility gray paint scheme, was the final VFP-206 airplane still in commission. It was the last Crusader to be in commission anywhere in the U.S. armed forces. This photoreconnaissance RF-8G was one of 144 Crusaders that had started life as F8U-1Ps.[1] Later redesignated RF-8A (under postunification nomenclature), it was one of seventy-three survivors that were rebuilt as RF-8Gs.[2] Unlike its parent, which would fly no more, the RF-8G was to have one more go. The next day, 30 March 1987, no-longer-commanding-officer Commander David G. Strong, USNR, would fly the airplane to its final home at Dulles International Airport. There it would await construction of a new exhibition facility of the Air and Space Museum.

Between John Konrad's first Crusader flight and Dave Strong's final trip in the airplane there would have elapsed thirty-two years and five

F8U-1, somewhere over the Western Pacific. (Author's collection)

days. There were 1,261 F-8 Crusaders in nine major versions, making it one of the more numerous, as well as one of the most long-lived, of the carrier fighters.

This occasion was a celebration of respect and affection. The airplane had earned both, with such high points as being the first production airplane[3] to achieve 1,000 mph in level flight and achieving the highest kill ratio of any fighter in the Vietnam War. It was also an occasion of sadness, not unlike the wake of a friend.

The audience was composed of people with close ties to naval aviation: active and retired military of all ranks, Navy Department civilians, and a sizable contingent from Ling-Temco-Vought, the corporate entity to which Chance Vought Aircraft now belongs. There were former F8U mechanics, commanding officers, test pilots, just plain pilots, and other friends and admirers. Present were almost too many admirals to count, including Whitey Feightner, Bill Houser, and Don Engen, then Administrator of the Federal Aviation Administration. John Konrad was there, looking as if he could climb into the XF8U-1 and do it all over again. In the old days, it would have been the occasion for a rip-roaring party sponsored by United Aircraft. This Crusader's wake would be more separate, diverse, and private, and a lot less fun.

Dave Strong's farewell remarks to his squadron were almost lost on the audience as, choked with emotion, he struggled through his prepared text and extemporaneous comments. The event was a double blow to the reconnaissance community. This reserve squadron was the last Navy squadron to be assigned a dedicated reconnaissance mission; henceforth, the reconnaissance job would be relegated to a sub-mission performed by line fighter squadrons.[4] A new reserve squadron would in time likely be born on the same spot, probably flying brand-new F-18s. But it was the end of an era.

It had started in 1952 with the Navy's requirement for a new carrier fighter. The specifications were evolutionary rather than revolutionary with an interesting additional wrinkle: the airplane was to be supersonic. Not transonic but really supersonic, and that in level flight. The requirement was far from outlandish, but it was a challenge. There was the residual notion that, by definition, a carrier airplane was inherently inferior to its land-based competition. No carrier aircraft had yet been a legitimate Mach 1 airplane, although Ed Heinemann's F4D Skyray came close. Chance Vought's candidate would be the F8U Crusader.

It has been reported that this was a last gasp for Vought; the company had not built a successful airplane since the F4U Corsair. It could be said that Chance Vought lost its place in line to Grumman and McDonnell. There was a discernible pattern to the Navy's aircraft procurement policy: buy them in pairs so that you always get one that works. The best-known pair is the Hellcat and Corsair; at the beginning of the Navy's jet era it was the Fury and Phantom; in the early 1950s it was the Banshee and Panther.

Vought's F6U Pirate didn't even come close to making either of those last two pairs a triumvirate.[5] I remember the F6U's reputation as being grossly underpowered, a true "ground lover." A friend and classmate, James L. "Jim" Holbrook, stationed at Patuxent earned the distinction of being one of the first naval aviators to make a nylon descent from a jet airplane when he abandoned a Pirate in midair near Atlantic City, New Jersey. He had good reason. On takeoff from Naval Air Station Mustin Field, Philadelphia, Jim had left his main landing gear on the sea wall that separated the airport from the Delaware River. He knocked it clean off by being not quite airborne before the end of the runway; Mustin was a tight fit even for a good jet airplane. Jim Holbrook's Pirate was still flyable, but to attempt to make it back to Pax and then belly-land the damaged airplane was not an attractive alternative. The prudent choice was to depart the airplane. He did, but it wasn't easy. Repeated pulls on the face curtain failed to fire the ejection seat. Finally, approaching desperation, he opened the cockpit canopy, rolled the airplane upside down, opened his seat harness, and fell—ungracefully— out of the cockpit. The parachute worked just fine.

Vought came closer with the next effort, the tailless twin-engine F7U Cutlass. This radical airplane constituted a significant design departure in a number of ways: its wings were swept; it had no horizontal tail; there were two twin vertical tails and two afterburning engines (a first for carrier airplanes). In its production version as F7U-3M, the Cutlass was the first naval aircraft to be armed solely with missiles. It also became the first airplane to release ordnance in excess of Mach 1.[6] With a maximum speed of over 700 mph and a combat ceiling of forty-five thousand feet, the Cutlass appeared to be the answer to a lot of Navy prayers.

But once again a Vought airplane was going to have many problems to solve. Considerable time would elapse before a Cutlass squadron reached the fleet, and when it did, it would be a case of too little, too late. Many of the difficulties had to do with the dual-redundant hydraulic system powering the flight controls; such an installation would become standard for high-performance jet airplanes, but in the F7U it was a first. The pioneering swept-wing, tailless design would present interesting stability and control problems, and the long, spindly nose landing gear was the source of unpleasant surprises.

The length of the nose strut was necessary to get the nose of the airplane close to the angle of attack necessary for takeoff without the necessity for excessive rotation by the pilot. Its static attitude was about 9 degrees. Takeoff required about 15 degrees. One result of such extreme angles of attack[7] was restricted pilot visibility in landing configuration; another was difficulties in ground handling. The problems were worse than anticipated. The solution is evident in the bulge of the protruding cockpit as seen in production aircraft such as the F7U-3M, one of many changes that marred both appearance and performance.

That long nose strut had even nastier consequences. The pilot in the cockpit sat fourteen to sixteen feet above the deck. In the simplest of failures, that height could equate to a long fall. In the event of a strut collapse—as caused by a failure of the nose gear locking mechanism or an actual strut fracture—on an arrested landing, the cockpit might whiplash onto the flight deck with considerable force. More than one pilot had his back broken that way. In one incident the impact fired the ejection seat cartridge; the parabolic arc of the seat terminated on the forward end of the flight deck, killing the pilot.

These difficulties made the Cutlass an excellent test bed for the F8U but did not bode well for the service history of the F7U. Only 330 were built. Part of the problem was engines. The Westinghouse engines the F7U was designed for either weren't delivered on time or failed to provide design thrust.[8] Other difficulties, particularly with the complex hydraulic system, led to an unacceptably high accident rate. The old Corsair nickname "Ensign Eliminator" was resurrected and reapplied to the Cutlass.

I remember a flight demonstration at the Naval Air Test Center, Patuxent River, Maryland, in June of 1950. Such flight demonstrations consisted of air show-like exhibitions of the various airplanes undergoing test. The demonstrations were calculated to impress visiting dignitaries, like congressmen, who might afterwards be disposed to spend more taxpayer money for airplanes. The standard pièce de résistance was a parade of high-speed fly-bys terminating in nearly vertical climbs.

In spite of its many developmental problems, the afterburning Cutlass was a consistent star of the show. One day I stood watching from the Service Test Division ramp next to a tall mustang lieutenant named Howard S. Packard. The Cutlass followed the Banshee, Panther, and FJ-1 Fury (the Fury had put on a particularly hot show, making it the F7U's closest competitor). The Vought test pilot, former Navy pilot Paul Thayer, came roaring across the field in full afterburner at minimum altitude, a real grass cutter. Opposite the reviewing stand on the far side of the field, he rotated the nose of the Cutlass skyward and initiated a series of maximum-roll-rate vertical aileron rolls. Observers could see the winking red of the two afterburners as the airplane rotated. It was spectacular; it became even more so.

The red dots were punctuated by another flickering trace of red. The F7U abruptly nosed over into level flight and commenced a gentle turn away from us toward the mouth of the Patuxent River. Thayer was in trouble; that third flicker was a definite fire. The airplane commenced a series of oscillations in roll, finally rolling completely upside down; a fully developed fire was easily visible. The airplane seemed to hesitate, then pointed earthward. It disintegrated in a fiery ball on impact into the Chesapeake Bay off Drum Point. A fraction of a second before the crash, there was a tiny white patch in the sky; the patch blossomed into Paul Thayer's parachute. He was at an uncomfortably low altitude, but he was safe.

There was an audible gasp from the observers on the ramp at Service Test followed by a stunned silence. The silence was broken by Lieutenant Packard's voice beside me: "Damn! I'd sure hate to follow that act."

At the time I was sure that Thayer was trying to do as Jim Holbrook had done: roll upside down to facilitate a manual bailout. The roll excursions could be explained by a failing hydraulic system, not surprising with an aft fuselage fire. Attached to Flight Test at the time, Jim Holbrook says that those roll excursions were uncontrollable. Thayer had ejected as soon as he could; this seat at least worked. Ralph Clark, Grumman's senior rep on site at the time, remembers it as I do. Thayer had the same problem that Jim had had in the Pirate and rolled on purpose. However it happened, he was upside down when he got free of the airplane, which explains the low altitude at which the chute opened.

That was Paul Thayer's last test flight, ever. He must have concluded that there were better things in life. He later became president of the company, not just Chance Vought but the whole Ling-Temco-Vought Corporation.

General Description

With the precedent of failure set by the radical designs of the F5U "Flying Pancake" and the F7U Cutlass, Russ Clark's design team selected a more conventional approach for the F8U—conventional,[9] but by no means conservative. They opted for a 42-degree swept-wing design even though there were no swept-wing carrier airplanes flying at the time. The F7U was used as a standard of "how not to." Improved visibility over the nose was a prime consideration, as was avoiding the problems associated with a long nose strut. There remained the difficulty of a swept wing's high angle of attack for slow flight and landing, however clever and effective high-lift devices such as large wing flaps and leading-edge droops might be.

The visibility and nose strut problems were solved by an innovative feature. The solution was simple in concept but visually bizarre: Vought built a variable-incidence wing; it was hinged at two points near the trailing edge. The wing was further secured to the airplane and moved up and down by a third attachment point, offset to one side near the leading edge of the wing. At that attachment, raising and lowering of the wing was accomplished hydraulically. With this arrangement the wing could be raised almost 7 degrees for landings and takeoffs. The fuselage could remain relatively level for slow-flight conditions with only a modest increase in angle of attack. Most of the increase in angle of attack was provided—directly to the wing, where it was needed—by the increased incidence.

It was peculiar looking. Taxiing on the ground with the wing raised, large inboard flaps drooping at the rear, and oversize leading-edge wing droops lowered to the landing/takeoff position, the F8U resembled some kind of prehistoric creature; its size and apparent clumsiness on the ground added to the illusion. It was a big airplane, and its heritage showed. Like other Vought airplanes—the F4U is an example—the Crusader in landing configuration looked as if various important parts were about to fall off.

The forward edge of the wing where it faired into the fuselage terminated in a flat flange of considerable thickness. This surface, which was exposed to view when the wing was raised, was usually painted a bright red, as an aid to the flight line crew in preventing the pilot from trying to take off with the wing lowered. As if a raised wing with appendages dangling fore and aft weren't obvious to any but the most obtuse observer!

The wing flaps and leading edge droops were linked to the wing mechanism so that they automatically lowered when the wing was raised and, similarly, retracted when the wing was lowered. The flaps were differentially controlled so that they also acted as inboard ailerons. The leading-edge droops were in two sections. The short-chord section was a so-called cruise droop, which provided a modest increase in wing camber for subsonic flight. The larger, full-chord segment drooped as a unit to a larger angle for landing and takeoff—25 degrees for the inboard segment and 27 degrees for the outboard segment. The cruise droop was a vital design feature[10] that provided subsonic maneuverability to the thin, supersonic wing at high altitudes and low "q" ("dynamic pressure," as discussed in an earlier chapter).

The variable-incidence wing, mechanized as a two-position wing, made it possible for all three landing gear struts to be short. They retracted into the fuselage. The high wing and the absence of a propeller ensured that ground clearance was not a problem. The F8U squatted close to the ground. Since it was not equipped with a tail skag, it was possible to drag the tail pipe by over-rotation on landing or takeoff.

The F8U's fundamental design was conventional, but it made good use of a host of innovations. It was one of the first production airplanes to make use of lightweight wiring. Difficulties with the backup hydraulic system in the F7U were alleviated in the F8U by providing a Marquardt ram air turbine or RAT that selectively powered an auxiliary hydraulic pump and/or a backup AC-DC generator for electrical power. Power was provided to the emergency hydraulic pump and generator by the "turbine," which resembled a small propeller.

The RAT was an interesting device. Normally housed forward in the right side of the fuselage, it was deployed by pulling a handle in the cockpit. Propelled by compressed air from a 900-cubic-inch reservoir, it flopped out into the breeze, there to remain until it was manually stowed on the ground. Part of the Crusader's GSE (ground support equipment) was an ungainly contraption designed to fit over the Marquardt unit for ground maintenance check of both emergency features. In 1960, VF-124, the West Coast RAG (replacement air group) squadron, had at least a couple of them. However, most fleet squadrons, including VF-191, did not; an alternative test method was to reserve the RAT for the final test on a post-major-inspection test flight. The unit produced a lot of drag as it stayed out for the rest of the flight. (Drag or no, the published maximum speed limit with the RAT extended was a respectable Mach 1.4—essentially no restriction at all for an F8U-1. The airplane probably couldn't even achieve that speed with the RAT extended.)

The F8U's designers made use of the best and most appropriate materials for the job, and that contributed to more innovation in the form of magnesium and titanium. Titanium is very strong for its weight. About 40 percent lighter than stainless steel, it is heat resistant in terms of melting temperature as well as retention of strength at elevated temperatures. It also has the advantage of being corrosion resistant; titanium doesn't rust! Unfortunately, it is expensive and difficult to work. There was titanium in the tail section and fuselage of the Crusader. The fuselage was also about 25 percent magnesium, the principal appeal of which is light weight. Magnesium was slow coming into structural use in airplanes because it tends to be brittle; for a long time it was considered impossible to forge or to cast into any but the simplest shapes. It is also extremely susceptible to corrosion, especially when used in conjunction with other metals. (Dissimilar metals in an electrolyte constitute a battery, as in electroplating one metal onto another. Aluminum and magnesium are dissimilar metals; salt water is an electrolyte, as is high-humidity salt air.) Corrosion control and corrosion prevention were continuing problems during the service life of the airplane.

With its thin, supersonic swept wings, the Crusader had the classic small World War II fighter wingspan of a little over thirty-five feet. It made up for that small dimension in the fuselage length necessary to accommodate the Pratt & Whitney J57 engine: 54 feet 3 inches. Weight empty in the early models was about 16,500 pounds, which compared favorably with the 21,000-pound U.S. Air Force F-100 Super Sabre, powered by the same engine. With over 8,000 pounds of fuel—all of it internal in the "main" and "transfer" fuel systems—that brings the airplane close to 24,000 pounds at takeoff gross weight. (That tracks with my recollection of "24,000" grease-penciled on the nose of my F8U-1 on the USS *Bonhomme Richard* [CVA-31]. The weight figure was intended for the catapult crew so that they could set the proper pressure in the steam catapult. The number represented the actual weight for that launch, not some hypothetical "spec" value.)

Bill Gunston reports the maximum takeoff gross weight of the F-8E at a maximum of 34,000 pounds and an empty weight of 19,000 pounds;[11] the difference is explained in part by the external stores and pylons carried by that later version and additional internal fuel.

The J57 was one of the most advanced and successful engines of its time; versions of it appeared in the F-101, F-102, B-52, A3D, and F4D. (See table 2.)

Power up for start. Starboard catapult, the Bonnie Dick. (Author's collection)

It is not unusual for later versions of an airplane to lose top-end performance. The culprits are usually increased structural weight and increased drag. Higher drag may result from bumps and bulges added to house extra equipment or to provide means of carrying external stores, like bomb racks and pylons. Increased surface area and span of wings, fins, and rudders are common in later versions. Take, for example, the F8U-2N and the F8U-2NE (original designations). They were essentially the same airplane with the same engine, but even with both in a "clean" configuration, the F8U-2NE was somewhat slower. I think the reason for the difference is evident in a side-elevation, or profile, view of the airplanes: the nose of the F8U-2NE had a bump.

All Crusaders had the same nose shape until the F8U-2NE. The F8U-2N was the first F8U to have a sophisticated search and track radar, the Magnavox APQ-83. That radar's small antenna "dish" fit inside the same nose as the APG-30 range-only gunnery radar in the F8U-1 and the APS-67 search and ranging radar in the F8U-1E and F8U-2. In order to achieve greater range performance, the succeeding APQ-94 in the F8U-2NE was given a larger-diameter antenna. That necessitated a big-

Table 2 F8U Performance

	Engine	Thrust	Top speed
F8U-1	J57-P4A	10,200 lbs MRT[a] 16,000 lbs CRT[b]	Mach 1.5
F8U-2	J57-P16	17,000 lbs CRT	Mach 1.7
F8E[c]	J57-P20[d]	18,000 lbs CRT	Mach 1.8
F-8D	J57-P20	18,000 lbs CRT	Mach 1.9

[a] Military-rated thrust (full throttle in basic engine).
[b] Combat-rated thrust (unmodulated afterburner thrust).
[c] Originally F8U-2NE.
[d] Bill Gunston (*The Illustrated History of Fighters* [New York: Exeter Books, 1981]) places the P-20A in the F-8E. Barrett Tillman (*MiG Master—The Story of the F-8 Crusader* [Annapolis, Md.: Nautical and Aviation Publishing Company of America, 1980]) puts the -P20 in the F-8E and the -P20A in the French F-8E(FN).

ger nose. The result was a visible break, a discontinuity, in the smoothly faired line from the tip of the nose cone through the windscreen and canopy to the aft fuselage. That bump may have been responsible for the tenth-of-a-Mach-number slowdown in the F8U-2NE. (Another bump provided by the housing for the infrared scanning head, at the top of the radome in front of the windscreen, didn't help either, but that device was on the faster F8U-2N as well.)

There was a story told in VF-124 that has the ring of truth. Bumps like that had apparently been studied before. Late in the design development of the F8U, Vought ran what were intended to be final wind-tunnel tests to verify performance. Top speed was a disappointment, about Mach 1.2, roughly the same as the F11F. The design at that time featured a nose cone with a pronounced inflection or discontinuity just before it sloped upward at the windscreen. That bump was determined to contribute to a performance-robbing shock wave. The design was changed to produce a smooth, almost straight line from the tip of the nose all the way back to where the cockpit canopy faired into the fuselage with equal smoothness—no bumps and no discontinuities.[12] Predicted performance leaped to about Mach 1.4, where it was supposed to be.

All three axes of the F8U's control system—stabilator, ailerons, and rudder—were powered by a dual-redundant hydraulic system. This was a more reliable replication of the control system in the F7U. The 3,000-psi hydraulic system consisted of three major parts: PC-1, PC-2, and

Utility ("PC" meant "Power Control"). Each system was designed to be as independent of the others as possible; each had its own hydraulic fluid reservoir, pump, filters, and the valves and plumbing necessary to circulate fluid under pressure in its own enclosed system. The big advantage over earlier designs was reliability. No single failure, like a failed master pump or a unique leak, could incapacitate the airplane. There were bonus effects relating to battle damage: a single hit would not render the airplane uncontrollable, unless the damage was severe enough to affect more than one system. Everything was confined within the same narrow fuselage, wrapped around the same engine. Some forms of catastrophic, noncombat failure could also do one in: an explosive failure or one involving fire in one system might inflict damage on the others. Nonetheless, the system was a giant step forward compared with previous airplanes. The basic elements of the F8U hydraulic control system are more or less emulated in all modern U.S. high-performance airplanes.

Pilot commands to the control system—that is, stick and rudder inputs—operated through linkages to operate valves that told the hydraulic system what to do. The trim system was electric. The controls anticipated to be the most used—pitch and aileron trim controls—were small rotatable wheels located at the top of the stick, convenient to the pilot's right thumb. The wheels operated electric potentiometers ("pots") that commanded a complex trim and control force "feel" system.

The longitudinal control system deserves special mention. The horizontal tail was a two-piece "slab," one on each side of the fuselage, each side controlled by its own actuator. There was only so much control travel, as in any control system. What "trim" did was to position—or in the case of landing or takeoff, pre-position—the stabilator somewhere in its range of travel. The idea is to "trim" the system to where the pilot's immediate control movements—by definition much less than total travel—are in a range where the control forces are manageable and comfortable. In the F8U, longitudinal control forces could be formidable. Consequently, there was a backup pitch trim system. It was actuated by a little tee handle on the cockpit console with appropriate emergency-type yellow stripes painted on its shaft.

Ensuring that the backup trim system was operable in case of failure of the primary trim system was a mandatory preflight item. Since trim position is at the expense of total available control travel, there was more at stake than pilot control "feel" considerations. If, for instance, the airplane was trimmed for hands-off supersonic flight, there might not be enough pitch ("elevator") control travel left to land the airplane!

The emergency trim system was there to ensure that the pilot could control the airplane under all flight conditions.

The F8U's 42-degree wing sweep was greater than that of many of its contemporaries; 35 degrees was more common and, according to some aerodynamicists, the minimum value for realizing the advantages of swept-wing design. Swept-wing aerodynamic characteristics were exaggerated in the Crusader. Prominent among these, for both swept and delta wings, is directional instability. (One might think of such designs as being dartlike. Darts, once thrown or dropped, seem to want to fly straight and true. But there is a difference: once in its travel, a dart is essentially "pulled" through the air by its mass, which is concentrated in the nose; a jet airplane, unless its engines are in forward-mounted wing pods, is essentially "pushed" through the air by the reactive thrust of its engines located in the tail or the aft fuselage.)

The commonest cure for directional instability is an efficient yaw damper. The Crusader had one. At high speeds it was noticeably busy. The faster a swept-wing airplane flies, the more it wants to diverge, to fly sideways. The cockpit of the F8U, at the front end of a long fuselage, can be thought of as dangling at the end of a boom projecting far ahead of the center of pressure. Accordingly, oscillations in yaw were amplified at the cockpit location: at maximum speed an F8U-1 would "walk" infinitesimally back and forth under the pilot's butt, giving the impression that the airplane was only marginally under control. All F-8s subsequent to F8U-1 and F8U-1E had twin ventral fins under the aft fuselage for improved directional stability.[13]

As always, stability is achieved at the expense of maneuverability. Theoretically at least, the F8U-1's turning performance was slightly better than that of its ventral-wearing siblings. I knew a couple of Crusader skippers who, anticipating close-in combat, discussed unbolting and removing the ventral fins of their F8U-2Ns for improved "dogfight" capability.

An effective 4-foot-by-3-foot speed brake was located at the bottom of the forward fuselage. Hydraulically actuated, it was controlled by an electric switch located on the throttle handle. Its location was such that a wingman in the tightest of parade formations could see its position and movement. That facilitated formation "station keeping" during even the most dynamic maneuvers.

The Crusader was one of the last of the pure "day fighters," implying a clear air mass, visual fighter. Its armament was designed for visual target acquisition and visual weapon delivery; that is a cumbersome but accurate way of saying that the pilot had to find his enemy, maneuver his airplane into a firing position, and fire his weapon(s) by using the

Mark 1, Mod 1 human eyeball. For a long time there was no provision for carrying or delivering anything but air-to-air ordnance. Primary armament was four Colt Mk 12 20-millimeter cannon stacked in pairs on either side of the fuselage, below the cockpit. The tips of the muzzles were visible through small, raised blisters displaced outboard just far enough to keep projectiles from creasing the skin of the fuselage as they departed the airplane. The Mk 12 gun was a mixed blessing. It could be very effective, but it took a lot of care and feeding. My last close association with the gun dates back to 1961; my A4M-pilot son vigorously complained about its idiosyncrasies as recently as 1987. The ammunition feed system bordered on being a mechanical nightmare. In the Crusader, the charging and feed mechanisms were driven by one of three aircraft pneumatic systems. The gun chargers and gun gas vent doors shared a 2,600-psi pneumatic system with emergency actuation functions of the landing gear, wheel brakes, cruise droop (7-degrees; the emergency landing droop—27 and 25 degrees—operated from a different pneumatic system), and the Marquardt unit. Since the gun chargers and gun vent doors were the only normal operating function on the system, they automatically dropped off the line when pressure dropped to 1,400 psi. That was great for preserving lifesaving emergency systems, but it was lousy for gun reliability. When you lost air pressure, the guns quit! Because of various malfunctions having to do with hoses and fittings, they lost pressure a lot.

Ammunition stowage, on the other hand, was an unmixed blessing. A little less than 150 rounds per gun could be accommodated in cans that fit into a rectangular compartment behind the cockpit. Access was through a hinged door with quick-opening fasteners on top of the fuselage. The cans were removable—they had to be, for loading and unloading ammunition. When the cans weren't installed, there remained a large, easily accessible compartment for stowing things like pilot luggage. There was not even a requirement for carrying ballast in place of ammunition for proper weight and balance. With all that room for carrying personal gear and over 8,000 pounds of internal fuel, producing an unrefueled range of thirteen hundred nautical miles, the F8U was a great cross-country airplane.

Infrared homing Sidewinder missiles could be carried on detachable rails on the side of the fuselage just ahead of the wing. The F8U-1, -1E, and -2 could carry only two missiles, one each on single rails on either side. The F8U-2N and -2NE carried Y-racks in the same positions capable of carrying two AIM-9 Sidewinders each. Up through the service acceptance trials of the F8U-2NE in 1962 and 1963, there was still no air-to-ground capability. Later airplanes, F-8Ds and F-8Es,[14] were equipped with wing "hard points," pylons and bomb racks capable of carrying and delivering low-drag bombs and other air-to-ground ordnance. The missile stations were adapted to handle Zuni air-to-ground rockets.

I left Patuxent too soon to participate in or witness the fun of air-to-surface development and testing. Part of defining a safe flight envelope for carrying and releasing ordnance, especially gravity ordnance like bombs, is "separation" testing. The idea is to determine the conditions—speeds, altitudes, aircraft attitudes, aspects, g-loads—under which a weapon will come off cleanly without banging into the parent aircraft. That doesn't sound challenging, but the aerodynamic and inertial effects of different, sometimes strange, shapes in improbable clusters underneath an airplane can produce startling results. One of the early tests consisted of dropping a sleek, pointed "low-drag" bomb from a Crusader. The bomb didn't want to leave the airplane. It came off the wing rack and hovered, wiggling, below it. Then, held in some way by the airflow between the fuselage and the rack/pylon combination, it "flew" laterally toward the fuselage, dipped neatly underneath, and came back up to strike the opposite wing. That was one surprised pilot! The chase pilot must have been even more surprised; he had a better view. The problem was eventually solved. Crusaders dropped many bombs from wing store stations.

There is an exception to my allegation of no air-to-ground capability in the early F8Us: the notorious rocket pack. The pack was faired into the bottom of the fuselage and hinged at the rear so that it could be opened for firing (the speed brake was hinged in the middle of the pack). There were sixteen chambers that could house up to thirty-two 2.75-inch folding-fin airborne rockets (FFARs). They were stacked two to a hole, one behind the other. The pack was designed to work in a semiautomatic mode. After proper arming, the pilot pulled the trigger, whereupon the front end of the pack opened the few degrees necessary for the rockets to clear the airplane. The rockets fired. After they exited the door, the pack automatically closed again. These "Mighty Mouse" rockets, designed to be fired in clusters, carried an explosive charge but were unguided. The idea was to get enough of them in the vicinity of a target to cause lethal damage. They could be an effective saturation weapon and were used extensively from wing-mounted pods in other airplanes.

It doesn't take much imagination to recognize the potential hazards in this installation. Suppose there was a malfunction in the automatic sequencing and firing circuits such that the rockets fired but the pack did not open. (The pack was located under the main internal fuel cell—not a nice place for an explosion or a fuselage fire.) Or suppose the back row of rockets received the firing impulse, but the ones in front in the same holes did not. (The rear ones would be able to exit the pack only by blowing their way through their neighbors, and the resulting fireball would certainly destroy both airplane and pilot.) Now imagine a somewhat more benign possibility: everything else works, but one of the front-row missiles either doesn't fire or has a hang fire. Same result; the difference in degree of the resulting fire and explosion would be irrelevant. The automatic sequencing system could be circumvented by a manual mode that permitted the pack to be opened to the firing position. The rockets could then be fired, and the pilot could close the pack manually in a sequence that he controlled. There was no solution, however, for the nasty firing failure modes.

I fired rockets from an F8U-1 once, at the rocket range at NAAS Fallon, Nevada; it was part of the VF-124 training syllabus. We took precautions. Sixteen rockets were loaded, but only in the front chambers. The packs were opened manually in the air as we entered the firing range. After we inspected each other's airplanes visually, to ensure that all the packs were in the extended position, we assumed a spread formation. Out of shallow glides we salvoed the rockets. Watching the little buggers head earthward in their erratic flight paths was exciting. The pattern of explosions when they hit the ground was impressive.

After that one run, individual airplanes closed back into a formation of sections and divisions. Again we performed mutual visual inspections. We looked for evidence of hang fires—the airborne equivalent of a smoking gun, except that the gun would still be loaded—then we manually restored the packs to their housed position. None of us wanted to fly home with a rocket quietly cooking away in the fuselage. We did not shoot for score; the exercise was a demonstration. Later, F8U rocket packs were wired in the closed position. In my time in the fleet, the rocket packs were permanently disabled. In later models of the airplane the idea was abandoned completely—packs were not even installed.

The photo planes, F8U-1Ps and RF-8Gs (remanufactured version), carried cameras instead of ordnance. The RF8-1Ps had five camera bays in a fatter, more rectangular fuselage than the standard Crusaders. The RF-8Gs had one less camera bay and the higher-thrust -P20 engine. Ventral fins were added to the RF-8Gs.

How It Flew

The Crusader represented a totally new flying experience, particularly for a pilot who had never before flown an afterburning airplane. In the fall of 1959 I was a student in the six-month course of the Armed Forces Staff College in Norfolk, Virginia. There I received orders to report to VF-124 as prospective commanding officer of VF-191. *Ecstasy* is inadequate to describe my feelings; after frustrating years of flying desks and riding ships, I had begun to believe that my chances of getting back into a fighter squadron, let alone commanding one, were disappearing.

I ran into an old squadron mate, Bob Hoppe (it was the first time I had seen him since his bailout from a crippled Bearcat ten years earlier). Bob was skipper of VF-84, the "Jolly Rogers," at NAS Oceana. VF-84 was the first F8U-2 squadron. "The first burner takeoff is the wildest ride you've ever had in an airplane," he told me; "I guarantee it."

He was right, but that didn't happen for a while. I recently discovered among my possessions a fat loose-leaf notebook. Its yellowing pages contain a series of lectures that constituted the F8U ground school syllabus at VF-124, NAS Moffet Field, California. I reported aboard in February of 1960. With my recent flying background—or lack thereof—I was not immediately to leap into the cockpit of a Crusader and charge off into the blue.

VF-124 was a big squadron. It had to be; there were always several flights of students—FRPs, or fleet replacement pilots—going through the course at any one time. Even though the RAG squadron had a large number of airplanes, when a weapons detachment was at Fallon, Nevada, at the same time another detachment was aboard a carrier for carrier qualifications, resources for other training at Moffet were strained. Throw in the inevitable weather delays, and it could be a slow process. Sixteen or so pilots who would make up the new-look VF-191 were there ahead of me. (The old squadron was still at sea, flying F11F Tigers.) I needed to hurry to catch up.

In addition to the F8Us, VF-124 owned a separate squadron's worth of F9F-8T Cougars. These swept-wing two-seaters were used primarily for the jet instrument syllabus. The instrument course, extensive in itself, was mandatory for all but the fortunate few who showed up with recent-vintage jet instrument qualifications already in their pockets. I was not among them. The Cougars also provided refresher training for pilots like me who had not been in a jet cockpit for a while. Less frequently, the Cougars were used for initial or refresher carrier landing training.

I flew both the refresher (without the carrier landings) and the instrument course, ten flights each, starting with the refresher. In that first refresher flight, with an instructor riding as safety pilot, I was surprised and chagrined to discover that I really needed a refresher; the proof was a singularly ragged eight-point slow roll, an ill-advised attempt to show off for the kid in the back seat. But the rest of the refresher training went well. I had had only one previous Cougar flight, in a single-seat F9F-6 back in 1953. Under the guidance of Lieutenant

Barr, I was soon comfortable in the F9F-8T. With his insistence on flying proper angle of attack all the way to touchdown, I avoided duplicating my only previous swept-wing landing attempt, the one resulting in blown tires at Alameda in the F9F-6.

I started "instruments" with a four-flight overlap with remaining refresher flights. The instrument course was a revelation. The world had changed since my last serious jet instrument flying in a Panther. That had been in the early 1950s. Now it was all TACAN[15] and GCA (ground-controlled approach). A whole new high-altitude structure had been invented since then. The new rules seemed complex, but once learned, the high-altitude structure was marvelously simple to negotiate, particularly in the western states. Nothing like the current low-altitude instrument structure in the northeast corridor, for instance, where it sometimes seems to take three people and a computer in the airplane just to handle the administrative load.

There was good reason for instrument training before commencing the Crusader syllabus. Weather is generally good in the San Francisco area, but there is a lot of coastal fog. Sometimes the fog is over land with the ocean clear, sometimes the other way around. Often, mornings and evenings featured bad weather, with the middle of the day bright and sunny. Even with more serious frontal weather, there frequently were sizable altitude segments free of clouds where different kinds of training could be accomplished. We needed the facility for making instrument departures and approaches even though the bulk of our air work was to be visual. There were two requirements to take advantage of such conditions: every pilot had to be proficient in instrument flying, and there had to be pieces of sky reserved for training, free of uncontrolled transient aircraft.

Before taking his first F8U flight each FRP had to have a valid jet instrument card; that took care of the first requirement. There was a sizable restricted area just off the coast, complete with a supersonic corridor, to meet the second requirement. There was also a low-altitude corridor connecting Moffet Field to that area. The TACAN approach was a straight, down-the-chute penetration from an initial fix twenty-five miles south of the field at twenty thousand feet to a low-altitude, five-mile "Gate." At Gate, GCA controllers either took over for a straight-in approach to the northern runway or boxed the approaching airplanes around for a GCA approach to the southern runway.

Since we flew in two-plane elements, departures and approaches were usually flown in section formation. Even in dense stratus clouds it is not difficult for a wingman to maintain visual contact with his leader, just a few feet away during an instrument approach or departure—as long as the wingman doesn't mind not being able to see where he's going! (On the other hand, it's a bad thing if he fails to maintain visual contact with his leader in the "soup.")

It was an efficient system for getting significant numbers of airplanes in and out of the airfield under IFR (Instrument Flight Rules) conditions. Since we in VF-124 shared the field with another large squadron, the A4D RAG, and fleet squadrons across the field, the system was a practical necessity.

The weather had to be really lousy before we were forced to shut down completely. I flew "actual" instrument (as opposed to "simulated" instrument) departures and penetrations on my last two Cougar flights in the refresher phase. Since there was always a qualified instructor in the airplane, the instrument syllabus could be flown on actual instruments when necessary from the beginning. The ability to fly in "instrument meteorological conditions" (the FAA's preferred terminology) is one reason I was able to complete the twenty flights of the two F9F-8T syllabus phases in sixteen calendar days. Compared with most flight training experiences, that was some kind of speed record.

It was another eighteen days before I first flew the F8U. In the interim were two solid weeks of the most thorough ground school and general preflight instruction I ever received before flying any airplane. Appropriately so because before the fleet introduction of the F4H Phantom II, the Crusader was arguably the most complex airplane in the American inventory.

With my head full of the technical specifics of this formidable bird, I found myself in the pilots' locker room for my first F8U flight. I suited up with a couple of jaygees similarly engaged. Nervousness and apprehension hung in the air almost palpably, with a touch—dare I say it?—of incipient fear. To recall an old joke, we were there because we were crazy, not because we were stupid.

Even suiting up to fly was a new experience. We wore the standard (cotton/synthetic blend) flight suits, dyed high-visibility international orange. Footwear was heavy-duty boots, infantry style, suitable for walking out of wherever we might go down in an emergency. We carried survival knives—no sidearms in the States. Over the flight suits we wore a strap-on g-suit. It worked the same as the fully integrated g-suit. A wide, girdle-like band fit snugly around the lower abdomen, containing a bladder that the airplane pumped up on demand in accordance with applied g-forces; the legs contained similar bladders around the calves and thighs. When inflated, they kept blood from pooling in the lower body—in other words, kept blood from flowing from the pilot's brain, thus preventing grayouts or blackouts. The g-suit plugged into the airplane's pressurization system via an air hose attached to the left side of the suit; the hose was a couple of feet long and so became the source of much ribald comment despite its location over the hip. Then there was the torso harness (the F8U was one of the first airplanes to have it). This device resembled a parachute harness—appropriately, since that was one of its functions. It also provided a means of attaching the pilot to the equivalents of a separate seat belt and shoulder harness via quick-disconnect fasteners. Instead of a traditional life vest hung or worn around the neck or chest, our life vests and miscellaneous survival gear were contained in an olive-drab "donut" clipped onto the harness at the waist.

The entire rig was awkward and uncomfortable, especially when donned for the first time. Everything we put on was brand-new issue. The heavy webbed nylon straps and the survival gear donut were especially stiff and unyielding. In time, after much flexing, bending, and soaking in sweat, the rig would loosen up, but getting dressed for flight that first time used up a lot of time and energy. One of my companions was Lieutenant (jg) Sam Flynn, who maintained a mumbling, grumbling commentary as he explored the multiple hooks, laces, fasteners, and straps. The upshot of his mostly self-deprecating remarks was that this was a ridiculous process for grown men to be going through. On the other hand, as he said, he probably wouldn't have to go through it very often; the pilot-eating monster he was about to climb into would undoubtedly send him back to the minor leagues where he belonged. (The last time I saw Sam was not in person. It was on national television, where Captain Sam Flynn appeared as a principal Navy spokesman after the first Libyan Exercise. That was the one where two Tomcats from the *Nimitz* shot down two Libyan MiGs inside Muammar Qaddafi's "Line of Death.")[16]

My instructor on that first flight, and for most of the F8U syllabus, was Lieutenant Commander James M. Heffernan, USN. Jim was to be my Exec and later to succeed me as commanding officer of VF-191. He became a good friend. Jim was an outstanding pilot. His temperament was ideal for teaching neophytes like me to fly the most demanding airplane then in the Navy's fleet inventory.

The drill on first flight was to proceed immediately to the supersonic corridor, then conduct the usual exploration of an airplane's handling characteristics, including slow flight, buffet investigation, and incipient stalls. This was accompanied by advice over the radio by the instructor/ chase pilot to keep the student out of trouble. The next step was to take the airplane out to its maximum speed—Mach 1.4 to Mach 1.5 in the F8U-1s that were usually used for first flights. The supersonic part of the exercise terminated with a series of 5-g turns. Nothing like getting right to it! The idea was to get that out of the way so that the new F8U

Jim Heffernan celebrates two thousand accident-free jet flight hours. (Author's collection)

pilot could devote his full attention to what he was supposed to be doing and not have part of his brain anticipating the mysteries of supersonic flight.

The remainder of the flight, and most of the next two flights, was spent in "circuits and bumps" around Moffett Field, learning to land the airplane. On those initial landing attempts, the airplane felt heavy rather than solid, even a little sloppy on the controls. There was a pronounced tendency toward Dutch roll. A friend of mine said that it reminded him of a TBM, the Grumman-designed Avenger torpedo-bomber of World War II. He described wallowing down the glide slope on final approach. That was after his first flight. My impression of the phenomenon was not as strong, although I could see what he meant. It was to be a while before I figured out how to avoid Dutch roll: don't initiate it by extraneous control inputs.

I was not immediately to verify Bob Hoppe's comment about the afterburner takeoff. My airplane was an F8U-1—an "Ace," not the "Deuce" (F8U-2) he referred to. The afterburner takeoff was reserved for a later syllabus flight, number 3 or 4. The F8U takeoff in basic engine at MRT (military-rated thrust) was impressive but not startling.

There was much that was strange and new to be experienced before I was to release the brakes and start to roll down the runway. I waddled out to the flight line in my nylon armor, hard hat and oxygen mask in one hand, knee pad and charts in the other. The row of gray shapes, shark noses pointing arrogantly skyward over the gaping maws of engine intakes, was impressive. If my head hadn't been so occupied with vital information, I might have found it frightening.

There was a reason the Crusader noses looked toward the sky. It was common in the Pacific Fleet to overinflate the nose gear oleos so as to increase the ground incidence/angle of attack. That put fuselage incidence close to that required for takeoff angle of attack, thus reducing a pilot's uncertainty as to just how much rotation was enough. The purpose was to reduce the number of tail cones damaged by dragging on concrete or asphalt—a predictable consequence of over-rotation on takeoff or landing. The resulting ground attitude looked peculiar, but it worked. The afterburner nozzle was lowered to what appeared to be perilously close to the pavement.

The raised position of the nose cone made reaching it a stretch for shorter pilots. It was necessary that it be reached, because one of the preflight checks was to ensure that the cone was properly latched. It was hinged at the top and could be opened for maintenance of the APG-30 range-only gunnery radar inside. It would not be good for the nose cone to come open in flight, located as it was in front of the cockpit's windscreen! The first thing a pilot did on approaching the airplane was to stand in front, stare at it contemplatively, and push upward at the bottom of the radome to see if it were latched. It was a little like greeting one's steed. I was much too busy for rumination on that initial flight—but at least twice in the first eight flights, I remember giving the machine its mandatory chuck under the chin and thinking, "All right, you son-of-a-bitch, are you going to try to kill me today?"

Entrance to the Crusader's cockpit was by a short ladder, housed in the lower fuselage on the left side and releasable by a switch, and two small footrests that could be unfolded in the mid- and upper fuselage below the cockpit. With VF-124's exaggerated nose-up strut oleos, not even tall pilots could comfortably reach the single rung of the boarding ladder; short pilots couldn't reach it at all without assistance. Enter Sailors' Ingenuity: VF-124's "metal benders" designed and constructed ladder extensions that could easily be inserted into, and removed from, the bottom of the airplane's integral ladder. They were painted red, the universal sign for "remove before flight." Accordingly, these extensions routinely stayed with the home base line crews, not the airplane, and

Temporary ferry pilot Jim Heffernan delivers the first VF-191 Crusader. Note the low nose wheel oleo before Pacific Fleet–style overinflation. (Author's collection)

at a strange field most of us had to be boosted up to where we could reach ladder and footrests, like a medieval knight getting a leg up onto his mount.

Another jury rig concerned the cockpit canopy. The Crusader's canopy was hinged at the rear and opened from the front, alligator style. When it was unlatched, it opened itself in a manner similar to many automotive tailgates, the motion initiated and damped by a self-contained hydraulic cylinder and strut. It was found that taxiing over rough pavement and certainly being exposed to jet blast from another airplane could blow the canopy clean off. This could happen even in the chocks from a passing airplane, especially aboard ship. Again, the metalsmiths came to the rescue. They designed a short piece of metal, hooked over at each end, that could grab the top of the lower canopy rail at one end and hook underneath the inside of the cockpit sill at the other. The device restrained the canopy's movement so that it could not open far enough to do damage. This piece of equipment we carried with us in the airplanes! Usually, once the engine was started we closed the canopies and kept them closed until engine shutdown after the flight.

I referred to the elaborate preflight and pretaxi procedures associated with the F8U. They were initiated for the most part by hand and arm signals given by the ground crew to the pilot. After the engine was started, the plane captain became the principal, the star, as if the preceding ensemble work merely led up to his performance. Responding to his gracefully esoteric movements and gestures, the pilot raised the wing, checked essential hydraulics, exercised emergency pitch trim, verified the condition of the stabilator damper, and on and on. To a layperson watching for the first time, the sequence was a series of surprises, and seemingly endless. The Crusader was not an airplane in which you could simply "light the fire; leap into the blue; suck up the gear; and you're flying a torch!"[17] On my first flight Jim Heff sat on my wing, as was the normal chase pilot procedure. Sometimes he was in a tight parade formation as for takeoff and en route cruise and climb, other times in a loose formation or, even wider, in a tactical spread. This time I was too busy to be aware of where he was or what he was doing, except for the takeoff.

The Crusader required a formal, by-the-numbers run-up sequence before takeoff that was reminiscent of what is still required for reciprocating engines. The older jets didn't require much after reaching the runway beyond simply pushing the "go handle." The final step in the F8U process was application of full power while holding the brakes. The pilot made one last survey of his gauges, checking pressures and temperatures. Of special importance was the engine pressure ratio gauge. The device took different forms in different models, but for each there was an acceptable range of engine pressure differentials for ambient temperature conditions. The object was to ensure that rated thrust, or nearly rated thrust, was available for takeoff and that engine operating temperatures—particularly exhaust temperatures—were within limits.

That completed, still with full power, I looked over at Heffernan. He held up his thumb. I returned the signal. I put my head against the headrest, then nodded forward, releasing brakes as I did so. That told Heff we were rolling and to follow suit. Once rolling, I bled off a few percent rpm, to give my wingman enough extra available thrust to maintain formation.

The airplane moved straight and true, accelerating nicely but not spectacularly. It certainly moved out faster than anything I had been in before. By the time I had digested the sensations, it was time to rotate. I eased the nose up to just the point I had been briefed.

The Crusader's gunsight consisted of a rectangular combining glass mounted in a bracket at an angle above a light and lens source. Viewed from the cockpit, it presented a large rectangle—the part that held the glass—and a smaller, empty rectangle that was the rest of the bracket structure. A predecessor Crusader pilot had figured out that the point at which a tail cone impacted the pavement coincided with a position where the pilot's visible horizon was well below that bottom horizontal bracket strip: if you never pulled the nose up high enough to see daylight under that piece of metal, you couldn't drag your tail. A very handy piece of information. That became a guide to use on approach and landing as well as takeoff. Experimentation had demonstrated that putting the middle strip, the one holding the bottom of the combining glass in the bracket, right on the visible horizon was ideal for takeoff. That's what I did. When the airplane was ready, it became airborne. I immediately raised the gear. The airplane's acceleration increased (maximum permissible gear-down speed was about 175 knots). Next came the wing. The maximum wing-raised speed was 220 knots, which was coming up fast.

I looked over at Jim, tucked in snugly on my right side. I gave him a head signal, moving the wing handle (located on the left console) forward as I did so. There was a transient trim change as the wing came down. The airplane seemed to compensate by itself.[18] Now the machines really began to move out! In visual weather we were able to climb immediately toward the training area. I was flying an F8U-1 that had not yet gone through its first top overhaul, then called PAR for "progressive aircraft rework"—a remote descendant of the Panther quickie overhaul program at Alameda.

The longitudinal trim wheel on the stick was black with worn white scribe marks on its circumference—the "old" system. Pitch control forces were substantial in the Crusader. For normal maneuvering, trim was used constantly. Longitudinal stability was weak to unpredictable for all but steady high-speed flight; the airplane was, after all, designed to fly supersonic. The problem was that the gain of the electric potentiometer the trim wheel activated was too high. It seemed impossible to get the setting exactly right. A Crusader pilot's badge of office was a hole in the thumb of his right flight glove, worn through the thin leather by constant movement against that trim control. (It has been reported that some pilots dramatized the effect, and called attention to their elite status as F8U pilots, by cutting the right thumb out of their gloves entirely. Better to have no thumb at all than a shabby one?[19] I never saw that done, but I owned a couple of pairs of gloves with shabby right thumbs.)

The problem was solved in the F8U-2 and subsequent models. A larger-diameter trim wheel—this time painted red, for some reason—was installed. The simple change in diameter meant that a linear control input on the rim, the circumference, moved the wheel through a smaller angle than the older wheel. The potentiometer responded to angular rotation. Thus, the input was smaller, less radical. It approached a smooth rather than coarse input. Vought may have substituted a "pot" with less gain, or variable gain, as well. The change made a world of difference in flying the airplane, and it put an end to worn-out flight glove thumbs!

There must be an inviolable rule applied to airplane modification programs, one dictating that whenever changes are installed in individual airplanes, an equal amount will be allocated for each. No favorites! I can find no other explanation for what was done—or not done—to the F8U-1Es. All PAR-overhauled F8U-1s that returned to service as -1s received the trim change; the F8U-1Es, whether new or overhauled, did not. The F8U-1Es were F8U-1s that had been equipped with the APS-67 radar. The radar constituted an extra expenditure, and so someone must have decided to save money somewhere. VF-191's airplanes were F8U-1s fresh out of PAR; a sister squadron, VF-211, got -1Es, new or overhauled, with the old trim system. Looking back on the fifteen months that followed, I recognize that my life, state of mind, and general joie de vivre in the airplane were enhanced by the difference. I wasn't given a choice. Had I been, the decision between a modestly better gunnery radar with a minimal search capability, on the one hand, and pitch trim system that made the Crusader a joy to fly instead of a sometimes trial, on the other, would have taken me about a millisecond to make.

Compared with other airplanes, getting to know the Crusader was to encounter characteristics that approached difference in kind rather than in degree. Climb performance in basic engine was substantially better than anything I had flown before. Afterburner climb was a totally new experience. Best climb speed in burner was around Mach 0.92, increasing at altitude to Mach 0.96. The pitch attitude made me feel as though I were lying on my back. By F-18 or F-16 standards both climb attitude and performance were unremarkable, but this was 1960, not 1990.[20]

I learned to use the cruise droop, which was operated by a bend of the wrist of my throttle hand. The droop control, integral with the throttle handle, had two click-stop positions. With droop extended subsonic maneuverability was reasonable up to forty thousand feet. At fifty thousand feet, especially in an F8U-1, performance tended to degrade to uncomfortably low indicated airspeeds, always on the verge of either stall or buffet boundary. I discovered that to maintain a simple, shallow-bank, racetrack CAP (combat air patrol) pattern at fifty thousand feet I needed to pop in and out of burner to get around the corners. Since fuel consumption in burner was roughly four times that in basic engine, that effectively ruled out fifty-thousand-foot CAP stations.

A good introduction to buffet onset was to perform consecutive turns with cruise droop extended and then with droop retracted. In the cruise configuration, establish the maximum rate level turn that was comfortable; then try to duplicate the turn with droop retracted. A rattling sound like nuts being thrown down the engine intake would be the first indication. If the pilot persisted in steepening his turn, the sound got louder with more obvious accompanying noises. Depending on how hard the pilot pulled on the stick, the airplane might diverge into a pre-spin gyration—an inevitable step a Crusader went through en route to a spin.

The spin characteristics of the F8U were similar to those of the F7U, although the Crusader is of conventional configuration compared with the tailless Cutlass. A more dramatic attention getter is that for a long time it was believed by aerodynamicists and pilots alike that the F7U could not be spun. They were wrong. It could indeed be spun, but no one ever found a way to get out of a spin. There were attempts, though. The first one was inadvertent. Clyde A. "Willie" Williams[21] got into the first recorded, or at least the first acknowledged, F7U spin. After several attempts at recovery, increasingly innovative as his altitude dissipated, Willie punched out (ejected). Afterwards he described his "spin" in great detail to more than one disbelieving audience: the F7U was unspinnable, they said, therefore he could not possibly have been in a spin. One such audience was the aircraft accident investigation board convened for that purpose. Vought subsequentially demonstrated in a wind tunnel that an F7U spin was possible. It was an unusual spin; to make it happen required unorthodox maneuvering, but it could be done. How to undo it remained a mystery. A film of F7U spin-tunnel tests became a frightening part of the F8U spin lecture at VF-124.

It was difficult to get into a spin in an F8U; it could be even harder to recover from one, once it developed. The first problem was to identify the spin as such in the first place and distinguish it from a pre-spin gyration. The symptoms of the pre-spin (or "post-stall"—an acceptable term for the same phenomenon) gyration were similar to those of a fully developed spin: the nose of the aircraft went through wild excursions in pitch concurrent with equally wild, uncoordinated excursions in yaw.

A true post-stall gyration could be preceded by an end-over-end tumble, a spectacular departure from normal flight. When it occurred, the pilot's instincts screamed that he was supposed to react to this phenomenon, but that was exactly what he should *not* do. At that point virtually any control input—besides reducing power, a prudent move— would lead to a spin. The right thing to do was to neutralize the controls and wait. If the pilot was too traumatized to be sure he could even find neutral, he should let everything go; the power control system would find neutral, or close enough, by itself. When the airplane was ready, it would stabilize, headed more or less down. At that point the pilot could retake command, climb back up to where he had started, and go about his business.

Recovery from a post-stall gyration is the same as for the end-over-end tumble: let go of everything and be patient! Almost any control input will precipitate a spin. But how do you know that you are in a gyration, not already in a spin? The critical question: Is the airplane turning consistently in one direction or not? A true spin, regardless of what oscillations are superposed on it, is characterized by a continuous turn in the same direction. The post-stall or pre-spin gyration is another matter. Think of a leaf falling to the ground: side-to-side oscillations, a relatively flat attitude. Impose on that picture violent up-and-down oscillations about another axis—call it pitch. That is the post-stall gyration.

But from his vantage point in the wildly moving cockpit, the pilot wouldn't be able to tell the difference between back-and-forth oscillations in yaw and consistent turning all the way around. The cockpit at the end of the long boom of the forward fuselage was not an ideal location for dispassionate observation and analysis. At the end of the significant lever arm that was the cockpit's distance forward of the aerodynamic center of pressure, the pilot would be whipped around as far as his harness and straps would permit. Back and forth, up and down; or was it round and back and round and up and down? The difference was important, but the beleaguered pilot would have difficulty determining what was going on. The only reliable indicator of that motion was the turn and bank indicator. That is what we were taught to use. If the needle stays on the same side of the neutral (zero-turn rate) position, the airplane is in a spin. In a gyration it will swing from side to side, showing a turn first in one direction, then the other.

Recognizing a spin is only the beginning. Once you're in one, how do you recover? The leaf analogy is still useful, except now the airplane is turning in its descent. Unlike the leaf, the airplane has forward motion,[22] but the spin is fundamentally flat. The mean angle of attack is high, 40 degrees or greater, too high for useful airflow over the tail surfaces or the wings.

Let's look at what conventional recovery techniques would accomplish. First, push the stick forward to get the nose down. That will rotate the leading edge of the stabilator upward. It was already stalled; now it's really stalled, moving nearly perpendicular to the relative wind. Rudder against the spin won't help either. The stabilator is low on the fuselage, effectively blocking and disrupting airflow to the vertical fin and rudder, so those surfaces are also stalled and ineffective. Aileron against the spin? To recover from a left spin means right aileron should be applied; that lowers the left aileron and raises the right one. But the right wing is on the outside of the spin, so there is not enough airflow over the top of that wing for the raised aileron to be effective. Not so the left wing: the drooped left aileron is not "flying," but it makes a great speed brake, encouraging the airplane to spin even faster to the left.

The solution is a less conventional approach. First, lower the wing leading-edge droop to landing configuration; the increased camber will enable the wing to "fly" at an increased angle of attack. (There is an emergency blow-down feature that enables that to happen with the wing lowered.) It is easier said than done. The control is integral with the wing raise/lower quadrant on the left cockpit console, with a safety latch to prevent its inadvertent use. Getting to the latch while bouncing around the cockpit is not easy! It might take two hands to move the safety tab and activate the control.

Next (we are still spinning to the left), move the stick all the way back and as far into the left-hand corner as you can get it. All the way; the last inch or so is important. That moves the stabilator all the way down so that it tends to stream into the relative wind, allowing air to flow over it and the rudder. Now perhaps something favorable can happen. The aileron control movement into the spin will move the out-

My sweat-dampened hair indicates that this is a postflight briefing to the flight deck troubleshooter. (Author's collection)

board, right, aileron down so that the "speed brake" effect is on the outside wing, tending to yaw the airplane to the right—that is, against the spin. Finally. Whew!

But it's not quite over. Again it's time for patience; recovery will not be instantaneous. Hold the controls the way they are, and the movements will damp out. As they do, neutralize the controls (you don't want to do the whole thing all over again in the other direction). The airplane will stabilize in a dive, perhaps with the assistance of forward stick as control returns. Recover from the dive and head for home. There, the blown down emergency droop will be obvious to your friends, and you will have the privilege of explaining how you got into that mess in the first place.

It should be obvious that the exercise is not one of the most fun things you can do in an airplane. In general Crusader pilots avoided even the possibility. The best way was to be conscious of buffet onset and, in the event of a post-stall gyration, stay off the controls.

Lieutenant Commander "Billy Burner" Brooks was my Maintenance

Officer. He was also an aggressive pilot, particularly in ACM (air combat maneuvering) and gunnery, and he spun the airplane at least three times. As Maintenance Officer he had the ability, and sometimes the opportunity, to have the hydraulics people restore the landing droop to its normal position without noising it about. (His jaygee wingman wouldn't dare squeal on him.)

In my initial Crusader training flight the only opportunity for approaching aerodynamic difficulties came on the supersonic run—not the run itself, but the 5-g turns at the end. Lieutenant Commander William M. "Bill" Russell, USN, was the senior ground school instructor. He conducted the spin course and frequently flew as the instructor pilot on students' initial flights. (The caliber of instructors and instruction in VF-124 at the time was the best I ever encountered in the Navy, and the Navy is characteristically good at that sort of thing.) He made sure we learned what was necessary without scaring the bejesus out of us— no mean feat in this instance.

Bill Russell described an experience. A fellow FRP, a few weeks ahead of me in the program, was a commander who was slated to be skipper of VF-211. He was the FRP on a flight in which Russell was the instructor and chase pilot. It went smoothly until the end of the supersonic run. The prospective commanding officer was zealous in following instructions. After the last of his high-speed turns he held 5 g's as he decelerated to subsonic speed. Suddenly, it was ass-over-teakettles! The soon-to-be skipper entered a classic end-over-end tumble.

Not to worry. They were two experienced aviators. The commander had been well briefed on what to expect and what to do under such circumstances. Nevertheless, Russell decided that it would be timely to inject his instructor's persona. "Uh, Commander, neutralize the controls," in his best low-key Chuck Yeager voice.

The other airplane continued to swap ends as it sank earthward. His patience beginning to unravel, Russell tried again, stronger this time. "Commander, neutralize the controls."

There was no visible or audible reaction. Bill's charge was now dissipating altitude at a furious rate; recovery could use up to ten thousand feet. Russell's emotions passed rapidly through strained patience to growing concern. He was working increasingly hard to maintain his own airplane in the vicinity of his student's. "Goddammit, Commander, neutralize the fucking controls!"

As if on command, the other airplane's oscillations slowed and then stopped. The Crusader bottomed out of a controlled dive and started a climb back to altitude. A well-modulated voice came on the air: "*Lieutenant* Commander, what the Christ did you think I was doing?"

When it was my turn, I experienced no such excitement. There was nothing complicated about the supersonic run, but there was a preferred entry technique. At about thirty-six thousand feet—the most efficient altitude for a turbojet engine—select afterburner. At high altitude and cruise speed the pilot felt an impulse against his back as it ignited. (At lower altitudes, the impulse would be stronger.) The chase pilot could usually confirm ignition from the accompanying visible smoke ring.[23] At the same time, ease the stick forward just enough to establish close to zero g. In that condition, relieved momentarily of supporting the airplane in the air, all available thrust is applied to acceleration. Do not push too hard or too long, however; if you do, you'll dissipate altitude in the process.

When burner was selected in the F8U, maximum thrust was commanded. (When burner was selected in the F-4, by contrast, it was to the fully modulated, lowest afterburner thrust, position[s].) There was a short segment of thrust lever (throttle) travel that could be used to modulate downward the amount of thrust. A lead airplane routinely decreased thrust so that a wingman, in this case the chase pilot, would be able to stay with him.

Having grown up with a combination of fact and fiction epitomized in the motion picture *Breaking the Sound Barrier*, I found the transition from subsonic to supersonic flight anticlimactic; nothing detectable happened except for the reading on the Mach meter.[24] The Crusader was as docile as a lamb and wonderfully responsive. It is true that, for reasons to be discussed later, it is virtually impossible to stall an airplane under g-load while it is supersonic. However, it is possible to decelerate so rapidly as to go subsonic—where the airplane will stall—very quickly. That is what had happened to my commander friend, above.

Forewarned with specific instruction as well as by the example of Bill Russell's sea story, I suffered no such misadventure. I was astounded and delighted at the performance, the feeling of power and control over this marvelous machine. This is not to say that achieving supersonic speed in that older airplane was instantaneous; it required several minutes of level flight to top out at above Mach 1.4.

I had no apprehension about the mandatory 5-g turns either, although I kept close watch on the Mach meter lest the indication decrease too quickly. I "unloaded" the airplane (reduced the applied g-forces) very carefully when it was time to de-select burner. Decelerating through the transonic region, there was a noticeable but controllable pitch change. This was the phenomenon that could cause inconvenience and surprise if coupled with high g's. I noticed the pitch trim phenomenon because I had been briefed to look for it; had I been preoccupied and flying in essentially 1-g flight, I might have missed the change completely. It was theoretically possible, going in the other direction, to exceed the speed of sound inadvertently, thereby hurling a detached shock wave toward the earth.

The "new frontiers" part of the initial F8U flight was over too soon. I was not too euphoric to take seriously the landings back at Moffett, but they were far down on any scale of excitement or unique challenge. I had made "first landings" in a number of different airplanes, but I had never before flown that fast—not even close. I was now a Crusader pilot and by virtue of the supersonic run eligible to receive my "1,000 mph" pin from Vought. (In the summer of 1956, Commander Robert W. "Duke" Windsor, USN, set a new world's record for production aircraft by flying 1,015.428 mph [statute] in an F8U-1. The successful attempt was officially observed by the National Aeronautics Association, the U.S. body representing the world organization for such matters, and the Fédération aéronautique internationale in France.[25] Dubbed Project One Grand by Vought Aircraft, the effort broke an existing record held by a North American F-100 Super Sabre. Vought commemorated the event by creating shield-shaped lapel pins bearing a crusades-like design. Each Crusader pilot was awarded a pin after his first high-speed flight. The pins were a source of pride among F8U pilots. I still have mine. I wear it on special occasions—like every time I feel like it.)

Professional Recollections

F8U pilots constituted a close-knit community different from that of any prior airplane in my experience. That was a result of the role of the RAG squadron as a kind of model-dedicated mother hen to the fleet squadrons. Similar relationships followed for other aircraft communities, as evidenced by annual events like the Intruder Ball (A-6) and Phantom Phling (F-4).[26] The VF-124 instructors, virtually all of whom were both flight and ground instructors, were unusual in their individual and collective abilities—unusual even for naval aviation, where they are expected to be uniformly good. Some number of the lieutenants had served in the FJ-4 squadron of Donald C. "Red Dog" Davis.[27] Allowing for some later exaggeration, that squadron racked up incredible gunnery scores flying that last version of the Fury.

In June of 1960 I relieved Commander Gerard F. Colleran, USN, as commanding officer of VF-191. After the change-of-command ceremony, Jerry Colleran complained, "I'm getting sick and tired of people telling me that I'm leaving the best job in the Navy. Dammit, I'm not dead yet!" Fourteen months later I was better able to empathize with his remark. In many ways, commanding a squadron—especially (allowing my prejudices to show) a fighter squadron—*is* the best job in the Navy. There

The last F11F Tigers of VF-191 depart Moffett Field for the boneyard at Litchfield Park, Arizona. (Author's collection)

are many other jobs with considerable rewards, but being a part of a fleet squadron in any capacity is an approximation of heaven on earth for an aviator. The expression "getting paid to have fun" comes to mind.

I was still in the RAG when I assumed command, which meant that for a short time I split my time between VF-124 and VF-191. The squadron was to operate out of a hangar on the other side of the field. The arrangement worked fine. The squadron was in good hands with Jim Heffernan. Besides, I was flying at a good rate with VF-124, while VF-191 was still awaiting airplanes. There were the last F11Fs to get rid of. A few of the old squadron pilots and maintenance people were around to prepare the airplanes for transfer and to fly them away as they were made ready.

My last major milestone in VF-124 was carrier qualification aboard the *Coral Sea* (CV-43). The *Coral Sea* was the third of the *Midway* class and had been modified to the full angled deck/mirror landing system/ steam catapult configuration. Her deck was narrow compared with the *Forrestal*-class carriers and later CVs, but the landing area appeared longer. More important for us F8U drivers, the hook-to-ramp clearance over the threshold of the landing area was ample, reportedly better than on her sisters—certainly better than the "27 Charlie" *Oriskany*-converted *Bonhomme Richard* (CVA-31), which was again to be my home away from home.[28] To lose one's hook against the ramp was better than a ramp strike with the whole airplane but not a happy experience.

Thanks to the patience and expertise of the VF-124 Landing Signal Officers, as well as to good weather, I got through carrier qualifications in good order. I didn't appreciate the extent to which I was spoiled by the experience until later in the year when I first negotiated the smaller deck of the Bonnie Dick. I learned to respect the phenomenon of Crusader speed instability in the groove. For many of us—there were exceptions, the fortunate few who can do no wrong in an airplane—if the throttle wasn't in almost constant motion, however minute the changes, one of two things would happen at a critical point in the approach: either the airplane would start to accelerate—putting a surprised pilot both high and fast at exactly the wrong time—or the bottom would drop out. A high sink rate would develop, confronting the pilot with the distinct possibility of coming face to face with the "spud locker," the flat, vertical part of the back end of the boat that is not designed for landing airplanes.

A sink rate late in the approach could be insidious in the Crusader, depending on how it developed. If it was gradual, the pilot might initially compensate by increasing angle of attack. That would have a further consequence of decreasing speed. The result could be that the pilot would be both nose-high and low as he approached the ship. Now he has a dilemma: if he decreases angle of attack to increase speed, he will go further below the glide slope; if he gets below deck level, it's the spud locker. He can add power unless induced drag, caused by the high angle of attack, has become so great that he does not have sufficient excess thrust to accelerate. How about afterburner? When afterburner is selected in the F8U, the first thing to happen is that the nozzle slams to the open position; only then does ignition occur. Generally the two are nearly simultaneous, but sometimes the burner does not light on the first attempt. With the tail pipe nozzle full open there will be a further, dramatic reduction in thrust. Late in an approach that sequence is a prescription for disaster. That is why there are Landing Signal Officers: if the pilot has failed to detect that he is getting into trouble, it is up to the LSO to recognize the problem early enough to wave him off.

As recent RAG squadron graduates, we in VF-191 were by edict and training considered to be 60 to 70 percent ready for deployment. Most of the remaining preparation would be devoted to additional carrier landings, tactics, and weapons training. For us, "weapons" meant guns. We managed three separate gunnery deployments before the real deployment to the Western Pacific (WestPac) aboard the Bonnie Dick the next spring. For that purpose we went to Yuma, to Fallon, and then back to Yuma. The first Yuma deployment was in July. (Next time you hear a national weather report in the summertime, listen for the high temperature; it will probably be in Yuma.)

Flying gunnery in the F8U was a strong contender for the most fun one can have in an airplane, but it could also be frustrating. Even good shooters could have persistent dry spells. I remember Fred Winton coming up empty as he led several flights during a VF-124 deployment to Fallon. Certainly pilot technique was a critical factor, but the airplane needed to be properly set up, "harmonized," as well—guns boresighted and radar and lead-computing sight carefully calibrated and aligned.

In theory, F8U gunnery was not much different from what some of us older hands had experienced in SNJs, Hellcats, Corsairs, and Bearcats; it was more similar to gunnery in the Panthers or even the FJs. In practice, there were significant differences related to speed and altitude. There was only one standard firing run taught in the Crusader program, a "high side." We shot at two altitudes, twenty thousand and thirty thousand feet; that was the towplane's altitude. Put the shooter's starting "perch" six thousand to eight thousand feet higher, and the runs became real screamers.

Our lead-computing sights were most effective at a two-to-one speed advantage. With the target banner being towed through the sky at a nominal 200 knots, this meant that the shooter was traveling at 400 knots. Those are indicated airspeeds. True airspeed for the shooter at twenty thousand feet is about 540 knots; at thirty thousand feet, more than 660 knots, which is greater than Mach 1. The airplane still flies on indicated airspeed because indicated airspeed is derived from our old acquaintance q, or dynamic pressure.[29] Dynamic pressure is what keeps the airplane in the air. However, an airplane turns in accordance with true airspeed. Turning radius is proportional to the square of the actual, or true, velocity. One can't turn as tight corners up there as at lower altitudes. The constraints of time, space, and geometry require that a narrowly bounded flight path be flown with great precision for effective gunnery performance at higher altitudes.

What constitutes effective gunnery seems to vary with time and with different airplanes, but there are constants. Ten percent hits out of total rounds fired is better than acceptable for towed banner or sleeve gunnery in virtually every airplane, especially if that performance can be achieved consistently. I mentioned earlier high scores on the order of 30 percent in Hellcats by good shooters like Frank Lawlor and Leo Krupp. Then there was the performance reported for Red Dog Davis's Fury pilots—90 percent or better was said to have been achieved, with scores in the 55–60 percent range not uncommon. (The only circumstances for which I had previously heard numbers that high involved pre–World War II Grumman F3F biplanes.) It was different in Crusaders, where 5 percent hits was an acceptable beginning of competence, 10 percent was downright good, and 20 percent was infrequent. The only pilot I knew to shoot 25 percent or better was "Billy Burner" Brooks. He did it one time at twenty thousand feet; it was during a formal qualification for score in which he was permitted only two firing runs.

There is no mold for fighter pilots, or pilots in general; there are popular conceptions and misconceptions generated by the public and the press. But if there were a mold for pilots, Bill Brooks would be out of it; if there were a mold for almost anything, Bill Brooks would be out of it. He was a husky five feet ten inches or so, with a crop of shaggy, dirty-blond hair; he kept it cut regulation short, but like the rest of him it always looked a little mussed. I never saw him without his horn-rimmed glasses, their lenses thick as Coke bottles. They seemed inconsistent with the Navy's standard requirement for uncorrected twenty-twenty vision, but I figured that it was between him and the Medical Department. If his eyes weren't up to standard, some of the rest of us could have benefited from the same affliction. Bill had the right idea about gunnery, and he had the scores to prove it. His idea was to go as fast as possible—at both twenty thousand and thirty thousand feet—as was consistent with flying the pattern. This meant flying supersonic, or at least high subsonic, even at twenty thousand feet, although supersonic speed at that altitude is difficult in an F8U, especially an F8U-1.

There is a reason why this idea works. The details can be confusing, but the concept is simple. Let's look at figure 3.

This V-g diagram is a convenient way to portray the operating envelope of an airplane. Aerodynamic, control, and structural boundaries define the limits. The two V-stall lines represent the g and V (velocity) combinations at which the airplane will stall, constituting an aerodynamic limit. The diagram is not symmetrical for positive and negative g's; the airplane is designed to fly right side up (at least most of the time). Each stall curve starts at a point, $+1$ g or -1 g, representing the lowest velocity at which the airplane can stay in the air. As speed increases, the airplane can pull more g's (as is necessary in a turn, for

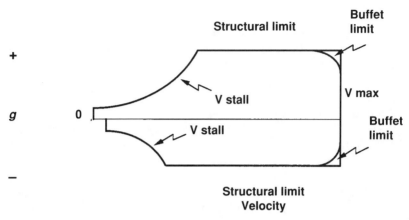

Figure 3: V-g Diagram.

instance) before stalling—that is, before the critical angle of attack is reached. That occurrence represents the peak of the lift-coefficient-versus-angle-of-attack curve, the classic definition of airfoil stall.

The condition can be met at any speed. The curves theoretically extend indefinitely, past either the structural limits, shown by the horizontal lines, or the ultimate speed of the airplane, Vmax, shown by the vertical line. Vmax may be defined by either performance—that is, thrust versus drag—or stability/control considerations such as buffet or controllability boundaries.

Figure 3 is a representative sea-level curve. The horizontal axis is real velocity, true airspeed, which at sea level is nearly equal to indicated airspeed. As we know, true airspeed becomes increasingly high compared with indicated airspeed as altitude increases. The ability of an airplane to achieve high speed—that is, aerodynamic performance—decreases with altitude (at least for conventional flying machines with air-breathing engines). Ultimately there is an altitude at which stall speed and maximum speed are equal; that is one way of describing an airplane's absolute ceiling. There is a family of possible V-g diagrams for an airplane, each valid for only one altitude.

For anyone trying to maneuver an airplane there is, therefore, special significance to the upper-left-hand corner of the diagram, where stall speed and structural limit intersect: below that speed the airplane will stall before the structural limit is reached; above that speed maximum g[30] is available for maneuvering. The greater the applied g, the smaller the turning radius, very important for either outmaneuvering an opponent or negotiating a complex gunnery run. Billy Burner had that figured right.

As pilot you would like the airspeed as low as possible (consistent with full available g) because turn radius also varies with the square of the velocity. With respect to turn radius, you could in effect lose on the peanuts what you make on the popcorn by carrying excess speed. There is an additional problem. The way a pilot increases g-force is to pull back on the stick, achieving a greater lift coefficient by increasing angle of attack. Unfortunately, drag coefficient, specifically induced drag coefficient, varies as the square of the lift coefficient. So at 6 g's the airplane wants to decelerate like crazy unless there is available excess thrust to compensate for the increase in drag. Bill Brooks was on top of that one too with his use of afterburner. But even with burner, the F8U (not having the thrust-to-weight ratio of today's machines— the F-16 and F-18 are examples) would still decelerate. This time Bill Brooks was one up. He invoked another phenomenon: regardless of g-load, an airplane cannot stall while it is supersonic. (It can, however, decelerate rapidly to subsonic speed.)

That one takes some explaining, but again the concept is simple. An airfoil producing lift at subsonic speeds can be likened to half of a venturi. A common example of a venturi is the throat of a simple carburetor. As entering air passes from the wide opening to the narrow throat, the pressure of the airstream drops and the velocity of the flow increases. That low pressure helps to draw atomized fuel from the carburetor jets. As the mixture passes from the throat into the intake manifold—that is, as the opening widens again—pressure increases and velocity decreases, just as Bernoulli said. Essentially the same thing happens as free airstream air negotiates the curved surfaces of an airfoil: low pressure on the upper surface of a wing produces the lift required to fly.

Figure 4 represents the pressure distribution of the cross-section of a lift-producing airfoil. The negative pressure on the upper surface multiplied by the wing's area defines the lift, which keeps the airplane in the air. As angle of attack is increased, the shape of the low-pressure envelope shifts toward the leading edge of the wing—initially into a bulge over the forward part of the chord—and the total area under the curve increases, for a while. Past the point of maximum curvature, like the narrow throat of the carburetor, the pressure becomes less negative (it increases). At the same time, the velocity over the after portion of the wing decreases (it loses energy). At some point, at the critical angle of attack, the airflow no longer has enough energy to follow the contour of the wing; it separates, and stall occurs.

What I have been describing is the *subsonic* venturi characteristic in which pressure decreases and velocity increases as air flows through a narrow throat; pressure increases and velocity decreases as air ex-

Lift

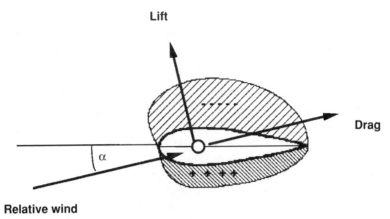

Drag

Relative wind

Figure 4: Subsonic Airfoil.

pands. But in *supersonic* flow, the rules change: velocity increases rather than decreases with expansion. High-velocity airflow will not separate. That is the basis for the first supersonic wind tunnels before anyone got to try it in a real airplane. If the flow could be made to reach supersonic velocity in the narrow throat of the tunnel, it would be even faster on the downstream side.

Figure 5 shows supersonic streamlines (instead of pressure distribution as in the previous figure) around an ideal supersonic shape.[31] The top panel represents symmetrical flow at zero angle of attack. Notice the leading- and trailing-edge shock waves and the expansion waves at maximum wing thickness. The bottom panel shows the same airfoil at a positive angle of attack so as to produce lift. Now there is an additional leading-edge expansion wave on the top surface. (They are all "shock" waves.) Airflow in the bottom panel will accelerate as it passes the leading-edge expansion wave and again as it passes through the midchord expansion wave.

Kinetic energy is proportional to the square of the velocity. This is not dead or dying air; it will not separate or stall. This means that a pilot can break an airplane apart with a flick of his wrist before it can stall—that is, if he can load enough g's to make that happen before the airplane slows down. The airplane tends to slow down quickly at high g because drag is rising proportionally with the square of the high lift coefficient that is producing the g's. Once it goes subsonic, the airplane may stall virtually instantaneously, which is what happened to Bill Russell's commander student a few pages back.

I don't think Bill Brooks went through all that in his head, but he was aware that if he could get supersonic in a critical part of his runs

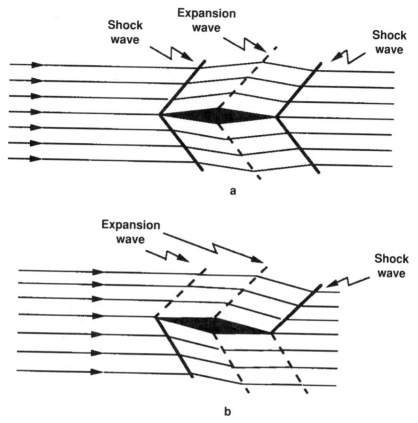

Figure 5: Supersonic Airfoil.

the increased available g would more than compensate for any square-of-the-velocity turn radius penalty in maneuvering the airplane. Even if he remained high subsonic rather than supersonic, he would be operating in that part of the V-g diagram where he was not stall-limited; he could maneuver up to the structural limit.

At twenty thousand feet it was marginal that a pilot could actually get supersonic in an F8U-1. At thirty thousand feet, it was essential to be supersonic in order to fly the run at all—essential, at least, if you wanted to stay in the same county with the banner. It was difficult enough to see and keep track of the banner when you were doing it right. From the perch position at either altitude, the six-by-twenty-foot piece of nylon mesh tended to blend in with the desert background that was the floor of most gunnery ranges.

The high-side run we flew was essentially the same as for other airplanes, except for the consequences of higher speeds and altitudes. It was critical that alignment be achieved with the towline well before the reversal turn so that smooth tracking could begin immediately. There was neither time nor room for large corrections; the gunsight needed a few seconds of settling time before producing usable lead computations.

The sight had a standard fixed reticle with the usual concentric rings, graduated in mils, and a pipper in the middle. There was a separate pipper, a single dot, that was driven by the gunsight. The separation between the fixed and movable pippers at any time was calculated lead angle. The pilot put the movable pipper on the target and kept it there; the calculating was done by an arrangement of gyros that precessed in accordance with the angular motion of the fighter as it tracked the target. The amount of precession was controlled by restraining springs. The correct amount of precession, or proper lead angle, was a function of range, so the spring tension was variable in response to a range input.[32] (That is why we had that little APG-30 ranging radar in the nose.) The moving pipper's separation from the fixed reticle varied in response to angle rates, primarily about the pitch axis, as the pilot tracked the target. The movable pipper's motion also varied in accordance with all other angular aircraft motion generated by the pilot: the more erratic the pilot's control movements, the more erratic the pipper's motion. It could be an elusive little bugger to place on target. We discovered early the importance of smooth tracking.

As in all sleeve or banner gunnery, the theoretical goal was for the firing airplane to pass through a point 90 degrees off the flight path of the target as firing range was reached. That was possible with some of the earlier metal monoplanes, but it certainly was not for any jet airplane I know, least of all the Crusader. Hellcats and Corsairs came close, but in the F8U we were lucky to have 15 to 20 degrees off the flight path of the target when we opened fire. The evidence lay in what we brought home, the holes in the sleeve. A good hit would leave an essentially round hole ringed by its identifying paint color. As angle off the flight path of the banner decreased, the holes would elongate. At the unacceptable extreme, where you were firing at the skinny edge of the back end of the banner, you put your friendly tow pilot above but definitely exposed to the line of fire. Our limit was six to eight inches of paint smeared around an elongated hole; that was close enough, thank you. The first time it happened, you bought the drinks. The second time, you were grounded.

Turning off the perch at the beginning of a run, the first thing a shooter did was to charge his guns, then locate the towplane far below.

(Our towplanes were frequently FJ-4s provided by a utility squadron; their usual color scheme was a dark blue fuselage—the old "sea-blue gloss" color of Hellcats and Avengers—and yellow wings.) Next, he followed the towline, or where he knew the towline should be, with his eyes until he saw the little white patch of the banner. Finding the banner could be the most difficult part of the whole run, depending on lighting conditions and background. The shooter would then drop his nose out of his turn until he was pointed at the towline, then reverse the turn and stop the nose wherever it was.

With luck the nose would be pointed close to the towline, slightly above or below but ahead of the banner. The pilot would let the pipper drift aft until the 100-mil ring was still well ahead of the banner. Then he would take his hand off the throttle long enough for a quick whack at a flat knob to his left. That started the radar searching. An illuminated needle wiggled back and forth before settling down; settling down signified range-lock.[33] Now the pilot let the moving pipper—substantially lagging the fixed reticle—drift aft toward the leading edge of the banner. He would be in a fairly steep dive and accelerating. Only careful corrections could be used to position and hold the dynamic pipper where it belonged, on or slightly forward of a circular mark in the middle of banner.

At a range of two thousand feet the pilot heard a preliminary 600-cycle tone in his ear. It was replaced by a 1,200-cycle tone. In range! As he fired, the gunsight images would bounce and shake with the vibration, no longer useful for anything. He might get a visual impression of tracers somewhere in the vicinity of the target. There wouldn't be time even to think about making a correction before an insistent beeping of the 1,200-cycle tone. Break away! The pilot would level his wings and the airplane would leap over the banner.

I recall an old hand describing the process. A newcomer asked a question: "If the radar doesn't lock, how do you know you're in range?"

The old hand looked at him. "If the radar doesn't lock, you probably won't hit your ass." He sighed. "Go back to stadiametric ranging. If you can, figure out how many mils twenty feet of banner is at twelve hundred feet and 15 degrees angle-off."

"That's not much help."

"Keep boring in until you're sure you can't recover in time. You're about to run into the banner."

"Then break away?"

"Shit, no. Start shooting. You just got in range."

VF-191 spent three weeks at Fallon in October of 1960 on a gunnery deployment. By the third week we were pretty good. Most of our problems had been solved or isolated. We were up there alone for the first week, then we were joined by the other squadrons in Air Group 19— VF-193, flying F3H-2 Demons; VA-192 and VA-195, flying A4D-2Ns; and VA-196, flying AD Skyraiders. It was the first time the air group that would deploy the following June was together in an operational environment. It was a good time operationally, and we got to know the pilots of the other squadrons we would be flying with.

As for us, the squadron recorded and calibrated everything, including individual airplane performance by side number and pilot. We cross-filed the data in such a way as to normalize pilot performance and airplane performance.[34] The weapon system "harmonization" process, with elements of sound engineering, fundamental physics, a touch of science, much hard work by the ordnance and fire control gangs, and more than a little luck, got most of our airplanes performing reliably. Some were better than others. I remember some specific side numbers.

I flew NM104 early the first week.[35]. The flight was average for the most part, but once there was that infrequent golden run. I was positive that I had all but blown the banner out of the sky on that run. But when we counted holes, I had three, out of two hundred rounds expended! With anticipation and frustration I looked at the gun camera film. It was not hard to isolate the run; it looked as good as it had felt. I was a little late establishing track, but everything else looked fine, up to and including guns firing. The film faithfully recorded the vibration and general bouncing about. It was not possible to determine where the tracers were going.

"There!" I exclaimed indignantly. "That should have got some hits."

Jim Heffernan at my elbow became Mr. Sensitivity, all sympathy and solicitude. He shook his head, showing a trace of sadness. "I don't know, Skipper. Maybe what you need to do is pick up the target early. You know, track a little smoother. Watch your angle-off. Don't shoot till you're in range. I bet you'll do better next time."

That airplane had a history.

With the advent of high-performance jet airplanes, the Navy reevaluated emergency landing procedures. With the big reciprocating-engined propeller planes, the usual recommendation had been to stay with the airplane rather than risk a bailout, especially at low altitudes. The new rule was to stay with the airplane only if you found yourself over a prepared runway in such an ideal position that you were 100 percent sure you could make it. Since there are few 100 percents in aviation, that usually meant "Get the hell out of the airplane," preferably without depositing it in a populated area.

The prior operator of NM104 was a Marine squadron. Some time previously—before the airplane's therapeutic visit to an Overhaul and

Repair facility for repair—one of that squadron's young men had vio-
lated the new premise: in extremis, he had planted the airplane on a
runway, wheels up. It seemed to have suffered surprisingly little damage.
However, in the process of either the landing or the repair of the damage,
something strange happened to the forward part of the fuselage of
NM104. Our ordnance gang made repeated attempts to boresight the
airplane. Finally the chief ordnanceman approached me with a frown
on his face: "Skipper, we got a problem with that bird. The front end
must be out of line." The only way it could be boresighted was to point
the guns so that on one side the bullets would likely tear through the
skin of the forward fuselage. That didn't explain why they couldn't boresight the two guns on the other side, but I wasn't the only one to have
a problem with NM104; nobody could hit with that airplane. The misalignment didn't seem to affect the way the airplane flew otherwise.

For reasons less apparent the good airplane on that deployment
was NM109. By the third week what had started as a kind of good luck
superstition—"That thing hit pretty good yesterday. How about giving
me 109?"—evolved into a pattern. A growing number of pilots made
good scores flying it. I flew NM109 on the last day we were at Fallon.
Everyone was trying one last time to establish a personal high score.
The pilot of NM109 on the flight before me was Lieutenant (jg) Eddelman. He didn't better his previous high, but he brought back a good
score. We laid the banner out on the tarmac and counted holes. He was
high man for his flight, with about twenty-two. They were all on the
last half of the banner.

By this time we were getting serious about this stuff. When I walked
out to NM109, the ordnancemen had the nose open for access to the
radar, and a petty officer was squinting through a boresight telescope
mounted on one of the guns, looking at a previously selected reference.

"Looks good to me, Chief. I wouldn't screw with it."

The chief nodded in agreement and looked at me. I thought again
about Eddelman's pattern, all on the back end of the rag. Eddelman
was one of our most consistent pilots and overall one of our best pure
airplane drivers. My off-the-wall reasoning was that the separation between the two pippers was too great.

"Tighten it one click,"[36] I said to the chief.

Standing at my side the squadron Ordnance Officer, Lieutenant (jg)
Bob Steelnack, looked at me without saying anything.

The flight went well. I felt there were two or three runs when I
might have really clobbered it. When the banner was laid out, I was
sure of it. The whole gunnery flight had done well. There were so many
holes I was surprised we hadn't shot the banner clean away. I had thirty
hits—two more than Lieutenant Gunnar Jenson, who then held the

Preflight, the writer in Bob Steelnack's airplane, starboard catapult of the Bonnie Dick. Note the boarding ladder extension in place. (Author's collection)

squadron lead for the day, and three more than Bill Brooks, whose usually smiling face was now marked by a frown. My hits were scattered evenly over the length of the banner. Steelnack looked at me as if I were a bloody genius.

I had one more flight, at thirty thousand feet. This time I didn't fly 109. Billy Burner flew it. I had thirteen hits, which was pretty good for thirty thousand feet. Brooks had eleven. I could tell it bugged him. He knew he was a better gunner than I; he knew it because it was true.

Later, something occurred to me, right out of the blue. About those pippers: Eddelman's hits were in the aft end of the banner because there was insufficient lead, not too much. My correction used the wrong pipper as a reference and was completely backwards! I decided not to share that gem of information with Bob Steelnack, nor with anyone else until now. There are times when it is better to be lucky than good.

In January we went to Yuma, Arizona, on another gunnery deployment, this time for two weeks. Naturally, we expected to pick up right where we had left off at Fallon. We were wrong. Overall we did all right, but we tried to do too much by preparing for our CompEx's (competitive exercises) at both thirty thousand feet and twenty thousand feet in the same short deployment. The magic was gone, for NM109 as well as for most of us. But not for Bill Brooks. In two runs he hit twenty-five out of one hundred rounds expended. That was better than anyone else I knew in the Crusader community of the time.

I heard of only one instance of gunnery scores significantly better than what VF-124 and other Crusader squadrons were achieving during that period. Commander Clyde H. Tuomela, with whom I flew at Patuxent, was a later commanding officer of VF-191, flying F8U-2NEs. Over a milkshake at the Tail Hook Reunion[37] in 1966 Clyde told me that on a recent gunnery exercise they had scores ranging as high as 45 to 50 percent hits.

"Clyde Henry, that's not possible."

He gave me a knowing grin. "Yes, it is. And we did it." His grin turned downright smug. "But there's a secret."

He wouldn't tell me what it was.

A few years later I ran into Clyde at another Tail Hook party. He had had several milkshakes before I saw him.

"You gonna tell me about those gunnery scores?"

On this occasion he gave me a broad smile. "Sure. Five thousand feet. We put the towplane at five thousand feet."

Remember that business about the advantages of high q and high indicated airspeed, preferably without excessively high true airspeed? It is all true, and it works. The combination of dense air and lower true airspeeds for both the towed banner and the shooters did wonders for maneuverability and increased firing time. The gunnery results he cited were like those for another airplane in another time. However, the pilots must have done things right to achieve such high scores.

CompEx's were part of the annual fleetwide competition to determine the best of the best for ships and squadrons in a variety of categories. The winners were awarded the coveted Battle Efficiency "E." Since CompEx's were a matter of official record, they were formally observed by dispassionate third-parties. A favorite source of observers was the Crusader mother squadron, VF-124. It worked for both parties. It filled a need for the fleet squadrons, and it was an opportunity for selected VF-124 instructor pilots to participate in a gunnery deployment. (It was the custom to include the observer in one or more practice firing flights.) But for a couple of years in a row, it appeared that observing for VF-191 could be hazardous to your health.

Fred Winton was our observer in January of 1961. We had been having a couple of mystery maintenance gripes on NM111 having to do

The Executive Officer of Marine Corps Air Station Yuma conducts a personal safety check of NM111. (Author's collection)

with the longitudinal control system—hardly a trivial matter. One pilot said that the stick seemed to hang up momentarily on takeoff. Maintenance couldn't find anything wrong. The next day Lieutenant Dick Richardson brought the airplane back after a flight and said that the stick had frozen on takeoff, scaring the bejesus out of him; somehow he broke it loose, after which it flew fine. "This hummer is *down*," he announced, "till somebody figures out what's wrong with it!" Maintenance took him seriously. They went through the whole system, including removing the panels on top of the turtleback where cables and push rods moved back and forth over the fuel cell to actuate hydraulic valves (those valves controlled the hydraulic actuators, which moved the horizontal stabilator). Again, they found nothing wrong and so put the airplane back in "up" status. As Jim Heffernan used to say, *"Ground checks OK* means you didn't find the problem!"

The next day Fred Winton flew NM111. Fred made his usual afterburner takeoff. After cleaning up the landing gear and putting the wing down, he pulled the nose up into a high-performance climb. As he approached his desired climb angle, he eased the back pressure to stop the nose from pitching higher. Or rather, he tried to; the stick wouldn't move. The nose continued to move upward toward the vertical. He pushed harder; still nothing. At that point, he demonstrated an aviation truism: for a fighter pilot there is no such thing as an unusual airplane attitude. If you can't get the airplane's nose down to the horizon by pushing, try something else. He rolled the airplane over on its back and pulled the nose to the horizon. The stick moved great in that direction! Once in level flight, Fred rolled the airplane back upright. There, to his surprise and relief, he discovered that the stick was free to move normally. This took scant seconds, but it was a heart thumper while it lasted. Displaying more dedication than good sense, he continued the flight, reporting his difficulty only after he landed.

Off came the turtleback again, and the troubleshooting approach now assumed fine-tooth-comb proportions. They found the difficulty. There were a couple of long leather sleeves enclosing the push rod linkages, apparently to protect the mechanism from picking up foreign matter or hanging up on a flange or other protuberance. In some way, never explained, a bolt had found its way inside one of the sleeves. Under just the right g-loading, it could fall into a position where it jammed the linkage. Apparently it was otherwise free to move, because it dislodged itself under negative g, or perhaps simply by movement of the control in the other direction. Scary! A guy could get killed that way.

The following year Lieutenant Commander Jack Snyder was the VF-191 gunnery observer at Fallon, Nevada. After the Compex he received the usual reward: he got to shoot, too. Coming off the perch in a run that commenced normally enough, he reversed his turn, aligned the pipper with the banner, and applied g to track the target. There was a loud bang. The windscreen shattered, the canopy left the airplane, and the ejection curtain came loose and flapped wildly in the breeze, the two handles threatening to become lethal weapons. Initially to prevent inadvertent ejection, Jack reached one hand to grab a handle, still flying the airplane with the other. The airplane did not seem to be responding. So, as he is reported to have explained later, "I had my hand on the curtain. I figured, hell, might as well use it." He did. The Martin-Baker ejection seat worked as advertised. Comfortable but confused in his harness under the nylon canopy of the parachute, Jack could see his airplane diving earthward. Peripherally he saw something else, another shape falling more lazily. The wing of his airplane! His two-position airfoil had evolved a third position, completely *off* his flying machine—three-point attachment, screw jack, and all.

Jack Snyder was to be rewarded further; he later became commanding officer of VF-191. When he received those orders, I wonder if he heard a little voice deep within him that said something like, "Isn't there another F8U squadron somewhere in this Navy?"

Personal Recollections

Every aircraft squadron in the Navy and Marine Corps has a colorful nickname designed to impress friends and critics. Sometimes there is an unofficial name in addition to the official nickname. Examples of official ones are Red Rippers, Jolly Rogers, Golden Dragons, Ghost Riders, and Wake Avengers.[38] On occasion informal ones become officially accepted, like the Black Sheep and Blue Tailed Flies.[39]

VF-191's official nickname was Satan's Kittens. The squadron insignia featured a raunchy-looking, fiercely aggressive black cat in a red cape, brandishing lightning bolts in one paw and a long-handled trident in the other. We had an apparently limitless supply of decals of the squadron insignia, which we left behind us on our travels to mark our passing, a practice embarrassingly reminiscent of an animal marking his territory—especially since many of the decals wound up on the walls of various johns. One of those johns was in a watering hole called Red's Place in Winterhaven, California, just across the state line from Yuma, Arizona. We were generous to Red's Place; one night we plastered those decals all over the place.

Red was a huge fellow with a red beard, a red complexion, and a disposition to match. Fortunately, his behavior was friendly in its quiescent state. His establishment was atmospheric to a fault. There was a small bar with dark, well-worn wood panelling. Memorabilia of all kinds hung from the walls and ceiling; most of the stuff was American Western, but Red was eclectic. The main room had the same decor. There was a U-shaped bar. A sexy, somewhat beat-up young woman usually held forth at an upright piano enclosed by the bar. The seats were tractor seats supported by huge springs. The seats and springs were shiny brass or plated with a convincing imitation. Among the paraphernalia hanging from the wall were a dozen or so fire hats. They were the real thing, red leather with impressive insignia on high frontpieces, dating from the 1920s or earlier. Earlier would be consistent with Red's truck.

Red owned a 1914 La France fire truck in good running condition.

It was a great-looking vehicle. The engine in full cry made a wonderfully ferocious noise. Outwardly in a good state of restoration, the machine had a serious flaw: a cracked engine block. But Red had found a workable solution. Since the truck was a tanker, the body was mostly water tank, with rails and ladders along the sides suitable for people to stand on or cling to. By running a hose directly from the tank into the engine's radiator, Red could drive the truck without overheating until he exhausted all the water in the tank; worst case, that meant close to an hour of steady, almost full-bore operation. A telltale whisper of steam would waft from the front end of the truck when it was in action.

A couple of our young men discovered Red's Place one Saturday afternoon during the July 1960 gunnery deployment to Yuma. Eager to share their find, they convinced Red to come out to the base in his truck and collect the rest of the available VF-191 pilots. Surprisingly, he did. Back in the bar it turned into a real party. With Red's knowledge, if not exactly permission, we left with one of his fire hats.

That fire hat became a kind of squadron symbol for a while, the basis of a short-lived tradition. Whoever the flight leader might be wore it whenever we visited a strange field for a deployment or extended visit. That usually meant me or Jim Heffernan. VF-193, Les Tarleton's Demon squadron, must have concluded that we were getting obnoxious or uppity. In October of 1960 when the air group was leaving Fallon to return to Moffett, someone looked out the hangar window and saw Les drive by in his F3H, wearing our fire hat. We were preparing to leave, too. Lefty Schwartz took off in hot pursuit, hoping to get on the ground at Moffett Field before Les. Notwithstanding the speed advantage of a Crusader over a Demon, Les had too big a lead to be caught in the short flight home. Over the next months the fire hat became the excuse for a lot of undignified high jinks between VF-193 and Satan's Kittens.

Lieutenant Commander Tom Wilson was responsible for VF-191's other nickname, the unofficial one. Tom was our Operations Officer. He had a good disposition and a quiet intensity that enabled him to get things done. However, his sense of responsibility sometimes led him to take things more seriously than he should. He had a sense of humor, always wry, sometimes off the wall, that saved him and us from the ravages of excessive stress. This was good, because he had a personal exasperation quotient that needed periodic relieving.

Air Group 19 was assigned to the USS *Bonhomme Richard* (CVA-31). Bonnie Dick was home ported not at nearby NAS Alameda at the other end of San Francisco Bay—which would have made sense—but at not-so-nearby NAS North Island, San Diego, five hundred nautical miles south, close to an hour's flight in an F8U. There was to be a change-

From aviation ordnanceman, first class, to aviation ordnanceman, chief, and the coveted "hat." The skipper is granted a minor role in the investiture. (Author's collection)

of-command ceremony of the carrier division to which the Bonnie Dick belonged. It was edicted that the air group be suitably represented by the air group commander and his staff and a contingent from each squadron. The formal occasion demanded dress uniforms, which included large medals and swords. The swords got Tom's attention.

In VF-191 we concluded that we could meet all of our training requirements if we could consistently maintain four ready airplanes throughout every training day. That amounts to a continuous, twelve-to-sixteen-hour day. A modest requirement of four available airplanes,[40] only 25 percent of complement, doesn't sound like much. But it gets tougher if you visualize the real requirement of having four airplanes ready to launch on a training flight at intervals of something over two hours throughout a working day; it was especially tough with a maintenance crew that was also in training and was operating under the relatively low priority for spare parts that was the lot of nondeployed squadrons.

Tom Wilson launches from the port catapult of the USS *Bonhomme Richard* (CVA-31). (Author's collection)

Operations Officer Wilson was responsible for devising, scheduling, and implementing the overall schedule. He recognized and dealt well with the normal hazards of his job: his absolute dependence on the output of Bill Brooks's maintenance gang; the sometimes unpredictable performance of the air station's fuel farm. But the change-of-command ceremony, not a normal hazard, caught him by surprise. There was never a good time to lose four airplanes for a whole day so four of us could stand on a flight deck in San Diego while a couple of admirals read their orders to each other.

Tom responded to the challenge in typically professional fashion. He concluded with some logic that as Operations Officer he was required to create and publish an Operations Order for VF-191's portion of the evolution. It would consist of a Movement Order and a Task Organization,[41] the latter to identify the participants and their relationship to each other. In addition to creating, publishing, and posting the Operations Order Tom attached an important two-page appendix. The appendix consisted of a detailed explanation, with diagram, of how to transport a U.S. naval officer's dress sword in the cockpit of an F8U. Tom's appendix filled a need: Crusader pilots were blessed with the airplane's usually more-than-adequate ammunition can compartment for transporting clothes and other gear, but even diagonally, an officer's sword in its scabbard and case wouldn't fit. Tom had figured out a way to squeeze one in, alongside the left cockpit console and along the channel up to the rudder pedals, where it would not significantly impede one's efforts to fly the airplane.

One annoying administrative chore for the Operations Officer of a squadron with supersonic airplanes was to be the de facto investigative officer for all sonic boom complaints. This meant that he got first crack at answering a form message from ComNavAirPac that began something like, "Were, or could any of your aircraft have been, in the vicinity of So-and-So at such-and-such a time on such-and-such a date so as to have been the cause of a sonic boom?" As keeper of the schedule, Tom had to ascertain who was where, when—and whether even with substantial straying from an assigned area one of our folks could possibly have been the culprit. There was no satisfactory answer to such a message other than "No way!" If it was even possible to have been there, the onus of proof of innocence seemed usually to be on the squadron. In point of fact, I don't think we ever received a complaint where we could have been guilty. This is not to say that no VF-191 pilot ever boomed anybody; we just never got caught, not in the States, anyway. There were repeat complaints of sonic booms from specific areas, but the leader of the numbers game was a small California town. It got our attention because the place was small. Also, it was so far from our usual haunts like Moffett, Alameda, and Fallon that our presumption of innocence was unquestioned.

Aboard the Bonnie Dick for good, we sailed for WestPac on 26 April 1961. We stopped in Honolulu, Hawaii, for the usual CinCPac (Commander in Chief, Pacific) briefings for the carrier division and ship commanders. One afternoon a group of us were at tables around the banyan tree in the court of the Moana Hotel. There were about eight pilots, a couple of chiefs, and as many first-class petty officers sitting around, some wearing newly purchased coconut palm hats and aloha shirts. Conversation was desultory to nonexistent. Tom Wilson, a stack of postcards in front of him, was writing diligently.

More from boredom than real interest, Jim Grey asked, "Tom, what are you doing?"

Without looking up, "I'm confessing."

"Confessing what?" Grey persisted.

"I'm confessing to the mayor of So-and-So" (our oft-boomed California town). Putting down his pen, Tom straightened in his chair. He read from what he had just written: "Dear Mayor of So-and-So, I can keep my guilty secret no longer. It was I who boomed your town. I have done it more than once. Many times since. . . ."

Tom read on to the end. There wasn't much more; it was just a postcard. He had signed it "The Mad Boomer." He looked around. "Anybody got any stamps?"

Guardianship of the fire hat invoked a high silliness quotient. Second from left, back row, Jim Grey views the proceedings with a typically jaundiced eye. (Author's collection)

Jim Grey's face lit up. (Jim was our dour one. His face rarely lit up. He was the perennial winner of the squadron's "Lovable Award" for the grump of the month.) "What a great idea," Jim said. "I'm going to get a postcard." Over his shoulder, "I'll check on the stamps."

Within minutes the rest of the pilots, me included, were writing our own confessions to the heinous crime of booming the same small, blameless California community. We continued the practice everywhere we went in WestPac, writing singular confessions always signed "The Mad Boomer." When someone embarked on a special errand, such as ferrying an airplane from the Philippines to Atsugi, Japan, the final admonition to him would be, "Don't forget to send your Boomer card."

My visions of immediately revisiting Japan were put on hold when I found that we would spend the initial part of the deployment operating in and around the Philippines. Since much of the ship's operating program involved multiple carrier launches and much deck respotting, it was decided to loosen things up by getting rid of some airplanes. Thus, VF-191 wound up with a semipermanent detachment of four to six airplanes at NAS Cubi Point in Subic Bay on the island of Luzon.

For the next three weeks we ran different people through the detachment for short periods, the airplanes and pilots constantly changing as well, while we operated back and forth from the ship on a daily flight-by-flight basis. Flying conditions were far from ideal in the middle of the Philippine monsoon season. There was not a satisfactory instrument approach into Cubi, which meant that before we ventured through the clouds, rain, and general muck of the weather into the mountain-sur-rounded bowl of Subic Bay, we wanted some idea of what the weather was really like in there. It was possible to slide in between clouds, descend below the last layer, and then find oneself in the middle of a driving rainstorm with no idea of where either the airfield or those hard, ugly hills were. The best that could happen was a fast climb out of there, wasting precious fuel and hoping that there would be enough to get back to the ship. That experience was to be avoided. Thus, it became our custom to request from the Cubi Point tower the present local weather before we committed to a descent.

Some higher authority in his wisdom had decided that since tower operators were not trained aerologists, it would be misleading for them to pass along their personal weather observations as if they were the real thing. So tower personnel were allowed only to read the previous hourly sequence, which was based on official observations taken on the hour by a rated weather guesser. The nasty thing about monsoon weather, however, is that it can change drastically in about twenty min-utes. It can go from relatively benign—an occasional piece of low scud, maybe a scattered layer of clouds at two thousand feet underneath a barely broken higher level at four thousand, with good visibility—to a you-can't-see-your-hand-in-front-of-your-face gully washer. It was more than irritating when the tower wouldn't give a straight answer before we let down into this sort of thing.

I remember Jim Heffernan's voice, patiently exasperated, on one such occasion. After being read what he recognized as the latest hourly weather sequence, some forty minutes old, he radioed, "Cubi Tower, are you allowed to look out the window?"

"Affirmative, Feedbag."[42]

"Would you please look out the window. Can you tell me if it is raining right now?"

Long pause. "Feedbag, our latest reported weather is—" The same sequence now more than forty minutes old, followed.

It was not surprising that on another day, when the weather was more forgiving, Cubi Point tower was hit by an inadvertent sonic boom. I don't know who that first perpetrator was, but it was not Jim. At least, I don't think it was. It was a minor revenge, but the idea caught on. The tower was boomed frequently if irregularly. The only other likely can-didate for such activity was a Marine Crusader squadron since departed, so there wasn't much question about where the guilt lay. It isn't normally possible to lay a shock wave precisely on a desired target. Accordingly, the noise was spread ecumenically throughout NAS Cubi: the family housing area, Officers' Quarters, the swimming pool, and other areas of base activity (there was no reported damage). When a shock wave is detached on purpose in a dive as opposed to level flight, there is often a double *whap whap* as shock waves come off both ends of the airplane.

At first the station Operations Officer filed his complaints routinely; they became increasingly vociferous as other reports came to him from different parts of the air station. For a while the air station commanding officer didn't get into the act. When he did and, predictably, lodged a complaint with Bonnie Dick's skipper, we backed off. But we didn't quit entirely.

Our enlisted detachment enjoyed the mini-confrontation and the notoriety that went with it. Someone in the detachment procured the

Early photo of the "new" VF-191. Background, Jim Heffernan is supporting the ready room ceiling. (I know, *ceiling* means something else aboard ship.) I am cutting the cake. Bob Steelnack is over my right shoulder. On the right, LSO Ken Wiley seems already to have his cake. Between us, Jim Grey wears a rare smile. Lefty Schwartz is center foreground. Over his left shoulder, the bespectacled one is "Billy Burner" Brooks. Tom Wilson is behind Lefty's other shoulder. Dick Richardson is left foreground in front of Hal Eddelman. Far left is Gunnar Jenson beside Bob Hillyard. The image on the cake appears to be a surfaced submarine, probably in honor of complaints of aerial harassment from our colleagues in the Silent Service. (Author's collection)

biggest piece of burlap I had ever seen and mounted it on poles outside the Quonset hut that served as our flight line shack. On it was painted, in large red letters, "The Mad Boomers." Tom Wilson's nickname was here to stay.

My tour of duty ended in August of 1961 when Jim Heffernan relieved me as commanding officer of VF-191. The change of command was on the hangar deck of the *Bonhomme Richard* in port in Yokosuka, Japan. I flew home to my new duty station, NATC Patuxent River, Maryland. The following spring I saw Jim briefly on a cross-country flight. I was able to combine the flight with a visit to the Vought plant in Dallas, Texas, for a Navy Pilots' Evaluation of the F8U-2NE. It was a circuitous route. VF-191 was then home ported at NAS Miramar, near San Diego. Jim was having a great time with the squadron. Always an excellent pilot, he was in a period where he seemed to excel in every phase of what he was doing. He was pleased with a recent gunnery deployment. Most of his satisfaction was with overall squadron performance, but his personal scores were the best ever.

A short time later I heard the news: Jim Heffernan had died in a crash at sea. He was flying back to Miramar from the ship alone, after completing refresher carrier landings. The weather was reportedly lousy

Change-of-command ceremony aboard the USS *Bonhomme Richard* (CVA-31), August of 1961, Yokosuka, Japan. Jim Heffernan accepts command of VF-191 and custody of the fire hat. (Author's collection)

but good enough underneath for carrier ops. Flying home in the soup was no problem. He was an excellent pilot with well over four thousand flight hours, much of it at night and on instruments from his night-fighter days. With the ship only a few miles offshore, he probably never got very high for the short flight—ten thousand feet, maybe. It was reported that the airplane came out of the low clouds almost inverted and went into the sea. After-the-fact speculation is not productive, but a slowly developing materiel failure, like a bad gyro, is as good a guess as any.

A few years later, after I had left the Navy, I ran into Lefty Schwartz at another Tail Hook Reunion. Lefty was the one who had tried to liberate VF-191's fire hat from Les Tarleton. We talked about Jim Heffernan. I asked Lefty if he knew what happened to the fire hat. He wasn't sure, but he thought he remembered somebody telling him that after Jim's death, Tom Wilson and a couple of other pilots took the hat up to the flight deck. Without ceremony they threw it over the round-down of the flight deck ramp, into the sea.

That sounds like Tom.

Chapter 10
Other Jets

F2H Banshee

*I*N THE FALL OF 1947, VF-17 at Naval Air Station Quonset Point, Rhode Island, underwent a major reshuffling of personnel in preparation for an important event. The squadron was to be the U.S. Navy's first jet squadron. They were to be equipped with the McDonnell FH-1 Phantom. As the prototype squadron, VF-17 would have training and development as well as transition responsibilities. Accordingly, ComAirLant equipped the squadron with seasoned, well-qualified pilots.[1] The airplanes fulfilled their training and transition functions well. VF-17 made the first operational fleet jet carrier landings, and the squadron conducted a limited jet indoctrination program for selected pilots of other squadrons. Lieutenant Bob Hoppe, our Operations Officer, and Lieutenant (jg) Al Wright participated for VBF-3; they were our most experienced carrier pilots after the squadron skipper and Executive Officer, both having flown Wildcats off CVEs during World War II.

The Phantom was a small airplane, about 10,000 pounds. It was powered by two Westinghouse J30 engines nested in the wing roots. They were rated at a mere 1600 pounds each, giving the airplane a reported top speed of 500 mph.[2] They were terribly noisy, real screamers on the ground. It was evident from the beginning that the Phantom was a low performer compared with its contemporaries. The much faster North American FJ Fury was close on its heels. Only sixty Phantoms were procured. In March of 1945, the Navy issued a letter of intent to McDonnell for the design and construction of a successor to be designated XF2D-1.[3]

The new airplane, the Banshee, was basically an enlarged Phantom. The wing root fillet location was retained for two Westinghouse J34 engines that produced 3,000 pounds of thrust each. The fuselage was lengthened for increased fuel capacity. The four nose-mounted .50-caliber machine guns were supplanted by four 20-millimeter cannon. Before production, the guns were moved to the bottom of the nose to prevent muzzle glare from blinding the pilot at night. Also before production, the designation of the Banshee was changed to F2H-1.[4]

McDonnell profited from being actively engaged with new jet fighters for the Navy at the end of World War II. Some traditional suppliers of Navy aircraft, producing rather than developing airplanes at war's end, bore the brunt of contract cancellations without the benefit of ongoing funded development.[5] That circumstance led to the availability of the Curtiss-Wright plant at Lambert Field, St. Louis, Missouri—a government-owned facility that had been built to produce propeller-driven Curtiss airplanes, not needed in the postwar era. The gamble James S. McDonnell took in entering the competitive military airplane business while the war was still going on was paying off. There were to be 892 production Banshees in six major models.

I visited the McDonnell plant while F2H production was in full swing. Fresh from the Naval Postgraduate School, where I had heard lectures on' manufacturing methods and production efficiency, I saw an operation that was right out of the textbooks. Materials that were to become F2H Banshees entered one end of the building. First parts, then subassemblies, then major assemblies moved as needed from the sides into the assembly line that moved down the center of the building. The final stage was the paint shop, complete with a small air-cleansing waterfall. Sparkling new, blue Banshee fighters rolled out of the door at that end of the building. When the finished airplanes first revealed themselves in sunshine under a clear blue sky, it was impressive. During the era when most F2Hs were being produced, the standard color for U.S. Navy aircraft was the dark "sea-blue gloss" of World War II. No other manufacturers' paint jobs were as shiny and durable as McDonnell's.

The airplane I flew out of Service Test at Patuxent was one of the early-production F2H-1s. It was just under 19,000 pounds with a wingspan of 41 feet 6 inches. The -1s lacked the tip tanks of the more numerous F2H-2s,[6] and the nose was shorter. The early airplanes had a feature to conserve fore and aft aircraft carrier deck space: the nose strut could be depressed to a kneeling position. With the Banshee's upswept tail and a kneeled nose strut, airplanes could be stacked nose-under-tail. To my knowledge the technique was never actually employed in service, and the feature was abandoned in later airplanes.

Other features were to ensure a long, productive service life for the Banshee. All of the F2Hs had rated service ceilings of around forty nine thousand feet, but in August of 1949, an F2H-1 was flown to fifty two thousand feet, setting an unofficial record for jet-powered aircraft.[7] The airplane's range and cruise characteristics made it one of the Navy's

F2H-1 Banshee. (USNI Photo Library)

F2H-2s from the USS *Essex* (CV-9) returning from a mission over North Korea. Piloting the aircraft on the right is Ensign, later Rear Admiral, Paul Speer, USN. (USNI Photo Library)

first tactical nuclear bombers. In October of 1954, Ensign Varner of VF-34 flew an F2H-2 nonstop from NAS Los Alamitos, California, to NAS Cecil Field, Florida—a distance of nineteen hundred miles—without refueling.[8] Banshees were used as escort fighters, photo planes, and fighter bombers throughout the Korean War. From mid-1952 until September of 1959, long-tailed F2H-3s were the standard carrier all-weather fighters.[9] The first fleet Banshee had been an F2H-1 delivered to VF-171 in August of 1948. In November of 1955 the Royal Canadian Air Force began receiving F2H-3s that were to go aboard the HMCS *Bonaventure*. When struck from the service lists in September of 1962, Banshees were the last Canadian aircraft carrier fighters.[10]

The "Banjo" had an impressively long service life, particularly for a straight-wing jet fighter during a period of dynamic development of airplanes and high-speed aerodynamics. It was happenstance that my first jet flight as pilot in command was in Service Test's F2H-1; it might just as easily have been the F9F-2 Panther. It would be difficult to justify a preference. The Banshee may have been somewhat more docile and predictable on the ground. Except for there being twice as many controls and the necessity for going through two starting procedures, the presence of an extra engine didn't make any meaningful difference in flying, or learning to fly, the airplane. In the Banshee, the Phantom II, and the T-39 Sabreliner, the only twin jets I have flown, the loss of an engine is noticeable only in terms of total thrust and speed. Not only is there no discernible thrust imbalance, no requirement for torque compensation; flight characteristics are basically unaffected. Without the necessity to become familiar with the complicated engine-out procedures endemic to twin-engine propeller aircraft, I was free simply to explore—and enjoy—the Banshee.

For years McDonnell was heavily into the supernatural and the spirit world as sources for airplane names: Phantom, Banshee, Goblin, Voodoo, and Demon among them. There were those who said that the company was right on the mark, in that some of those airplanes were downright spooky! The origin for the comments was certainly the F2H. The remarks were not intended to be derogatory—I never met a Banshee pilot who didn't like the airplane—but it did make funny noises!

Transitioning propeller pilots were unfailingly impressed by the difference in the sound level and sound quality in the newfangled jet airplanes, and the Banshee was archetypical. The pilot sat well forward of the two engines, which were isolated and partially insulated by being nestled in the wing roots rather than the fuselage. At a relatively low 3,000 pounds of thrust each, the J34 engines were quiet; they whined rather than screeched or roared. The pilot, remotely positioned in the cocoon of his pressurized cockpit, could hear things that in his previous experience had been drowned out by the roaring monster of a big radial engine a few feet from his lap. He could hear things like his own breathing through the oxygen mask and the diluter-demand regulator, the whine of the gyro instruments, the rushing pressurization air—and another sound that was anomalous, a kind of pop-pop-popping, a most un-airplane-like noise. More than one first-time pilot became apprehensive when he first discerned that audible signature of a small reciprocating pump located somewhere in the pressurization system.

Then there were the aerodynamic sounds. Compared with most airplanes the Banshee felt light, even loose, especially that early version without tip tanks. It also felt smooth and agile, as if inviting the pilot to maneuver. With application of g-forces, particularly at altitude, buffet and the beginnings of buffet announced themselves with buzzings, rattlings, and groans difficult to describe. One could get deep into buffet before anything exciting occurred, but the airplane constantly warned the pilot that something was going on.

Slow-flight and stall characteristics were pleasantly unremarkable. If the aircraft had any bad habits, I didn't discover them in my brief encounter. Not that I didn't try. This is a fast, high-altitude airplane, I told myself; it's time to wring it out with some acrobatics! Obviously those maneuvers should be performed at high altitude, I reasoned. Wrong! I forgot about the aviator's old friend "q."[11] If a pilot wants maximum available g's, as he must when performing vertical maneuvers like loops and Immelmanns, he should be at the lower altitudes where denser, thicker air and available airspeed will support them. But I didn't process what I knew about aerodynamics: I tried my first loop with the bottom at twenty thousand feet! Somehow I made it around, but it wasn't easy. As I passed through the vertical to on-top, I played the pitch forces gingerly, using the buffet noises as a gauge as to how hard I could pull. I was close to stall when I got on my back and started down the other side, but I made it.

On subsequent attempts, and for the Immelmann, I moved down to fourteen thousand feet at the bottom. The maneuvers still required care, but I performed them successfully. It was not until later, back on the ground, that I began to appreciate that I had been operating in the wrong flight regime for what I was doing; the proper altitude for the low point would have been closer to nine thousand or ten thousand feet. It is a tribute to the airplane's aerodynamic qualities, considering its relatively low available thrust, that I was able to accomplish those maneuvers at all.

Landing the airplane was a piece of cake. The briefing had prepared me for a lack of either challenge or unpleasant surprises. It had not prepared me for the pleasant surprises. The airplane handled well in landing configuration. On final approach there was some wiggling around—not quite a Dutch roll—caused, I am sure, by my own over-controlling. As I got close to the ground I eased the nose up, preparing for my usual approach-to-stall landing. Before I could quite get there, I found myself executing the best roll-on landing I had ever experienced. Not only that, it was repeatable. After a few tries I decided that the Banjo could make anybody feel like a good pilot.

The Banshee had an entirely different overall feel than the more solid, slower F9F-2 Panther. There was an impression of lightness and flexibility compared with the Grumman product. The wings visibly flexed up and down, as in a DC-3,[12] especially, I have been told, with tip tanks.

The F2H was a remarkable airplane. Pilots are ingenious when it comes to finding things to complain about in an airplane, but I don't think I ever heard anyone who had flown a Banshee bad-mouth it. The worst I recall is a fatigue problem late in its service life. It came to light after an accident in which the number four (the slot man) in a Marine acrobatic team flying F2H-2s was killed. Already under g-load in the recovery from a maneuver at low altitude—and in rough air from the three airplanes in front of him—he hit turbulence. A wing failed catastrophically.

Inspection of other airplanes revealed systematic structural fatigue cracks in a number of the high-flight-time air frames. Until the problem was fixed, the airplanes were restricted to a little over 3 g's. It certainly had something to do with all that wing flexing. Structural fatigue damage was, and is, among the more difficult things to predict in an airframe: just how many flexes is too many? The problem is compounded for airplanes whose airframes are subjected to the intermittent pounding of carrier landings. All airplanes are affected, however, if they stay in service long enough. Some years ago, even the ageless DC-3s had fatigue and corrosion problems affecting the main wing spars.

We are much smarter about structural fatigue now than we used to be, for civil as well as military airplanes. Sometimes it doesn't seem that way; the public is made increasingly aware of the phenomenon through reports in the media. But we are flying more high-flight-time airframes than ever before, and we know more about fatigue problems than ever before. People in the industry are doing a lot of airframe inspecting and fixing. It gets reported.

F3D Skyknight

In late 1945, the Navy discussed its need for a carrier-based night fighter with four manufacturers: Douglas, Curtiss, Grumman, and Fleetwing.

F3D-2 Skyknight. (USNI Photo Library)

These discussions led to the single-engine day fighter that became the F9F Panther; for Douglas the result was the twin-jet two-place F3D Skyknight. It was to be seven years before Douglas delivered the first Skyknight to VC-3[13] at Moffett Field, California.

This first jet carrier night fighter—more properly called an "all-weather fighter"—was a midwing side-by-side design with two West-inghouse J34 engines semisubmerged in pods in the lower fuselage. Initially they were WE-24s developing 3,000 pounds of thrust. The later F3D-2s were powered by J34-WE-36 engines, which produced 3,400 pounds of thrust. That welcome change turned the airplane from a "ground lover" into something merely underpowered. The gross weight of the F3D-2 was 26,850 pounds. There were 28 F3D-1s built and 237 F3D-2s.

All production versions had straight, midfuselage-mounted wings. (Three units of a swept-wing version were built, but there was no pro-duction—yet another casualty of the failed engine division of the West-inghouse Electric Company. The F3D-3, like the F3D-2, was designed around the J46 engine, which never reached production quantities.) The side-by-side seating for the two-man crew and the sliding canopy panel overhead, providing entrance to and egress from the cockpit, precluded standard ejection seats. The Heinemann team's design solution was a tunnel from the cockpit through the center of the fuselage. The crew accessed the tunnel through a normally pressure-tight door. In a bailout emergency they opened the door, slid down the tunnel, and exited through the opening left by a detachable, blow-away panel in the bottom of the fuselage. The big twin-engine carrier-based bomber, the A3D, had a similar arrangement.[14]

Armament was four 20-millimeter cannon. The Westinghouse APQ-35 search and track radar was housed in the large nose behind a plastic radome. There was an autopilot, also by Westinghouse. The presence of an autopilot was unique for carrier aircraft of the time, but it was a good idea from the standpoint of pilot fatigue. The F3D was designed for good endurance and range—which translates to time in the air—but there was only one set of controls. The other crew station was dedicated to radar and weapon system management. This feature too was to be duplicated in the A3D.

The state-of-the-art electronics in the Skyknight were extremely capable, but their sophisticated design included many discrete parts and, worse yet, many vacuum tubes. Reliability was low, and the various system elements were difficult to maintain.[15]

Driven by design requirements laid on by the Navy, the F3D was a large airplane. Compared with contemporary carrier jet fighters, everything about it was large, including the tail hook and the wheels. I have reason to be aware of, and grateful for, those large 32-inch wheels, but nothing as interesting as Mr. Heinemann's experience. I know that they were 32-inch wheels only because of a story he tells in his book *Ed Heinemann—Combat Aircraft Designer.*[16]

During the early design phase of the A3D Skywarrior, which was to be the Navy's principal all-weather nuclear weapon delivery airplane, Mr. Heinemann was visited by a colonel friend, later a U.S. Air Force general. Understandably, Ed Heinemann was having some difficulty designing an airplane to meet demanding performance specifications and at the same time have room in its bomb bay for something called Fat Man; the weapon, one of the two types dropped on Japan at the end of the war, was 5 feet by 5 feet by 183 inches. Not a nuclear physicist but having some knowledge of weapon as well as airplane design,[17] Mr. Heinemann was sure that there was a better way to go. Why not design a smaller bomb? To make his point with the colonel, he used a convenient dimension for the cross-section, the 32 inches of the F3D wheel diameter. Quickly sketching, he "shrunk" his conceptual airplane around the new payload, his hypothetical bomb. The result was a dramatic reduction in size and weight. The colonel was impressed—and surprised. Heinemann did not appreciate the extent of that surprise until he received some visitors from the government. Polite, persistent, and very thorough, they plied him with questions for some time. When they left, seemingly not entirely satisfied with his answers, their problem was simple: how could this airplane designer, however prominent and well respected, know the precise dimensions of the new atom bomb that was secretly under development?

By the time F3D-2 deliveries were being made to the two Navy all-weather fighter squadrons on each coast, the decision had been made to go with the long-tailed Banshees whose better performance had already been proven aboard aircraft carriers. The Skyknights were relegated to a training role in the Navy, although they served actively and with distinction with the U.S. Marines in Korea.

Recognizing that the F3Ds were underused, Gordon Snyder, in his capacity as Aircraft Assignment Officer at ComFAir (Commander, Fleet Air) Alameda, intercepted a brand-new F3D-2 that was destined for VC-3 at Moffett Field. He assigned the airplane to FASRON 8 (Fleet Air Support Squadron Eight) at NAS Alameda, where it immediately became available for staff pilots' proficiency, training, and logistics flights.

With its large, comfortable cockpit, state-of-the-art ergonomic control layout and design, and the best cockpit lighting I had ever seen, it made a glorious two-man transport. Its 400-knot-plus cruising speed cut the three-and-a-half-hour flight (via Beechcraft) to ComAirPac headquarters in San Diego to a little over an hour. Besides that, it was a great airplane to fly. Referring to its docility, Mr. Heinemann once described it as an "old man's airplane"; maybe so, but it wasn't exactly shabby as a young man's airplane either!

In the middle of 1953—when airplanes were being delivered to the fleet but production was still in full swing in St. Louis—a structural problem was discovered in the F2H-3s and F2H-4s. The problem was not severe, and the fix was relatively easy to implement. Cracks were discovered in the aft bulkheads of the long tails. The bulkheads needed to be inspected, fixed if necessary, and then reinforced to prevent new damage. All airplanes were affected. To simplify things administratively, it was decided to "deliver" all the airplanes to the Navy on paper and then do the repair; physical delivery of the aircraft would follow. Airplanes already in the fleet were to be scheduled for recycle and repair back at St. Louis.[18]

The decision resulted in a management and score-keeping task for the Navy—somebody in the Navy. ComAirPac didn't want it, so they gave the job to ComFAir Alameda, where I was Airframes Officer. By January of 1954, ComFAir's meager fiscal-year travel budget was already extended. We couldn't afford a commercial airline ticket to McDonnell in St. Louis for me to make an urgently needed planning visit. The solution was for me to use the F3D for transportation.[19]

I left from FASRON 8's flight line early one morning while it was still black air out. I had hoped to make a refueling stop in Denver and arrive in St. Louis by afternoon—too late for a meeting that day, but ready to start bright and early in the morning. I had a couple of strikes against me. In an excess of zeal, the line crew had turned up the engines as part of the preflight to make sure that all systems were functioning properly (not a usual practice with jet airplanes of the day). That was fine, but they neglected to top off the fuel tanks afterwards. I could still make it to Denver, however, if I had sufficient tail wind, not an unreasonable expectation for a flight from west to east at jet cruising altitudes.

I monitored my progress between checkpoints rigorously, hoping that my ground speed would confirm the necessary wind velocity. No such luck; I couldn't make it to Denver without refueling. Somewhere west and south of Salt Lake City I revised my flight plan and headed for Hill Air Force Base in Ogden, Utah. It was a beautiful clear day. As I approached the field, I had trouble identifying the runways—for good reason. They were covered with snow, albeit with a few patches of black macadam showing through. With the beginnings of apprehension, I called for landing clearance, optimistically assuming that the field was operational.

The tower controller responded matter-of-factly with the usual numbers and a clearance to land. Nary a reference to runway condition. Obviously, they were all right. My landing was normal. I had the good sense to let the airplane run straight on the white stuff with no extraneous control inputs. My only real concern was getting stopped before the end; the F3D may have been a ground lover, but it was heavy and it rolled forever. When I slowed down sufficiently, I tried the brakes, v-e-r-y gingerly. The aircraft slowed obediently. It became a little skittish turning off the runway, but once on the taxiway I proceeded sedately toward the transient flight line.

Thank God for those big wheels and Douglas brakes, I thought.

My thoughts were interrupted by the tower. "Navy Jet 12345 [not the real Bureau number], how is the runway braking action?"

"Hill Tower, Navy Jet. Not good, but it's usable."

"Thanks, Navy Jet. You're the first person to land here in five days."

And thanks to *you*, Air Force, I thought.

The flight on to Denver was uneventful. The Denver naval reserve ground crew got me turned around in good order, and I was not irretrievably behind schedule when I strapped in for the leg to Lambert Field, St. Louis—until I tried to start the left engine, that is. The line chief soon confirmed that my problem was "no ignition." But why no ignition? That determination would have to await the ministrations of the night-check crew. I was stuck for the night.

Things didn't start out much better the next morning. Night check had determined that I had a bad ignition microswitch in the throttle quadrant. That was sort of good news; at least it wasn't the igniters. But there were no spare switches to be had. The day crew beat the bushes most of the day looking for a usable substitute, to no avail.

Late in the afternoon, the first-class aviation mech in charge approached me. Having observed my growing frustration, perhaps he felt sympathy. "Lieutenant, if you really want to get out of here, I think we can do it."

My spirits rose. "Hey, let's do it."

He seemed to hesitate, then looked at me kind of sideways. "It isn't going to be your basic, regulation repair."

"Will it work?"

"It'll work."

"Do it."

And he did. The solution was to wire around the failed microswitch with a piece of plain, single-strand insulated wire. In the middle of the wire my friendly mechanic inserted a spring-loaded toggle switch, so unsophisticated in appearance that I wondered if it would meet the standards of even a neighborhood hobby electronics supplier. The hard part for the mechanic was digging into the throttle quadrant to locate the proper attachment points without doing further damage. Since the switch needed to be activated only once per engine start, it was safely dormant the rest of the time. It did look lousy, however, this length of loose wire floating around near the base of the throttle. At the proper time for engine ignition I had to let go of everything else, hold the switch with one hand, and close the contacts momentarily with the other.

It was late afternoon when I finally left Denver. NAS Denver was one of the first fields I ever saw with ten thousand feet of usable runway. It is a good place to have long runways; the field elevation is over five thousand feet, where the air is thin. The F3D felt as if it was going to use every inch of that ten thousand feet of pavement. I actually got airborne after about eight thousand feet.

I arrived in St. Louis after dark that evening without further incident. The naval reserve personnel who were the station keepers at NAS St. Louis[20] couldn't perform a proper repair either in the two days I was there. My only requirement was that, if they couldn't find the right parts, they leave my jury rig in place. They did, and that is what I used to start the left engine for the remainder of the trip. The business part of my visit was successful and unremarkable, as was my return to Alameda.

In some respects one of Douglas's less successful airplanes, the

F3D had a long and not undistinguished service life. It never made it as a carrier all-weather fighter, but the Marines employed it successfully in Korea. Flying a Skyknight on the night of 2 November 1952, Major William Stratton and his radar operator, Master Sergeant Hans Hoagland, shot down a YAK-15, the first recorded jet-versus-jet kill at night. The airplane also saw service as a night intruder throughout that conflict. VF-101 used the F3D as a trainer for F-4 Radar Intercept Officers. The Skyknight was in use with the Marines as an electronic countermeasures aircraft in the Vietnam War until its retirement from service in 1969.[21]

A4D Skyhawk

In late October of 1957, shortly after I joined the staff of ComCarDiv-3 (Commander, Carrier Division Three), I overheard Rear Admiral Frank O'Beirne talking to his Chief of Staff. He was relating that Captain Jimmy Mills's son-in-law had been killed flying a VA-153 A4D Skyhawk on a night-bombing training flight out of NAAS Fallon, Nevada. Frank O'Beirne was a product of that close-knit prewar community of naval aviators in which everybody knew everybody else. Accordingly, he knew Captain James H. Mills, Jr., USN, the commanding officer of NAS Alameda, well. As a lieutenant commander in the much larger postwar Navy, I did not know Captain Mills, nor had I known the son-in-law, Lieutenant Robert Thayer Rich, USN. I reacted to the tragic news as one does to the loss of a fellow flyer, known or not. But the incident was to assume a more personal significance for me later.

"Heinemann's Hot Rod,"[22] The marvelous Skyhawk, was conceived in 1951. Fleet deliveries of A4D-1s commenced to VA-72 in the Atlantic Fleet in September of 1956, followed shortly by deliveries to VA-93 in the Pacific Fleet. As I write, the U.S. Marine Corps is phasing out the A-4Ms, the last combat Skyhawks in the U.S. inventory. The airplane lives on in the form of TA-4F/Js in the U.S. Navy's Advanced Training Command, as well as in almost too many configurations to count in various air forces throughout the world. New Zealand is currently modifying its A-4s with a new radar, among other changes, for yet another extension of service life. A4D production commenced in 1954 and ended with the last Skyhawk coming off the production line in February of 1979.[23] A summation of A-4 production figures cited by René Francillon yields a total of just under three thousand for all major versions.[24] That doesn't begin to tell the story because, like cats, some A-4s led many lives.

The airplane owes its existence to the postwar need for delivery platforms for the atomic weapons that were to be the basis of the nu-

A-4Ms of VMA-214. The appearance of this best performer of the in-service A-4s is marred by the unsightly equipment bay hump. Barely visible over the nose, the in-flight refueling probe now has a bend to keep it away from the engine intake. (USNI Photo Library)

clear deterrent force. Ed Heinemann's original concept had been for a lightweight interceptor. The Skyhawk was the first light attack airplane to be built from the keel up as a nuclear bomber. The form it took was a product of Ed Heinemann's genius, and of his frustration with the trend of constantly growing aircraft weight and size to meet combat missions. He was convinced that there was a better way. The A4D was the result.[25] That the A4D met its primary requirement is his validation. That the airplane did so many other jobs well is evidence of the breadth and scope of his genius.

The Skyhawk had a low-mounted, delta-planform wing of only 27 feet 6 inches' span, less than that of any World War II fighter I know. The vertical fin and rudder faired smoothly from the turtleback of the fuselage.[26] The high horizontal tail consisted of a conventional stabilizer with trailing-edge elevator. The short wingspan obviated the necessity of folding wings for stowage on aircraft carriers. The airplane sat on long, spindly landing gear that folded forward. The forward-folding feature made possible a gravity rather than pneumatic or hydraulically actuated emergency landing gear system—a good example of saving weight and avoiding complexity. (I have heard the landing gear described as having been "designed" by the Mk 7 bomb, at the time the smallest of the so-called tactical nuclear weapons. The gear had to be wide enough to provide clearance to allow the bomb to hang on the fuselage centerline station and long enough to provide ground clearance, even when the oleo struts were compressed by the impact of a carrier landing.) The combination of a nose wheel free to swivel, a high center of gravity, and a relatively small wing area made the airplane a handful to land under some crosswind conditions. But most of the time the A-4 was about as hard to land as a kiddie car (one of its nicknames, by the way).

Design gross weight was initially 12,000 pounds, considered by virtually all the "experts" to be an impossible goal. After the Navy added a few extra requirements, like JP jet fuel instead of AvGas and a bigger bomb, the weight ante increased to 14,500 pounds, and there it remained for the agreed design configuration. For the first flight of the A4D-1 on 22 June 1954, Mr. Heinemann cites a "gross weight" of 19,910 pounds and a "combat weight" of 15,876 pounds; again, the differences are explained by defined configurations.[27] (In the Bureau of Aeronautics at the time, I recall someone claiming as little as 10,000 pounds for a stripped, empty A4D. However accurate or inaccurate, the number stuck in my head because it was so close to the 9,000 pounds I had heard similarly quoted years before for the small F8F Bearcat.)

From its introduction, the Skyhawk was a wonderfully easy and enjoyable airplane to fly. Pilots accepted it enthusiastically. However, its primary mission as a light nuclear bomber injected spice and more than a little risk into the game. Most of the weapon delivery tactics were developed by VX-5 and entailed maneuver combinations discouraged by prudent pilots since the beginnings of aviation, like putting vertical maneuvers, such as loops and Cuban eights, together with high speeds and very low altitudes.

Among those delivery techniques were "toss bombing" and "over-the-shoulder" bombing. Toss bombing is almost self-explanatory.[28] The pilot makes a grass-top approach and commences a pull-up at a selected point. As the aircraft's nose passes through a preselected pitch angle— usually between 35 and 50 degrees—the bomb is released manually or by computer, whereupon it proceeds in a parabolic arc toward the target. The trajectory makes it possible to utilize any of the variety of fusing options built into every weapon. The pilot's job gets even more interesting after weapon release. He continues the pull-up through the vertical, over the top and down the other side—so far like the first half of a loop. Once pointed well down, say at a 45-degree angle, he stops the nose and rolls upright, still descending. He continues his descent in a classic Cuban eight maneuver, leveling off when at minimum altitude to exit the target area.

Over-the-shoulder bombing is similar, except that the pull-up point is the target itself and the bomb is released as the delivery airplane is headed skyward, close to the vertical. In this case the weapon flies a much narrower parabola and comes down, if all goes well, right on the target below. The probability that the airplane's and the weapon's post-launch trajectories will intersect in space and time are, happily, minimal, although you can be sure that the possibility has entered the mind of virtually every pilot who ever performed the maneuver. This isn't the sort of thing one practices with live nuclear weapons, but flying the maneuver with full-size shapes was part of the program.

Both maneuvers were designed to accomplish several objectives. The low-altitude approach was chosen to optimize the pilot's chances of penetrating a heavily defended target area; "popping up" for the actual weapon delivery minimized his exposure to hostile fire, as did getting back down to low altitude as soon as possible. The over-the-shoulder delivery was considered the more accurate method, but it required flying directly over the target, around which the heaviest concentration of anti-aircraft weapons could be expected.

For each maneuver, escaping the effects of the delivered weapons themselves was a major consideration. Each of the principal effects—blast, thermal, and radiation—is threatening to the delivery airplane. Thermal reaches the airplane almost instantaneously, closely followed by radiation. The pressure waves move through the air much more slowly, in accordance with the physics of supersonic airflow, but the movement is still very fast compared with that of an airplane. (The objective of almost all explosive weapons is to cause damage with overpressure. From a weapons-effectiveness standpoint, pressure is the most effective agent; it is also the most controllable.) All of these effects are minimized for a low-flying airplane proceeding away from a target at high speed while presenting a minimum cross-section, tail-on aspect. Thermal effects can be further reduced by reflective rather than absorptive paint schemes.

Fortunately, none of these weapons was ever dropped in anger. The A-4s successful combat history was as a general purpose, light attack airplane, delivering "conventional" (non-nuclear) ordnance.

The nuclear weapon delivery maneuvers were practiced, however, and they took their toll in the early years of A4D employment. A limited night/all-weather capability was introduced with the A4D-2N, which first flew in 1959. Such features as a terrain-follow radar, autopilot, angle-of-attack-indicating system, and enhanced LABS (low-altitude bombing system) were introduced. These added features reduced the early accident rate of the A4D, which for a time was badly inconsistent with its good flying qualities and general ease of operation.

It is difficult to explain a spate of accidents in an otherwise docile airplane, especially when there is no dominant mechanical or aerodynamic cause. Operating practices, human error, and just plain bad luck all contribute. Aerodynamic characteristics are certainly a factor. Once it diverged from controlled flight, the small delta wing of the A-4 needed time and space—which equates to altitude—to get flying again. Those low-altitude weapon delivery maneuvers A4D pilots flew were referred to as "goofy loops" for good reason: they represent the only circumstance in my experience where pilots were encouraged to perform acrobatic maneuvers in a vertical plane close to the ground.[29]

It was to be some years before I flew the A-4, but I observed it at close hand on a cruise to the Western Pacific in 1957 and 1958. ComCarDiv-3 rode the *Ticonderoga* (CVA-14) for most of that deployment. The embarked light jet attack squadron was VA-93, flying A-4s. It was an excellent carrier airplane, and VA-93 did an outstanding job with it. (In 1960 when Tom Sedaker was my air group commander in Air Group 19, he carrier-qualified in the A-4. Afterwards he remarked, "Hell, my nine-year-old son could bring that thing aboard ship!" I can't accept that it was quite so easy, but many pilots made it look so.)

On a summer evening in 1958, in the Officers' Club at NAS Alameda, a classmate introduced me to a beautiful, dark-haired girl. A year and a half later, Jacqueline Marie Mills Rich and I were married. A few months after that happy event, Marie and I and our (my adopted) daughter Diana drove up to my new duty station, NAS Moffett Field. We were greeted by a column of black smoke rising from a housing development adjacent to the airfield where an A-4 had just crashed.[30] I could only imagine the reaction of my bride sitting beside me on her return to the former home field of VA-153, which had been Bob Rich's squadron. For anyone susceptible to omens or Greek tragedy, this was not the most encouraging of signs, at least I was going to be flying not A-4s but F8Us, for whatever encouragement that provided. (Do enlightened adults really react that way? You bet they do, once they have experienced the lightning bolt. We were less than thrilled years afterwards when our son flew A-4s in Advanced flight training; Marie concedes that she found it a kind of unfair triple jeopardy when he also flew A-4Ms in VMA-211, his first tactical squadron.)

I finally flew the A-4 at Patuxent in 1962, an A4D-5 (later A-4E) out of Service Test. This was the first version of the airplane in which the Pratt & Whitney J52 engine replaced the Curtiss-Wright J65, an American version of the British-designed and -developed "Sapphire." The original J65 produced only 7,700 pounds of the promised 8,000 pounds of thrust; available thrust stayed at about that level through the early A4D-2Ns until the J65-16C produced 8,500 pounds. The initial J52s did not provide significantly more thrust. The A-4Ms finally got a substantial

A4D-5 (A-4E) on the Weapons Test ramp at Patuxent. (USNI Photo Library)

increase in thrust with the J52-P-408 engines, which delivered 11,200 pounds, commencing in April of 1970.

The A4D-5 had the same longer nose as the A4D-2N, along with various other improvements including an improved ejection seat and additional wing-mounted weapon stations. The latter was an acknowledgment of the change in the aircraft's primary role from nuclear to conventional weapons delivery.

There were three other improvements that the Test Center people consistently favored and that the procurement folks in the Bureau of Aeronautics consistently resisted. They resisted for a valid reason: there was no money available to pay for them. The argument was perhaps valid for program managers,[31] but it was not willingly accepted by other pilots. The three proposed changes were a steerable nose wheel, wing spoilers, and nonskid brakes (that was the original nomenclature; *antilock* brakes is the more appropriate term in use today).

Each of the features was nice to have individually. Taken together, the three provided important relief in a scenario that goes like this: An A-4 lands on a long runway in generally benign conditions. The sun is shining. The runway is dry. The wind is about 40 degrees to the left of the runway heading at 10 knots or so, occasionally gusting to 20 knots. Shortly after touchdown one of those gusts hits the airplane. The A-4 tries to weathercock downwind (as an A-4 will) toward the leeward side of the runway. The pilot tries to correct with left rudder; the airplane starts to correct back to the left. Before the pilot can back up the effort with left brake, the left wing rises, responding to the centrifugal force of the curved path. Whoops! He throws in left aileron to get the wing—and that upwind wheel and brake—back down on the ground to regain control. No luck. Now he is out of aerodynamic control—no rudder or aileron effectiveness, the wrong wheel up in the air, and a swiveling nose wheel that is still on the ground but not controllable. All he can do is sit there and enjoy the ride until he runs off the runway. It is too late to add power. Besides, he is pointing in the wrong direction. Depending on how fast he is traveling, it might be prudent simply to shut down the engine and hope for the best.

In the usual such occurrence, damage was minimal except to the pilot's pride. It could happen to the best of them. It happened to Lieutenant Commander Jim Tyson one day at Patuxent, just as I have described. Jim had a mere two thousand hours in model at the time! He was a fine pilot who was later to head the U.S. contingent of the multinational team that evaluated the Hawker-Siddeley Kestrel, the predecessor of the VSTOL Harrier that is flown by the U.S. Marine Corps as the AV-8.

Any one of the three changes would solve the problem. If all three were used together, the problem would not develop in the first place: the steerable nose wheel would prevent the initial swerve; the wing spoilers would keep the wing, and the wheel, down where they belonged; the antilock brakes, even if applied too vigorously, too soon, would be effective for directional control. No sweat!

All three modifications got into subsequent airplanes, but not the A4D-5. Not on my watch, anyway.

The maneuverability and agility of the A-4s became legendary almost from the beginning. I remember coming upon a lone A-4 north of the Test Center one afternoon. He was there, so I made a run on him. I was flying an F8U-2N, the best performer of the entire Crusader series, but over the next ten minutes I never got a fair shot. No matter what I did, every time I approached gun range, there was his nose—and his 20-millimeter cannon—pointed right at me. I gave it the whole nine yards: vertical maneuvers, high and low yo-yos, rolling scissors (Oops! Don't try any kind of scissors with this guy!), and every gunnery pass I could think of. Nothing worked. I couldn't even honestly claim a decent Sidewinder shot. The Navy recognized that A-4 capability when they chose it as an Aggressor aircraft for the Fighter Weapons School. The Skyhawk is only now being phased out of that role in favor of the F-16N Falcon.[32]

The airplane Jim Tyson ran off the runway was an A4D-2N that belonged to Service Test. There were a couple of minor evaluation projects piggybacking on the airplane in addition to the primary one (in Service Test the major program almost always had something to do with the engine). One of these secondary evaluations involved an experimental voice warning system. Almost as an afterthought in my preflight briefing came the suggestion, "Oh, you might give us a write-up on this one too." Such systems have since become common in automobiles as well as in airplanes, but in 1962 it was a new idea. The concept was to augment written checkoff lists with a human voice that would automatically get the pilot's attention and provide necessary information when something malfunctioned, or when the pilot forgot to do something important like lower the landing gear prior to landing. The aviation psychologist who invented the device decided on a female voice, for a couple of reasons: in the predominantly male military aviation environment, the female voice was calculated to be an especially effective attention getter, and its higher pitch would make any message more understandable, easier to read, over the ambient noises of jet airplanes.

I was given another oh-by-the-way piece of information: for some reason, landing gear actuation in this airplane was slow. Just be patient, I was told. It worked fine. It just took longer than normal.

The flight was undemanding and uneventful; the most stressful part was writing down a few numbers at appropriate times. After getting permission to enter the traffic pattern and land, I broke left over the duty runway, stood the airplane on its wing, and whacked off the power. As I slowed through the gear-down speed, I slapped down the landing gear handle and waited to perform the next event, which would be to lower the flaps. In the interests of not overburdening the hydraulic system, I waited for the barber pole in the indicator to be replaced by the wheels-down symbol. Like the man said, it took a while.

I was startled to hear a matter-of-fact female voice: "You have an unsafe indication on your landing gear. Check the landing gear indicator. If it is still unsafe, please recycle."

This was repeated twice. Then "she" started to recite the emergency landing gear lowering procedure. (Now *that* was one I knew by heart, for the A-4 and every other airplane I had ever sat in!) As "she" continued, the pacing of the delivery increased, the pitch of the voice rose. Jesus, I thought, I'm about to have a hysterical woman on my hands. And I'm all alone in the airplane!

I could stand it no more. I heard my own voice: "Shut up, you stupid bitch! *I'm* flying this goddam airplane."

Just then the gear locked into place. Three little wheel symbols magically appeared on the indicator. I found myself looking around to see if anyone had heard my unseemly outburst.

I dutifully wrote my evaluation, omitting any reference to my one-way conversation with "her." D. Z. Skalla told me that another pilot, Lieutenant Commander Russ Farley, and I were the only ones who didn't like the device. I guess that made us the duty Male Chauvinistic Pigs, an expression that hadn't been invented in 1962. I thought that my objections were reasonable: a male voice might be less traumatic to a male pilot in an emergency situation in which articulation and comprehension were not necessarily the critical factors. But Russ and I remained in the minority; the systems abound today, using female voices. (In describing a system idiosyncrasy in the AV-8B, a close male relative recently referred to such a voice warning in his own airplane. It seems that Harrier pilots call it, simply, "The Bitch.")

F-4 (F4H) Phantom II

In December of 1960 VF-191 was temporarily operating out of NAS Miramar for carrier landing buildup operations aboard the USS *Bonhomme Richard* (CVA-31). Miramar was the home field for VF-121, the F3H Demon RAG (replacement air group) squadron, which was being reequipped with F4H-1 Phantom IIs. It was there that I had my first look at this new airplane about which I had heard so much. Three things impressed me right off: it was noisy as hell; it went like the very dickens; and it was as ugly as sin. There are some pilots, most of them F-4 drivers, who extol beauty as one of the virtues of this remarkable airplane. In the eyes of the beholder? The F-4 has enough outstanding attributes that a lack of beauty is by no means disqualifying.

My first thought was that the Phantom II was a brute-force solution to a number of aerodynamic problems. It wears design compromises like egg on its face. The nose droops as if it had been mildly smashed down in a boxing ring. The wing outer panels point skyward in exaggerated dihedral. The two slabs of the stabilator flying tail sag in anhedral as if attached by an inefficient model airplane builder. There are good and sufficient reasons for each feature, but beauty is not among them.

This is how René Francillon refers to the F-4:

"Few aircraft of Western design have come close to the superlative McDonnell Phantom II in terms of quantity produced (the 5,000th F-4 was delivered on 24 May, 1978), and in the late-seventies the veteran McDonnell aircraft was still the most numerous and powerful fighter in the non-communist world. Furthermore, even though it will be progressively supplanted by newer aircraft, the F-4 will remain in service with some air forces until the early-nineties. Quite a remarkable achievement by a combat aircraft for which the design was started in 1953.[33]

Conceptually, the F4H started with design studies in 1953 for a twin-engine replacement for the Demon, which suffered from persistent power plant problems throughout its service life, specifically the lack of the right power plant. The project came to life with a Navy letter of intent in October of 1954 for a long-range twin-engine attack aircraft. Two YAH-1s were ordered. In May of 1955 the Navy changed its mind once more, and the airplanes were completed as all-weather fighters. The airplanes were to be powered by General Electric J79 engines. Armament was to be four Sparrow air-to-air missiles, making the F-4 the first U.S. Navy, as well as first U.S., all-missile fighter.

I have seen photographs of an early mock-up of the design in which the family resemblance to a twin-engine F3H Demon is striking. Extensive wind-tunnel testing revealed stability and control problems with this Mach 2-plus airplane that dictated many changes, some of which are implicit in the visual recognition characteristics referred to above.

When I observed my first F4H takeoff at Miramar that December day in 1960, fleet deliveries had already commenced. F4Hs were concurrently well into the Navy's extensive service acceptance and development trials at the Naval Air Test Center (NATC), Patuxent River, Maryland, the Naval Ordnance Test Station (NOTS), China Lake, California,[34] and the Naval Missile Center (NMC), Point Mugu, California. The Phantom II had been selected in the all-weather fighter competition over Vought Aircraft's F8U-3 Crusader II. Even in those days, hard-over Crusader enthusiasts were reluctantly acknowledging the potential of the F-4's versatile design over that of the single-mission F8U-3.

René Francillon refers to twenty-three separate F-4 configurations covering virtually every tactical airplane mission known to man, excepting obvious oxymorons like long-range patrol, antisubmarine warfare, and transport. Ten different nations are cited as operators of the aircraft, not including the three U.S. services, Navy, Air Force, and Marines.

With only two exceptions, all Phantom IIs were powered by General Electric J79 engines ranging from the J79-GE-2and 2A in the F4H-1F (F-4A) to the J79-GE-17 in the Air Force F-4E and -10 in the Navy F-4J. The early engines produced 16,100 pounds of thrust per engine in afterburner. That is the figure I recall in the Patuxent test airplanes in the early 1960s, later engines delivered 18,000 pounds and more. The exceptions to the GE engines are the power plants in the two British airplanes, the Royal Navy F-4K and the Royal Air Force F-4M, both powered by afterburning Rolls-Royce RB.186 Spey turbofan engines. The F-4K 201 engine produced 20,515 pounds of thrust "with reheat," in British terminology. The F-4M used Spey 202 turbofans with the same thrust rating. I was recently informed by a longtime McDonnell engineer

This F4H-1F (F-4A) was flown by Commander Larry Flint, USN, to an altitude record of 98,560 feet on 6 December 1959. (USNI Photo Library)

that the F-4K was the fastest of the Phantom IIs. With the most powerful engines of all the Phantom IIs, it is believable.

That must have been fast indeed. On 22 November 1961, Lieutenant Colonel R. B. Robinson set an absolute speed record of 1,606.3 mph by flying an F4H-1F two runs over a defined 15/25-kilometer course. A reasonable assumption is that the runs were made close to the tropopause—approximately thirty-seven thousand feet—where turbojet engines are most efficient; that equates to Mach 2.4. Francillon identifies sixteen world, national, and unofficial records set by F-4s in 1959, 1960, and 1961.

In 1962 and 1963 it was my job to categorize and compile the various Test Division reports that were to constitute the official report of the Navy Board of Inspection and Survey service acceptance trials of the F4H.[35] The contractor's performance demonstrations were formally observed by the Flight Test Division as part of the stability and control and performance trials, a Flight Test responsibility. The Flight Test report was clear and succinct: there were five contract performance guarantees in categories covering parameters like speed, range, endurance, and rate of climb, and the F4H had failed to meet each and every one of them. Obviously, what we have here is an unsatisfactory airplane, right? Of course not; not with that record-setting performance. (This is my favorite example of why "contract guarantees" and other specifications should be considered in proper context, if not taken with the proverbial grain of salt. A specification is, after all, a combination of a best guess and a wishful-thinking description of something that has not yet been built.)

Standard U.S. Navy airplanes were primarily F-4B and F-4J aircraft. Although other designators were used for the products of the various modification and rework programs, Navy airplanes were all based on one or the other of those two. The principal Air Force airplanes were F-4Cs, F-4Ds, and F-4Es. The F-4Cs were essentially F-4Bs with some Air Force–peculiar changes (some of these were improvement changes that the Navy chose not to incorporate because of cost). Air Force airplanes were also distinguished by the addition of a set of flight controls in the rear cockpit. The F-4Ds emphasized the air-to-ground role, while the F-4Es were primarily interceptors with the GE 20-millimeter "Gatling gun" installed on the bottom of a smaller-diameter nose section. Thus the Air Force expressed its dissatisfaction with the idea of a missiles-only fighter.

All the fighter versions of the airplane except the F-4E housed a 32-inch radar antenna within a large radome for the guidance of the semiactive AIM-7 Sparrow III air-to-air missiles. The various models of Westinghouse radars also provided search, acquisition, and track capabilities for Sidewinder infrared missiles. In the F-4E with its smaller nose, the radar additionally furnished fire-control data for air-to-air gunnery. Only the Navy F-4Js and the British F-4s had a radar look-down capability with the Westinghouse AWG-10 pulse-doppler radar weapon system and the AWG-11 and -12, the latter two tailored especially to meet U.K. requirements. A radar look-down capability can be considered critically important for effective control of the temperamental Sparrow III and only slightly less so for aerial combat using Sidewinder missiles. The AWG-10 was the first airborne doppler fighter radar to see extensive operational service. With over ten thousand parts in the early days of discrete-component, solid-state electronic devices, it was difficult to maintain (reminder: reliability is inversely proportional to the number of parts).

In Vietnam the Navy emphasized Sidewinder for fighter-to-fighter combat, while the Air Force relied more on Sparrow and, with the F-4E, the high-rate-of-fire 20-millimeter cannon.

The same McDonnell engineer who informed me that the fastest F-4s were Royal Navy F-4Ks talks of observing preparations for flight over Vietnam by a leading Air Force ace. What impressed the McDonnell rep was the thoroughness and overall care exercised by the air-and ground crews with the Sparrow missiles. This pilot's AIM-7 missiles were effective in combat; many AIM-7s were not. In roughly the same time frame Lieutenant (jg) Randy Cunningham, USN, was being effective with Sidewinder—five confirmed kills' worth of effective. Both missiles could work and work well. But it was not always so, and it was not easy getting there.

In the mid-1960s the fighter communities of both the Navy and the Air Force expressed apprehension about the effectiveness of gunless fighters, armed only with existing AIM-7 Sparrow and AIM-9 Sidewinder missiles. The Tactical Air Command and the U.S. Navy Operational Test & Evaluation Force (OpTEvFor) embarked on a joint venture to evaluate the effectiveness of these missiles against fighter-type maneuvering targets. We knew that Sidewinder could be effective because of early successes of Nationalist Chinese fighters operating out of Taiwan against Mainland Chinese MiG-15s. The first results were two kills for two missiles fired! Then there were a couple of hiccups: zero for two (in that engagement, both intended targets executed hard turns while the missiles were in the air). Sparrow, designed and tested for long-range[36] intercept of nonmaneuvering targets, was a complete unknown against maneuvering targets.

The timing for such an investigation could hardly have been better. VX-4 at NMC Point Mugu, California, OpTEvFor's fighter development squadron, was well along in the mandatory service suitability evaluations of AIM-7E Sparrow III and Sidewinders AIM-9C and AIM-9D.

With the exception of the anomalous AIM-9C,[37] the Sidewinder family of air-to-air missiles are infrared heat seekers. Wonderfully simple in concept, the original Sidewinder[38] was an on-the-cheap development conceived and executed by energetic, arguably brilliant Navy civilian scientists and engineers at NOTS China Lake. The standard inventory Sidewinder in the early 1960s was AIM-9D, one step removed from the missiles used by the Twiwan Chinese. AIM9-D was a significant developmental change, with a bigger rocket motor and an improved infrared sensor. The new sensor was much more sensitive and had a narrower beam. (Infrared is closer to visible light in the electromagnetic spectrum than radio frequencies. "Narrow" in infrared terms is a very small angle compared with radar beam widths.)

The bigger motor of AIM-9D promised advantages in both range and maneuverability, while the new sensor provided a greater ability to detect targets at longer ranges and over a broader range of target aspects. As heat seekers, Sidewinders were essentially rear-hemisphere, tail-chase weapons; they were most effective looking at airplane tail pipes, especially afterburning tail pipes. Any increase in missile capability in off-angle detection and tracking to include a target's entire rear hemisphere, perhaps even part of the forward hemisphere, would have been a welcome improvement. (The all-aspect capability of current Sidewinders was still in the future.) Increased sensitivity helped.

As always, there was a price to be paid for performance enhancement. The new sensor had to be pointed very precisely in order to acquire its target. The narrower the beam width, the more difficult the process becomes; a skinny, invisible "pencil" beam waving in space can be difficult to control. It resulted in plenty of false alarms. Sidewinders tell the aircrew that they "see" a target by emitting a growling sound through the pilot's—and in the two-seaters, the Radar Intercept Officer's—earphones; a sensitive infrared sensor can emit as convincing a growl from a hot-spot reflection of the sun on a cloud as from an airplane target.[39]

The enhanced sensitivity of AIM-9D was made possible in part by nitrogen cooling of the sensor in the missile's head, and that cooling system had to be put somewhere. In Navy aircraft it was located in the airplanes, a solution that required suitable plumbing and connections at each Sidewinder missile station. Having acquired Sidewinder later than the Navy—(it was, after all, a Navy missile)—the Air Force chose to have the cooling self-contained in each missile, thus avoiding expensive and time-consuming airplane modification. But that had a price too. For a long time Air Force missiles did not have the larger motor; also, when armed in flight and not fired, such missiles had to be reworked on the ground prior to the next flight.[40]

Since the bulk of inventory missiles were Sidewinder AIM-9Bs, that missile was the first to be tested in the joint evaluation. The OpTEvFor name for the project was OV-69 (Operational Evaluation Project 69). Coincidentally, sixty-nine missiles were fired by Navy and Air Force pilots at various targets, mostly live drones, including full-size targets such as drone F9F-6 Cougars, at different test sites.

The initial results were not encouraging. They warranted a meeting in the Pentagon, which I attended. The primary audience was two admirals, one of whom, a highly regarded combat veteran of World War II in the Pacific, was head of DCNO (Deputy Chief of Naval Operations) for Air's military requirements section for naval aircraft and weapons. The purpose of the meeting, which we had called, was to deliver bad news: under some conditions, a target maneuver of as little as 2 g's could defeat Sidewinder AIM-9B. The presenters of the news, were Lieutenant Commander Dick Seymour and Lieutenant John Disher, chief projects officer and project pilot, respectively, from VX-4.[41] Also in the audience were Captain Swede Vejtasa, Commander George Watkins, and Commander Randy Prothro. Swede showed obvious concern, George Watkins was dismayed, Randy Prothro was near apoplexy—we had just told these two senior officers that the only inventory missile currently available for their new all-missile fighter was ineffective in fighter-to-fighter, dogfight combat! Displaying commendable calm, the two admirals thanked us and departed. I like to think they were displaying the quality of unflappability that admirals are supposed to have. Within a couple of weeks, other tests confirmed that AIM-9D was a hellaceously capable dogfight missile. Whew! We dodged that bullet. OV-69 was dedicated to missile capability, not total weapon system performance. Accordingly, we figured out ahead of time, through computer analysis and accessing previous studies, what the missiles should be able to do. Then the most demanding of probable combat situations were reduced to closely controlled live firing missile tests against maneuvering drone targets. AIM-7E Sparrow, the newest of that missile family at the time, also proved to be a capable weapon in the maneuvering-target environment.

The real world was different. Knowing that a capability exists is not the same as recognizing when a favorable firing position has been been reached or, even more difficult, knowing how to reach a favorable launch position when one is out of envelope. Initially, missile fire control solutions were simplistic, based on long-range, nonmaneuvering target geometry. They were not helpful in short-range, maneuvering situations. In the case of Sparrow weapon solutions, they were in fact frequently incorrect in a maneuvering environment. That and reliability problems caused a lot of missiles to miss their targets.

I recall a message from the Commander, Seventh Fleet, following an incident with the Communist Chinese south of Hainan Island, on the eve of our participation in the Vietnam War. The message was sent after Navy airplanes had, in one description, "blackened the sky with missiles" with no productive results: "Even the best missiles will not achieve kills when fired outside of [the effective] envelope." Twenty-some years later, things are different. Missiles are better and more reliable. Sensors like radar and infrared are better, and both fire control solutions and their presentation to aircrews are more accurate and more useful. In fact, the weapon systems as a whole have become almost as reliable and effective as they are portrayed in Tom Clancy's books!

The period of the Vietnam War, however, was not without its frustrations. Not all of them were related to equipment and hardware; our political leaders contributed mightily. "Rules of Engagement" became a particularly touchy subject. It sometimes seemed as if they had been devised by the enemy specifically to render our forces ineffective. Pilot reaction may be exemplified by the following:

Lieutenant Commander Kyle Woodbury was chief project pilot in VX-4. He was in indignant conversation with Lieutenant Commander Peter Marshall, the Royal Navy exchange pilot. It wasn't a conversation so much as a bitch session concerning the latest Washington "whiz-kid" idiocy that had been visited on our pilots. A mission over Vietnam had been compromised by unrealistic tactical restrictions, and one of our airplanes was shot down.

A squadron lieutenant passing by overheard a reference to Rules of Engagement. Like a good junior officer, he was eager to learn from his superiors. He asked what they were talking about. Kyle and Peter exchanged glances.

"It goes like this," Kyle began. "When you see a nun riding down the middle of the road on her bicycle, you don't strafe her." He paused for effect. "Not unless she commits a hostile act. Now, if she turns into you on that bicycle, that's a hostile act. Then you strafe her!"

He turned toward Peter. "Isn't that right, *Lefft*enant Commander?"

Her Majesty's representative replied, "Bullshit! War is hell. Strafe her anyway."

As our involvement in Vietnam became more imminent, ComOpTEvFor rightly concluded that fleet squadrons needed more tactical air-to-ground weapon information than was available to fleet squadrons. VX-5, OpTEvFor's attack development squadron, needed an F-4 with which to devise tactics and generate bombing/weapon delivery tables for a complete spectrum of air-to-ground weapons. As OpTEvFor's Air Warfare Division representative, I flew from OpTEvFor headquarters in Norfolk to visit the CNO Aircraft Assignment Officer in the Pentagon.

My request for an airplane was greeted with, "You'll turn that perfectly good fighter into a bomber over my dead body!" Having some identification with the fighter community of pilots, I could feel a level of empathy, but not enough to compensate for the failure to accomplish my objective. However, my Pentagon colleague and I were to be overtaken by events. A lot of bombs were dropped from F-4s on North and South Vietnam. VX-5 ultimately got its airplane, but not that day.

The F-4s I flew, starting in the fall of 1961, were two of the forty-seven F4H-1Fs. The *F* designation indicated special power plants; not so special, they were equipped with an early version of the J79 engine because of unavailability of the J79-8s that went into the rest of the F4H-1s. The -1Fs were also characterized by a skinny nose that housed the APQ-50 radar in lieu of the Westinghouse APQ-72, with its larger antenna, in later aircraft. Both of the airplanes I flew belonged to Service Test.

It wasn't easy to get in my few flights. The Service Test F-4 flight schedule was more wish-list than serious plan. The early J79 engines were plagued with problems. It seemed as if operating time between failures was measured in minutes rather than hours. Time between en-

A Service Test F-4B (F4H-1) returns to base, NAS Patuxent River, visible over the top of the fuselag. When the picture was taken in 1968, the long runway was among the longest in the world at 11,800 feet. (USNI Photo Library)

gine overhaul or major maintenance action wasn't much better. The airplanes spent a lot of time in the hangar.

The airplane indoctrination and checkout procedures as practiced were somewhat more extensive for the F4H than for some other airplanes I have flown, but they were hardly rigorous. They chose to send me out solo on my first flight rather than risk the life and limb of a Radar Intercept Officer in the back seat. Commander David M. Longton chased me in an FJ-4.[42] (If they wouldn't risk a RIO Officer, you can bet no pilot wanted to sit in that back seat without flight controls!)

On the second and subsequent flights it was back to the flight test business. I had an RIO this time, a skinny Marine warrant officer, Gunner Meyer. As he worked his wonders with the sophisticated radar, I watched mostly mysterious symbols dance across my repeater display in the front cockpit; I never became proficient in the use of that radar, but it was a virtual order of magnitude better than either the simplistic APG-30 in the F8U-1 or the Navy-developed APS-67 in the F8U-2. The big advantage for me in having the gunner along, however, was his help in locating knobs and switches that I might have had difficulty finding.

I was not so fortunate on my third flight. It was not a radar flight, so I was again alone. Because of some discrepancy I got off late; when I came back to land, it was dark. I dutifully threw the switches for the airplane's internal and exterior lighting. The exterior lights included an add-on, a newly installed red rotating beacon with its own independent switch. The tower gave me a bad time about not seeing my lights. The controller finally conceded that he could see what he presumed to be the rotating beacon, but no other lights. I took two wave-offs before he decided that he could see me well enough to let me land. Back in the chocks I found my problem. In the air I had been all over that cockpit, throwing every switch in sight that had anything to do with lights. The key expression is *in sight*. There was an external lights master switch located on the outboard side of the left engine's throttle. If you didn't know it was there, you would never find it; you certainly couldn't see it. Gunner, where were you when I needed you?

On my fifth Phantom II flight I flew for the first and only time in a full pressure suit.[43] As part of Crusader training all pilots had been given a thorough indoctrination in the full pressure suit, including a simulated flight in a low-pressure chamber to greater than eighty thousand feet. Each of us was issued a full pressure suit that was maintained in the aviation physiology lab of the duty station to which he was assigned. I don't know that any Crusader squadron actually used the full pressure suits in service; certainly no F8U-1 squadron did. There was little need, since that airplane could barely fly at fifty thousand feet in basic engine. (Actually, it flew all right, but maneuverability was severely limited. Performance in afterburner was quite sparkling up to sixty thousand feet, but flying that high was rare and of short duration.)

The whole idea of the full pressure suit was to protect against a sudden loss of cockpit pressurization at extreme altitudes. Most of the time the cockpit environment was such that oxygen was barely required. For instance, an F8U-1 cockpit was pressurized to sixteen thousand feet at an altitude of forty thousand feet. Pressurization diminished with higher altitudes. Sudden and catastrophic loss of pressurization was indeed possible, however, and the consequences were not pleasant. A shattered or separated cockpit canopy would do it, as would a simple flameout at altitude. The physiological results could vary from breathing difficulty, even with 100 percent liquid oxygen, to symptoms of the "bends" as bubbles of nitrogen precipitated out of the blood, perhaps to lodge in joints or, worse, in some critical part of the cardiovascular system—like the heart.

Then there was a really scary possibility. At ambient altitudes above seventy thousand feet, human blood boils. One bubble to the heart or the brain, and that's all she wrote! And there is no such thing as a one-bubble boil. To drive that point home, in the graduation exercise for pressure suit training—the one where they put you in a tiny chamber and evacuated it to simulate eighty thousand feet or higher—it was common to place an uncovered beaker of water in there with you. The liquid contained a red dye that made a convincing simulation of human blood. I guarantee it got a pilot's attention when that stuff began to boil, and it boiled furiously. It was a brave man indeed who didn't at that moment manifest serious concern for the integrity of his pressure suit, the only thing keeping his very own real blood in a docile state. Never mind that the technicians were adamant in their assertion that a hole in the suit the size of a silver dollar mattered not a wit, that the incoming airflow would more than compensate for what was lost through the hole. It didn't help that the chamber itself bore an uncanny resemblance to the gas chamber used by the State of California for executions.

The graduation "ride" in the chamber was the first time I ever put on the suit, and I hadn't worn one since—until now, for my fifth flight in an F4H-1F. Again, it was a nonradar flight, so I was alone. The flight itself was undemanding, featuring just one zoom climb to about seventy-seven thousand feet. No big deal, really; that was well under the record, set by an F4H, in excess of one-hundred thousand feet.

The most difficult part was mastering the technique so that I could attain even as much as seventy-seven thousand feet. In concept it was not difficult, although optimizing the process took more practice than I was able to devote to the task as well as a knowledge of the right numbers to hit. I had been briefed on the numbers. The idea was to attain a particular supersonic speed, then pull up into a pitch attitude, or a series of predetermined pitch angles correlated to Mach/airspeed, so as to produce the ballistic trajectory calculated to produce the highest altitude.

Ballistic trajectory is the proper expression. Sometime after passing through sixty thousand feet the machine quit flying like a conventional airplane. A little higher, and aerodynamic flight controls became completely ineffective. The airplane behaved like a bullet. Best let it do its thing until the parabolic trajectory led it down, back into denser air where things became normal again. Letting it do its thing included the engines. Don't mess with those throttles!

Passing through a still higher, even less dense altitude, every warning light in the cockpit came on. The annunciator panel lit up like a Christmas tree. The engines' tail pipe temperatures got so low it was problematical that they were still operating, that the fires were still lit. Concurrently, the cockpit pressurization bled off to nothing. My pressure suit inflated like a balloon. I felt like a cross between that rotund, layered figure in the Michelin tire advertisements and a toddler stuffed into immobility in a snowsuit.

The TACAN (tactical air navigation) indicator needle began to circle aimlessly. That was my guidance home! Dismay born of my Crusader training took over. My backup navigation system usually resided in that other airplane on my wing. But I had no wingman; all I had left was my VHF radio. I looked down as the nose finally pointed earthward.

Earthward? All I could see was a solid undercast; the earth was invisible beneath the clouds. I knew I was somewhere within twenty-five miles south of Patuxent, over the Chesapeake Bay in the supersonic restricted area, but nothing more specific. I could call Patuxent Approach Control for vectors, but if my radio quit too, I might be in trouble. In a Crusader, once that TACAN quit it was gone for the day; likewise the radio. Both were located in an avionics package some feet behind the cockpit, underneath an access panel secured by umpteen patent fasteners. The popped circuit breakers that could restore life to failed systems were as inaccessible as the moon.

As these thoughts flashed through my mind, things began to return to normal. The engines again operated quite normally. Flashing lights ceased to flash. The illuminated annunciator panel quietly went back to sleep. As cockpit pressurization returned, my pressure suit deflated. I could move again. The TACAN seemed to shrug its shoulders as it went back to work, pointing faithfully toward Patuxent as it clicked off the intervening mileage. I proceeded back to base and landed without incident.

Come to think of it, everything I had observed had been carefully explained to me and anticipated in the preflight briefing. That is what happens when the air is so thin that airborne flying machines don't fly and air-breathing engines have little to breathe. O me of little faith.

The airplane I flew on the pressure suit flight was F4H-1F, Bureau Number 145315. It was one of forty-seven small-nose F4Hs that were decreed to be unsuitable for deployment as regular fleet airplanes. That condemned it and others of its ilk to semipermanent status in the test and development community.[44] This airplane earned its keep. It spent most of its life carrying two different kinds of engines. On one side, the right side as I recall, it carried a J79-2 or -2A. On the other side it carried the current engine under evaluation, eventually the J79-8 that powered most of the F4H-1s (F-4Bs).

Many Service Test F4H flights were dedicated to exercising the engine under investigation in specific operating conditions, looking at variables like power settings, airspeeds, altitudes, and dynamically induced changes in state. That last included changing power settings from idle to full afterburner and back. Lieutenant Commander D. Z. Skalla was the project officer for several projects on 145315 when I flew it. Having come back with an incomplete test card on a prior flight—I ran low on fuel and out of time before I hit all of the points—I found myself on a subsequent flight with time to spare. Out of loyalty to D. Z.—after all, it was his airplane I was flying—I decided to make up for my earlier omission. I fumbled through my knee pad, thick with "idiot cards" (checklists) for various airplanes, looking for the earlier test card. I couldn't find it. No problem; I was sure I remembered the most critical test point.

That previous test card had been devoted to jam accelerations and throttle chops, even including a couple of dramatic engine shutdowns. A point of particular interest—one of the ones I had failed to hit—was a chop from full afterburner to idle at a Mach number in excess of 1.3. I guess the idea was that an engine that could survive that trauma could survive anything.

I hit the test point this time all right. But out of carelessness or confusion, I somehow managed to get the throttle around the horn and shut the engine down completely—from full afterburner to shutdown, doing in excess of Mach 1.3, yet. If the planned point was a severe test, this one was a monster. Starting at forty thousand feet, I used up about fifteen thousand feet getting the engine restarted. Happily, the engine did just fine. D. Z. thought it was funny. I don't think he would have been as amused if I had blown the engine. In the final report there was a point scatter diagram. Out there all by itself, far to the right, was the The Point. I was glad it didn't have my name attached.

The Phantom II was an impressive flying machine that substantially outperformed the Crusader. The F8U-1s and -2s were Mach 1.5 to Mach 1.7 airplanes; the fastest Crusader[45] was the F8U-2N (F-8D), at Mach 1.9. The F4Hs, even the thin-nose F4H-1Fs with their 16,100-pound thrust engines, were honest Mach 2.4 to Mach 2.5 airplanes, (although they later were flight restricted at the high-q and high-Mach-number ends of the spectrum for stability and control and structural reasons).

An afterburner takeoff in a Crusader was exciting, from the bang of afterburner ignition to the definite impact of suddenly applied acceleration. That was partly because the J57 engine afterburner was ignited at full burner. It could be modulated down from there. The J79 engines in the Phantom II ignited at the low end of the afterburner range. Thus, the airplane lacked that initial whack of the Crusader. Instead, it manifested a growing, surging, irresistibly increasing thrust as one went through what felt like four different stages of power. The airplane really moved out! Whereas the Crusader takeoff could seem like a ride with the wild one, with the airplane barely under control, the Phantom II felt solid as a rock all the way.

At high-q the airplane was easily controllable and maneuverable, but it felt stiffer, less agile than the Crusader. It got to altitude incredibly quickly in burner, climbing at an impressively high pitch angle. Subsonic performance at altitude was somewhat disappointing. It wasn't the numbers it achieved that was the problem; it was the way it felt and the way it flew. The airplane was designed as an interceptor, not a dogfight fighter, and it showed. With aerodynamically thin wings, before the installation of leading-edge wing flaps and the upside-down, slotted stabilator, it didn't turn for beans. Even a modest wing dip produced strange noises—shades of its Banshee ancestor—and detectable incipient buffet. If it had been a Crusader talking to its pilot, the message would have been clear: "Watch that, Mister. Keep it up, and I'll do something unpleasant to you."

But it wasn't a Crusader. The airplane could be flown deep into buffet without turning on its master. It took time, but the appearance in the Phantom II community of people like Sam Flynn demonstrated what an effective maneuvering fighter it could be, in the right hands. Aerodynamic changes like the leading-edge flaps and the slotted stabilator didn't hurt. The F-4 is in many ways a brute-force solution to aerodynamic and performance problems. It sometimes requires brute-force handling by its pilots it to make it achieve its optimum performance level.

The Phantom II is a marvelous airplane. It will be a long time, if ever, before anything like the F-4s service record is again attained. Given the trend of escalating costs of airplanes and lower production rates, a good guess is never. And the story is not over yet. F-4s have a lot of miles and a lot of flight hours left in them. The survivors are rapidly phasing out of U.S. service, but they continue to fly in other parts of the world. Some of them are brand-new. As I write, Mitsubishi Heavy Industries in Nagoya, Japan, has not yet completed its licensed production run of F-4EJs.

I am reminded of the rallying cry of diehard Skyhawk pilots: "A-4s forever!" I don't know about forever, but the Phantom II is certainly going to make it into the twenty-first century.

Chapter 11
The Little Guys

FOR YEARS I WAS OF THE "My airplane is the greatest; yours is [expletive deleted] garbage!" school of airplane evaluation. Perhaps not quite that bad, but having been spoiled for about twenty-three years by the best that the American taxpayer and the U.S. Navy could provide in the way of airplanes, I was slow to appreciate what general aviation has to offer. My attitude was that if I could no longer fly a supersonic airplane, fully fueled and maintained by somebody else, then to hell with it. Low-speed aerodynamics, here I come! That translates to "Buy a sailboat," which I did, twice. I enjoyed them both, but the time came when I ran out of crew. I was varnishing more and sailing less. With uncertainty and low expectations, I approached the small end of the general aviation spectrum, the "Little Guys." That was fifteen years ago, after a nearly nine-year hiatus from piloting anything faster than a thirty-five-foot cruising sailboat.

A generally held perception in the airplane industry when World War II ended was that the family airplane would become so common as to complement, if not partially replace, the family automobile. The idea was that those thousands of military pilots and aircrewmen, once returned to civilian life, would be so aware of what airplanes could do and would be so attracted by their attributes that the small airplane segment of general aviation would grow enormously. Even wartime nonaviation personnel had been exposed to so much information and misinformation about the contribution of airpower to victory that they must be impressed and curious. The "I can do that!" (fly, that is) syndrome just had to be vibrating out there in the potential customer hinterlands.

There were those in the industry who envisioned an airborne Everyman's transportation phenomenon like the Model T Ford. The notion may have been born of a combination of wishful thinking and desperation. The big guys in the business had been cranking out airplanes by the thousands for four years or more; then the military market disappeared almost overnight. What were they going to do next? The "big iron" folks, the bomber builders, embarked on a war for dominance in the transport field—Boeing, Douglas, Consolidated (soon to be Convair, later General Dynamics), Lockheed, and the rest. The purely military builders of smaller "tactical" airplanes had a different problem. A few tried to hang in as government producers. The jet airplane had just appeared. Also, postwar nations who still felt the need for an air force were going to have to refurbish their fighter fleets if nothing else. For the rest, diversify!

Grumman, while fighting to retain its position as a supplier for the Navy, branched out in some surprising directions. Aluminum canoes? I don't know if they ever made money, but they are still out there. North American took the general aviation bait. They built the Navion and tried to sell it as Everyman's P-51 Mustang. The design ultimately was sold to Ryan. There is no evidence that anybody ever made money with it.

The anticipated explosion in the personal airplane market never occurred. The companies who came closest to realizing the opportunities were not the big guys but the trainer manufacturers. Beechcraft, which had built thousands of military versions of the smallish Model 18 transport, and Cessna, with a comparable production run of the twin-engine bomber and navigation trainer known affectionately and derisively as the "Bamboo Bomber"—lots of plywood in that one—came closest.

Beechcraft managed to miss the mark but nevertheless started production of a family of airplanes that is still going strong today. As strong, that is, as any in a badly depressed general aviation marketplace. They came out with the first V-tailed Bonanza. These many years later its descendants and derivatives are still the class act among single-engine personal airplanes. Beechcraft's late-1940s advertising picture of a family, conservative middle class, gathered smiling around their brand-new V-tailed Bonanza in front of their nice suburban house with its manicured lawn, a piece of a middle-sized American car—Buick? DeSoto?—showing in the background, never quite became reality. The concept was flawed, but economics, as always, defined a real marketplace. Beech sold a lot of those airplanes.

Most of the real newcomers, with their grand schemes of personal airplanes, fell by the wayside. A numerous and notable failure that almost survived is the Ercoupe in its various guises and ownerships. (Ercoupe was another design with many foster parents.)

Beech represented the high end of the scale. Their smaller airplanes were always bigger and more expensive than the Piper and Cessna

The ubiquitous Cessna 172. This fairly recent-vintage 160-hp Skyhawk has the classic Cessna look. The two-seat C150/152 trainers are similar in appearance except for a shorter cabin. (Author's collection)

counterparts. Rockwell (formerly North American) made a valiant run, but their various Navions, Commanders, and so on seemed too closely targeted at the Beech segment of the market. For sheer numbers and variants of airplanes the "Little Guy" field belongs to Piper and Cessna.

Sadly, today the battlefield is empty; as of this writing, no one is producing a small four-place single or a simple two-place trainer.[1] Oh, perhaps when the orders build up, there will be a small production run of something. You either have to exercise the tooling occasionally or mothball—or destroy—the whole affair. Lord knows what happens to the work force while this is going on. Almost by default, then, Pipers and Cessnas are the airplanes that most of us learn to fly in today. A contemporary version of that Bonanza—"Everyman's airplane"—can cost a quarter of a million dollars or more. The reasons are manifold and complex, certainly beyond the scope of this discussion. A good starting place for corrective action, however, is "product liability" as interpreted in our courts.

The Cessnas

In 1975, as often as not the beginning was a Cessna 150. It was for me. My checkout pilot was a regular Army captain aviator named Jim Smith.

In short order he got me through the Cessna 150, the T-41 (a C172 with a big engine and a constant-speed propeller), the Piper PA28/140, and the 180-hp Piper Arrow. Since I had not had the foresight to transfer my military credits to Federal Aviation Administration rules—(except my original Commercial Pilot ticket)—within the two-year eligibility period, I also needed an instrument ticket. Jim Smith helped me there too. Once I acquired that rating—which I considered essential if I were ever to use a small airplane for serious transportation—I flew the C150 for most of the preparation for my instructor certificate. Presently I do most of my primary, private pilot, instruction in the C150's close cousin, the C152.

These airplanes are incredibly honest, perhaps to a fault. They are so honest and forgiving that I sometimes have apprehension when a pilot is experienced only in Cessnas. There is a whole spectrum of exciting flying experiences that the Cessna pilot will never know; that is good until he first gets into an airplane that has not been so sanitized.

These Cessna airplanes are lightly constructed to the point of seeming flimsy. However, they are strong, durable machines. It is the non-essentials, like interior appointments, plastic door panels, instrument panels—even door locks and hinges—that take a beating in service. For the most part, nothing important ever gives way. A door that pops open in flight can always be reclosed. I concede that the seat track locking mechanism—the one that restricts the fore and aft position of the seat—has a less-than-perfect service history. It can be disconcerting for the pilot to find himself moving sharply away from the yoke with which he is trying to control the airplane. The one thing he better not do is try to move himself forward by pulling on that same yoke. But by now the seat track has been adequately AD'd—that is, issued an FAA Airworthiness Directive requiring an inspection or "fix"—and everyone who flies the airplanes knows to check the mechanism. If the startled pilot subjected to the indignity of a suddenly unlocked seat can bring himself to leave the yoke alone, the inherently stable airplane will obediently seek its last trim speed, presumably something greater than stall speed. It may take a while to settle down, of course. The airplane doesn't have a brain, just good longitudinal stability; the oscillations will damp out in time. In the meantime the pilot should be able to move himself back into position by grabbing something other than the tempting handle provided by the yoke.

It is too bad that a fledgling pilot cannot begin in the air, thus postponing the unpleasantness associated with maneuvering a flying machine on the ground. Airplanes are at best awkward to handle as wheeled vehicles, and the Cessnas are no exception. They do have nose gear steering through a limited arc, which can be influenced rather than actually controlled with differential braking. The bad news is that the steering operates through bungees, which become incredibly loose and sloppy in service. ("Bungee" in this sense is not the real thing, as in bungee cord. More often it is some form of spring. The expression derives from the old days in aviation, when real bungees were actually used to produce stick "feel" or force stability where it might otherwise be lacking. In a real sense every airplane designed, even today, represents some form of replication of what pilots by instinct, training and experience expect. As pointed out earlier, there is at least a little bit of Stearman, DC-3, and, yes, even S.P.A.D. in every airplane you are likely to fly or ride in.)

The Cessna nose gear strut oleo does not ameliorate this ground steering problem, especially when the oleo strut needs servicing. In the interests of providing a fail-safe, landing gear that would be economical to produce, the Cessna company selected a springy, tubular, main landing gear suspension system. It works, and it is very durable. (The expression *main landing gear* is actually both redundant and inaccurate. The two big wheels and whatever strut and load-carrying system they are attached to constitute, in fact, the "landing gear." That other, generally smaller, wheel attached to either end of the airplane is technically part of the "alighting gear.")

The Cessna nose gear makes for generally sloppy ground steering. You soon learn to establish a rudder position, see what happens, and then make a correction. Let the airplane seek what it wants to do, then help it do what you want it to do. Not a bad approach to flying in general. An oleo strut is essentially a fancy shock absorber, what our British cousins more accurately call a "damper." That is precisely what it does: under load it depresses proportionally and then damps out oscillations. A bad shock absorber on a car can be lethal in a hard turn; the rest of the time it merely contributes to a bouncy, essentially undamped ride. A bad or overinflated nose gear shock on the nose gear of an airplane, however, can contribute to oscillations of increasing amplitude—such that on, perhaps, number three you might find yourself driving the propeller onto the concrete.

The airplane variety is somewhat more sophisticated than its automotive counterpart. It has a hydraulic oil side in which, under load, fluid must pass through orifices, thus limiting how quickly the strut can depress. On removal of the load the fluid is metered back through the same orifices. So far it is the same as the automotive variety. But the true oleo strut also has an air side: it is, in fact, charged with compressed air. The combination gives the oleo strut the ability to absorb without damage higher dynamic loads than the automotive version. The air side of the strut in service is more difficult to maintain. After all, it is generally more difficult to contain a gas than a liquid. On the other hand, recharging from an available compressor is not difficult. Hydraulic leaks are less frequent, but potentially they represent more extensive maintenance action. With even a partial failure or leak there is the possibility at least of a loose, sloppy feel on the ground. So it is with the small Cessnas. There is some sensation, particularly for the novice, of the airplane trying to go in several directions at once.

One of the remarkable things about "all those Cessnas" is their ubiquity—think of the AMC jeep of World War II—and their versatility. A young West German recently flew a C172 Skyhawk from somewhere in Finland to Moscow and landed in the middle of Red Square.[2] (Even considering his somewhat skinned-out airplane with added long-range fuel tanks, I marvel at the feat: I still remember flying a fairly recent-vintage C172—with standard tanks and typically flaky fuel gauges—to the airplane's nominal four-hour endurance limit in the face of a fierce headwind such that my ground speed frequently sank to the highway speed limit.) Go where you will, anywhere in the world, and you will find Cessna airplanes. Some are trainers; many are C172s in their various guises; there are many C182s and Skywagons. The old-timers are there too, with designators ending in 0 instead of 2, suggesting that the third wheel might be on the other end of the airplane. I focus on the small end of the line on purpose. You can find the high end of the line, up to the newer, fancier Citations, on any well-equipped commercial airfield anywhere along with the Gulfstreams, Lears, Falcons, Diamonds, and Jetstars. The small airplanes are there too, but they also exist on deserts, grass fields, ranches, the veldt, the pampas, the outback—any remote area where a small airplane might be more useful than a jeep or a Land Rover. One might speculate that the Cessnas—the Pipers too—have assumed the role of earlier, pre–World War II machines like the Chichesters and Beryl Markham's "Gypsy Moth." The modern equivalents perform better and more reliably than those machines, however capable they were for their time.

I flew my first C150 in November of 1975. It was not a new airplane then. My last flying had been about eight years earlier—in a T-33. The Cessna appeared very light on the controls, responsive, stable but rather loose. After all that time it was probably I who was loose. That is not, however, an inaccurate description of the airplane's feel based on a number of subsequent hours. Up to a standard rate turn—about 3 degrees per second—you could fly with your feet on the floor. Anywhere near normal cruise speed, the airplane wanted to fly in coordinated flight. There was some incipient wander inherent in the aircraft that could be easily damped if one merely hung onto the controls. The stall characteristics were so honest that it was difficult to determine when stall actually occurred. What was true of the C150s in that sense is true of the early C152s and even more true of the later C152s with their curled, low-induced-drag wing tips. The Cessnas improved with subsequent models. Not only the feel, but the stability and overall control harmony were better in later versions.

By *stall* I refer primarily to approach-to-landing stalls.[3] That stall is the one with the greatest potential for serious mischief. The airplane does not want to stall. It complains. It wiggles. The controls get soft and ineffective. The airspeed indicator reads something less than 40 knots. All the while, the little reed-operated stall warning horn is yelling in your ears. Recovery is a really big deal: all you do is relax the back pressure on the yoke, just a little. You couldn't have got the airplane into that situation in the first place if you hadn't been pulling back like crazy. The stall recovery is so nearly instantaneous that much of the rate of descent will go away even before you think to add power.

So where is the problem? The problem is that the scary stall, even spin, situations occur when the pilot is otherwise distracted. Unbelievable as it may sound, obvious warning signs are sometimes ignored. It is possible to be in a fully developed stall where the only obvious signal, besides low airspeed, is an excessive rate of descent. If the pilot fails to recognize that he is stalled, he can get very close to the ground. Then his solution to the excessive rate of descent may be to pull back on the yoke even further—with predictable bad results.

The small Cessna airplanes are designed to be safe and forgiving, and they are. At some level, however, these very qualities may mask what is really going on; the airplanes still require the full attention of the pilot. I have some apprehension that the result is to breed a false sense of security. (Other good general aviation airplanes have been designed with the same goals—the old "Everyman's airplane" syndrome. The Ercoupe I mentioned earlier was a yoke-only airplane in its earliest incarnation—no rudder pedals. It couldn't stall, therefore it couldn't spin.[4] But what happens if you outfox the designer of an unstallable, unspinnable airplane? If the designer inhibited control authority so as to keep you out of a spin, you may not have enough control authority to recover from the spin if you somehow manage to get into one.) Cessna must own the all-time, longtime safety record for small airplanes. For that very reason, Cessna pilots transitioning to the products of other manufacturers perhaps should treat the new birds as if they represented a whole different way of life.

The other classic stalls (departure and accelerated)[5] in the C150/152 series have a more easily identifiable "break"—signifying the precise moment at which stall occurs—and are just as easily recoverable. You may want to be a little more brisk with the yoke to recover from one of these. Unless you manage to be exceptionally ingenious in your entry, the accelerated stalls tend to move in the "over-the-top" direction, which just happens to be toward the wings-level position you are probably trying to achieve on recovery. Spins are no longer part of anyone's required syllabus, but the small Cessnas don't like to spin any more than they like to stall. However, they will spin. Recovery is simple, straightforward, and quick. If you don't get the yoke all the way back and then hold pro-spin controls for at least a quarter of a turn, the airplane may not spin at all, especially to the right.

Things don't change much as you move upward in the current Cessna line. The C172s—in all their incarnations, retractable and otherwise—the military versions like the T-41, the various reengined machines with up to 230-hp engines, and the C182 family all behave very much as you might expect from a simple upscaling. The machines get roomier. The doors get bigger, but they still appear to be relatively fragile. Control forces get somewhat heavier. In particular, there is a tendency toward nose-heaviness at low airspeeds.

Among the variations included above are big engines in a C172. More powerful translates to heavier. A concomitant to the feeling of "heavier" control forces is an increase in apparent stability about all three axes. It is predictable. First, there is the increase in inertia that comes with more mass. A prime characteristic of inertia is that an object, whatever it is, wants to keep doing whatever it is doing, such as maintaining speed and altitude; that is one definition of *stability*. There may also be a modest contribution of the "pendulum" effect that exists in all high-wing monoplanes—the tendency of a mass suspended by a lifting device or surface, in this case a high wing, to seek a position such that the center of the mass is directly below the center of whatever force is trying to lift that mass. Conversely, in a low-wing monoplane if you tip the airplane far enough, like 90 degrees, it may want to keep rolling rather than to right itself. With all the aerodynamic and mass-distribution techniques involved in a modern airplane, the pendulum effect may be minimal, but it does exist.

When I get to the C182, I have exhausted my Cessna experience. It must be noted, however, that the C182 and its cousins and competitors are at the low end of the threshold for the first real four-place airplane of the "Little Guys" I have mentioned. Four seats do not a four-place airplane make. I will offer, without defense or substantiation, a theory: based on design gross weight, four FAA-size passengers/occupants— by definition 170 pounds each—the obligatory "100 pounds" of baggage,

This 1972 C182, with a 230-hp Continental engine and long-range tanks, provides serious transportation for up to four people with baggage. The avionics suite includes dual navigation/communication radios, one with ILS (instrument landing system) glide slope, ADF (automatic direction-finder) receiver, and transponder with encoding altimeter. No DME (distance-measuring equipment), but it has Loran (long-range navigation). (Author's collection)

and a full "standard" fuel load, there is no such thing as a four-place airplane with less than 230 hp.

I have not flown the more exotic Cessnas, even those lineal descendants of the machines we have been examining like the C210 Centurion. The closest I have come is the C177 Cardinal, a kind of aberration among the smaller Cessna airplanes, in many ways most un-Cessna-like. The only version I flew was a 180-hp C177R (*R* for retractable). The flying characteristics of the later Cardinals, such as the one I flew, were more traditionally aerodynamic in their responses than the earlier ones. They were sharper reacting than the Cessna airplanes we have been discussing, particularly in roll. I have been told that there was a wing change somewhere along the line—in the interests of giving the airplane a more traditional Cessna feel—sometime after the early 160-hp versions of the Cardinal, which reputedly were underpowered. The C177R was a slicker machine than most of its cousins. The lack of wing struts reduced drag, and the lower profile with its sharply raked windscreen gave it more of a sports-car than family-sedan look. Marginally faster than the C172, the Cardinal gave the impression of being a more capable airplane overall. The performance difference wasn't really that great, but it felt substantially better, especially with a constant-speed propeller. With retractable landing gear, it was a racy-looking bird indeed.

About that landing gear. I remember the first time I saw a retractable-gear Cessna "single" in flight; it reminded me of a ballad from the big-band era, "They Won't Believe Their Eyes." When the gear started to come up, I thought I was watching something vital disintegrate before my eyes. For the benefit of those who have not observed this phenomenon, imagine, if you will, the appendages of the offspring of a couple of praying mantises, each of which had some genetic defect that fit not at all well with the defect of the other. Once the gear is retracted, the airplanes—Cardinals, Centurions, retractable Skyhawks, Skylanes, and the rest—look pretty slick.

On the ground, the retractables bear a strong resemblance to their fixed-gear sisters—except that the gear looks a little naked, as if someone had inadvertently left off the strut and wheel fairings. Everything retracts into the fuselage, of course; with a relatively thin-wing high-wing monoplane, there isn't any other place to hide the wheels. This means that there is much twisting, turning, and spatial translation going on when the gear is actually in motion. For those accustomed to more conventional retractable-gear installations, the Cessna system is not a confidence builder, but it works fine in service. There may have been the occasional Airworthiness Directive—almost no airborne system or subsystem is immune to that—but to my knowledge there have been no significant problems.

My Cessna experience is limited to the modern era. I was, however, minimally exposed to a representative of a somewhat earlier time. A friend of mine, a retired naval aviator and flight surgeon, also a practicing ophthalmologist, decided that he had to have an airplane. Being recently retired from the Navy and trying to establish a civilian practice, he found that he couldn't afford a new airplane, or even a new-used one. However, he found a C170A. In the A and B versions, these machines were built from the mid- and late 1940s to about the mid-1950s.

I have seen descriptions of the Cessna line wherein the 170s were grouped with the C172s. I believe that creates a misleading impression. The 170s look a lot more like the C120s and C140s, to which they were close cousins, than like the 172s. The most obvious distinguishing feature is that the small wheel is on the other end of the airplane. The difference is more than esthetic. There is that characteristic, relatively narrow Cessna wheel track width supporting a long fuselage with the whole thing terminating in a rather large, businesslike tail wheel. That tail wheel is a lot more reminiscent of a C180 Skywagon than any of the domesticated tricycle-gear airplanes we have addressed so far.

There were other end-of-an-era attributes in the doctor's airplane: the avionics were an ecumenical mix of tubes and discrete-component solid-state devices. For those not able to remember vacuum tube avionics, they worked by exception rather than by rule. As for discrete-component avionics, late-1960s/early-1970s television sets were more reliable than the similar gear in most airplanes (and those television sets spent a lot of time in the shop). Military specification and FAA TO'd (Technical Order) radios and navigation equipment of the period were characterized more by high prices than increased reliability. "Coffee-grinder" tuning was common in this C170 airplane; the occasional click-stop channel-selection devices represented the new breed, installed well after the airplane had left the factory.

Modern era or no, this was a different kind of airplane. The C170A had no vacuum pump. The gyros were powered by an honest-to-God venturi hanging out in the breeze. No breeze, no gyros! What that means is that the gyros were dead until you attained flying speed. This is not so bad, but it also means that they didn't tell the truth until they had been up to speed for a while. Not a big deal, because nobody was about to make an actual instrument takeoff in one of those machines—no prudent person, at any rate.

I was invited to go along with Dr. John on the maiden flight in his "new" airplane. The idea was to see if we could even fly it. We pre-flighted the airplane, got it untied, and, after a couple of unproductive attempts, got it started. I had the first turn in the barrel. That is, I got to taxi out of parking—on grass, of course—and then find the narrow macadam taxiway, which I negotiated to the runway. I made the first takeoff and landing.

It wasn't that simple. I am too short to see over the nose of many airplanes, especially those that sit on their tails. I could almost, but not quite, see well enough to taxi the C170 straight ahead without S-turning. It was tough enough to get out of the parking place. The brakes were not really up to steering by differential braking. The "steerable" tail wheel was just barely steerable. I managed to achieve controllable forward motion out of the chocks, get the airplane pointed generally in the direction of the taxiway, which had to be out there somewhere, and miraculously find the pavement. I didn't do any damage, but the airplane was a horse to taxi. That desirable feeling of confident mastery over my steed eluded me. I was surviving, but nothing about this exercise justified the apparent confidence of my companion. I was theoretically aboard to help him stay out of trouble!

We got to the run-up area without conspicuous embarrassment, went through the checkoff list, and took off. The relatively modest full power available for takeoff presented no torque problem; that was just as well, because there were enough other considerations affecting directional control to keep me occupied. There was a seemingly interminable period between the application of takeoff power and attaining aerodynamic rudder control. I went through an almost orderly process of damping out my own tendency to overcontrol with rudder, then applied an approximation of appropriate back pressure on the yoke. Finally, I shook the surly bonds of Lee Field and got airborne.

Once in the air things got better. I have read descriptions of the flying qualities of the 170s that compared them favorably with the 172 Skyhawks and later 182 Skylanes. I don't disagree. I do object, however, to any implication that they are demonstrably similar. All the normal "good" attributes are there; they are honest airplanes, easily controllable with straightforward stall characteristics, easily recoverable. But similar to the Skyhawks? Not really, in my judgment. The performance may be close, but the handling qualities are not. That really is intended as a compliment to Cessna's later efforts, certainly with no derogation of this particular earlier effort. Along with other attributes, a late Skyhawk, complete with an avionics suite that a military pilot of my generation might find mind-boggling, is an instrument platform that practically flies itself. The 170 not only requires more attention, it requires more muscle. This became evident when I tried to land the aircraft.

Nothing traumatic occurred. This is not to deny that I had to pay a lot more attention to making a decent approach and landing than I had anticipated. It is comfortable for a pilot to sit there, monitoring the progress of the airplane as it flies the approach, making an occasional gentle correction until the machine finally sighs itself onto the runway. But that isn't the way it went. I had to work harder on the corrections, and the control forces were heavier than I was familiar with in current Cessnas, even though I achieved reasonable longitudinal trim before commencing the approach. ("Longitudinal" is redundant here. I doubt that any C170 ever had rudder trim, let alone aileron trim.) The flare and landing, tail wheel notwithstanding, were not difficult, although the pitch forces seemed heavier than I associate with a C172 and more comparable to a T-41 (a military C172 with a big engine) or a C182 Skylane. On the other hand, I may have been especially sensitive to the control forces and the airplane's responses because of that extra requirement for directional control: the little wheel was at the back end of the airplane.

My landings were survivable. When my friend took over his own airplane, his landings were good.

The Pipers

My experience in Piper aircraft, hours in model and variety of models, is less than my experience in Cessnas. My first ride in a Piper airplane resulted from a desire expressed by my son, then twelve years old. The occasion was a free demonstration ride out of Lee Field south of Annapolis, Maryland. The airplane was a PA28/140 Cherokee, about as standard as you could get for an FBO (fixed-base operator) who had Pipers instead of Cessnas.

It was 1972, and that machine was not new. I don't know how old it was. For years I wondered if the 140s had ever been new; those I have seen suggest that they all came out of the factory at least six years old. That can't be true, though, because they were produced from 1963 until that very year. In 1972 with some modifications, including a dorsal fin and a different rudder, the 150-hp 140s became Cruisers and Flite Liners, although most people still called them Piper 140s.

This was the first general aviation airplane I had ever really looked at. "Piper" to me had meant the Cub, which surprisingly I had managed to miss completely, and a couple of Tri-Pacers seen only at a distance. I barely knew that this metal monoplane existed. It was not a toy but a businesslike, capable machine. Among other things, it looked seriously useful. I did not at the time recognize that the presence of four seats was misleading; it wasn't a real four-passenger airplane. But dual yoke configuration was clearly the way it is supposed to be—none of your throw-over-control nonsense. The absence of brakes on the passenger side appeared to be a reasonable cost-saving option. The instrument panel was more than adequate, its gauges readable, their size not inconsistent with what I was used to. This was a one-NAV/COM configuration, which as far as I was concerned made it an instrument airplane; one communications radio and one navigation receiver were all that the squadron airplanes I flew in the Navy ever had.

In my brief stint at the yoke of my first Piper the control forces seemed heavy for such a small airplane, especially in roll. I expected some stiffness in pitch; that is one way to create the appearance of good longitudinal stability. My subsequent experience in Pipers of that vintage has diminished my surprise but not the impression. Firmly entrenched in my sailboat period, I was not inclined either to switch allegiance or to acquire another money-sink hobby. I was, however, motivated to ask the price of such a machine and was impressed that the figure was substantially less than for my sailboat, about twelve thousand dollars.

My next encounter with a Cherokee 140 was three years later. It was one of the first airplanes I checked out in after I started flying again. It appeared to have some real advantages. It was certainly cheap to rent, about ten dollars an hour "wet" (that is, including the cost of the gasoline). But it still had those misleading four seats, and if that first demonstrator 140 had seemed to have a few hours on it, this later

Army flying club airplane was downright ancient. And it manifested in one machine most of the features I like least about Pipers. (Perhaps I was getting fussy. By this time I had flown four other general aviation airplanes—including another in the Cherokee line, the Arrow, to which I shall return. I have both respect and affection for the Cherokee line, even if not all the characteristics of all the versions are always attractive.)

This flying club airplane, in late 1975, was my introduction to what I think of as the Piper "grunt start." I don't know the origin of the 140 designation. At the time I assumed that it referred to the rated horsepower of the engine, but I was wrong. Likely it was powered by a version of the same Lycoming O-320 engine that also appears in the C172 series and some less long-lived machines like the Grumman-American Cheetah. In those days, and for a long time thereafter, that engine was rated at 150 hp; today, in both Piper Warriors and late-model Skyhawks, it is rated at 160 hp. It is a marvelous engine. The whole family of derivative, horizontally opposed, carburated, air-cooled Lycoming four-bangers is impressive. They are durable, reliable, and maintainable, frequently in the face of substantial and sustained abuse. They are also easy to start—at least most of the time, and in most airplanes. This Cherokee 140 was a notable exception.

Cessna designs tend to cram everything into a tight, efficient, virtually inaccessible nose package around and behind the engine. All the important stuff is there, well organized and well ventilated. It works, but you almost have to disassemble the front end of the airplane to see what is going on. You can't really see anything unless you remove the cowling. With the right-size Phillips-head screwdriver and a large number of dzuz or camloc fasteners later you can indeed see the whole thing; reverse the procedure, and you might even get in the air the same day.

Most Pipers use a different approach. The cowlings can be opened much like the hood of an old-fashioned automobile, and from either side, yet. (As I said earlier, some Navy airplane mechanics were still referring to similar access openings as "Buick doors" well into the 1950s.) This feature existed in the early 140s and is characteristic of many of the Cherokee line to this day. Once it's open, you can see everything. Not only that, the engine compartment is intentionally kept simple. Whereas in a Cessna the battery is stuffed into such a narrow space that you can barely see it through the oil dipstick access panel, in a Piper the battery is not even in the nose package; it is under or behind the rear seat or, depending on configuration, behind a bulkhead in the fuselage. From a structural, power plant, and weight and balance viewpoint, it is an altogether great idea. Electrically, however, it is really lousy, and the older the airplane, the lousier the idea.

The problem has to do with line loss. In simplest terms, the longer a conductor—such as an electric wire—the greater the voltage drop across its length. All these small Pipers, then as now, have twelve-volt electrical systems. The biggest electrical load is characteristically that drawn by the starter when turning over the engine incident to starting. What is the source of the electricity for that load? As everybody knows, it is a smallish, aviation-rated wet-cell storage battery. It is not too different in most respects from the device that starts the large-engined family automobile, except that it costs a lot more and is probably smaller—which means less capacity.

This particular Cherokee 140—which obviously made enough of an impression for me to belabor the point—was, I think, the fifth general aviation airplane I had been introduced to. In fairly short order I had flown a C150, C172, Piper PA28/180R Arrow, and Cessna T-41. The checkout instructor in each case was the same Captain Jim Smith, USA, already identified. The starting procedure for this airplane was essentially the same as for the other small-engined airplanes, although in practice there were a couple of attention-getting differences. In some of the Piper airplanes, it is not enough simply to move the ignition key past "both" (for both magnetos) to "start"; you must also push as you turn the key. As airplanes and keys get old, this is not necessarily easy. If you don't get the key all the way over and all the way in, you don't make electrical contact. Nothing happens. Once you do manage to make electrical contact, what happens may be unpredictable. Based on my experience in other airplanes, the propeller is supposed to start to turn, perhaps briskly, or at least more or less consistently at some rate. Not so that 140. What ensued was somewhere between a spasmodic twitch and a grunt; I prefer to call it a grunt. Without any discernible cranking speed, the last thing a pilot expected was that the engine would actually start. Miraculously, most of the time it did. But we all can appreciate, "most of the time" doesn't quite do it.

Initially, I thought that I had made a wonderful discovery in this airplane. Albeit not a true four-person airplane, the 140 made a more convincing show of cross-country capability than a C150; it might provide inexpensive one-hour transportation for a day trip to Ocean City. But after a checkout ride and a couple of other flights in that machine, I decided that the last thing in the world I wanted to do was take it somewhere where I might really need a start, only to find myself one critical grunt short.

A couple of years later a fellow instructor, G. P. Morgan, purchased another vintage 140, one of those upscale versions called a Cruiser. It looked to be in better shape than my flying club heap, and it had a number of design and cosmetic improvements. However, it was another relatively old airplane with some of the same characteristics, including the grunt start. Morgan's airplane really did have, for the most part, better cranking speed than the 140 I had flown, but I distinctly recall one- and two-blade cranks on starting. A good measure of my confidence is that I never intentionally shut down the engine of any Piper 140 away from my home field. Some of us are chicken.

In the time period subtended by my exposure to these Piper 140s, I got my instrument and flight instructor ratings. For each, I did much of my preparatory flying and the check ride in a PA28/180R Arrow. (To put things in perspective, in 1977 that airplane rented for $20.50 per Hobbs hour "wet."[6] How have we gone so wrong so fast? Try to find one today for less than $60.00 an hour, even in a flying club.) The retractable-gear Arrow was a relatively plush, comfortable, capable airplane. Like most of the species it came with a bag of essentially reliable instruments. With reasonable cruise speed and range, the Arrow represents a lot of the best in general aviation. That includes the relative old-timer I flew as well as its even more capable descendants.

Even with the Arrow I would reiterate my personal adage about four-seat versus four-place airplanes. The Arrow, like its competitors, is capable of serious transportation for up to four souls. Piper has taken a constructive step in the direction of saving us from gross weight problems by putting a partial fuel "tab" in each tank. That makes it easy for the pilot to fill to about thirty-five gallons of fuel instead of the full usable total of about fifty. The fifteen-gallon difference in fuel converts to ninety additional pounds of useful load. I don't know if Piper did it first, but that healthy practice of providing easily visible partial fuel tabs is also followed by Gulfstream-American, née Grumman-American, née Aviation, in the Traveler/Tiger/Cheetah series; also Mooney and others. With all that help, why are there still over-gross-weight takeoffs in these airplanes? It's a wonder.

All of the Piper low-wing monoplane singles bear a strong family resemblance to each other. This is especially true of the Cherokee series, from the lowly 140 with its second seat row added almost as an afterthought, to the most complex 200-hp turbocharged Arrow. (I should make it clear that my use of "Cherokee" is confined to the smaller four-bangers with no more than about 200 hp. I have no experience in the bigger six-cylinder machines, although I much admire them, and in time I hope to change that lack of experience.) The Pipers also look a little more like what we have been led to expect of airplanes, more like regular airplanes than the distinctively designed Cessnas. They all are

The PA28/161 Warrior is representative of the line of four-cylinder Piper Cherokees. With only 161 hp, it is not a true four-passenger airplane. (Author's collection)

of conventional, riveted aluminum construction. The early ones all have the famous, or infamous, "Hershey Bar" wing (the wing planform has the same shape as the candy bar). They have an all-moving horizontal "stabilator" instead of a conventional stabilizer/trailing-edge elevator combination. They are roomy and comfortable inside. The ample instrument panel is well laid out. The 140s and Warriors most often used as trainers in their usual configurations have a lot of empty instrument panel space; their more sophisticated cousins use the available space for as much avionics as personal preference and bank accounts will permit.

In the early versions, Piper went for a price-saving alternative that, as an instructor, I have always deplored: only the pilot has brakes. (In the Warriors and beyond, Piper rectified this omission.) For normal personal flying, excluding extremis situations, this older brake arrangement works fine. The Piper hand brake is easily accessible to either pilot. Not only that, its design is like that of a "fly-off" emergency brake in a traditional sports car: you just grab it and pull. (It doesn't lock unless you push a thumb-operated lock. Once it is locked, a little additional pull will unlock it.) The only thing you can't do is differential braking, but with the wide landing gear and extremely effective nose gear steering, that hardly matters. That nose gear steering is permanently engaged. In the older machines, the linkage was either solid, a virtual "hernia bar," or it merely felt that way. The later versions have a fairly stiff bungee-type linkage. In either case, you can't really check it or the rudder control unless the airplane is moving. That makes it a good idea to check the steering/rudder as well as the brakes as soon as you start out of the chocks.

The seats have also undergone improvement with time. For a shorty like me and for most female pilots, the older machines make you feel like you are sitting in a hole, barely able to see over the instrument panel. That can cause problems. I know one pilot who taxied a Cherokee 180 right into an engine cowling that had been inadvertently left on the ground; the cowling had been removed for the preflight inspection. The 180 was an exception to the open-from-either-side Buick door configuration, although the cowling did have the usual Piper latches as well as numerous dzuz fasteners. (How the cowling got left there is another story.) From the cockpit this pilot couldn't even see the top of the cowling well enough to tell that there was a significant piece of the airplane missing. I used to carry a boat cushion to sit on for extra height. Some of my students use both seat and back cushions. The improved Warriors and beyond have multiple adjustments, usually in both crew seats.

About that "Hershey Bar" wing. The Cherokees have a wide, conventional oleo strut landing gear. There may be something interesting about the way the structural carry-through structure distributes the main gear landing loads to the main spar and hence to the rest of the airplane. Perhaps I make excuses for poor technique, but I have found that in a full-stall or approach-to-stall landing it is a lot easier to get a firm *thunk* at touchdown than the sigh so easily attainable in a Cessna. The airplanes' stall characteristics are benign to the point of being difficult to recognize. As with some of the Cessnas, it is possible to get into a fully stalled condition where the best recognition features are very low airspeed and a high rate of descent. That is not necessarily a good thing, especially when close to the ground. One does have to work at it to get into that precarious condition. The audible stall warning not only works well but is an effective attention getter. It is worth recognizing, however, that Mr. Piper's 140s are bigger than C152s, and stall recovery can require more altitude.

There is more to the story. In the smaller Cherokees I have flown, including fairly late-model Warriors, the control shaft attached to the control yoke is straight for most of its length. The last inch or so bends up. If, in the attempt to get full back yoke, you pull down as well as back, you may not get full control deflection. You may be pulling against that little upward bend. If you pull up as well as back until you do get full throw and hold it there, the airplane will start a rocking motion in

The PA28/161 Cadet two-seat trainer is anomalous among the airplanes in this chapter in that it is currently being produced. Essentially a two-seat Warrior, the Cadet has one less cabin window, reminiscent of the Cherokee 140s. (Author's collection)

pitch. It will keep doing that, losing altitude all the while, until you release back pressure. Now you are stalled! This works with either the "Hershey Bar" or the new wing. (The "new wing"? In 1973 Piper replaced the Cruiser/Flite Liner 140s with the Warrior and the 180D with the Archer. Each airplane ultimately incorporated a new wing featuring Frise ailerons, which greatly improved aileron response. The "new wing" tapers outboard of the flaps and has a five-foot greater overall wingspan. It does not seem to provide greatly altered stall characteristics, but I find it a lot easier to approximate a grease-on landing in these aircraft. At least some of the time.)

Unfortunately, there is an expensive Airworthiness Directive that is applicable to a large number of the Cherokee family, particularly the older ones. The inspection is of the wing spar. This AD results from the investigation of at least one fatal accident and the discovery of fatigue/stress-raising cracks in the main spars of some other airplanes. It is a one-time inspection that is causing significant financial grief to a lot of owners. After a few months it will be history, except for some thinner wallets. It goes without saying that there is no consequent reflection on the overall quality of these fine airplanes. It does, however, represent an exciting facet of private aircraft ownership![7]

The Grumman-Americans

The Grumman-American family of two- and four-seat single-engine airplanes came from the innovative design brain of Jim Bede. He fathered a variety of machines characterized by a lot of performance for their size and price tag. The original was the two-seat Yankee trainer. Initially conceived as a kit airplane, the Yankee and its four-seat cousin, the Traveler, were produced in the early 1970s by American Aviation. (This is the same Jim Bede who offered in kit form a small turbojet-powered general aviation airplane. That endeavor was a controversial but interesting failure. A few flying prototypes were built, one way or another, before the whole exercise collapsed in the midst of legal and airworthiness hassles.)

By late 1976, Grumman Aerospace had bought the line and was producing upscale versions of the Yankee and Traveler under a new dedicated company, Grumman-American. This was part of an effort by Grumman to establish an entire, diverse line of general aviation airplanes to go with the limited-production expensive-to-produce business Gulfstreams. It was an interesting try while it lasted. There were two upgraded Yankees, the sporty TR2 and the flashy little Lynx. The Traveler derivatives were the Tiger and the Cheetah. The company also got as far as the introduction of a slick, high-performance light twin before discretion, not to mention good business sense, led to a sell-off of the entire line. In keeping with the Grumman tradition of cat names for its airplanes, the twin was called the Cougar.

The new owner was a self-proclaimed "big-iron" entrepreneur named Allen Paulson. The company became Gulfstream-American. The name is the key. It is reputed that the Gulfstream series is what Mr. Paulson was really after—that and a modern production facility for a Paulson brainchild, a radical centerline twin. As part of the deal, the Gulfstream name was retained and, it is rumored, some significant Grumman Aerospace support of the endeavor was to continue. A predictable result of all of this is that the Cougar never reached significant production, and the single-engine line was permitted an early death.

There is more here than a history of corporate shenanigans. The relatively short alliance of ex–American Aviation people and Grumman Aerospace engineers and managers had significant influence on both airplane design and marketing. The relationship between the two factions was uneasy at best. On the one hand there was Grumman, a traditional manufacturer of high-performance military airplanes. That represents a very competitive business characterized by much smaller profit margins than is generally understood. However, production runs can be large. The total dollar amounts involved are enormous. On the other hand there was American Aviation, representing the equally competitive general aviation market where dollar volume is relatively small. Production runs are driven by customer acceptance, which can vary wildly and dynamically over changing time frames. This is much different from production runs that can be decided, going in, by a contract signature. The results of this short-lived liaison provided a lot of excitement for the customer, while it lasted.

A new dynamism was immediately injected into the old American Aviation line of airplanes. This in part sprang from the different design and marketing philosophies of Grumman, one of the surviving giants of the airplane business. It was also, I believe, heavily influenced by the fact that Grumman was primarily a supplier of military airplanes. The personalities and background of the two people at the top were by no means a trivial part of the equation. The president was one Corky Meyer, who had become a Grumman test pilot during World War II. Corky was chief test pilot for years before becoming a vice president of the parent company. His engineering test pilot background and long association with military aviation, especially naval aviation, reputedly had two effects: an apparent reluctance to "freeze" a design and let it stay frozen; and an inclination to apply military marketing techniques to a line of small general aviation airplanes.

His number two—I never did get his various titles sorted out—was Allan Benjamin Lemlein, a Marine major fighter pilot who had joined Grumman in the early 1950s. (Notice I did not call him an "ex-Marine"; there is no such thing.) Al Lemlein was a production-oriented engineer who was the last program manager of the ill fated F-111B at Grumman. This was the failed Navy version of the infamous TFX, one of the lasting tributes to the military procurement perspicacity of Robert Strange McNamara. Anyway, Al's background carried a somewhat stronger requirement for purely business judgments than Corky's, but Corky was the boss. That is where the fun came in.

American Aviation had produced the AA1 Yankee trainer and its somewhat fancier cousin, the AA1B TR2. I don't believe Grumman-American ever built the Yanke. I did see a couple TR2s with the Grumman logo on the tail, suggesting that there was some production run. If so, it probably took place before the manufacturing facilities were moved to the Gulfstream plant in Savannah, Georgia. The TR2 got some aerodynamic, engine, and cosmetic changes that turned it into the AA1C Lynx. These included a later version of the Lycoming O-235, rated at 115 hp and requiring 100 octane fuel, and a larger horizontal tail.

It is worthy of note that the Bede designs of these airplanes are, if nothing else, different. The structure is aluminum, bonded over honeycomb, which provides a smooth, rivetless surface. The cylindrical fuel cell doubles as a structural member. The ailerons are actuated by torque tubes driven by a linkage that included a short bicycle chain, complete with a sprocket wheel, in the fuselage. The flaps are conventionally operated, electric. In the two-seaters, the fuel gauges for the two tanks are plastic, manometer-like tubes with little red balls that look for all the world like miniature ping-pong balls. The tubes are mounted on either side of the cockpit, right where they can be hidden by the pilot's and passenger's knees, but that hardly matters because with those round fuel cells they are inaccurate as hell. Flight controls and instruments are conventional. The panels and other controls are well laid out with plenty of room for a full instrument package, as in the more sophisticated four-seaters. The four-seaters, derived from the Traveler, have more conventional fuel tanks and gauges. The basic airframes, however, are similar.

The laminated main landing gear struts are both springy and, by their load-carrying capacity, forgiving—hence the "face-saver" appellation dreamed up by some Grumman publicist. The nose gear consists of an interestingly bent piece of tubing that also has excellent load-absorption characteristics. It terminates in a nose wheel that is free to swivel about 60 degrees from straight ahead. How do you steer the airplane? Just like tail-wheel airplanes and most tricycle-gear airplanes used to be steered: by differential braking. This initially unnatural-feeling technique, once acquired, is very effective. Most pilots hate it during the learning process; then they love it.

There is another side to the springy, undamped struts on all three wheels. A bounce on the main gear only is fine, especially if you keep the yoke back, where it is supposed to be. It takes a good hit for the machine actually to bounce back into the air. Even if it does, it will come right back down. The only damage may be to the pilot's ego. You can even get away with "three-pointers." However, if after that first impact with the runway you let the yoke come forward, you can get into some excitement. The airplane will want to porpoise if you let the yoke move forward. If you attempt to stop the oscillations by corrective movements of the yoke, you are almost certainly doomed to failure. Along about oscillation number three, you are going to do bad things to the propeller. All this can happen while employing a landing technique that you can survive in most Cessnas and Pipers with nary a tremor. This is why some people call these airplanes "twitchy."

I mustn't leave out an important design feature that has nothing to do with flying qualities. These airplanes all have sliding canopies, providing excellent visibility. That makes them different from the competition, probably a little more difficult to get into and out of. The two-seaters in particular, where the entire canopy is transparent plastic,

Refueling stop, Accomack County Airport, Melfa, Virginia. The Grumman-American AA1C Lynx is representative of Jim Bede's two- and four-place singles. The four-seaters have a longer cabin with another window. The eighteen-year-old holding the tow bar behind the wing of N31NA is Captain R. B. Linnekin, Jr., USMC. In the background, Orville Wright, no relation, tops off N30NA. (Author's collection)

provide a view comparable to a fighter's bubble canopy. Couple that with having to climb in and out, rather than entrance and egress through a pedestrian door, and you have the basis for an advertising campaign that, if Corky Meyer didn't invent, he certainly endorsed. "Fly your own private fighter," the Lynx advertising said. To make the fantasy more convincing, they offered a Battle of Britain paint job, a 1930s U.S. Navy paint job, and a third one, a North African World War II desert camouflage scheme.

The aura, if not the offer of semicustom paint schemes, extended to the Cheetah and Tiger as well. These two four-seaters shared the same airframe, significantly cleaned up aerodynamically from their Traveler predecessor. They also had plusher interiors, euphemistically if inaccurately compared in the advertising campaign with that of the Gulfstream, then as now the class act of the business jets. The Cheetah was more the lineal descendant, sharing the same 150-hp Lycoming O-320 engine as the Traveler and Cessna 172. Among the obvious changes were the elimination of the Traveler dorsal fin and modifications to the

The instrument panel and cockpit layout of this 1975 150-hp American Aviation Traveler (the Grumman-American successors were Tigers and Cheetahs) are typical of the more enlightened general aviation four-place singles. Note the accessible fuel tank selector, bottom center, with integral, legible gauges. The businesslike avionics stack includes dual navigation/communication radios (with glide slope), ADF receiver, transponder with encoding altimeter, DME, and built-in intercom. (Author's collection)

engine cowling, particularly the frontal area and air intakes. Both airplanes are good performers, the 180-hp Tiger comparing favorably with then-contemporary Piper Arrows and measurably, if not significantly, faster than Piper 180s.

The commercial history of this family of airplanes and their in-service reputations amount to your basic mixed bag. It is evident that, even in the relatively halcyon 1970s, the omens were not favorable. I feel less reticent about commenting on their qualities as flying machines. I did a lot of my early instructing in two different AA1C Lynxes, about three years' worth, and I liked them. During most of the same period I had access to a brand-new straight-from-the-factory Tiger. I liked that airplane even more. It had a complete bag of digitally tuned Narco avionics that worked reliably and well. Given the inherent limitations of a small, naturally aspirated (that means no supercharger) general aviation airplane, it was wonderfully capable. In terms of redundancy and versatility, I get to the P-3A Orion[8] before I can cull from my Navy experience a machine I flew regularly that had more avionics that worked consistently.

The Grumman-American airplanes are relatively light on the controls and essentially more responsive than their Piper and Cessna cousins. Control harmonization is good. Stability about all three axes is at least satisfactory. The impression of sparkling performance is partially a product of the handling qualities, although pound for pound, horsepower for horsepower, they did outperform the competition. There is nothing spooky or surprising about them. They lack some of the extraordinary fail-safe characteristics of other airplanes. An easy comment is that they fly more like "real" airplanes. Historically, "real" airplanes include a lot of undesirable to downright nasty characteristics that don't need to be emulated in modern airplanes. However, I don't believe there is anything inherently disqualifying about airplanes that require basic aeronautical skills and some minimum concentration span. These airplanes have, at this point, a poor accident record, particularly the trainers.

From the Yankee through the TR2 to the Lynx there is not a lot of wing area. The wing stalls honestly with a recognizable break. Recovery is normal and traditional. However, there is no appreciable float. The airplane doesn't fall out of the sky, but one should pay special attention while landing. Roll-on landings are not recommended because of that springy "face-saver" gear.

Probably the worst feature is that the trainers are marginally underpowered. In order to give the machines something approximating a minimal cross-country capability, Grumman-American offered a "cruise" propeller as well as a "climb" propeller. I was shipmates with two versions of the Lynx, produced about a year apart. They both were reputed to have climb propellers verified by serial number. The first airplane, with a full fuel load and two standard FAA 170-pound occupants, had a theoretical 19 pounds left over before exceeding maximum recommended gross weight. The second one, identical even down to the old-time Navy paint scheme, had the same Lycoming engine, for some reason rated at 118 hp instead of 115 hp, but that airplane as configured had only 9 pounds to spare. Both of these airplanes had specification takeoff and climb performance, but just barely.

The second was a comparative dog on hot days from the beginning. There was little or no margin for error or carelessness. This means that there was no problem operating off ten thousand feet or better of wide runway at Baltimore-Washington International Airport. (We actually ran training flights out of that major airport for a couple of years. We were not alone. Hinson's Cessna operation is still there.) But go over to Suburban (at Laurel, Maryland), two thousand feet surrounded by trees, or Freeway, about the same amount of narrow up-and-down sidewalk-like runway, and you better be careful. In spite of the serial number, I remain unconvinced that the second Lynx did not have one of those pesky "cruise" propellers.

I remain enthusiastic about this line of airplanes. I missed flying the Yankee and the Cheetah—the Cheetah, remember, is identical to the Tiger except for the engine—but I would generalize that engine effects are predictable, particularly with respect to performance, and therefore should not provide any unpleasant surprises to a pilot. I am fond of the trainers, particularly for new, start-from-scratch students with no previous experience. It is always dangerous to generalize from small statistical samples, but I never knew, or knew of, any student who started in the little Grummans who didn't transition easily to other airplanes. On the other hand, I have known many pilots for whom the transition from other airplanes to the Grummans varied from challenging to downright exciting. This can be especially true of pre–private license pilots who started their training in other airplanes. It took me a couple of examples before I realized that some unlearning followed by some new learning is desirable, even for post-solo, cross-country phase students who started in Pipers or Cessnas.

An example of a high-time pilot who needed some extra attention in transition was a Navy lieutenant commander A-7 pilot. I figured that all we needed for an airplane checkout was a couple of passes around the pea patch. Not so. This guy was one of the new breed. He was an experienced Vietnam combat veteran with a couple of thousand hours of flight time, but only about a hundred hours of it had been in propeller aircraft and that experience had been years ago. Going from large to small can be interesting in almost any field (I remember from my childhood tales of retired ship captains getting into sometimes fatal difficulties in small sailboats). The principles may be the same, but the details can be troublesome. A swept-wing, jet-powered carrier airplane is different from a small, straight-wing reciprocator. Moreover, the disciplined, hard-learned habit patterns from the one may not be directly transferable to the other.

The carrier pilot, for instance, has completed his landing cockpit checklist by the time he reaches the 180-degree position, opposite where he intends to land. He establishes approach angle of attack and the appropriate rate of descent. He flies a roughly semicircular path to final approach, picks up the "meatball" in the "mirror" (optical glide slope, really a sophisticated, space-stabilized Fresnel lens), and drives the bird until he hits the runway/carrier deck. There is no flare and no approach-to-stall landing, that which we try to achieve in the little guys. When done right, the result is a precision landing to a spot with about a 20-foot per second descent rate at impact. The landings are firm but surprisingly gentle. (At least for runway landings; carrier landings, of course, are not gentle. It is worthy of note that, after years of design and development experience, carrier airplanes do not bounce.)

My lieutenant commander friend had initial problems with both flare and touchdown. Knowing his background, I came up with what I thought was a brilliant solution. Reenter that "fail-safe" landing gear: if it's that bloody strong, I thought, let's land the airplane carrier style! So we did. But I had forgotten something. That gear is also springy, virtually undamped. On the first try we bounced about ten feet in the air, practically out of airspeed. Apparently that was not such a brilliant idea. Coolly, calmly, two sets of hands and feet all over the cockpit, we managed to keep the machine airborne for another try. It took two periods of what our British friends call "circuits and bumps" before he relearned what he had had no use for since Primary flight training in a reciprocating-engine T-34.

Sometime in the fall of 1977, I talked to Ralph Clark of Grumman's Washington office. I had known Ralph since the early 1950s, when he was a Grumman service representative at the Naval Air Test Center, Patuxent River, Maryland. He left there as the head of the Grumman operation to go to the Washington billet. I had kept in periodic contact with him through the years. Naturally, I waxed semi-ecstatic about these little airplanes and our good relations with the factory people in Savannah. His response was something like, "Enjoy it while you can. We're losing money on every one we make!"

Even before the oil embargo, with resulting precipitate rise in fuel prices, and the growth of the "product liability" monster, the small airplane business was a real dogfight. Who knows what contributed to what? Al Lemlein, mildly complaining, suggested that Corky Meyer should stop having fun tinkering with design so that they could get on with firm production configurations. Amid rumors of friction between ex–American Aviation and Grumman personnel, Allen Paulson moved in with "Gulfstream Aviation." Corky Meyer went on to other things. Al Lemlein stayed on with the new company. Allen Paulson shut down production of the small airplanes. There were subsequent attempts to sell the line to another producer but apparently no takers. That, sadly, was that.

The Mooneys

My Mooney experience is mostly confined to one model and one airplane, a Mooney 201H, leased to the flying club where I do most of my flying. I have a little time in the slightly upgraded Mooney 205. There was nothing "slight" about the upgrade that produced the 201, however. Since the Mooney Mite in 1947, Mooneys have enjoyed the reputation of being quicker than the competition. Mooneys as we know them began in about 1955 with the four-place 150-hp retractable-gear Mooney Mk20. In 1958 the Mk 20A received the 180-hp Lycoming engine. The result was a remarkable cruise speed, about 180 mph—remarkable, that is, for a four-seat four-banger. Many familiar Mooney features were included. The vertical tail was on backwards (swept the "wrong" way). The fuselage was narrow and relatively tight for even normal-size occupants. The resulting low frontal area was one of the contributors to its speed.

There were some now happily abandoned features The "hernia bar" landing gear actuating system was later replaced by an efficient electrohydraulic system. The wooden wing was replaced by a metal one in 1960. After a production hiccup and management changes not uncommon in the business, the company resumed production in the mid-1970s. The airplanes are essentially variations on the same theme, with changes in the direction of fuselage stretching and aerodynamic cleanup in the various models. The 201 is a much-aerodynamically-cleaned-up version of the Executive, which was a stretched Chaparral, derived in turn from the Ranger.

The 200-hp 201 appeared in 1977. In addition to speed-enhancing devices like sealed control surface hinge gaps, it had a sloped windshield, flush rivets, and a new cowl. The 201 nomenclature represents a maximum "cruise" speed of 201 mph. Actually, *top speed* may be a more accurate phrase, but the top end of the current Mooney line are still arguably the fastest four-bangers around, certainly providing the most performance for the dollar. One of the performance enhancers is the ram air alternate induction feature that bypasses the air filter.

In the 201—formally designated M20J—the fuel-injected Lycoming IO-360 engine, complete with balanced crankshaft, is representative of other installations using the same engine. As in the Piper Arrow installation, it is not the easiest engine to start when cold; it is a bear to start when hot. When in doubt, treat it as if were flooded. If you don't, it soon will be flooded.

The handling qualities of these airplanes are consistent with their comparatively sparkling performance, although I found the one I flew a little stiffer in pitch than I expected. This relates to the longitudinal trim system, which involves moving the entire horizontal stabilizer up and down as opposed to a trailing-edge trim tab. Actually, that design approach was not uncommon in various mid-1930s biplanes. The Mooneys have a reputation, in my view unearned, of being so "slippery" as to be difficult either to slow down to proper approach speed or to land

Mooney 205SE. Fast, slippery, comfortable, and well equipped, this is a capable airplane. The cabin is tight for heavyweights, but with only 200 hp, more than two and a fraction heavyweights shouldn't be in the airplane anyway. The "5" means that the airplane is four miles per hour faster than the predecessor 201H. (The basic model designation for each is M20J.) (Author's collection)

precisely after having slowed down. They are not inherently high drag, to be sure. The flaps are more efficient as lift producers than drag producers. However, that shouldn't take much getting used to for a pilot who is not irreversibly locked into habit patterns associated with higher-drag machines. Stall characteristics are predictable and straightforward. There is little doubt when stall occurs. Recovery does require some action by the pilot, like releasing back pressure on the yoke long enough for the airplane to start flying again. Failing that, a wing drop may occur. I imagine that, if one let things go long enough, an honest-to-goodness spin would ensue.

In keeping with the overall upscale approach, most of these airplanes have impressive avionics suites. Certainly the ones I am familiar with do. The only real drawbacks to these altogether fast, comfortable, capable airplanes are the relatively tight cabin, however luxuriously appointed, and the limitations on load/passenger-carrying ability shared by all four-seaters with 200 hp or less.

I am sometimes surprised at the way manufacturers choose to cut costs. Like the early Cherokees, the Mooneys to this day—perhaps not all but certainly the 201 and 205—have brakes only on the pilot side. In this class of airplane one is not likely to be conducting Primary flight training, but a checkout in a relatively "hot" airplane is indeed part of the equation. It is surely possible that an instructor pilot might see the need to take over control incident to a less-than-sterling landing attempt. Having access to brakes in such a circumstance would be nice. The Cherokees at least have within reach of both crew stations the MG/Jaguar-type "fly-off" emergency hand brake; the front passenger seat in the Mooneys has nothing. Brakes may be an optional installation for the right seat, but I have never seen one.

I am reminded of the experience of a good friend of mine who, as part of his preparation for his upcoming instructor pilot flight test, devoted an entire period of practice touch-and-go landings to familiarizing himself with operations from the right seat. He was alone in the airplane. Once in the air, he released his restraining belts, put the bird on wing leveler/autopilot, and slid into the right seat. About five landings later, on roll-out as a matter of fact, he decided to stay down. Only when he saw the end of the runway—grass overrun and all—coming up did he recall that he had no available means of stopping the airplane! Fortunately, he had landed on speed at the other end of three thousand feet of runway. He was quite slow by the time he ran out of pavement. The worst damage was to his ego and to the freshly mowed grass overrun; there was minor sheet metal damage to the relatively complex Mooney landing gear fairings. It is not recommended that one taxi Mooneys where ground clearance or surface smoothness is at all in question. It is also not recommended that one fly from the right side when all alone in the airplane.

The CITABRIAs

For those whose first flying experiences were in stick-and-throttle tandem-seated airplanes, especially with tail wheels, there is something irresistible about the genre. Anyone who fits that description is almost certainly some kind of old head, probably with a high nostalgia quotient as well. Guilty as charged! It is not that the CITABRIAs are exactly replacements for Stearmans, but they represent the last general production aircraft available that have these attributes, plus being certified for at least limited acrobatics. ("Citabria" is "Airbatic" spelled backwards.)

The CITABRIAs bear a strong family resemblance to their lineal ancestor, the old Aeronca "Bathtub." They are really quite different airplanes, however, starting with the new design in about 1964. Early versions were powered by the same 90-hp Continental engines as the Cessna 150. My CITABRIA experience is confined to the 7ECA, powered by the 115-hp Lycoming O-235 described earlier in the Grumman-American Lynx. By the time I became acquainted with the line in the 1970s they were being manufactured by the Champion Division of Bellanca.

Bellanca 7ECA CITABRIA—the last production, acrobatic-certified general aviation airplane. CITABRIA and its siblings are no longer being produced. (Author's collection)

There are a number of interesting variations on the basic theme. They are all wooden-spar, fabric-over-tubular construction. The basic CITABRIA was also offered with a 150-hp Lycoming, some with fuel injection. The DECATHLON had a different wing, shorter wingspan and longer chord, specifically designed for acrobatics. Having, in my declining years, given up any notion of extended cross-country exploration, I confess that I have a yearning bordering on lust for a DECATHLON. Good sense, I think, has so far prevailed, strengthened by the realization that with no production support these airplanes are all orphans. Beefed up control cables and, significantly, ball bearings in the pulleys are reported to result in lighter control forces than in the CITABRIA. I cannot verify that from experience, unfortunately, but I can certify that CITABRIA control forces are surprisingly heavy in acrobatic maneuvers.

A somewhat longer-wing version, called the SCOUT, was available with a 180-hp engine and various other structural and aerodynamic modifications. The changes sound as if they were intended to improve STOL (short takeoff and landing) characteristics and to ruggedize the machine for more demanding service. The American West comes not so much to mind as Canada or whatever is meant by "the bush."

The basic CITABRIA is an honest, undemanding airplane—once you get used to the idea of a tail wheel, that is. It is at the same time substantially more airplane than the revered Piper Cub without the brute-force requirements of a Stearman. Among the niceties is that even shorter pilots can see over the nose well enough to taxi without all that confounded S-turning. There isn't enough power for the classic three-point takeoff. One does indeed have to get the tail up to encourage acceleration to takeoff speed. Of course, that gives one a much better view of where one is actually going during the takeoff roll. The forward visibility isn't that good. Directional control with rudder is almost immediately available, certainly by the time there is enough airflow over the empennage to permit raising the tail. That is altogether a good thing because you don't really want to try to steer a tail-wheel machine with brakes. Not with takeoff power.

The control pressures for normal flying are light. Control force harmonization is good. Visibility is excellent for a high-wing monoplane. Most of these airplanes have a transparent "greenhouse" over the crew seats, permitting good upward visibility, a necessity for even rudimentary acrobatic flight. The obvious consequences of tandem versus side-by-side seating really need to be experienced to be appreciated. How many pilots have had to fight the tendency to drop the right wing to improve visibility past a large passenger when making right-hand turns to landing? It is really neat to be able to look straight down from either side of a narrow fuselage! (Visibility out of airplanes is a subject that could easily generate more discussion than is appropriate here. The topic has a long history. In an earlier chapter I referred to a prewar naval aviator giving an indoctrination lecture to some midshipment. He chose the following as one of the most significant pieces of information he could offer: "The big thing about airplanes is that you can't see out of them nearly as well as you think you can. There is always a piece of somebody or a piece of the airplane between you and what you are trying to look at.")

The simpler versions on the low end of the CITABRIA line, like the 7ECA, have no flaps and a fixed-pitch propeller. With a fuel system essentially on/off, there isn't much of a checkoff list to worry about except for mixture and carburetor heat. The airplanes are not only light on the controls, they are themselves light. Not to worry about no flaps for losing unwanted altitude, however. The airplanes slip beautifully to either side. They do not, like some other contemporary airplanes, run out of control authority before their pilots run out of ideas. It is desirable, however, to approximate recommended approach speed to avoid having to demonstrate one's prowess at slipping away altitude. For most landings, an actual full-stall landing, tail wheel hitting first if possible, is the preferred technique. Landings are controllable, repeatable, and correctable—all nifty characteristics. Once committed to touchdown, one best get the stick all the way back against the seat pan and keep it there to ensure that the airplane's behavior remains docile. The big advantage of the full-stall landing, of course, is that the airplane is through flying. If the stick moves forward prematurely, the machine may reconsider and try to get back into the air—or do something else like trying to swap ends. Such possibilities are the traditional bogeymen of tail-wheel airplanes. Nonetheless, you would be hard-pressed to find a tail-wheel machine more tolerant of minor pilot derelictions than the CITABRIA family.

Although as a family these airplanes are a far cry from the Cubs and Aeroncas of which they are lineal descendants, there is enough family resemblance—including some operational characteristics—to validate the judicious exercise of techniques peculiar to that class of airplanes. I refer specifically to the roll-on, "wheels" landing. I appreciate the reasons for it; I just never have mastered the technique of the wheels landing in a tail-wheel airplane. Oh, I can do it all right on demand, even well enough almost to satisfy Joe Susi. Joe is a longtime full-time instructor in one of the clubs where I do lot of flying. If there is anything one can do in a small airplane, Joe can do it. He insisted that I demonstrate competence in the dreaded wheels-landing technique before declaring me "safe" in a CITABRIA. He was sanguine enough when I did it from the back seat—a prerequisite for certifying me to instruct in the aircraft—but he wasn't all that calm when I did my first "wheelie" at Suburban Airport in Laurel, Maryland, from the front seat.

Not surprising, really. When I was in the back seat, landing on that same two-thousand-foot sidewalk surrounded by trees, he could see what was going on. When I was in front and he was in the back seat, he couldn't see squat. "Squat," in this euphemistic sense, includes any part of the runway. If he could see any part of the narrow runway from the back seat, we had to be over grass, certainly not over pavement. That is the only time I have ever felt Joe on the controls, all the while trying to pretend that he wasn't.

The advantage of a wheel landing in a small tail-wheel airplane has to do with a combination of light weight and low stall/flying speed, such as 35 to 40 mph. It is not unusual for ambient surface wind to approach a significant fraction of those speeds.[9] I could almost visualize people grabbing onto various parts of a small airplane to keep it from blowing over after landing in a strong wind. I could certainly appreciate the difficulty facing a pilot in getting such an airplane on the ground and slowing it down so that somebody *could* grab onto it. The idea is to get the machine on the ground at sufficient speed to keep the controls effective, therefore assuring relative immunity from gust effects until one is slow enough to get off the runway and/or get help from co-operative colleagues on the ground. Personally, I think when you up the landing airspeed 10 knots or so you might as well do a full-stall landing and take your chances. If something bad is going to happen, it probably will happen before you are slow enough for anyone to help. The wheels landing is still taught as a good thing to do on windy, gusty days.

This family of airplanes were, before they went out of production, the last American general production airplanes to be certified for ac-robatic maneuvers. A disclaimer is now in order. Lest someone treat this as a "how to" section, there are a couple of important footnotes. First, if any other than required crew members are aboard an aircraft engaged in acrobatic flight, all occupants must be wearing properly certified and current parachutes. Second, this is not stuff to mess around with unless by properly qualified pilots with adequate and appropriate supervision.

My aerobatic experience in this breed is confined to a 115-hp 7ECA CITABRIA. Loops are probably the most straightforward and the easiest maneuvers to perform in the airplane. Control forces are relatively light throughout, and the transparent greenhouse over the cockpit makes it easy to find the horizon when you are going over the top on your back. The more extreme version of lazy eights that the military calls wingovers is easy in terms of control response and control lightness, but it is a coordination challenge. More arcane maneuvers like the cartwheel and falling leaf are not particularly difficult.

Roll maneuvers in CITABRIAs are a different story. This includes slow rolls, aileron rolls, snap rolls, Immelmanns, split-S maneuvers, Cuban eights, and the rest. Here my problem may be an incomplete memory. How heavy were those Stearman control forces? The last time I did these maneuvers in a Stearman I was twenty-three years old, and pumped up with youthful adrenaline as well. By the time I left that airplane, everything in it was easy. But I found roll maneuvers difficult to do well in the CITABRIA.

The snap roll was not unduly difficult to initiate, although it did require full control deflection energetically applied. I had trouble getting the rolls stopped in a consistently wings-level attitude. I know I did not have the same problem with the Stearman. Since the recovery part of the maneuver is more one of timing and control response than athletic strength, I conclude that it is in fact more difficult in the CITABRIA. The same comments apply for the split-S, which is after all a half snap roll on top of—at the beginning of—a half loop.

A true slow roll, especially in a relatively low-powered, high-drag airplane, is an exercise in precise application of exquisitely coordinated control positioning. The modern jet pilot has no idea how good he has it. Those "slow rolls" you see military pilots do at air shows are really aileron rolls. They have powered controls and yaw dampers. The pilot simply slaps the stick over toward the side of the cockpit. The bird goes round so fast it doesn't have a chance to deviate from a point. In the airplane we are talking about, it all happens very slowly. And that "coordination" I mentioned is really systematically applied cross-controlling. The upshot is that you must apply full aileron deflection and keep it there while you are, at the same time, continuously varying pitch and rudder controls. It ain't easy! I suspect this is a coin flipper between the two airplanes. I know the Stearman took effort. I did it better in those days, but I was stronger then. Similar problem with the Immelmann, which is a half slow roll on the top half of a loop. Part of the difficulty is to arrive at the top of the loop with enough airspeed to complete the roll!

I imagine that with a shorter wingspan, more powerful engine, preferably with a constant-speed propeller, and niceties like ball bearings in the pulleys, the story would be quite different. I have heard that it is. That sounds like a DECATHLON. One of these days I hope to fly one.

Notes

Chapter 1. N2S Stearman

1. A turn and bank indicator is really two instruments in one, a turn-rate indicator and a slip or skid indicator. The turn-rate part is a constrained gyro that precesses proportional to the rate of turn. The precession drives a needle on the face of the instrument. The other part is simply a ball enclosed in a curved tube filled with a damping liquid, usually alcohol. It indicates side forces on the airplane, the same forces you would feel if you had an appropriately sensitive posterior. If the ball is in the center, you are in "coordinated" flight, which means that the airplane is flying through the air in the direction in which it is pointed—that is, neither "slipping" nor "skidding" to one side. Under that circumstance, turn rate is in fact proportional to bank angle, hence "turn and bank indicator."

2. The mat at NAS San Diego was partially bounded by two runways as early as the 1940s, but it was used by F4U Corsairs and AD Skyraiders throughout the Korean War. Propeller-driven S2F antisubmarine aircraft and Skyraiders continued to use the mat through the late 1950s.

3. "Controversial" for good reason. In common with Old Wives' Tales and other Old Aviators' Tales, it is correct for carefully defined conditions but by no means all of the time.

4. An airplane "stalls" when the wing loses a substantial portion of its lift. That is, the airflow over the wing has become insufficient to produce the pressure differential, above and below the wing, that produced the lift in the first place. The perceived cause of a stall is low airspeed. The real cause is exceeding something called the "critical angle of attack." "Angle of attack" is the angle at which the wing "sees" the air it is flying through.

5. *V* was the first available letter in *heavy* after the hospital ships got the *H*, the ammunition ships got the *E* (for explosive), and the noncombatant ships got the *A* (for auxiliary). The *A* was shared by the CAs. These heavy cruisers also wanted the *H*.

6. The public lands of the United States were divided into "sections" of one square mile each—640 acres. In some of our flatter, less topographically

varied states—initially "territories" made up of congressionally edicted "public lands"—the section lines became the boundaries for roads, farmers' fields, railroad lines, and whatever else required easily defined and recognizable limits. Boundaries for areas smaller than sections were marked as a subgrid within the section lines. The result as seen from the air in states like Iowa is a wonderful, quiltlike panorama, a vast rectangular grid. It is possible to get thoroughly lost using that grid for what used to be called "contact" navigation.

7. With respect to the Hellcat, for which the maneuver was forbidden, the snap to the left was sloppy and awkward; I found it impossible to do one to the right. As for the Bearcat and Corsair, I was never tempted to try.

Chapter 2. SNJ Texan

1. James C. Fahey, ed., *The Ships and Aircraft of the U.S. Fleet—1939* (Falls Church, Va.: Ships and Aircraft, 1939).

2. Ibid., *Two-Ocean Fleet Edition* (1941). The NJ-1's range has dropped to 685 statute miles.

3. "Gorgeous George" became the first carrier pilot, so far as I know, to reach one thousand arrested landings. It is a tribute to the tempo of operations in the modern carrier Navy that the figure has become a commonly achieved milestone. George was also the first (primarily) fighter pilot I ever knew to reach ten thousand flight hours. George Watkins's first tour of aviation duty was in torpedo bombers, TBM Avengers.

4. In describing the requirements for a Commercial Pilot certificate (FAR 61.129), the FAA refers to "an airplane having retractable landing gear, flaps and a controllable pitch propeller." That requirement has given rise to the terms *complex* and *simple* airplanes, although they are neither defined nor specifically referred to by the FAA. The terms *constant-speed*, *variable-pitch*, and *controllable-pitch* as applied to propellers can be considered interchangeable.

5. A much-used colloquialism meaning "you're behind" or "you're too far aft."

6. It may be acknowledged that round instruments are being replaced in the more exotic—and expensive—new airplanes by elaborate CRT displays, many in full color.

7. World War I–type "synchronization"—many World War II airplanes used the same system.

Chapter 3. F6F Hellcat

1. See Martin Caidin's *The Ragged Rugged Warriors* (New York: Bantam Books, 1966), passim. I have been told in strong terms that my "intelligence circles" knew all about the Zero; it was the "operating forces" who wouldn't listen. Same result. The Zero was a nasty surprise when it came time to fight it.

2. Barrett Tillman, *Hellcat—The F6F in World War II* (Annapolis, Md.: Naval Institute Press, 1979).

3. Ibid., pp. 238, 239.

4. If I let it go at that, some reader is going to accuse me of not knowing "the rest of the story." One or more of the buildings that housed F6F production at Bethpage were constructed using steel salvaged from the New York City Second Avenue "El" elevated railway system. As the Grummans' structural integrity became apparent, the story got started—perhaps tongue in cheek—that the steel was actually used in the Hellcats.

5. "Fast carriers" really means Task Force 58 or 38, depending on who was in charge. When it was Admirals Spruance and Mitscher, it was 58; when it was Admirals McCain and Halsey, it was 38. Either way it consisted of four to five task groups, each built around four aircraft carriers. At war's end, it had the capability of putting close to two thousand airplanes in the air.

6. Remarkable in many ways, the treaty was intended to stop a naval arms race among the maritime powers. The keystone of the agreement was a 5–5–3 ratio of capital ships of the United States, Great Britain, and Japan. "Capital ships" were battleships and battle cruisers. Great Britain and the United States both had large battle cruisers building on the ways that had to be either scrapped or completed as something else. Aircraft carriers, considered to be either not combat ships or not effective offensive weapons, were not restricted. That is how the *Lexington* and *Saratoga* became our first large carriers. The treaty also restricted tonnage, armament, and protective armor of some classes of ships. Heavy cruisers ("heavy" refers to guns, not tonnage; 8-inch guns constitute a heavy cruiser; 6-inch guns, a light cruiser) were restricted in both gross tonnage and protective armor. Light cruisers were not. That is why U.S. "light" cruisers, starting with the *Brooklyn*, were larger and better protected than some of our treaty-compliant heavy cruisers.

7. The exception was small Corsair night-fighter detachments on some of the carriers, notably the USS *Enterprise*. Literally in the middle of the Pacific Ocean, they would send one guy south and one guy north. In my CIC (combat information center) watch station aboard the *Louisville*, I used to listen to the fighter director net and think those pilots must be the two loneliest people on the face of the earth. There may be something wrong here. If the airplane is too dangerous for daytime squadron operations, how come they are throwing these guys into the air in a coal-black night? With the intention of recovering them on a blacked-out aircraft carrier? In the middle of the same coal-black night? Who was in those cockpits? Charles A. Lindbergh? Orville Wright? God?

8. Later Rear Admiral Yates, Captain Earl Yates was the first commanding officer of USS *John F. Kennedy*.

9. Tillman, *Hellcat*, pp. 24, 25.

10. A typical but certainly not the sole or most accurate source of fighter performance is Bill Gunston, ed., *The Illustrated History of Fighters*, (New York: Exeter Books, 1981).

11. "Domestic" here refers to indigenous aircraft, built by Europeans to fight in Europe. The U.S. airplanes tended to be "different" both from the European machines and among themselves. Their reputations, which is part of what this is about, also varied widely from theater to theater. The European

"dog" that was the early P-38 was a roaring success in the hands of the likes of Major Richard Bong in the Pacific. That circumstance is a principal reason for the myth of European air war superiority. The P-39 Airacobra, on the other hand, was a dog wherever it flew, although the Soviets had considerable success with it in an air-to-ground role.

12. Gunston, *Illustrated History of Fighters.*

13. Tillman, *Hellcat.*

14. Ibid., appendix D.

15. I unintentionally provided the comic relief for my gunnery flight one day by referring to "jamming on" 35 inches of manifold pressure. The engine was capable of producing more than 50 inches.

16. "Our" as used above is unintentionally parochial. Although certainly valid for Navy/Marine Corps tactics, the same tactical notions must have occurred at about the same time in other services, notably the U.S. Army Air Corps.

17. As my artist wife points out, oil paint takes a long time to dry completely, even after it reaches the tacky stage where it can be handled.

18. A mil is a milliradian, one-thousandth of a radian, the commonest unit of angular measurement used in gunnery and fire control applications. One degree of angle is approximately 17.5 mils.

19. For the benefit of the uninitiated, and at the risk of sounding condescending to the rest, an automatic weapon fires continuously as long as the trigger is depresed. So-called automatic pistols like the Colt .45 and the Beretta are really semiautomatic. They automatically eject spent cartridges and reload the firing chamber, but there is only one round per trigger pull.

20. The depression was still real, and jobs were not plentiful. Not all graduating naval aviation cadets were immediately put on active duty.

21. Tillman, *Hellcat.*

22. Ready rooms always had plenty of blackboards. Do you suppose somebody decided that fighter pilots understood pictures better than the written word? Naah!

23. Betty was the type of airplane Admiral Yamamoto was riding when he was killed—or executed, or assassinated, depending on one's point of view.

Chapter 4. F8F Bearcat

1. Some detractors of the aircraft carrier still insist that carrier aviation *is* show business.

2. In the U.S. Navy all LSO signals, except for the mandatory "cut" and "wave-off," which were commands, were advisory in nature. They told the pilot what he was doing, not what he was supposed to be doing. In the Royal Navy our British cousins, even though they largely followed and emulated U.S. Navy procedures, did it differently, exactly backwards: their signals told the pilot what he was supposed to do. That added a certain spice to early "cross-decking" operations where Americans landed on British carriers and vice versa. It is my understanding that the British ultimately adopted our system.

3. As late as my mid-1950s three-year tour in the Structures Branch of the old Bureau of Aeronautics (BuAer), now Naval Air Systems Command (NavAir), the specification for carrier aircraft was a "limit load" sink rate of 14 feet per second and "ultimate load" sink rate of 20.8 feet per second. Limit load is the maximum repeated load that can be tolerated throughout the specified service life without deformation or structural failure. Ultimate load is the minimum load at which structural deformation or failure may occur. A rate of 14 feet per second is a pretty good jolt, even without the deceleration of an arresting wire. The mid-1950s was well into the jet era and the beginning of the high-performance swept-wing jet era. The above values were later raised to about 18 and 26 feet per second, respectively. In the propeller aircraft, sink rates of about 10 feet per second were routinely experienced and might be considered normal. This is not to imply that higher sink rates were not experienced; they were.

4. Bill Gunston, ed., *The Illustrated History of Fighters* (New York: Exeter Books, 1981).

5. Ibid.

6. See Barrett Tillman, *Hellcat—The F6F in World War II* (Annapolis, Md.: Naval Institute Press, 1979).

7. A big reason for the delay in exceeding the record, in those days before afterburners, was the long takeoff run required by the early jets. The Bearcat got into the air in about 114 feet by running (bouncing) over a two by four laid transversely across the runway (according to a Grumman legend that I have no reason to doubt). A wind of about 14 knots down the runway didn't hurt.

8. The traditional Grumman approach, as on Wildcats, Hellcats, and Avengers, was to fold essentially the whole wing except for a short stub at the fuselage through the use of angled hinges. Legend has it that Leroy Grumman conceived the idea while playing with a bent paper clip and a desk eraser.

9. Gunston, *Illustrated History of Fighters*.

10. Everything is relative in aviation. When later exposed to power control systems, I came to regard the F8F's roll response as pedestrian and characterized by heavy control forces.

11. That is not as vague as it sounds. For takeoff, which by definition is a full-power exercise, preset trim settings vary from important to critical. On landing, which is mostly head out of the cockpit, the pilot simply dials in what is required by feel. He doesn't know what the trim setting is because he has no need to look down at the numbers. He only knows if he doesn't have proper trim!

12. October 27th. Teddy Roosevelt was the strongest presidential Navy supporter before Franklin Delano Roosevelt. It was Teddy Roosevelt who sent the Great White Fleet around the world. When Congress denied him funds, he said that he had enough money to send them halfway around; if Congress didn't come up with the rest, there they would sit. He got the money.

13. The wires in their arrestment position were supported by mechanically operated "fiddles" that raised them a few inches above the deck, giving the tail hook something to grab onto.

14. "Overhaul & Repair." The lineal descendant is called NAD (Naval Air Depot).

15. The usual version of Bacardi went for $1.25 a fifth in Guantánamo. The more prestigious Anejo cost a lofty $2.00. Hatuey was the local beer, named for a historical indigenous chief. His likeness dominated the logo on the bottle. Some years later, when a Navy fighter squadron was based at "Gitmo's" Leeward Field, they chose the likeness for their squadron patch and airplane decals.

16. Oil dilution was accomplished on engine shutdown in anticipation of a cold start. A quantity of fuel would be injected into the engine oil system to lower the viscosity. On starting, the fuel quickly burned off, leaving the engine lubricant at its original, proper viscosity.

17. "Fixed-base operator," a general aviation term.

18. "Remaining over night." RON was the message acronym transmitted back to base when you and your airplane were unavoidably detained somewhere.

19. The low-frequency range had four legs, usually arranged orthogonally (they intersected at a 90-degree angle). The four quadrants defined by the legs were alternately designated *A* or *N* for the Morse code letter transmitted in that quadrant. The legs themselves emitted a steady tone, the result of superposing the codes for $A(\cdot\text{-})$ and $N(\text{-}\cdot)$. Hence the expression "on the beam."

20. *Barge* if the visitor were of flag rank, *gig* if a captain by rank or command, or *launch* or *boat* in most other instances. My use of the arcane *sha'n't* is not accidental. The Royal Navy invented and formalized the whole process.

21. James L. Holloway III, Naval Academy class of 1943, later Chief of Naval Operations.

22. VBF-3 became VF-32 under a new numbering scheme adopted in the fall of 1948.

Chapter 5. F4U Corsair

1. As opposed to "Operational" Training in my day—our "Advanced" had been in SNJs.

2. The team's preferred nickname, dating back to the 1950s. The "Angels," as I was told by Sheldon Omar "Lefty" Schwartz some time later, is used only by uninformed outsiders.

3. I demur only because I don't believe it is reasonable to compare things that are not comparable. The Bearcat show had great attributes, among them that the airplanes were in full view during the whole show, almost within the field boundaries. Later airplanes had different attributes. The complexity, imagination, and difficulty of today's maneuvers, developed through the years, are incomparable in the Bearcat frame of reference.

4. Every Rhodes in the Navy is automatically "Dusty," unless he figures out some way to avoid it.

5. I use *aviator* instead of *pilot* in acknowledgment of Ernest Gann's repeated observation that there are a lot more pilots than aviators.

6. I had only recently achieved the one-thousand-flight-hour milestone. That's a respectable experience level, but it was low for a second-tour lieutenant (senior grade) pilot—especially low for a flight instructor.

7. James C. Fahey, ed., *The Ships and Aircraft of the U.S. Fleet—Two-Ocean Fleet Edition* (New York: Ships and Aircraft, 1941; rpt. Annapolis, Md.: U.S. Naval Institute Press, 1976).

8. Barrett Tillman, *Corsair—The F4U in World War II and Korea* (Annapolis, Md.: U.S. Naval Institute Press, 1979). Bill Gunston's *The Illustrated History of Fighters* (New York: Exeter Books, 1981) places the first flight in 1939. There is little question that Tillman's version is correct, but it illustrates the confusion that can exist among multiple sources, even well-intentioned ones. Gunston was covering a whole class of airplanes. Tillman was researching just one airplane, and in its country of origin at that. The significant fact is that this remarkable airplane is a 1938–39 design.

9. Any association with the ill-fated Brewster Buffalo would guarantee "maligned." Obsolescent at inception, obsolete by first production, that airplane almost made enemies of good friends like the Australians.

10. "Carrier on-board delivery." These airplanes provide personnel and material transfers from shore to ship and ship to shore. The early CODs were converted tactical types. Dedicated COD airplanes came later.

11. *Bill Mauldin in Korea* (New York: Norton, 1952), p. 143. Mauldin recorded another memorable line. Many of the Korean War pilots were reserves called up as intact squadrons. They were not exactly little kids. Mauldin watched and was impressed by jet carrier recovery operations. "Hard Hats," impact-resistant helmets, were still new. He commented on the shiny gold helmets and, upon their removal, the "pilots' bald heads glistening in the sun" (p. 150).

12. Tillman, *Corsair*. See also Edward T. Maloney and Thomas E. Doll, *Chance Vought F4U Corsair* (Fallbrook, Calif.: Aero Publishers, 1967).

13. Tillman, *Corsair*, appendix C, "Specifications," pp. 196, 197.

14. Gunston, *Illustrated History of Fighters*. William Newby Grant, *P-51 Mustang* (London: Bison Books, 1980; U.S. ed. Secaucus, N.J.: Chartwell Books).

15. It is not a significant exaggeration to refer to the separate Air Force as "the house that SAC built."

16. Forrestal was a former naval aviator. He had personal knowledge and experience applicable to both jobs—not the norm then or now.

17. There are some of us older maritime types who see a pattern: Some time after the live rounds stop flying about, carrier aviation and the Marine Corps become too expensive or difficult to justify and therefore become expendable. Then something unpleasant happens somewhere in the world. The first folks on the scene are carrier airplanes and Marines. Later, the Army and Air Force become involved. The crisis abates. Naval aviation and the Marines again become targets for the budget cutters, until the next crisis. Check it out. The first significant air strikes in Korea after the North Koreans invaded were executed by Air Group 5 off an *Essex*-class carrier, the USS *Valley Forge* (CV-45). That the carrier was even in the theater is a tribute to a wisdom beyond the control of the budgeteers. It was a few Marines and a typically excellent Army airborne unit who kept us from being driven off the Korean peninsula. That was the Pusan Perimeter. As a naval type I am not saying that the Army

is typically excellent; I am acknowledging that their good guys are at least as good as other folks' good guys.

18. Imagine the difficulty of getting money out of Congress for a fleet of new jet airplanes when an important defense scenario involved an airplane with a propeller, let alone an airplane that first flew in 1939!

19. Negative stability is not mentioned here, for good reason. When encountered in an airplane, usually in some flight regime the airplane was not designed for, negative stability makes for fanny-over-the-fantail gyrations, or "Watch out! This thing can kill you."

20. Maloney and Doll, *F4U Corsair*, p. 43. The same picture includes SC-1 Sea Hawks and F6F Hellcats.

21. VC-3 provided night-fighter detachments for Pacific Fleet carriers from a mixed bag of F4U-5Ns and night-fighter-configured Banshees.

22. A significant exception was Lieutenant Guy Bordelon. Operating from Korea, on loan from the USS *Princeton* (CV-37), he became an ace with five night kills of various intruding enemy propeller aircraft. According to Barrett Tillman's *Corsair*, he left his airplane ashore for the Air Force to use as night intruder. Reportedly, the aircraft was soon "totaled" by an Air Force pilot. The armistice soon terminated Air Force interest in Corsair night fighters.

Chapter 6. F9F Panther

1. The Bureau of Aeronautics was part of the Navy's system of technical bureaus. The Bureau of Ships and the Bureau of Ordnance were others. Their descendants have names like Naval Air Systems Command and Naval Sea Systems Command. The Bureau of Aeronautics, BuAer, was the Navy's procurement agency for airplanes.

2. In the Navy, F9F-2 and F4U-4 are "models"; torpedo, patrol, attack, and fighter are "types." To the Federal Aviation Administration and the U.S. Air Force, DC-3, C-47, and P-51 are "types." Accordingly, their pilots must be "type certified" rather than checked out or qualified in "model," as in the Navy.

3. The organization of the test divisions of the NATC underwent remarkably little change through the years until they were superseded by the current, mission-oriented test directorates. Before that occurred, Flight and Tactical Test were combined into Flight Test; Electronics and Armament Test became Weapons Test. "Test Pilot Training" has been the "Test Pilot School" for many years.

4. A principal source is Bert Kinzey, *F9F Panther*, Detail & Scale vol. 15 (Fallbrook, Calif.: Aero Publishers, 1983). Also, Bill Gunston, ed., *The Illustrated History of Fighters* (New York, Exeter Books, 1981). It can be inferred that the night fighter was temporarily shelved rather than canceled. The later Douglas F3D Skyknight, one of Ed Heinemann's many designs, seems to meet the Navy's originally specified night-fighter requirements very nicely.

5. The MiG-15s were powered by Nene engines, either British or Russian built. In the middle of an engine problem of my own in 1952, I was told that while the United States received two Nene engines the Russians received

twenty-five. I can't verify the number, but a transfer of Nene engines was made in accordance with the Anglo-Soviet Trade Agreement of 1946. I suppose the United States didn't need to buy as many of the same engines that Pratt & Whitney was going to build, but in view of the hostile behavior of the MiGs south of the Yalu River, I did not see the circumstance as an overly friendly gesture by our British cousins.

6. The F2H-2 Banshee was powered by two Westinghouse J34-WE-34 axial-flow engines rated at 3,250 pounds of thrust each. The F9F-2 was powered by a single Pratt & Whitney J42-P-6 rated at 5,000 pounds dry, 5,700 pounds with water injection; the F9F-5 by a single J48-P-6 rated at 6,250 pounds dry, 7,000 pounds with water.

7. The dark side was that a Banshee tip tank cost almost exactly the price of a new Cadillac. They were seldom jettisoned.

8. VF-51's skipper was Commander A. D. Pollock; CAG-5 was Commander Harvey P. Lanham. I was in Test Pilot School (then Test Pilot *Training*) with both of them. Dave Pollock was later killed in an unsuccessful emergency landing attempt, flying an F3D undergoing tests at Patuxent.

9. The primary power/thrust instrument was the engine tachometer, calibrated in percent rpm. One hundred percent represented approximately 10,000 rpm—far different from reciprocating engines, for which a typical maximum rpm might be on the order of 2,800.

10. I by no means have total recall. H. J. "Shoney" Schonenberg, longtime Grumman employee and now in charge of Grumman's historical museum, dug out a pilot's handbook to refresh my memory.

11. Design limit load for most of the propeller fighter and dive-bomber/ attack airplanes was 8 to 9 g's. The SBD's limit load has been reported as even higher. Jet fighters tend to run from a 6-g to 9-g limit load, usually closer to 6. Stall speed for propeller airplanes is characteristically lower than stall speed for jet airplanes. Slower, stronger airplanes have a tighter turning circle than faster, less structurally strong airplanes. For the fighter pilot there is an important conclusion: Don't get in a level turning contest with a slower, stronger airplane. If you do, he will soon be in your tail quadrant if not actually on your tail, perhaps in about two turns.

12. Unlike today's 100 percent liquid oxygen systems, gaseous oxygen was mixed with cockpit air by a regulator as a function of cockpit altitude.

13. Best glide speed and best endurance speed can be expected to be close to the speed that provides best ratio of lift over drag (L/D). Glider (more properly "sailplane") design optimizes L/D.

14. I attempted to verify the story with Bob Elder, a likely candidate for the protagonist since he was flying Panthers in VF-5 at the right time. He couldn't provide substantiation, but he offered several examples of fuel exhaustion, or near–fuel exhaustion, where folks glided substantial distances to successful emergency landings. It sounds pretty scary to me!

15. In lay terms, the symptomatic consequences of oxygen deprivation. In 1950, we were still using the term *anoxia*, which roughly translates to no, or the lack of, oxygen.

16. It should be noted that the Navy and the Air Force were even then far from cavalier on the subject of oxygen. There was an aviation physiology test activity co-located with Service Test. It had an altitude ("low-pressure") chamber to simulate high-altitude flight in which all of us were indoctrinated before being permitted to fly. The indoctrination included the pressure-breathing and communication activities. It is de rigueur in any altitude chamber ride for one fortunate "volunteer" to take off his mask so his colleagues can see how fast he loses functional capability without oxygen. The volunteer will have no recollection afterwards of almost instantaneously going stupid before reaching the incipient passout stage. I don't want to leave an impression of a cruel experiment; an aviation medical specialist, usually commissioned, frequently an M.D., hovered over the volunteer. The subject was given a routine task to perform, like counting a deck of cards. The flight surgeon had mask in hand, watching for his patient's eyes to glaze. One minute the subject is doing fine; the next thing you know his hand freezes in midair, still clutching one of the cards.

17. In the old days they were called aviation machinists' mates—"mates" because the top of the rating line, the warrant officers, were the "machinists."

18. A striker is an airman who is "striking" for, working toward, a particular technical rating. An AMAN, for instance, is an airman who is a designated striker for AM3, aviation structural mechanic, third class (petty officer).

19. As a very new boy in the squadron, I neither saw nor participated in the actual demonstration; I didn't even make the trip. I got close enough to a rehearsal, however, or at least to its consequences. I was Assistant Officer of the Watch for NAAS Oceana when two VF-3 Hellcats collided during a practice formation tail chase loop. I had to follow the ambulance and crash crew to the site. From low altitude the airplanes' ground impacts were close together. I arrived in time to see one pilot loaded into the ambulance, an identifying tag tied to one bare toe. He had got out of the airplane, but too low for the parachute to open. The wreck of the other airplane, surprisingly intact, was in a level attitude on the ground. It was burning, the pilot still inside. Two fatalities.

20. As in the Battle of Midway.

21. The press coverage was unusual in itself. The Korean War was largely ignored in the press after the winter of the Chosin Reservoir, vastly different from the wall-to-wall saturation coverage of the Vietnam War. In view of the nature and quality of much of that coverage, being ignored wasn't all bad. If there were any Korean villages wantonly burned by American servicemen, the American public was spared watching it happen in living color over dessert.

22. For reasons unknown, the crane's name was always "Tilly."

23. I still have trouble applying the word *War* to what was alternatively referred to, especially by the United Nations, as a *Police Action*. A viable definition of a war is a conflict that our political leaders have serious intent to win. Korea didn't qualify.

24. Alan R. Millett, *Semper Fidelis—The History of the United States Marine Corps* (New York: Macmillan, 1980).

25. I verified a suggested technique for detecting enemy ground fire: Turn off the cockpit pressurization before making a run. Then you could hear the

gunfire, sometimes before you could see either tracers or exploding puffs of smoke. Even if you couldn't locate the source, you knew to jink like hell.

26. The standard complement of Task Force 77 was two CVAs on station in the Sea of Japan. In the days of straight-deck carriers, we needed to maintain a "ready deck" all the time in case of emergencies or other unscheduled aircraft recovery. That made two ships the minimum. There were three carriers for short periods during changeovers. Occasionally we got up to four for a special operation.

27. "Undermine" was *Essex*'s call sign.

28. Hutch took the interesting ones, but he also took all the missions he could squeeze in. He figured it was his job to fly as many as possible.

29. Limited Duty Officer. Many of them came up through the ranks, which is what makes a mustang officer. LDOs are characterized by expert technical skills.

30. That translates to an octane-equivalent rating of 115 for normal use and 145 with water injection. The fuel is unavailable in today's market.

31. The standard was an extension of the octane scale, a measure of anti-knock capability. Obviously, octane can't be more than 100 percent of itself—any more than athletes can produce "110 percent" of their own capability!

32. "Class alpha" damage, to be disposed of, "stricken" from the Navy's records, hence "strike."

Chapter 7. F9F-6/8T Cougar

1. Bill Gunston, ed., *The Illustrated History of Fighters* (New York: Exeter Books, 1981).

2. Mach number is the ratio of a speed or velocity to the speed of sound. Mach 1.0 represents the speed of sound, which varies with altitude.

3. Gunston, *Illustrated History of Fighters*.

4. The benefits of swept wings are most apparent in transonic flight. In many respects thin, straight wings are preferable for supersonic flight—hence the straight wings of Yeager's Bell X-1, Douglas's research aircraft D558-1, and Lockheed's F-104 and F-94.

5. Gunston, *Illustrated History of Fighters*.

6. Ibid.

7. The appropriate designation for a new Navy fighter by North American would have been F2J.

8. Bert Kinzey, *F9F Cougar in Detail and Scale* (Fallbrook, Calif.: Aero Publishers, 1983).

9. Ibid.

10. Nobody bothered to tell the Blue Angels, who flew the Cougar from December of 1954 to April of 1955.

11. Gunston, *Illustrated History of Fighters*.

12. Kinzey, *F9F Cougar*.

13. Ibid.

14. This was before the term *program manager* was used. The Aircraft

Division was the home of what were known as Class Desk Officers for the various Navy airplanes.

15. The F10F went the flying tail one better; it had a real flying tail that sort of flopped around until, on takeoff roll, enough air flowed over its surfaces to unstall it. The F10F flying tail proved especially interesting on catapult launches.

16. The area rule recognized that compressibility effects manifested themselves where there was a sudden increase in surface area, such as where wings join the fuselage. This could be avoided by giving the fuselage a pronounced wasp waist—not altogether avoided, but drag rise could be decreased and pushed further toward Mach 1.0.

17. This is *not* the same as the drag rise associated with compressibility. This one is purely subsonic aerodynamics.

18. A curve like that of the figure is called a drag polar, a useful tool for the performance engineer. The drag polar is the basis for prediction and estimation of aircraft performance.

19. An accelerated stall is a stall occurring in greater than 1-g flight, as out of a hard turn.

20. No relation to classmate "Gorgeous George" Watkins.

21. A large part of Westinghouse's defense business during that period was aircraft engines, not electronics. All those F2H Banshees, and the relatively few F3D Skyknights, were powered by Westinghouse J34 engines.

22. q is dynamic pressure, a key aerodynamic parameter that is involved in the production of lift, drag, and, consequently, aerodynamically produced structural loads. $q = \frac{1}{2}\rho V^2$, where ρ is air density and V is true airspeed. Essentially, q is what an airspeed indicator reads (indicates), based on a quixotically pragmatic assumption that air density is always that of sea level. "Indicated" airspeed and its cousin "calibrated" airspeed aren't much help in telling you how fast you are actually traveling through the air, but the airplane will always stall (in 1-g flight) at the same reading on the indicator, regardless of altitude. Thus, an airspeed indicator is really a q-meter calibrated in knots or miles per hour. q actually does have the units of pressure, which makes an airspeed indicator a special kind of pressure gauge.

23. I was the guest of "D. Z." Skalla, a test pilot for Westinghouse in Baltimore; I had known "D. Z." since the Patuxent years, first in Service Test and then when he was assistant director of the Test Pilot School. The meeting was in honor of George Spangenberg, who was also the guest speaker. George was for years the Navy's chief aerodynamicist in BuAer. He was articulate, strong willed, and (some alleged) opinionated. With this combination of qualities, he helped the Navy maintain a leadership role in modern, high-technology aviation. In the process he also helped keep carrier aviation vital and innovative in a period of dynamic changes. Highly regarded, he was an effective, credible witness before the various armed forces committees on Capitol Hill. George had friends and colleagues throughout the industry. Four Grumman test pilots flew down from Long Island in the company's Beechcraft Baron for the dinner. One of them was Chuck Sewell, whom I had known in 1962 as a Marine major, an

across-the-street neighbor at Patuxent; Chuck was destined soon to become Grumman's chief test pilot.

24. That comment did not apply to me, a guest of SETP for the evening; I was pretending to be an engineer for a living.

Chapter 8. AD Skyraider

1. This is a game everybody can play. Old Skyraider pilots will always come up with a couple you never heard of before. Captain Rosario "Zip" Rausa, USN, barely got through my list before he added The Big Machine and Pedigreed Pulverizer. Able Dog represents the letters *A* and *D* from the military phonetic alphabet in use when the Skyraider was first built. Martin's competing airplane similarly should have been called Able Mike instead of its actual nickname, Able Mable.

2. Postunification nomenclature under the new McNamara system.

3. J. M. Bruce, comp., *Spad Scouts SVII–SXIII*, Arco-Aircam Series no. 9 (New York: Arco Publishing Company, 1969).

4. Ibid.

5. SBD stands for *s*cout *b*omber by *D*ouglas. The popularly used term *dive-bomber* was the pilots' preferred mission description. *Scout* reflected the Navy's perception of the primary mission of airplanes as scouting for an over-the-horizon battle fleet, an extension of the traditional mission of cruisers and, in earlier times, sailing frigates.

6. The original Helldiver was the strut-and-wire-braced biplane flown by Clark Gable and Wallace Beery in a 1930s motion picture *Hell Divers*. The SB2C's immediate predecessor was the SBC, a relatively clean biplane featuring faired struts and retractable landing gear.

7. Edward H. Heinemann and Rosario Rausa, *Ed Heinemann—Combat Aircraft Designer* (Annapolis, Md.: Naval Institute Press, 1980).

8. In comparison, the total buy of Martin's AM Mauler was 151.

9. Military specifications act as a vehicle for conveying military requirements to a manufacturer. As such, they are a yardstick against which an end product can be measured. They can also be distorted into a kind of military wish list. This can occur when hardware experts in the Bureau of Aeronautics and Military Requirements people in the offices of the Chief of Naval Operations become overly influenced by the optimism of articulate contractor marketeers. It really is a judgment call. In that sense a specification, such as a current PIDS (Prime Item Development Specification), can be compared to the output of crystal ball gazing. However sophisticated the process, a specification is an attempt to describe something that has not yet been built. In terms of the government's attaining the best product, it is a toss-up as to which is worse, specify too little or too much. The spec writers simply must do the best they can with the information available to them.

10. Rosario Rausa, *Skyraider—The Douglas A-1 "Flying Dump Truck"* (Annapolis, Md.: Nautical and Aviation Publishing Company of America, 1982).

11. The nonmoving stick works because it is a *force* control rather than a

displacement control. I once asked John Fendley, chief test pilot for Westinghouse in Baltimore, how long it took him to get accustomed to such a device in the F-16. With no discernible hesitation he replied, "About thirty seconds."

12. It should be acknowledged that neither I nor, so far as I know, anyone else ever ran any formal comparative tests among those airplanes. These remarks are not only subjective, they describe long-past experience. I have not retained the test log I was required to submit for the flight, so I don't have even my old notes to refer to.

13. The prospective passenger must of course meet the requirements for riding in military aircraft. That usually meant a current Department of Defense employee, military or civilian, or a reserve or retired military or DOD employee.

14. They marked the old colored airways: green or amber, depending on whether the direction was mostly north/south or mostly east/west.

15. There is a lot of good stuff available about flying in that era, much of it gathering dust on library shelves. It includes works by the contemporary Ernest K. Gann, almost any account of Charles A. Lindbergh's early flying, and, of course, Saint-Exupéry himself.

16. "Remaining over night because of mechanical/maintenance problems" is a close enough translation.

17. As an old squadron buddy, then Lieutenant J. G. Jack Armstrong, used to say, "The only difference between night flying and day flying is that at night you can't see!"

18. The Main Navy and Munitions Buildings were World War I temporary buildings made of brick. The "W" and "N" buildings were World War II temporary buildings made of wood. I shudder to think what World War III temporary buildings might be made of. Perhaps we shouldn't bother to find out.

Chapter 9. F8U Crusader

1. *R* for reconnaissance (which includes photo), *F* for fighter, number eight in lineal sequence of U.S. fighters since unification. This is the old U.S. Army Air Corps system. In the F8U-1P, *F* is for fighter, *8* means the eighth fighter design by Chance Vought with its manufacturer's designator, *U-1* indicates the first major modification of the model, and *P* stands for photo.

2. Barrett Tillman, *MiG Master—The Story of the F-8 Crusader* (Annapolis, Md.: Nautical and Aviation Publishing Company of America, 1980).

3. An aircraft carrier airplane at that, to the joy and satisfaction of naval aviators.

4. Rear Admiral Tommie F. Rinard, USNR, Commander, Naval Air Reserve Force, made it clear in his remarks that this "kit" approach to recce and photo would not be popular among reconnaissance professionals.

5. The successful F8U would constitute half of such a pair with the F11F Tiger. Unfortunately for corporate peace of mind, Vought did not know that going in.

6. Tillman, *MiG Master.*

7. An unavoidable characteristic of any low-aspect ratio, roughly delta planform airfoil.

8. The Cutlass was one of at least three airplanes that suffered from the eventual failure of the aircraft engine division of the Westinghouse Electric Company. The Pratt & Whitney J57 was a substitute for a Westinghouse engine in the F4D Skyray. McDonnell seemingly acquired a lasting enmity toward Westinghouse after bargeloads of engine-less F3H-1 Demons took a midnight ride down the Mississippi River for disposal. (These airplanes had been deemed uneconomical to complete with alternative engines. Press accounts made much of the fact that the airplanes were moved under cover of darkness.) The alternate Allison J71 never provided sufficient thrust for design performance in the F3H-2N production versions.

9. Tillman, *MiG Master*.

10. This feature was important enough to be retrofitted into the F-4 Phantom II in the form of leading-edge "slats." Before that, the airplane was a subsonic dog. At forty thousand feet it felt as if it could hardly turn at all. Audible wing buffet began at quite shallow bank angles.

11. Bill Gunston, ed., *The Illustrated History of Fighters* (New York: Exeter Books, 1981).

12. This meant that rearward visibility was poor to nonexistent. Perhaps the designers rationalized that the performance was so good that no one could catch or keep up with the airplane from behind. True or not, the idea recalls a remark attributed to Ettore Bugatti at a time when his Bugatti automobiles were consistent Grand Prix winners and the toast of the Continent. Someone had the effrontery to complain about the brakes on his racers. "Le Patron" is alleged to have responded, "My cars are built to go, not to stop!"

13. Virtually all high-performance airplanes have some form of ventral fins or their equivalent. In some designs they are movable to provide increased span (and effectiveness) at really high speeds, as in the F8U-3. The "Crusader III" was an entirely different airplane that never saw production, the loser in a formal competition with the F4H Phantom II. The F4H did not have ventrals, but the drooping "anhedral" (opposite of dihedral) of the stabilator fulfilled a similar function.

14. I use the aircraft designations appropriate to the period in which each model was most used. All versions except the F8U-1 were reworked or remanufactured at some time. They are designated by suffixes such as *J,H,K,* and *L*. Except for the RF-8G photo planes, the later the alphabetical position of the suffix, the older the original version. F8U-1Es were remanufactured as F-8Ks, F-8Es as F-8Js.

15. Tactical air navigation system—in operation essentially identical to VORTAC, with which it is compatible. VORTAC is a combination of Omni (VOR, VHF omnidirectional radio) and DME (distance-measuring equipment).

16. Almost instantly, T-shirts appeared aboard the *Nimitz* with the legend "Navy 2, Libya 0."

17. Those are the words of a P-80 pilot. Air Force, of course.

18. Wait a minute! Did the wing really come down? It did with respect to the fuselage. But what was holding the airplane up in the air? That's right, the wing. Then, doesn't it follow that what really happened is that the fuselage

moved up to meet the wing that was holding it (the fuselage) in the air? The question was a favorite for argument among Crusader pilots. The answer is as pragmatically important as the answer to that other question: If a tree falls in the forest when no one is around, does it make a sound?

19. Tillman, *MiG Master.*

20. The F8U-2N at Mach 1.9 was in the same top-end speed category as those airplanes. The significant difference is the newer airplanes' ability to accelerate and turn—to change state rapidly, which is a way of referring to energy conversion. The F-15, the F-14, and the aging F-4 are capable of Mach 2.3 or better.

21. Then–Lieutenant Commander Willie Williams was Exec of VBF-3 when I reported aboard in 1946.

22. It was determined by Vought that a Crusader will not spin at an indicated airspeed greater than 170 knots. That sounds like a useful piece of information: stay faster than 170 knots, and you will never spin. Unfortunately, there are situations where the F8U's airspeed decays at 70 knots per second or greater.

23. That was a sometimes useful feature in protecting oneself against unplanned hassle opponents. If you happened to be looking in the right place, you could see a burner puff a long way off, well before the airplane itself was discernible. It could be a dead giveaway that someone was initiating a run on you.

24. During my stint in the Bureau of Aeronautics certain other airplanes revealed transition characteristics that were not desirable. The F4D had a transonic pitch oscillation. The solution was a "Mach box" in the control system. The FJ-4, which was not supersonic in level flight (it was the last of the FJ series; its closest Air Force equivalent was the F-86F), manifested both aileron and rudder "buzz" at transonic or close to transonic speeds before critical aerodynamic changes were incorporated.

25. Tillman, *MiG Master.*

26. The annual ball was an idea too late for the Crusader squadrons. A few years ago I was at NAS Oceana, Virginia. On the grass in front of the Officers' Club was what appeared to be a mint-condition F8U in VF-191 colors. Closer inspection revealed that, far from mint, it had been cosmetically "restored." It was a hulk that had been doomed to spend its final days as a practice object for the fire crews. The occasion for its display was the second "First and Last Crusader Ball." There has been a "last" Crusader Ball every year since.

27. Later Admiral Donald C. Davis.

28. The last *Essex*-class carriers to see first-line service with the fleet were so-called *Oriskany* conversions. The third major modification to the USS *Oriskany* (CVA-27) resulted in a new designation: CVA-27C. This prototype modification included the latest version of the angled deck, mirror landing system, and steam catapults. *Essex*-class ships were needed to meet Navy commitments pending completion of larger ships. The Navy needed first-line fighters on those ships. The F4H wasn't carrier suitable for operating off the small *Essex* hulls. The Crusader was. That created an interdependent relationship between such

ships as the *Essex, Oriskany, Hancock, Ticonderoga*, and *Hornet* and the F8U. The end came when the *Hancock*, VF-191, and VF-194, the last two fleet Crusader squadrons, left the active scene.

29. $q = \frac{1}{2}\rho V^2$. Lift $= C_L \frac{1}{2}\rho V^2 S$, where C_L is lift coefficient, ρ is air density, V is velocity, and S is the area of the lifting surface. A 4-g turn, for example, requires that lift be increased by a factor of 4 over straight-and-level (1-g) flight. That can only come from increases in speed or lift coefficient. (q has the units of pressure lbs/ft^2. ρ is mass density, with units of slugs/ft^3 or lb-secs^2/ft^4. Velocity's units are ft/sec. Multiply ρ by V^2 and you get lbs/ft^2.)

30. For a modern fighter or attack airplane that maximum may be on the order of 6 g's. Some airplanes, such as the F-16, have higher limits. Limit load is the maximum permissible repeated load. Ultimate load is 50 percent greater; you are not supposed to hit that one even once, because the airplane is allowed to bend or break there.

31. The double-wedge shape is ideal for supersonic flow, but you don't see it on real airplanes; skinny and pointy airfoils abound, but not double-wedge airfoils. The reasons is that for the most part supersonic airplanes are subson'c airplanes that fly supersonically only for short periods. Subsonic airfoil theory has a strong influence on their design. In that respect supersonic airplanes are analogous to diesel submarines, which are not true submersibles but surface craft that can operate submerged for short periods of time.

32. The device was based on the Mk 7 gyro precessing sight invented by Dr. Draper at MIT during World War II. It was the sight used aboard our ships on thousands of 20-millimeter gun mounts.

33. How did the radar "see" the nylon banner? By two means: a metallic thread woven through the nylon mesh, and a little reflector attached to one end of the tow bar.

34. All manually; this was before the availability of computers.

35. The N signified an AirPac as opposed to AirLant squadron (AirLant used A; I don't know why AirPac didn't use P). M was the identifier for Air Group 19 in the Pacific Fleet. A 100 series number for individual airplanes indicated the first squadron in the numerical hierarchy and by tradition suggested a fighter squadron. If the rule were consistently applied, the first two squadrons would be fighters with 100 and 200 series numbers. In practice side numbers usually went with the last digit of the squadron's designator. Hence, VA-192 had numbers in the 200s and VA-195 had numbers in the 500s.

36. There were about six click stops that could be used to adjust the spring tension that controlled the amount of precession in the lead-computing gunsight. Increasing the tension would inhibit the precession, thus decreasing displayed lead.

37. The reunion is the annual bash, usually in Las Vegas, of the Tail Hookers, an organization of naval aviators ostensibly existing for the furtherance of carrier aviation. The original purpose was an excuse for a big party.

38. The Wake Avengers are VMA-211, a Marine attack squadron that is the lineal descendant of the Marine fighter squadron at Wake Island. The squadron was overwhelmed, along with the other defenders, by greatly superior Japanese air and sea forces at the beginning of World War II.

39. During the Korean Unpleasantness, VF-153 was a Panther squadron. Most Panthers were painted the traditional "sea-blue gloss," although a few were unpainted aluminum. Through a set of circumstances one VF-153 airplane was disabled on one end and another airplane on the other end. Panther tails—the whole aft fuselage—came off as a unit when a few nuts were loosened; they were also interchangeable. In a visually impressive exchange, one of VF-153's aluminum airplanes received a blue airplane's tail and so became the Blue Tail Fly. The squadron retained the name at least through the period of the gray A4Ds they acquired after becoming VA-153.

40. *Available* meant not down for maintenance action, which could vary from a serious mechanical problem or a scheduled periodic inspection to replacing worn tires or swapping radios. Fueling delays didn't count; they were beyond squadron control. They nevertheless got in the way of the Operations Officer's training schedule every bit as much as the lack of available airplanes.

41. The fundamental structure of the Task Organization would be identical to that of somewhat larger Task Organizations, like Task Force 58 in World War II.

42. Feedbag was our less-than-glamorous squadron call sign.

Chapter 10. Other Jets

1. The action made the unit top heavy in rank as well as experience. It was a disappointment to those junior, inexperienced pilots who were transferred to make room for them. Their dreams of being pioneer jet pilots were dashed aborning. No matter the reason, such an apparent rejection constitutes a jolt to any pilot's ego. It was our gain in VBF-3. Ensigns Joe Canto, "Red" Smith, and Jim Petty, who came to us from VF-17, were good pilots and good people.

2. James C. Fahey, ed., *The Ships and Aircraft of the U.S. Fleet—Victory Edition* (New York: Ships and Aircraft, 1945; rpt. Annapolis, Md.: Naval Institute Press, 1976).

3. Ibid.

4. At the time of the letters of intent and initial contracts for the Phantom and the Banshee, Douglas Aircraft, normally the resident D in the Navy nomenclature system, was not under production contract with the Navy. By the time production orders were let for the Banshee, Douglas was again under Navy contract. Hence the H for McDonnell. The Phantom was originally the FD-1, later the FH-1.

5. René Francillon, *McDonnell-Douglas Aircraft since 1920* (London: Putnam, 1979).

6. Fifty-six F2H-1s were produced.

7. Francillon, *McDonnell-Douglas Aircraft.*

8. Ibid.

9. F2H-3s and -4s were essentially identical airplanes designed specifically for the all-weather fighter role. The tails were eight feet longer than that of the F2H-2, and the nose was extended to accommodate airborne intercept radars.

The -4s had somewhat larger engines and a Hughes instead of a Westinghouse radar. In all, 250 F2H-3s were built. There were 150 F2H-4s, most of which went to the Marines.

10. Francillon, *McDonnell-Douglas Aircraft.*

11. As noted in an earlier chapter, $q = \frac{1}{2}\rho V^2$, where ρ is air density and V is true airspeed.

12. There is the apocryphal tale of the nervous, and elderly, female passenger on her first airplane ride. Concerned about the visible up and down movement of the wing tips of the DC-3—it seemed to her that they should be more rigidly attached—she stopped the co-pilot in the aisle on his way to the cockpit. To alleviate her concern but less than sensitive to public relations niceties, he reassured her, "Hell, lady, they're supposed to do that. If they didn't, the wings would break off."

13. Francillon, *McDonnell-Douglas Aircraft.*

14. At a time when part of the A3D's mission required flight at extremely low altitudes, the cynics said the nomenclature stood for "All Three Dead."

15. That would not change dramatically until the large-scale use of integrated circuits, microchips, and digital devices many years later.

16. Edward H. Heinemann and Rosario Rausa, *Ed Heinemann—Combat Aircraft Designer* (Annapolis, Md.: Naval Institute Press, 1980).

17. He was responsible for the Aero 1A shape that defined the contour of many externally carried airborne tanks and pods as well as the entire series of low-drag bombs. Those bombs are still in the U.S. inventory these many years later.

18. The simplification was that one category of repair was eliminated: "forward fit" (which required a production line break-in). We were dealing with two categories of "retrofit" as it was.

19. Sometimes it isn't a question of how much money is available but how much is in what pocket. The Skyknight's fuel was paid for out of operating funds.

20. "NAS St. Louis" was a tenant activity at Lambert Field occupying a flight line and a compound across the field from the McDonnell plant.

21. Francillon, *McDonnell-Douglas Aircraft.*

22. Also known as Scooter, Tinker Toy, Baby Bomber, Bantam Bomber, Might Mite, and others.

23. Heinemann and Rausa, *Ed Heinemann.*

24. Francillon, *McDonnell-Douglas Aircraft.*

25. A4D, *a*ttack, *4*th by *D*ouglas, became A-4 under the new nomenclature system.

26. The fuselage line was badly disrupted by a hump containing additional electronics in the late A-4Es, the -4Fs, and the -4Ms. Mr. Heinemann deplored the change on esthetic and engineering grounds, to no effect.

27. To be meaningful, aircraft weights must be precisely defined as to actual configuration. This is especially true of light attack airplanes, which can accept many combinations of bombs, rockets, special-function external pods, fuel tanks, and so on.

28. Also described as "loft bombing" in lower-performing airplanes like the A-1, where the standard maneuver was "medium angle loft." That went with a special variant of nuclear weapon that had its own integral rocket assist in the aft end.

29. Other than the special circumstance of flight demonstration teams, that is.

30. The engine had seized up in the landing pattern from oil starvation. On this occasion there was an obvious mechanical cause.

31. It is only fair to point out that the cognizant officer in the Bureau of Naval Aeronautics, or Bureau of Naval Weapons, or later Naval Air Systems Command, was a naval aviator, experienced in the same generic kind of airplanes as in the aircraft program he was managing. That is why he was chosen for the job. Unfortunately, he was also the guy who was supposed to make the dollars come out even. Given the choice, he would have preferred to be flying his airplane at Patuxent and demanding improvement changes along with the rest of us.

32. *N* identifies the Navy-unique model of that airplane as flown by "Top Gun" instructors.

33. Francillon, *McDonnell-Douglas Aircraft*.

34. The Naval Ordnance Test Station is located east of Inyokern, California, north and east of Palmdale and Edwards Air Force Base, just west of Death Valley. NOTS was a Bureau of Naval Ordnance activity. When BuOrd and BuAer were combined into BuWeps (Bureau of Naval Weapons), NOTS became the Naval Weapons Center (NWC), China Lake.

35. The Board of Inspection and Survey (BIS) is a Navy-peculiar institution formed in the last century to assess the condition of ships in the deteriorating post–Civil War Navy. BIS persists to this day as a statutory body reporting directly to the Secretary of the Navy. It is the final legal arbiter as to the service acceptability of major equipments like ships and airplanes. BIS reports have contractual clout.

36. "Long" range is relative. Sparrow is a medium-range air-to-air missile. Phoenix is a long-range missile.

37. AIM-9C or SARAH (semiactive radar homing) was the invention of a brilliant Ph.D. at China Lake, Dr. Tom Amlie. (In the same time period, AIM-9D was called IRAH—infrared active homing.) SARAH's principal problem was that it used for guidance reflected noncoherent (nondoppler), short-pulse radar energy. Its ultimate failure was due more to the laws of physics than to any want of zeal or talent. Dr. Amlie, when I last heard of him, was prominently positioned on the civilian staff of the Secretary of Defense. He has become an especially vocal and articulate critic of fighter radars.

38. For knowledgeable North Americans the name is indicative of its place of origin. Sidewinder is the common name of a desert species of rattlesnake noteworthy as much for its style of locomotion as for the potency of it venom.

39. Ordnancemen check out installed missiles on the deck/ground by shining a flashlight at the heads.

40. Happily, such difficulties are in the past. The AIM-9Ls and their equivalents and descendants in Air Force and Navy service today are equally capable.

41. Both were to become admirals. Vice Admiral Richard Seymour would later be Commander, Naval Air Systems Command, in charge of all naval air weapons procurement.

42. The FJ-4 was similar in appearance to the Air Force F-86F and, I believe, one of the finest non-afterburning fighters ever built. Dave Longton participated in the F4H assault on time-to-climb records in the spring of 1962. He set the zero-to-6,000-meter record. Longtime astronaut (then Commander) John W. Young set two other records in that same exercise.

43. U.S. Navy full pressure suits were similar in appearance and function to the pressure suits worn by the Mercury astronauts.

44. The existence of 145315 and its fellow F4H-1Fs in R&D status was one of the reasons I later had trouble getting an F4H-1 (F-4B) for VX-5.

45. The fastest real Crusader. The F8U-3 was an entirely different airplane.

Chapter 11. The Little Guys

1. Amendment: Piper has undertaken limited production of the Cadet, essentially a stripped, two-seat version of the Warrior. At the time this book was going to press, production had ceased. When last heard from, Piper was again out of business and up for sale. A French firm was prominent among potential buyers.

2. On 28 May 1987, a West German teenager named Mathias Rust flew a "borrowed" Cessna 172 from an airport in Finland across over five hundred miles of heavily defended Russian territory before landing in Red Square in Moscow. To add insult to injury, he buzzed the place first, guaranteeing an interested crowd when he touched down. By some coincidence, no doubt, this borrowed airplane was equipped with long-range fuel tanks.

3. It is difficult to keep up with the FAA. They have gone back to calling that one "power-off stall."

4. Pitch control authority was deliberately inhibited to prevent the pilot from exceeding the "critical angle of attack." Ailerons and the rudder were mechanically linked so as to ensure coordinated, ball-in-the-center flight.

5. This too has recently changed. The accelerated stall has been deleted as a requirement. The departure stall has been replaced by a "power-on stall."

6. The Hobbs is essentially a clock that measures aircraft operating time.

7. I find it interesting that, when something is found untoward in automotive design, the manufacturer is held responsible for necessary corrective action, frequently as implemented in a government-directed "recall." But when something is found wrong enough to warrant an Airworthiness Directive in an airplane, the owner gets to pay. I can't have it both ways, I know; I just got through bemoaning the economic constraints on general aviation manufacturers. But how about a deal? We get rid of the excesses in "product liability" and then we make the airplane manufacturers pay for their own mistakes. Piper by no means has an exclusive on this industrywide phenomenon.

8. Even the P-3 may not be that good an example because its early Litton inertial platform had a bad habit of falling over on its side after a few hours.

Fortunately, that airplane had a backup vertical reference, without which there would have been no gyro horizon. Not a trivial matter in a jet-type penetration approach in the middle the night.

9. If an airplane lands at 35 knots directly into a 35-knot wind, it would be landing at zero ground speed—an unlikely but theoretically possible occurrence.

Index

ABOUT THE AUTHOR

Captain Richard Linnekin, USN (Ret.), graduated from the U.S. Naval Academy with the class of 1944 in June 1943, a year early under the accelerated wartime program. After serving for a year in the Pacific theater aboard the USS *Louisville* (CA-28), he entered flight training at NAAS Ottumwa, Iowa, in October 1944. He received his wings in Corpus Christi, Texas, in November 1945, thereby missing the excitement and hazards of World War II carrier aviation.

Over the next twenty-two years he served in various fighter and training squadrons, flying the standard—and numerous—assortment of trainer, fighter, and attack aircraft that composed the fleet during that period. This included the big, round-engined airplanes used in World War II, the early jet aircraft of the Korean War period, and the Mach 2, swept wing, supersonic aircraft that the U.S. Navy flew over Vietnam. His successful but not unique career in naval aviation can be considered typical of that of many of his peers who also partook of the airplane riches at their diposal. These airplanes ranged from the fabric-covered, wooden spar Stearman to the Mach 2.3 Phantom II.

Captain Linnekin's less typical association with testing, development, and design of aircraft and airborne weapon systems has allowed him to view these machines both in the context of their own time and as they relate to the present. A graduate of the U.S. Navy Test Pilot School, he holds a degree in aeronautical engineering from the U.S. Navy Postgraduate School. He recently retired, for the second time, after twenty-three years with the Westinghouse Defense and Electronics Center in Baltimore, Maryland, where he worked as a systems engineer and program manager on fighter and attack aircraft radar and airborne missile fire-control systems. He now lives in Annapolis, Maryland.

The **Naval Institute Press** is the book-publishing arm of the U.S. Naval Institute, a private, nonprofit professional society for members of the sea services and civilians who share an interest in naval and maritime affairs. Established in 1873 at the U.S. Naval Academy in Annapolis, Maryland, where its offices remain today, the Naval Institute has more than 100,000 members worldwide.

Members of the Naval Institute receive the influential monthly magazine *Proceedings* and discounts on fine nautical prints, ship and aircraft photos, and subscriptions to the quarterly *Naval History* magazine. They also have access to the transcripts of the Institute's Oral History Program and get discounted admission to any of the Institute-sponsored seminars regularly offered around the country.

The Naval Institute's book-publishing program, begun in 1898 with basic guides to naval practices, has broadened its scope in recent years to include books of more general interest. Now the Naval Institute Press publishes more than sixty new titles each year, ranging from how-to books on boating and navigation to battle histories, biographies, ship and aircraft guides, and novels. Institute members receive discounts on the Press's more than 375 books.

Full-time students are eligible for special half-price membership rates. Life memberships are also available.

For a free catalog describing the Naval Institute Press books currently available, and for further information about U.S. Naval Institute membership, please write to:

Membership & Communications Department
U.S. Naval Institute
118 Maryland Avenue
Annapolis, Maryland 21402-5035

Or call, toll-free, (800) 233-USNI. In Maryland, call (301) 224-3378.

THE NAVAL INSTITUTE PRESS
EIGHTY KNOTS TO MACH 2
Forty-five Years in the Cockpit
Designed by Charles West
Set in Century Book, Futura Condensed Oblique, and Helvetica
by Maryland Composition Company, Inc.
Glen Burnie, Maryland
Printed on 50-lb. Glatfelter Decision Opaque Smooth White
and bound in ICG Western Kennett Natural
by The Maple-Vail Book Manufacturing Group
York, Pennsylvania